Financial Models Using Simulation and Optimization

A Step-by-Step Guide with Excel and Palisade's DecisionTools Software

Wayne L. Winston

Kelley School of Business
Indiana University

Published by:

Palisade Corporation
31 Decker Road
Newfield, NY USA 14867

(607) 277-8000
(607) 277-8001 (fax)
http://www.palisade.com (website)
sales@palisade.com (e-mail)

Preface

As we all know, technology is changing the world and the rate of change is increasing daily! Until recently, it was difficult for anyone except a Ph.D. who had some computer programming expertise to solve complicated finance problems. Today the power of Microsoft Excel and Excel add-ins such as @RISK, Evolver, TopRank, and PrecisionTree makes it possible for people with a good business education and reasonable spreadsheet skills to tackle problems that were viewed only a few years ago as the province of the "rocket scientists". Thanks to Microsoft and Palisade you no longer need a Ph.D. to solve many complicated financial problems! The purpose of this book is to show advanced undergraduates, M.B.A's and most of all **practicing finance professionals** how to use the power of Excel and Palisade Add-ins to solve complicated financial problems.

Organization

We begin in Chapter 1 with an introduction to Excel's what-if capabilities. Then (Chapters 2-12) we introduce Excel's data analysis capabilities. In Chapters 13-26 we utilize the Excel Solver and the Palisade's add-in Evolver to solve complicated optimization problems. In Chapters 27-37 we introduce the simulation add-in @RISK and emphasize how @RISK can be used to model the **profitability of new products**. In Chapter 38 we introduce the Palisade decision tree add-in PrecisionTree. In Chapter 39 we introduce the Palisade sensitivity analysis add-in TopRank. Chapters 40-54 detail how the Lognormal random variable and the risk neutral approach can be used to value **financial derivatives**. We also discuss how to do a value at risk (VAR analysis) for many financial derivatives. Chapters 55-58 introduce the reader to the exciting world of **real options**, in which option theory is used to evaluate corporate investment opportunities. Chapters 59 and 60 discuss two interesting topics, M^2 and the Kelly Growth criteria, that can be used to improve management of investment portfolios. Chapters 61 and 63 discuss how to integrate macros (including Solver) with @RISK. Last (and not least) Chapter 62 tells the reader how to simulate the NCAA tournament! Most material in this book has never been in print. It is my hope that financial analysts will find the material in this book aids them in making better business decisions.

How to Use the Book

There are several core chapters that **must** be read. Every reader should look at Chapters 1, 2, 3, 6, 16, 17, 27, 28, 40-42, 45, 47, 55, and 56. Beyond these chapters, the prerequisites for each chapter are listed below:

Chapter	Prerequisite
24	23
30	29
49	48
52	51
53	12, 51,52
63	61

Each chapter is written (as much as possible) in a modular fashion. All files discussed in the book are included on a CD-ROM. The step-by step and teach by example approach should make the book suitable for self-study or executive education classes. Indeed, the author has used portions of the book to teach executives at Eli Lilly, GM, NCR, PriceWaterhouseCoopers, Bristol-Myers Squibb, and Deloitte & Touche. The book has been successfully class tested for several years in a second year MBA elective course (Decision Support Systems). Hopefully, the book will be used as a supplement to many finance courses and will spawn new courses such as "Financial Applications of Management Science."

Acknowledgements

This book has been a lot of fun to write. I am grateful to Palisade Corporation for publishing the manuscript in such a timely fashion. The support of my K510 classes, the participants in the 1998 TMSS workshop at Dartmouth (particularly Steve Powell), and my family has been unwavering. Let me know what you think. I can be reached via e-mail at Winston@Indiana.edu or by phone (812-855-3495).

Wayne L. Winston
Bloomington, Indiana
August 1998

Table of Contents

Section II-@RISK Functions 485

Chapter 1: Sensitivity Analysis with Data Tables

Introduction to Solver and Goal Seek

In many business situations there are several inputs or **parameters** which influence **outputs** of interest. Here are some examples:

Inputs	Outputs
Interest rate and cash flows of project	Project NPV
Advertising and price	Demand and profit earned from product
Temperature and pressure	Yield of a chemical process and quality of product

Sensitivity analysis is concerned with determining how changes in inputs affect the outputs. The Excel **data table capability** makes it easy to perform sensitivity analysis on one or two inputs at a time. If we want to find a value of a single input which yields a desired level of an output then Goal Seek is useful. If we want to determine a combination of inputs which optimizes (maximizes or minimizes) an output then the Excel **Solver** or the genetic algorithm Evolver can solve your problem. We now look at three examples of data tables in action. All three examples will utilize data tables. Our first example will also utilize Goal Seek. Our second example will introduce us to the optimization capabilities of Solver.

Example 1.1 In the sheet NPV of the file *datatable.xls* you are given the cash flows for two projects. Time 0 is today, Time 1 a year from now, etc. We would like to determine how the relative NPV's of the two projects depends on the interest rate (r). Currently cash flows are discounted at a rate of 10% per year.

Figure 1.1

	A	B	C
1			
2	r	0.1	
3	Time	Project 1	Project 2
4	0	-50	-100
5	1	10	90
6	2	20	80
7	3	30	70
8	4	40	60
9	5	50	50
10	6	60	40
11	7	70	30
12	8	80	20
13	9	90	10
14	10	100	5
15	NPV	$240.36	$226.03

Solution   First we will compute in B15 and C15 the NPV of each project. Then we will use a **one way data table** (see Figure 1.2) to determine how changes in the interest rate change the NPV of each project.

Figure 1.2

	F	G	H	I
1				
2	r	NPV 1	NPV 2	NPV1 - NPV 2
3		$240.36	$226.03	$14.33
4	0.01	463.148	338.5089	124.6391703
5	0.02	429.3769	322.9834	106.3934655
6	0.03	398.3899	308.3508	90.03909536
7	0.04	369.9225	294.5449	75.37756236
8	0.05	343.7378	281.5052	62.23259691
9	0.06	319.6241	269.1766	50.44748942
10	0.07	297.3913	257.5086	39.88276443
11	0.08	276.8691	246.455	30.41415017
12	0.09	257.9043	235.9735	21.9308037
13	0.1	240.3591	226.0253	14.33375738
14	0.11	224.1093	216.5748	7.534557332
15	0.12	209.0431	207.5891	1.454068628
16	0.13	195.0594	199.0379	-3.97857448
17	0.14	182.0667	190.8936	-8.826892022
18	0.15	169.9825	183.1303	-13.14787165
19	0.16	158.7317	175.7244	-16.9926858
20	0.17	148.2466	168.6539	-20.4073248
21	0.18	138.4654	161.8986	-23.4331564
22	0.19	129.332	155.4395	-26.10742079
23	0.2	120.7955	149.2592	-28.46366909

A one-way data table lets us vary the value of one parameter in a spreadsheet. The values of the parameter are placed in the left-hand column of the table range (F4:F23). In the row above the first value of the input parameter we move over one column (to cell G3) and enter formulas we want recalculated for each value of the input parameter. Then we call up Data Table and select the desired Column Input Cell. The formulas in the first row of the table range will then be repeatedly calculated for the values of the input cell in the first column of the table range. Here's how things go:

Step by Step   **Step 1: In cells B15 and C15 compute the NPV of each project at 10% by entering in B15 the formula**

$=B4+NPV(\$B\$2,B5:B14)$

and copying the formula to C15. Remember the =NPV function assumes payments are received at end of a year, not beginning of a year.

Step 2: Enter possible values for interest rates in F4:F23.

Step 3: In G3:I3 enter formula we want to keep track of

(G3) = B15 (NPV of Project 1)

(H3) = C15 (NPV of Project 2)

• *(I3) =B15-C15 (Difference in Project NPV's).*

Step 4: Select the table range F3:I23 and select Data Table. Fill in dialog box as follows:

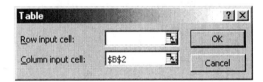

Basically, Excel first places a .01 in B2 and calculates each project's NPV and the difference in the project NPV's. Next Excel places a .02 in B2 and makes the calculations, etc.

You will now obtain the table in Figure 1.2. For example, we find for an interest rate of 8% (look at row 11) Project 1 has an NPV of $276.87, Project 2 has an NPV of $246.46, and Project 1 has an NPV $30.41 higher than Project 2.

From this table we may conclude:

• Increases in the discount rate decrease the NPV of both projects.

• For low interest rates Project 1 has a larger NPV and for high interest rates Project 2 has a larger NPV. This is because Project 1 has most of its cash flows later and Project 2 has most of its cash flows earlier. Somewhere between a 12% and 13% discount factor both projects have the same NPV. (see below)

Remarks

If you do not want your data table to recalculate each time the spreadsheet is changed, select the Excel Tools menu *"Options"* command and check *"Automatic Except Tables"* Calculation tab. If you choose this option you will need to hit F9 to recalculate your data tables.

Using Goal Seek to find the "Indifference Point"

For what interest rate are we indifferent between Projects 1 and 2? In short for what interest rate do Projects 1 and 2 have the same NPV? This can be determined with Goal Seek. Goal Seek let's us find the value of a "changing cell" which makes a "set cell" assume a desired value. We begin (*see sheet Goal Seek of datatable.xls file*) by setting up in cell E5 is the difference in the Project NPV's (B16-C16). Then we tell Goal Seek to Set cell E5 (difference in NPV's) to 0 by changing the interest rate (cell B3). Goal Seek reports that for a 12.2% interest rate both projects have the same NPV.

Figure 1.3

	A	B	C	D	E
2					
3	r	0.122567			
4	Time	Project 1	Project 2		NPV1 - NPV 2
5	0	-50	-100		$0.00
6	1	10	90		
7	2	20	80		
8	3	30	70		
9	4	40	60		
10	5	50	50		
11	6	60	40		
12	7	70	30		
13	8	80	20		
14	9	90	10		
15	10	100	5		
16	NPV	$205.35	$205.35		

The Goal Seek window is as follows:

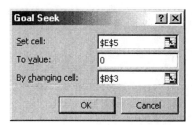

Goal Seek	? X
Set cell:	$E$5
To value:	0
By changing cell:	$B$3

OK   Cancel

Remarks

You may increase the precision of Goal Seek by selecting Excel Tools menu *"Options"* command and changing *"Precision"* on the Calculation tab to a number very close to 0. For example, if you set Precision = .00001 Goal Seek will find an interest rate for which NPV of Project 1 - NPV of Project 2 is within .00001 of the desired value (0).

Two Way Data Tables and an Introduction to Solver

If we want to determine how an output is affected by changes in two inputs we simply put values for the inputs across the first row of the table range and down the first column of the table range. Our output formula must be placed in the upper left-hand corner of the output range. Here's an example (*see sheet sales of file datatable.xls*):

Example 1.2 A product costs $3 per unit to make. Possible prices include $1, $2, … $10 and possible amounts to be spent on advertising are $20,000, $40,000, $60,000, … $180,000. It is estimated that demand for the product (in thousands of units) is given by:

$$Sales = 70 + .2 * A^{1/3} - 7P + \sqrt{A * P}$$

where A is in $000's. Investigate how demand and profit depend on price and advertising.

Solution Our work is in the sheet Sales of file *datatable.xls* as shown in Figure 1.4.

Figure 1.4

	A	B	C	D
1	Demand=70+.2*A$^{1/3}$-7P+sqrt(A*P)			
2	A in $000 P and C in $ss demand in 000's			
3	A	$ 127.15		
4	P	$ 10.00		
5	C	$ 3.00		
6	Demand	36.66379943		
7	Profit	$ 129,496.60		

Step by Step **Step 1: First select the range A3:B5.** Then use Insert Name Range to define range names A, P, and C_ for B3:B5 respectively. Thus when we type a C_ in a formula,

Excel treats it as the value entered in B5, etc. Note Excel cannot name a range C or R; it inserts the _.

Step 2: In cell B6 we compute demand (in thousands of units) with the formula

=70+0.2*A^(1/3)-7*P+SQRT(A*P).

Step 3: In cell B7 we compute profit (in dollars) with the formula

=1000*B6*(P-C_)-1000*A.

Note that the value of A in cell B3 is in $000's, so in computing profit we must multiply A by 1,000. Also, demand in B6 is in 000's so we need to multiply the value in B6 by 1000 to get total units sold.

Step 4: We are now ready to determine how changes in price and advertising change demand. We have entered trial values for price in B10:B19 and trial values for advertising (in $000's) in C9:K9. The output formula (=B6 for demand) is entered in B9. We select our table range of B9:K19 and select Data Table TWO WAY. Then we fill in our dialog box as follows:

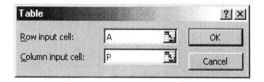

After hitting OK Excel repeatedly computes demand (in 000's of units) by inserting the values of A in row 9 and the values of price in column B into B3 and B4 respectively. We find, for example (see Figure 1.5) that when a price of $4 is charged and $20,000 is spent on advertising demand is 51,487 units.

Figure 1.5

	A	B	C	D	E	F	G	H	I	J	K
8											
9	Demand	36.66	20	40	60	80	100	120	140	160	180
10		$ 1.00	68.015	70.009	71.529	72.806	73.928	74.941	75.871	76.735	77.546
11		$ 2.00	62.867	65.628	67.737	69.511	71.070	72.478	73.772	74.974	76.103
12		$ 3.00	57.289	60.638	63.199	65.354	67.249	68.960	70.532	71.995	73.367
13		$ 4.00	51.487	55.333	58.275	60.750	62.928	64.895	66.703	68.384	69.962
14		$ 5.00	45.543	49.826	53.103	55.862	58.289	60.481	62.496	64.370	66.129
15		$ 6.00	39.497	44.176	47.757	50.771	53.423	55.819	58.021	60.070	61.993
16		$ 7.00	33.375	38.417	42.277	45.526	48.386	50.969	53.343	55.552	57.626
17		$ 8.00	27.192	32.573	36.692	40.160	43.213	45.970	48.505	50.863	53.077
18		$ 9.00	20.959	26.658	31.021	34.695	37.928	40.850	43.535	46.033	48.378
19		$10.00	14.685	20.684	25.278	29.146	32.551	35.628	38.455	41.086	43.556

From this table we learn the following:

- For a given level of advertising, a price increase will decrease demand at an increasing rate. To see this, look down each column of the table. You will find demand decreases, and the rate of decrease is increasing.

- For a given price level, an increase in advertising increases demand at a decreasing rate. To see this, note that as we move across each row, demand increases, but the rate of increase slows. The diminishing returns from advertising is due to the $A^{1/3}$ term in the demand function.

- At higher prices a given advertising increase will have a larger effect on demand. For example, when we increase advertising from $20,000 to $40,000 we find that at a $1 price sales increase by almost 2000 units and at a $10 price sales increase by almost 6000 units.

Step 5: We now construct a two- way data table to determine how variation in price and advertising affect profit. Our table range is B25:K35. Our output function (=B7, which is profit) is placed in cell A25. Our row and column input cells are as before. The resulting table is in Figure 1.6.

Figure 1.6

	A	B	C	D	E	F	G	H	I	J
23										
24	**Profit**									
25	$ 129,496.60	20	40	60	80	100	120	140	160	180
26	$ 1.00	-156030.0	-180017.1	-203057.9	-225612.1	-247856.6	-269881.9	-291741.3	-313469.8	-335091.3
27	$ 2.00	-82867.4	-105628.3	-127737.4	-149510.9	-171070.5	-192478.4	-213771.7	-234974.3	-256102.9
28	$ 3.00	-20000.0	-40000.0	-60000.0	-80000.0	-100000.0	-120000.0	-140000.0	-160000.0	-180000.0
29	$ 4.00	31487.2	15333.1	-1725.1	-19249.7	-37071.7	-55104.6	-73297.2	-91616.0	-110037.9
30	$ 5.00	71085.8	59652.3	46207.0	31723.5	16578.0	962.8	-15008.0	-31259.9	-47741.5
31	$ 6.00	98492.0	92527.8	83269.9	72312.0	60269.6	47457.9	34063.8	20208.9	5977.8
32	$ 7.00	113500.2	113668.8	109107.5	102104.4	93543.3	83877.0	73373.8	62208.7	50502.9
33	$ 8.00	115960.0	122862.7	123459.4	120800.0	116062.9	109851.8	102524.5	94314.3	85382.9
34	$ 9.00	105755.7	119945.9	126125.2	128167.5	127569.9	125099.0	121209.9	116198.6	110270.8
35	$ 10.00	82795.1	104787.9	116945.1	124022.3	127857.7	129392.5	129185.5	127600.4	124889.6
36	Max Profit	115960.0	122862.7	126125.2	128167.5	127857.7	129392.5	129185.5	127600.4	124889.6

In row 36 we computed the maximum profit for each advertising level by copying from C36 to D36:K36 the formula

$=MAX(C25:C35).$

We find a price of $10 and $120,000 spent on advertising yields the largest profit ($129,393).

Using Solver to Maximize Profit

We found the profit-maximizing combination of price and advertising with a trial and error search of a data table. Excel contains a Solver that can be used to systematically solve **optimization** problems. An optimization problem has three parts:

- A **target cell** that we wish to maximize or minimize.

- A set of **changing cells** which the Solver is free to vary.

- A set of **constraints** that restrict the values of the changing cells.

An optimal solution to a Solver model is the set of changing cells that **yields the best value of the target cell among all sets of changing cell values which satisfy all constraints.**

In our problem the Target Cell is profit (B7). Our changing cells are A and P. We will assume price is constrained to be at most $10, but any level of advertising is possible. Before showing you how to use Solver, we must define **linear functions** and a **linear Solver model.** A function of our changing cells is linear if changing cells only occur multiplied by constants and added together. Thus $2A + 3P$ is a linear function of our changing cells but $A^{1/2} + P$ is not a linear function of the changing cells.

A Solver model is **linear** if the target cell as well as the left-hand and right-hand side of all constraints are linear functions of the changing cells. Our model is not linear because the target cell (profit) is not a linear function of A and P. Solver is guaranteed to find an optimal solution for linear models, but may fail to find an optimal solution for nonlinear models. Fortunately, for our model Solver does find an optimal solution. For nonlinear models, Evolver, an optimizer which uses genetic algorithms, is often useful.

Starting Solver

To invoke Solver select the Excel menu "Tools" "Solver" command. If Solver is not available, select the "Tools" "Add-ins" command.

If Solver still does not show up you need to reinstall Office or Excel with the Custom option.

To use Solver to find the combinations of price and advertising that maximize profit :

Step by Step

Step 1: Select cell B7 (profit) as target cell.

Step 2: Select cells A and P as changing cells.

Step 3: Add constraint that P<=10. You will obtain the following Solver dialog box.

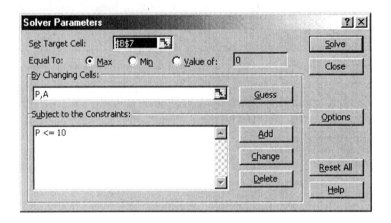

Step 4: Click *"Options"* **and select** *"Assume Non-Negative".* This ensures that the Changing cells will assume non-negative values. Do not check *"Assume Linear Model"* because model is not linear. Set Tolerance to 0 to ensure that Solver finds an optimal solution and does not stop when it obtains a *Target* cell value which is say, within 5% of optimal solution.

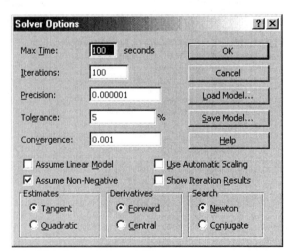

Step 5: Click *OK*, and click *"Solve"*. We find the optimal solution in Figure 1.4. Profit is maximized at $129,496.60 by charging a price of $10 and spending $127,150 on advertising. Note the data table found a very similar answer but Solver searched over all price and advertising levels and found a slightly better answer.

Two-way Data Tables and Decision Making Under Uncertainty

The following example illustrates how to use two-way data tables to make better decisions when facing an uncertain environment. Recall that the **mean** of a random variable is the "average value" assumed by a random variable when each outcome is weighted by its probability of occurrence. Also recall the **variance** of a random variable is the average squared deviation of a random variable from its mean (again the average is taken by weighting each outcome by its probability of occurring). The **standard deviation** of a random variable is the square root of the random variable's variance. Usually decision-makers want a high expected value and a low variance. This is because variance is a measure of risk or uncertainty and decision-makers dislike uncertainty. Here is an example of how data tables can be used to facilitate decision-making under uncertainty. (*See Figure 1.7 and sheet Capacity of file datatable.xls.*)

Example 1.3   In the year 2000 Eli Daisy must determine the capacity level for a new drug. The drug will sell for 10 years at a price of $7 per unit. The unit cost of producing the drug is $4. It costs $15 to build each unit of annual capacity. For example, building 100,000 units of annual capacity costs $1.5 million. Even if capacity is unused, it costs $1 per year to maintain each unit of capacity. Annual demand is uncertain, but it is assumed that demand will be the same each year and is governed by the following probabilities:

Annual demand	Probability
100,000	.1
200,000	.2
300,000	.3
400,000	.2
500,000	.1
600,000	.1

What amount of capacity should Eli Daisy build?

Note: To simplify this example, we will ignore the time value of money.

Solution

This problem involves **decisions** (the possible capacity levels of 100,000-600,000) and uncertain **states of nature** (annual demands of 100,000-600,000). The key to this problem is to set up a **payoff table** that gives the profit earned for each decision-state of the world combination. This is a job for a two-way data table! To make our work easier to follow, we have created the range names listed in B3:B9 We begin by computing the profit for one decision-state of the world combination, and then use a data table to create the entire payoff table.

Figure 1.7

	A	B	C
1	**Capacity Planning**		
2		Name	Value
3	Unit cost	uc	$4.00
4	Sales price	p	$7.00
5	Unit Building cost	f	$15.00
6	Annual maintenance cost per unit of capacity	m	$1.00
7	Annual Capacity Level	c	300000
8	Annual demand	d	100000
9	Years	t	10
10	**Revenue**		
11	Unit sales	100000	
12	Total Revenue	$ 7,000,000.00	
13	**Costs**		
14	Building	$ 4,500,000.00	
15	Maintenance	$ 3,000,000.00	
16	Unit costs	$ 4,000,000.00	
17	Total costs	$ 11,500,000.00	
18			
19	**Profit**	$ (4,500,000.00)	

Step by Step

Step 1: **Observe that annual sales will equal the smaller of capacity and annual demand.** Therefore in B11 we compute annual sales with the formula

$=MIN(d,c\_).$

Step 2: **In B12 compute our ten year total revenue with the formula**

$=B11*t*p.$

Two-way Data Tables and Decision Making Under Uncertainty

Step 3: In cell B14 compute building costs with the formula

$=c\_*f.$

Step 4: In cell B15 compute total maintenance costs with the formula

$=t*m*c\_.$

Step 5: In cell B16 compute unit production costs for the ten years with the formula

$=t*B11*uc.$

Step 6: In cell B17 compute total costs with the formula

$=SUM(B14:B16).$

Step 7: In cell B19 compute total profit with the formula

$=B12-B17.$

Step 8: We now set up a data table (see Figure 1.8) to determine profit for each action-state-of-world combination.

Figure 1.8

	F	G	H	I	J	K	L	M
5	probabilities	0.1	0.2	0.3	0.2	0.1	0.1	
6	profit	demand						
7	$ (4,500,000.00)	100000	200000	300000	400000	500000	600000	Mean profit
8	100000	500000	500000	500000	500000	500000	500000	$ 500,000
9	200000	-2000000	1000000	1000000	1000000	1000000	1000000	$ 700,000
10	300000	-4500000	-1500000	1500000	1500000	1500000	1500000	$ 300,000
11	400000	-7000000	-4000000	-1000000	2000000	2000000	2000000	$(1,000,000)
12	500000	-9500000	-6500000	-3500000	-500000	2500000	2500000	$(2,900,000)
13	600000	-12000000	-9000000	-6000000	-3000000	0	3000000	$(5,100,000)

Our table range is F7:L13 and our output cell F7 contains the formula =B19 (profit). Our column input cell is c_ (capacity) and our row input cell is d (demand). We find for example, that 300,000 in capacity with 200,000 in annual demand will yield a loss of $1.5 million. See cell H10.

Step 9: Expected profit for, say a capacity of 200,000 would be

.1(-2,000,000) + .2(1,000,000) + .3(1,000,000) + .2(1,000,000) + .1(1,000,000) + .1(1,000,000) = $700,000.

To compute expected profit for each capacity level enter the formula

=SUMPRODUCT($G$5:$L$5,G8:L8)

in M8 and copy it to M9:M13. The =SUMPRODUCT formula will multiply pairwise (and then sum up) two rows or columns of numbers. We find a capacity level of 200,000 units yields largest expected profit.

Step 10: In Figure 1.9 we find the variance and standard deviation of profit for each order quantity.

Figure 1.9

	F	G	H	I	J	K	L	M	N
15	Squared deviation	100000	200000	300000	400000	500000	600000	Variance	Std dev
16	100000	0	0	0	0	0	0	0	0
17	200000	7.29E+12	9E+10	9E+10	9E+10	9E+10	9E+10	8.1E+11	900000
18	300000	2.3E+13	3.2E+12	1.4E+12	1.4E+12	1.4E+12	1.4E+12	3.96E+12	1989975
19	400000	3.6E+13	9E+12	0	9E+12	9E+12	9E+12	9E+12	3000000
20	500000	4.36E+13	1.3E+13	3.6E+11	5.8E+12	2.9E+13	2.9E+13	1.404E+13	3746999
21	600000	4.76E+13	1.5E+13	8.1E+11	4.4E+12	2.6E+13	6.6E+13	1.809E+13	4253234

In G16 we compute squared deviation of profit for 100,000 capacity and 100,000 demand from mean profit for 100,000 capacity with the formula

=(G8-$M8)^2.

Copying this formula from G16 to G16:L21 computes squared deviation from profit for each capacity-demand combination.

In cell M16 we compute the variance or averaged squared deviation from mean profit for 100,000 capacity with formula

=SUMPRODUCT($G$5:$L$5,G16:L16).

Copying this formula from M16 to M17:M21 determines the variance of profit for each capacity level. Copying the formula

   =SQRT(M16)

from N16 to N17:N21 computes the standard deviation of profit for each capacity level. Note that as capacity increases, riskiness of profit increases. Clearly a capacity level of 200,000 is superior to a capacity level of 300,000 or higher. This is because a capacity level of 200,000 has a higher average profit and less risk than higher capacity levels. An extremely risk-averse corporation, however, might prefer a 100,000 unit capacity level to 200,000 capacity because it has no risk.

Two-way Data Tables and Decision Making Under Uncertainty

Chapter 2: Simple Linear Regression- Estimating Fixed and Variable Cost

There are many situations in which we want to predict the value of a variable (the **dependent variable**) from the value of one or more **independent variables**. In this chapter we will discuss how to make such predictions when there is one independent variable. We will conventionally let Y = Dependent Variable and X = Independent Variable. Here are some examples where it is important to be able to predict the dependent variable from the value of the independent variable.

Example 2.1   In Figure 2.1 we are given past sales of Microsoft (*see the file Micro.xls*). Can we use this data to forecast future sales? This is known as fitting a **trend** to data.

Solution   The independent variable (column A) is usually the year (first year is year 1, second year is year 2, etc.). The dependent variable (column B) is sales. Data for Microsoft is displayed in Figure 2.1. Year 1 is 1984 and sales are expressed in millions of dollars.

Figure 2.1

	A	B
3	Year	Sales
4	1	98
5	2	140
6	3	198
7	4	346
8	5	591
9	6	804
10	7	1183
11	8	1843
12	9	2759
13	10	3753

In Figure 2.2 we have plotted this data. We have also included a curve that fits the data well. The slope of this curve increases as YEAR increases, so no straight line could fit this data as well as the curve in Figure 2.2. (Recall that a straight line has a constant slope). Microsoft's growth is an example of exponential growth. We will return to our study of exponential growth in Chapter 3.

Figure 2.2

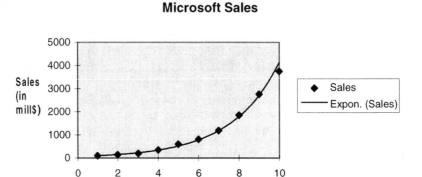

Example 2.2 The return of most stocks is closely tied to the return on the market. It is very important in finance to try and predict the return on a stock (dependent variable) from the return on the market (independent variable). Note that

$$Annual\ Return = \frac{NextYear's\ Price + Dividend - LastYear's\ Price}{Last\ Year's\ Price}$$

In Figure 2.3 we have given the annual return on Eli Lilly stock (*file Lilly.xls*) and the annual return on the market for the years 1985-1994. We would use column E as the independent variable and column F as the dependent variable.

Figure 2.3

	B	C	D	E	F
3	Year	Closing Stock Price	Dividends	Market Return	Return on Lilly
4	1984	$ 16.50	0.75	0.0627	
5	1985	$ 27.88	0.8	0.3216	0.738182
6	1986	$ 37.13	0.9	0.1847	0.36406
7	1987	$ 39.00	1	0.0523	0.077296
8	1988	$ 42.75	1.15	0.1681	0.125641
9	1989	$ 68.50	1.35	0.3149	0.633918
10	1990	$ 73.25	1.64	-0.0317	0.093285
11	1991	$ 83.50	2	0.3055	0.167235
12	1992	$ 60.75	2.2	0.0767	-0.24611
13	1993	$ 59.38	2.42	0.0999	0.017284
14	1994	$ 65.63	2.5	0.0131	0.147356

In Figure 2.4 we have plotted the line that "best fits" this data (more on the meaning of "best fits" later in the chapter). We see that there is a linear relationship between the return on the market and the return on Lilly, but the wide dispersion of the points about the best fitting line indicates that we do not have a "perfect" linear relationship. Other factors besides the return on the market must be governing the return on Lilly.

Figure 2.4

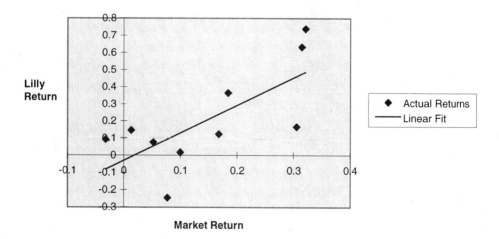

Lilly Return vs. Market

Fitting a Straight Line to Data

We now discuss how to fit a straight line to data. The following example will get us started.

Example 2.3 Chipco, a small computer chip manufacturer, wants to be able to forecast monthly operating costs as a function of the number of units produced during a month. They have collected the 16 months of data in Figure 2.5 (file *Chipco.xls*).

Figure 2.5

	A	B	C
3	Month	Units Produced	Total Cost
4	1	500	131000
5	2	600	135000
6	3	400	104000
7	4	300	76000
8	5	800	186000
9	6	900	190100
10	7	600	150000
11	8	400	98000
12	9	300	78000
13	10	200	60000
14	11	400	108000
15	12	600	152000
16	13	700	158000
17	14	500	134380
18	15	300	86000
19	16	200	60002
20	17	400	

Determine an equation that can be used to predict monthly production costs from units produced.

Solution When trying to relate one variable to another, we always begin by constructing a scatterplot. This will tell use whether a linear (or nonlinear) relationship is reasonable.

Plotting the Data

Step by Step **Step 1: Select the range B3:C19.**

Step 2: Select Chart Wizard Icon and choose X-Y Scatterplot Option (Choice 1).

You will obtain the scatterplot in Figure 2.6.

Figure 2.6

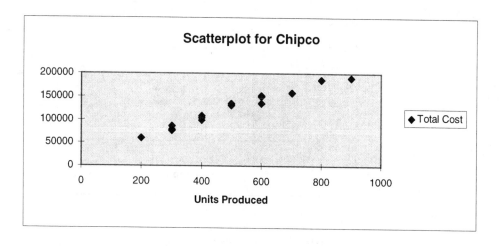

Finding the Least Squares Line

Figure 2.6 makes it clear that there is a strong linear relationship between Units Produced and Monthly Cost. When we fit a line using a single independent variable to predict a dependent variable, we are running a **simple linear regression**. Now that we have found that there is a straight-line relationship between Units Produced and Monthly Cost, we want to find the line that "best" fits the data plotted in Figure 2.6. The best line is usually defined to be the line that minimizes the sum of the squared **vertical distances** from the line to the data points. (You might want to think about why we do not minimize the sum of the vertical distances from the line to the points!). This line is called the **least squares line**. There are at least three ways that you can use Excel to find the least squares line. For now, we give you two methods.

Step by Step

Step 1: Select your scatterplot and click on the data points until they turn Gold.

Step 2: You can now select *"Chart" " Add Trendline".*

Step 3: Check the boxes for *"Display equation on chart"* **and** *"Display R-Sq Value."* You will now obtain Figure 2.7.

Figure 2.7

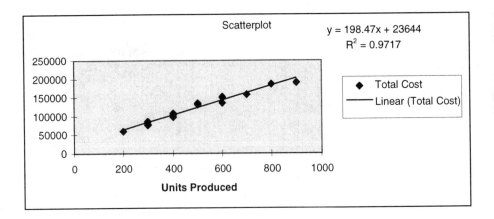

We now see the least squares line. The line is

$$COST = 23,644 + 198.47(UNITS\ PRODUCED).$$

This line has an intercept of 23,644 and slope of 198.47. For any least squares line the intercept is the predicted value for Y (the dependent variable) when X (the independent variable) equals 0. In this example the intercept of $23,644 would be our prediction of cost when 0 units are produced. This is an estimate of Chipco's **fixed cost** of monthly operation.

The slope of any least squares line is the predicted increase in Y corresponding to a unit increase in X. For our example the slope of $198.47 is interpreted as saying that the **variable cost** of producing each additional unit is estimated to be $198.47.

Another way to get to get the least squares line is to use the Excel =INTERCEPT( ) and =SLOPE( ) functions.

Step 4: To obtain the Intercept for Chipco's least squares line enter in cell C22 the formula

$$= INTERCEPT(C4:C19, B4:B19).$$

Excel returns 23,643.8 (see Figure 2.8).

Figure 2.8

	A	B	C
22	Intercept		23643.8
23	Slope		198.4651

Step 5: To obtain the slope for Chipco's least squares lines enter in cell C23 the formula

$= SLOPE(C4:C19, B4:B19).$

Excel returns 198.47 (see Figure 2.8).

Observe that the first argument in the = SLOPE ( ) and = INTERCEPT() functions is the range where the Y-data is and the second argument is the X-range.

Making Predictions with the Least Squares Line

We next show two ways to use the Least Squares Line to make predictions for Monthly Cost (see Figure 2.9). For example, for Month 1:

Predicted Cost = 23,643.8 + 198.4651(500) = $122,876.35.

Figure 2.9

	A	B	C	D	E	F
3	Month	Units Produced	Total Cost	Predictions from Trend Function	Predictions from Equation of Line	Residuals
4	1	500	131000	122876.35	122876.35	8123.655
5	2	600	135000	142722.85	142722.85	-7722.85
6	3	400	104000	103029.84	103029.84	970.1629
7	4	300	76000	83183.329	83183.329	-7183.33
8	5	800	186000	182415.87	182415.87	3584.13
9	6	900	190100	202262.38	202262.38	-12162.4
10	7	600	150000	142722.85	142722.85	7277.146
11	8	400	98000	103029.84	103029.84	-5029.84
12	9	300	78000	83183.329	83183.329	-5183.33
13	10	200	60000	63336.821	63336.821	-3336.82
14	11	400	108000	103029.84	103029.84	4970.163
15	12	600	152000	142722.85	142722.85	9277.146
16	13	700	158000	162569.36	162569.36	-4569.36
17	14	500	134380	122876.35	122876.35	11503.65
18	15	300	86000	83183.329	83183.329	2816.671
19	16	200	60002	63336.821	63336.821	-3334.82
20	17	400		103029.84	103029.84	

Step 1: In cell E4 predict Month 1 total cost with the formula

$$= \$C\$22 + \$C\$23^*B4.$$

Copying this formula to the cell range E4:E19 computes the predictions for month 2-16 (*see Figure 2.9*)

Step 2: Excel contains a built-in function (= TREND( )) which can be used to construct predictions from regressions. = TREND is a special kind of function, called an array function. To construct forecasts for Months 1-16 move the cursor to D4 and select the range where you want the forecasts to go (D4:D19). Now type in cell D4 the formula

$$= TREND(C4:C19, B4:B19, B4:B19).$$

Hit *<Ctrl><Shift><Enter>* (not just *<Enter>*!) and your forecasts will appear in D4:D19. Don't worry about the {. The { signifies that you have entered an Array function. The first argument of =TREND is the Y-Range for the data used to the fit the line. The second argument of =TREND is the X-Range for the data used to fit the line. The third range is the X-Range for the data for which you want to make predictions. Note that columns D and E match (they better!!).

Suppose, that during month 17, 400 chips were produced. How can we determine a prediction for monthly cost? We could use either of the following approaches.

Step 3: Copy the formula in E19 to E20. This yields a prediction of $103,029.84.

Step 4: In D20 type the array formula

$$=TREND(C4:C19, B4:B19, B20).$$

After hitting *<Ctrl><Shift><Enter>* Excel will yield $103,029.84.

Remarks

1) A regression should not be used to make forecasts for values of the independent variable which differ greatly from the observed values. For example, our regression probably has little validity for predicting costs during a month in which Chipco produces say, 10,000 units. This is because our data does not include any month with a similar production volume.

2) If you believe that a regression should go through the point (0,0) you can ensure this by checking the INTERCEPT = 0 box on the OPTIONS part of INSERT TRENDLINE.

Analyzing the Errors or Residuals

An important concept in evaluating predictions is the **error or residual** from each observation. For each observation we define the **residual** by *Residual of Observation = Observed Value of Y - Predicted Value of Y*. If we had a line perfectly fitting the points all residuals would equal 0. Thus a "good-fitting" line should have most residuals near 0. We compute the residuals for Chipco's data in the range F4:F19 of Figure 2.9.

Step by Step

Step 1: Compute Month 1's residual in cell F4 with the formula

$$= C4 - D4.$$

Copying this formula to the cell range F5:F19 computes the residuals for Months 2-16.

For any least squares line, the residuals will sum to 0 (why is this reasonable?) We will return to our discussion of the residuals when we discuss the accuracy of regression forecasts.

How Good is the Fit?

Figure 2.7 yields R^2 = .9717. What does this mean? For any simple linear regression R^2 is the percentage of variation in the dependent variable (cost) explained by the independent variable (units produced). Thus variation in units produced explains 97.17% of monthly variation in costs. This means that only 2.8% of variation in monthly cost is unexplained by variation in units produced. We can also find the value of R^2 with the =RSQ function. For the Chipco example, entering in cell C25 the formula:

=RSQ(C4:C19, B4:B19)

would yield .9717. (See Figure 2.10).

Figure 2.10

	A	B	C
24	Std. Error		7261.642
25	RSq		0.971736

How Accurate are our Predictions?

When we use a simple linear regression to predict a dependent variable, a natural question is how accurate are our forecasts? The key to answering this question is s_e = **standard error of the estimate**. s_e is a measure of the standard deviation of the residuals. It will be the case that

- For approximately 68% of all observations the actual value of the dependent variable will be within s_e of the predicted value. (or | residual | $\leq s_e$ 68% of time)

- For approximately 95% of all observations the actual value of the dependent variable will be within $2s_e$ of the predicted value. (or | residual | $\leq 2s_e$ 95% of time)

- For approximately 99.7% of all observations the actual value of the dependent variable will be within $3s_e$ of the predicted value. (or | residual | $\leq 3s_e$ 99.7% of time)

In Figure 2.10 we find s_e = 7262. We found this by entering in cell C24 the formula

$= STEYX(C4:C19, B4:B19).$

Excel yields s_e = 7262. Column F of Figure 2.9 shows that all for observations actual cost is within $2s_e$ = \$14,524 of actual cost while 11/16 = 69% of actual costs are within s_e of actual costs. Any observation for which our prediction is off by more than $2s_e$ is called an **outlier**. Outliers should be examined carefully because they may represent inaccurate information or be caused by factors not considered in the regression. For example, an outlier on the high side could have been caused by a plant strike. For our data, Chipco has no outliers.

Probability Statements about the Dependent Variable

Given the value of the independent variable, we can even make probabilistic statements about the value of the dependent variable. The key is to note that if $x = x_o$, then the actual value of y will be approximately normally distributed with:

Mean = predicted value of y when $x = x_o$

and

Standard deviation = s_e.

The following illustrates the use of this idea.

Example 2.1
(continued)   During a month in which 500 units are produced what is the probability that monthly costs will exceed $145,000?

Figure 2.11

	A	B	C
			Prob(Costs
27	Production	Predicted costs	>=$145,000
28	500	122879	0.001158526

Solution   In cell B28 we compute (see Figure 2.11) the mean cost when 500 units are produced in a month with the formula:

$$=A28*198.47 + 23644.$$

We obtain $122,879. We now know that during a month in which production equals 500 units, monthly cost will follow a normal distribution with mean (in B28) $122,879 and a standard deviation (in C24) equal to $s_e = 7,262$. Now in cell C28 we obtain the probability that monthly cost is at least $145,000 with the formula:

$$=1 -NORMDIST(145000,B28, C24, 1).$$

We obtain .001. This tells us that if we make 500 units in a month and costs exceed $145,000 something is wrong!

Remarks

The Excel function $=NORMDIST(x,\mu,\sigma,1)$ will yield the probability that a normal random variable with mean μ and standard deviation σ assumes a value less than or equal to x.

Regression with the Analysis Toolpak: Hypothesis Testing in Regression

Using the Regression option from the Analysis Toolpak provides us with a lot more information about the relationship between x and y. To illustrate, here's how to run a regression with the Analysis Toolpak for the Chipco example (see Figure 2.12).

Step by Step

Step 1: Select *"Data Analysis" "Tools" "Regression"*.

Step 2: Select the Y-Range as C3:C19.

Step 3: Select the X-Range as B3:B19.

Step 4: Check the *"Labels"* box.

Step 5: Check the *"Residuals"* box.

Step 6: Check the *"New Sheet box for output"* (call the sheet regression).

In cell B5 we find $R^2 = .9717$. In cell B7 we find $s_e = 7261.64$. In cell B17 we find the intercept (23,643.8) for the regression and in cell B18 we find the slope (198.47) for the regression. In the range C25:C40 we obtain the residuals for the 16 observations. The predictions for the 16 observations are in the cell range B25:B40.

Figure 2.12

	A	B	C	D	E	F	G	H	I
1	SUMMARY OUTPUT								
2									
3	*Regression Statistics*								
4	Multiple R	0.985767							
5	R Square	0.971736							
6	Adjusted F	0.969717							
7	Standard E	7261.642							
8	Observatic	16							
9									
10	ANOVA								
11		*df*	*SS*	*MS*	*F*	*Significance F*			
12	Regressio	1	2.54E+10	2.54E+10	481.3237	3.05661E-12			
13	Residual	14	7.38E+08	52731447					
14	Total	15	2.61E+10						
15									
16		*Coefficients*	*andard Err*	*t Stat*	*P-value*	*Lower 95%*	*Upper 95%*	*Lower 95.0%*	*Upper 95.0%*
17	Intercept	23643.8	4716.829	5.012648	0.00019	13527.20286	33760.405	13527.20286	33760.40529
18	Units Proc	198.4651	9.046186	21.93909	3.06E-12	179.0629264	217.86724	179.0629264	217.8672385
19									
20									
21									
22	RESIDUAL OUTPUT								
23									
24	*Observatio*	*icted Total*	*Residuals*						
25	1	122876.3	8123.655						
26	2	142722.9	-7722.85						
27	3	103029.8	970.1629						
28	4	83183.33	-7183.33						
29	5	182415.9	3584.13						
30	6	202262.4	-12162.4						
31	7	142722.9	7277.146						
32	8	103029.8	-5029.84						
33	9	83183.33	-5183.33						
34	10	63336.82	-3336.82						
35	11	103029.8	4970.163						
36	12	142722.9	9277.146						
37	13	162569.4	-4569.36						
38	14	122876.3	11503.65						
39	15	83183.33	2816.671						
40	16	63336.82	-3334.82						

Testing the Significance of the Linear Relationship

The **linear regression model** postulates that

$$y = \beta_0 + \beta_1 x + (error\ term)\ (2.1).$$

The error term is assumed to have a mean of 0. This represents the fact that points scatter about the true regression line ($\beta_0 + \beta_1 x$). Like the mean and variance of a random variable, β_0 and β_1 are unknown population parameters that we try to estimate. The intercept of our least squares line is an estimate of β_0 and the slope of our least squares line is an estimate of β_1. The DATA ANALYSIS regression analysis enables us to test the following hypotheses:

$H_o: \beta_1 = 0$ *(no significant linear relationship)*

$H_a: \beta_1 \neq 0$ *(a significant linear relationship).*

Note that if H_o is true then (2.1) becomes y = β_0 + (error term). This would mean that for all values of x our prediction for y would be the same number (β_0). This is the meaning of "no linear relationship". To choose between H_o and H_a we look at the t-statistic in D18 (21.93) and the p-value (3.06E-12) in E18. We reject H_o if p-value<α = level of significance. Thus for any level of significance we would conclude there is a significant linear relationship between units produced and monthly cost. This is consistent with the tight scatter of the points about the least squares line in Figure 2.7. For reasonable sample sizes (at least 30), a t-statistic exceeding 2 in absolute value will be significant at the .05 level. Often in regression we use α = .10. This is to avoid missing a possibly important linear relationship.

Chapter 3: Fitting Exponential Growth-Estimating the Growth Rate of Microsoft

Often a scatterplot will indicate that x and y are related, but not in a linear fashion. For example, in Figure 3.1 we try and fit a "trend curve" to predict sales of Microsoft (y) as a function of years after 1984 (x). It is clear that the slope of this graph is increasing. Thus fitting a straight line is unreasonable. When the slope of a curve is increasing it is often reasonable to fit an **exponential curve** of the form

$$Y = ae^{bx} \quad (3.1)$$

to your data. The file *exponential.xls* plots examples of (3.1).

Figure 3.1

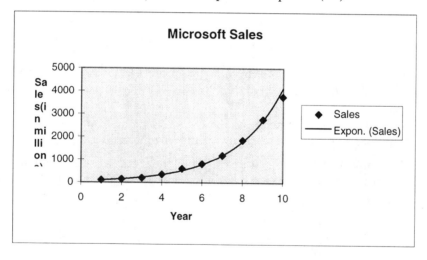

In Figure 3.2 we plot $y = 2e^{3x}$. Note that e = 2.7182 (approximately), and we compute, say e^4 in Excel by entering

=EXP(4).

Figure 3.2

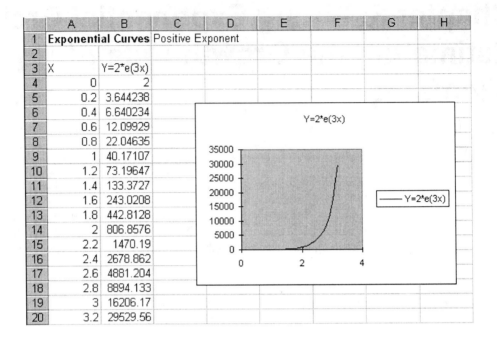

	A	B	C	D	E	F	G	H
1	**Exponential Curves**	Positive Exponent						
2								
3	X	Y=2*e(3x)						
4	0	2						
5	0.2	3.644238						
6	0.4	6.640234						
7	0.6	12.09929						
8	0.8	22.04635						
9	1	40.17107						
10	1.2	73.19647						
11	1.4	133.3727						
12	1.6	243.0208						
13	1.8	442.8128						
14	2	806.8576						
15	2.2	1470.19						
16	2.4	2678.862						
17	2.6	4881.204						
18	2.8	8894.133						
19	3	16206.17						
20	3.2	29529.56						

Note that as x increases y increases. Also, the slope of this curve increases rapidly and the curve gets steep quickly. This is an example of the fact that for b>0, the slope of $y = ae^{bx}$ increases as x increases.

In Figure 3.3 we plot $y = 2e^{-1.5x}$. As x increases, y decreases. Note the slope of this curve increases towards 0 as x increases. This is an example of the fact that for b<0, the slope of $y = ae^{bx}$ increases towards 0 as x increases.

It is important to note that for an exponential curve a unit increase in x causes our prediction for y to increase by a factor of e^b. To see this note that:

Prediction for y for $x = ae^{bx}$

Prediction for y for $x + 1 = ae^{b(x+1)}$.

Thus (Prediction for y for x + 1)/(Prediction for y for x) = $\dfrac{ae^{b(x+1)}}{ae^{bx}} = e^b.$

Figure 3.3

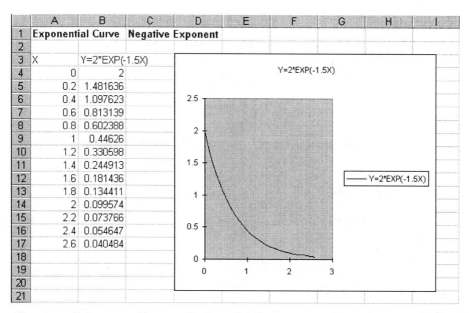

	A	B	C	D
1	Exponential Curve	Negative Exponent		
2				
3	X	Y=2*EXP(-1.5X)		
4	0	2		
5	0.2	1.481636		
6	0.4	1.097623		
7	0.6	0.813139		
8	0.8	0.602388		
9	1	0.44626		
10	1.2	0.330598		
11	1.4	0.244913		
12	1.6	0.181436		
13	1.8	0.134411		
14	2	0.099574		
15	2.2	0.073766		
16	2.4	0.054647		
17	2.6	0.040484		
18				
19				
20				
21				

Thus a **unit increase in x results in a fixed percentage increase in y of (e^b - 1)**. This implies that as x grows larger a unit increase in x will (for b>0) result in the same percentage increase but a larger absolute increase in y!

The easiest way to fit an exponential curve to data is to use the INSERT TRENDLINE FEATURE and choose EXPONENTIAL. When trying to fit the growth of a company's sales or profits, an exponential curve often will fit data quite well. We illustrate this in the following example:

Example 3.1   Figure 3.4 (*file Micro.xls*) gives the annual sales for Microsoft (in millions of dollars) for the years 1984-1993 (1984 = year 1). Here we will:

a)   Fit an exponential curve to this data.

b)   Use the percentage you estimate that Microsoft will grow each year.

c)   Give a prediction for 1995 Microsoft sales.

Figure 3.4

	A	B
3	Year	Sales
4	1	98
5	2	140
6	3	198
7	4	346
8	5	591
9	6	804
10	7	1183
11	8	1843
12	9	2759
13	10	3753

**Solution –
Part a)**

To fit an exponential curve proceed as follows:

**Step by
Step**

Step 1: Select the cell range A3:B13 and create an X-Y plot (Option 1).

Step 2: Click on the points until they all turn gold.

Step 3: Now select *"Chart" "Add Trendline"*, and highlight *"Exponential"*.

Step 4: Click the *"Options"* tab and select *"Display Equation on Chart"* and Display R-SQ.

Step 5: Hit OK and you will obtain (see Figure 3.5) the curve of the form $Y = e^{bx}$ that best fits your data.

We will discuss the interpretation of R^2 later. For now observe that the best fitting exponential curve is $y = 63.681e^{.4171x}$.

Figure 3.5

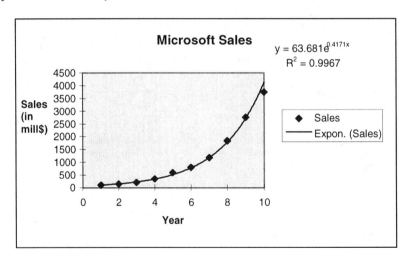

We estimate that (if past trends continue) Microsoft will grow by a factor of $e^{.4171} = 1.52$ from one year to the next. Thus past data indicates that Microsoft has grown at 52% per year.

To predict 1995 sales for Microsoft we need to compute $63.681*e^{.4171(12)}$. We do this in cell E14 of Figure 3.6 with the formula

=63.681*exp(A14*.4171) = 9500.37 (about 9.5 billion dollars).

Recall that the = TREND function could be used to generate predictions from a simple linear regression. Similarly, the = GROWTH function can be used to generate predictions from exponential growth. To generate a prediction for 1995 sales simply type in cell D14

=GROWTH(B4:B13, A4:A13, A14)

and hit <Ctrl><Shift><Enter>. The first argument of the = GROWTH function is the range where the dependent variable data used to fit the exponential curve is located. The second argument is the range where the independent variable data used to fit the exponential curve is located. The third argument is the range where new values of the independent variable(s) for which we want to make a prediction are located. We obtain 9502.98. This answer is slightly more correct than our answer in cell E14. In E14 we used a rounded off equation. Cell D14 uses the exact, non-rounded equation to produce forecasts.

Meaning of R^2 in a Nonlinear Regression

When we fit a nonlinear curve to data, the R^2 value reported by Excel is difficult to interpret. Before discussing the meaning of the R^2 value reported by Excel in exponential curve fitting we need to discuss logarithms.

Figure 3.6

	A	B	C	D	E	F	G
1	MIcrosoft Exponential Trend				MAPE	0.051833084	
2		in millions of $		Year 1 = 1984		Estimated s_{pe}	0.064791
3	Year	Sales	Net Income	LN(SALES	PREDICTED SALES	Absolute percentage error	
4	1	98	16	4.584967	96.6416403	0.013860814	
5	2	140	24	4.941642	146.66228	0.047587718	
6	3	198	39	5.288267	222.573049	0.124106307	
7	4	346	72	5.846439	337.774388	0.023773445	
8	5	591	124	6.381816	512.602662	0.132652011	
9	6	804	171	6.689599	777.920109	0.032437675	
10	7	1183	279	7.075809	1180.56292	0.002060083	
11	8	1843	463	7.51915	1791.60918	0.027884327	
12	9	2759	708	7.922624	2718.92621	0.014524752	
13	10	3753	953	8.230311	4126.21223	0.099443708	
14	12	1995 Forecast		9502.98064	9500.372097		

Logarithm and Exponential Functions

If b^x = a we say that $x = Log_b$ a = x or "x is the logarithm of a to the base b". When the base is e, we write Ln instead of Log. Ln a = x implies that e^x = a. Some examples follow.

Log_{10} *10,000 = 4 (because 10^4 = 10,000)*

Log_{10} *.001 = -3 (because 10^{-3} = .001)*

Ln e^4 = 4 (because e^4 = e^4).

To obtain a logarithm to base 10 use the =LOG10 function. Thus:

=LOG10(10000)

yields 4. To obtain a logarithm to base e (a natural logarithm) in Excel use the =LN function. Thus

= LN(exp(4))

yields 4.

We will repeatedly use the following rules:

Log(x*y) = Log x + Log y   (3.2)

Log (x^a) = a Log x. (3.3)

$e^{Ln x}$ *= x (3.4).*

- To illustrate (3.2) note that $Log_{10}(10^5*10^3)=Log_{10}$ *(10^5) +$Log_{10}(10^3)$ = 5 + 3= 8.*
- To illustrate (3.3) note that *Ln (e^5) = 5 Ln(e) = 5*1 = 5.*
- To illustrate (3.4) let x = e^8. Then

$$e^{Ln e^8} = e^8 = x.$$

We can now explain the meaning of the R^2 value Excel obtains when we fit a power trendline. Let's suppose that (3.3) is indeed valid. Thus y = ae^{bx}. Taking natural logs of both sides yields

Ln y = Ln a + bx.

Thus if (3.1) is valid, then a plot of Ln y against x should yield a linear relationship. The R^2 value obtained by Excel is the R^2 value for the least squares line obtained when fitting the points (x, Ln y).

To illustrate this we created Ln (Sales) in column D of Figure 3.4. First we entered in cell D4 the formula:

$$= LN(B4)$$

and then copied this formula down to D13. Next we created a scatterplot with the selected range being A4:A13, D4:D13 (to do this select A4:A13, hold down the control key and then select D4:D13). The resulting plot in Figure 3.8 shows a strong linear relationship, as expected.

Figure 3.7

	A	B	C	D
3	Year	Sales	Net Income	LN(SALES
4	1	98	16	4.584967
5	2	140	24	4.941642
6	3	198	39	5.288267
7	4	346	72	5.846439
8	5	591	124	6.381816
9	6	804	171	6.689599
10	7	1183	279	7.075809
11	8	1843	463	7.51915
12	9	2759	708	7.922624
13	10	3753	953	8.230311

Figure 3.8

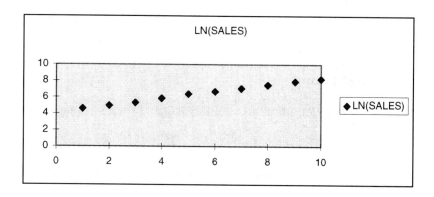

:

Accuracy of Forecasts

Recall from Chapter 2 that we expected around 95% of our predictions from simple linear regression to be accurate within $2s_e$. For a nonlinear model, it is more difficult to determine the accuracy of our forecasts. We proceed as follows:

Step by Step

Step 1: For each observation compute the absolute percentage value of the error (as a fraction of the actual value).

Step 2: Average the absolute percentage errors to obtain the MAPE = Mean Absolute Percentage Errors.

Step 3: Estimate the standard deviation of your percentage errors by

$$Estimated\ s_{pe} = 1.25 * MAPE .$$

Step 4: You can expect around 95% of your predictions to be within $2s_{pe}$ of the actual value.

Example 3.1 – Part c)   If past trends continue, you are 95% confident that a forecast for Microsoft sales based on trend will be accurate within how many millions of dollars?

Solution   Following the above procedure we proceed as follows:

Step by Step

Step 1: Compute the absolute percentage error for 1984 in cell F4 with the formula

$$=ABS(B4 - E4)/B4.$$

Step 2: Copy this formula down to F13 to compute absolute pecentage errors for 1985-1993.

Step 3: Compute the MAPE (5.2%) in F1 with the formula

$$=AVERAGE(F4:F13).$$

Step 4: In G2 compute the estimated standard percentage error (6.5%) with the formula

$$= 1.25 * F1.$$

We can now state that if past trends continue 95% of our forecasts should predict Microsoft's annual sales within 2(6.5%) = 13%. Year 5 (1988) is an outlier.

Chapter 4: The Power Model-Fitting the Learning Curve

Another nonlinear curve that models many business situations is the **power function** described by:

$$Y = ax^b \ (4.1).$$

In Figures 4.1-4.3 we display three examples of the power function.(*see File Power.xls*)

Figure 4.1

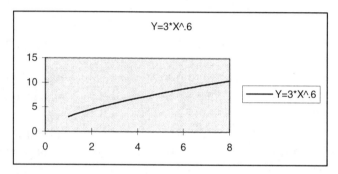

In Figure 4.1 we graph $y = 3x^6$. Notice as x increases y increases but the slope decreases and the curve gets flatter. This will occur when a>0 and 0<b<1. In Figure 4.2 we graph $y = 3x^3$. Note that as x increases y increases but the slope increases and the curve gets steeper. This will occur when a>0 and b>1.

Figure 4.2

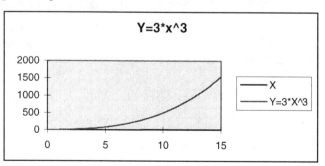

In Figure 4.3 we graph

$$y = 3x^{.5}$$

Observe that as x increases y decreases but the curve gets flatter (this means the slope is increasing). This will occur when a>0 and b<0.

Figure 4.3

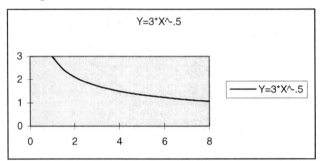

As with the exponential model, we can use the *Chart Add Trendline* feature to fit the Power model. (Note: If any x value is less than or equal to 0, the Power Trendline will not work!)

Example 4.1   In Figure 4.4 (*file Fax.xls*) you are given the number of Fax machines produced in the US during the years 1982-1988 and the unit cost of producing a Fax during each of these years.   With this example you will:

a) Fit a curve that can be used to determine how cost of producing a Fax depends on the number of Faxes already produced (this is an example of the **learning curve).**

b) Given that 1,000,000 Fax machines will be produced in 1989 develop a forecast for the cost of producing a Fax during 1989. Comment on the accuracy of the forecast.

c) If the cumulative number of Faxes produced doubles, by how much will per unit cost of making a Fax decrease?

Figure 4.4

	A	B	C	D	E	F	G	H
1	Learning curve FAX data						MAPE	0.058
2							Est s_{pe}	0.072962
3	Year	Production	Cumulative Production	Unit Cost	LN(CUM PROD)	LN(UNIT COST)	Predicted Unit Cost(power)	Absolute %age Error(power)
4	1982	64000	64000	$3,700.00	11.07	8.22	$3,955.84	0.07
5	1983	70000	134000	$3,416.00	11.81	8.14	$3,280.57	0.04
6	1984	100000	234000	$3,125.00	12.36	8.05	$2,848.54	0.09
7	1985	150000	384000	$2,583.00	12.86	7.86	$2,512.66	0.03
8	1986	175000	559000	$2,166.00	13.23	7.68	$2,284.68	0.05
9	1987	400000	959000	$1,833.00	13.77	7.51	$1,992.74	0.09
10	1988	785000	1744000	$1,788.00	14.37	7.49	$1,712.62	0.04
11	1989	1000000	2744000		14.82		$1,526.87	

To begin we must compute in column C the cumulative number of Faxes produced at the end of each year.

Step by Step – Part a)

Step 1: For 1982, we just enter in cell C4

   $= B4$.

Step 2: To compute the cumulative number of Faxes made by the end of 1983 enter in C5 the formula

   $= B5 + C4$.

Step 3: Copying this formula to C6:C10 computes the cumulative number of Faxes made by the end of 1984-1988.

Step 4: Construct a scatterplot after selecting the range A4:A10, C4:C10. You will obtain the plot in Figure 4.5:

Figure 4.5

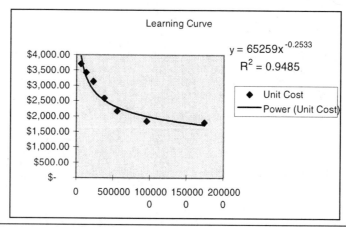

The curve looks similar to Figure 4.3 so we will try and fit a Power function. Click on your data points until the points turn gold. Now select *"Chart"* *"Add Trendline"* and choose *"Power"*. Click the *"Options"* tab and select *"Plot Equation"* and *"Plot R-SQ"* value. We find (see Figure 4.5) that the best fitting Power function is

$$y = 65259x^{-.2533}.$$

The fit appears to be good but not perfect. We created predicted unit costs in column G . First create a prediction for 1982 unit costs in cell G4 with the formula

$$= 65259*c4\wedge-.2533.$$

Copying this down to G5:G10 creates predicted unit costs for the years 1983-1988.

Step by Step – Part b)
To create a forecast for the unit cost of making a Fax in 1989 just determine cumulative production for 1989 by dragging down the formula in C10 to C11. Then create the prediction for the 1989 unit cost by dragging the formula in G10 to G11. We obtain a predicted unit cost of $1,526.87. To estimate a measure of accuracy we proceed as follows:

Step 1: Compute absolute percentage errors in column H. For 1982 compute the absolute error in cell H4 with the formula

$$=ABS(D4-G4)/D4.$$

Copying this down to H5:H10 computes the absolute percentage errors for the years 1983-1988.

Step 2: Compute the MAPE (5.8%) in cell H1 with the formula

$$=AVERAGE(H4:H10).$$

Step 3: Compute the estimated standard percentage error (7.3%) in H2 with the formula

$$= 1.25*H1.$$

We are 95% sure that a prediction for unit cost of producing a fax will be accurate within 2(7.3%) = 14.6%. Note that we have no outliers.

Solution –
Part c)
Note that the unit cost of producing the x'th unit is given by
65,259$x^{-.2533}$. The cost of producing the 2x'th unit is given by $65,259(2x)^{-.2533}$. Thus the
2x'th unit's cost will be a fraction $\dfrac{65,259(2x)^{-.2533}}{65,259x^{-.2533}} = 2^{-.2533} = .84$ of the x'th unit's cost.

We call this an 84% learning curve. This means that every time cumulative production is doubled unit costs drop by 16%.

Remarks

Taking natural logs of both sides of (4.1) yields

$Ln\ y = Ln\ a + b\ Ln\ x.$

Thus if (4.1) holds the points (Ln x, Ln y) will exhibit a straight-line relationship. The R^2 value obtained on the Trendline graph is the R^2 for the regression with Ln x as independent variable and Ln y as dependent variable. After computing Ln(CUM PROD) in column E and LN(UNIT COST) in column F we obtained the scatterplot in Figure 4.6.

Figure 4.6

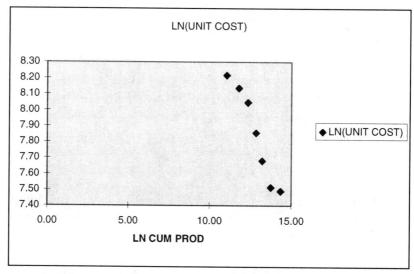

Note a strong, but not perfect linear relationship.

Which Curve Fits Best?

Recall from Chapter 3 that an exponential curve with b<0 also gets flatter as x decreases. How do we know the power curve better fits the Fax data than a power curve? **When comparing curves to see which curve best fits the data, simply choose the curve with the lowest MAPE.** This is reasonable, because a MAPE of 0 would represent a perfect fit of the data.

Example 4.1 (continued)

Does an exponential curve predict unit cost from cumulative production better than the power curve?

Solution

We have already found the MAPE for the best power curve to be 5.8%. To generate the MAPE for the best fitting exponential curve we need to create predictions for units cost and then generate absolute percentage errors for each year. (See Figure 4.7)

Figure 4.7

	G	H	I	J
1	MAPE	0.058		0.123432
2	Est s_{pe}	0.072962		
3	Predicted Unit Cost(power)	Absolute %age Error(power)	Predicted Unit Cost (exponential)	Absolute %age Error(exponential)
4	$ 3,955.84	0.07	3214.646	0.131177
5	$ 3,280.57	0.04	3117.643	0.087341
6	$ 2,848.54	0.09	2984.123	0.045081
7	$ 2,512.66	0.03	2794.488	0.081877
8	$ 2,284.68	0.05	2588.424	0.195025
9	$ 1,992.74	0.09	2172.686	0.185317
10	$ 1,712.62	0.04	1540.889	0.138205
11	$ 1,526.87			

In column I we use the =GROWTH function to generate the predictions from the best exponential curve. Select the range I4:I10 and type in I4 the formula

=GROWTH(D4:D10, C4:C10, C4:C10).

Hitting <Ctrl><Shift><Enter> will yield the predictions in Column I of Figure 4.7. Computing the MAPE in Column J tells us that the best exponential curve will have a MAPE = 12.3%. This shows the power curve gives us a much better fit!

Other Trend-line Functions

We now briefly describe the other functions that can be fit with the ADD TRENDLINE capability.

- The **Logarithmic** function fits a relationship of the form $y = a + bLn(x)$.

- The **Polynomial** function fits a relationship of the form

$$y = b_0 + b_1 x + b_2 x^2 + \ldots b_n x^n$$

  where n = 2, 3, 4, 5, or 6 (see Chapter 7). This is an example of **multiple regression**, which will be discussed in Chapters 6-8.

- The **Moving Average** function creates a prediction for y by averaging the last n observations.

Chapter 5: Fitting an S-Shaped Curve

Often when plotted over time the sales of a product will follow an **S-Shaped Curve**. This will be the case if sales start by increasing slowly, then increase sharply and final level off at some upper limit L. A sales pattern of this type is likely to occur for a product that follows **the product life cycle**. Often the diffusion over time of the number of companies producing a product also follows an S-Shaped Curve.

Fitting an S-Shaped curve to the first few months or years of data is important because it enables a company to estimate L, the maximum sales level for the product. Fitting the S-shaped curve also enables us to estimate how long it will take for sales to level off. Such information can be very useful in capacity planning and strategic planning. Figure 5.1 plots the sales of answering machines (in millions) for the years 1983-1991.

Figure 5.1

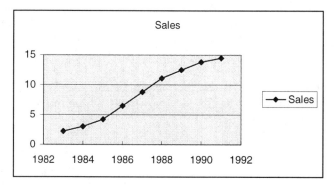

We now discuss two S-shaped curves (the Pearl and Gompertz curves) which can be used to fit S-shaped curves. We let t be our independent variable and Y be our dependent variable.

The Pearl Curve

The **Pearl or Logistic** curve states that

$$Y = \frac{L}{1 + ae^{-bt}} \quad (5.1)$$

After noting that $\dfrac{Y}{L-y} = \dfrac{e^{bt}}{a}$ it can be shown that if (5.1) holds then

$$Ln(\frac{Y}{L-Y}) = -Ln(a) + bt \quad (5.2).$$

This implies that if Y follows a Pearl curve, then a plot of $Ln\dfrac{Y}{L-Y}$ against t should yield a straight line. Equation (5.1) also implies that as t grows large, Y will approach L. We call L the **upper limit** for Y. To fit a Pearl curve to data we assume a value for L and use Excel to find the values of a and b for that value of L which best fit (5.1). Then using the "best" a and b for each L, we use a data table to find the value of L which yields the best predictions for Y (in the sense of minimizing MAPE). For a given L we find the a and b that best fit (5.1) by running a regression with $Ln\dfrac{Y}{L-Y}$ as the dependent variable and t as the independent variable.

Looking at (5.2) we see that applying the Excel =SLOPE function will yield an estimate for b and the Excel =INTERCEPT function will estimate -Ln(a). This leads us to estimate a as $e^{-\text{Intercept}}$.

The Gompertz Curve

The **Gompertz curve** states that

$$Y = Le^{-be^{-kt}} \; (5.3).$$

From (5.3) it follows that $\dfrac{L}{y} = e^{be^{-kt}}$. Taking the logs twice of both sides of this equation shows that if Y follows a Gompertz curve, then

$$Ln(Ln(\tfrac{L}{Y})) = Ln(b) - kt \; (5.4).$$

Again as t grows large, Y approaches its upper limit, L. Note from (5.4) that if Y follows a Gompertz curve, then there will be a straight line relationship between $Ln(Ln(\tfrac{L}{Y}))$ and t. To fit a Gompertz curve to data we assume a value for L and use the = SLOPE and = INTERCEPT functions (on a regression with dependent variable $Ln(Ln(\tfrac{L}{Y}))$ and independent variable t) to find the "best fitting" a and b for a given L. The = SLOPE function will estimate -k and = INTERCEPT function will estimate Ln b. Thus our estimate for k = -(Slope of regression) and our estimate of b will be $e^{Intercept}$. Then we use (5.4) to generate predictions for a given L. Finally we use a data table to find the L yielding the smallest MAPE.

The following example illustrates the fitting of an S-shaped curve to data.

Example 5.1   The file *Gompertz.xls* (see Figure 5.2) contains telephone-answering sales for the years 1983-1991. Fit an S-shaped curve to this data.

Figure 5.2

	A	B
2	Year	Sales
3	1983	2.2
4	1984	3
5	1985	4.2
6	1986	6.5
7	1987	8.8
8	1988	11.1
9	1989	12.5
10	1990	13.8
11	1991	14.5

We begin by finding the best fitting Pearl curve. See Figure 5.3.

Solution
Figure 5.3

	A	B	C	D	E	F
1	**Pearl**	Answering Machine				
2	Year	Sales	Year'	LN(Y/(L-Y))	Prediction	Absolute %age error
3	1983	2.2	0	-1.83621123	1.983057	0.09861
4	1984	3	1	-1.46633707	3.114534	0.038178
5	1985	4.2	2	-1.03301501	4.676222	0.113386
6	1986	6.5	3	-0.37948962	6.618745	0.018268
7	1987	8.8	4	0.2006707	8.74503	0.006247
8	1988	11.1	5	0.8177099	10.77018	0.029713
9	1989	12.5	6	1.27296568	12.45894	0.003285
10	1990	13.8	7	1.83621123	13.71792	0.005948
11	1991	14.5	8	2.26868354	14.5803	0.005538
12						
13						
14						
15	L	16				0.035464
16	-ln a	-1.95563				MAPE
17	b	0.535606				
18	a	7.068349				0.035464
19					15	0.063938
20					15.2	0.050573
21					15.4	0.0425
22					15.6	0.038675
23					15.8	0.035656
24					16	0.035464
25					16.2	0.035952
26					16.4	0.036373
27					16.6	0.036743
28					16.8	0.038143
29					17	0.039466
30					17.2	0.040688
31					17.4	0.041823
32					17.6	0.042883
33					17.8	0.043875
34					18	0.04577
35					18.2	0.048086
36					18.4	0.05037
37					18.6	0.052528
38					18.8	0.054572
39					19	0.056513
40					19.2	0.058359
41					19.4	0.060117
42					19.6	0.061795
43					19.8	0.063399
44					20	0.064934

Step by Step

Step 1: Enter the sales data in the cell range A3:B11.

Step 2: Enter the values of t (t = 0,1,2…, 8) in the range C3:C11.

Step 3: Enter a trial value for L (15) in cell B15.

Step 4: Create the dependent variable $Ln\dfrac{Y}{L-Y}$ in the range D3:D11. To do this enter in cell D3 the formula

   $= LN(B3/(\$B\$15-B3))$,

and copy this formula down to D11.

Step 5: Compute the estimate of -Ln (a) in cell B16 with the formula

   $= INTERCEPT(D3:D11, C3:C11)$.

Step 6: Compute our estimate of b in cell B16 with the formula

   $= SLOPE(D3:D11, C3:C11)$.

Step 7: Compute our estimate of a in cell B18 with the formula

   $= EXP(-B16)$.

Step 8: In the cell range E3:E11 we compute our predictions for Y by using the relationship $Y = \dfrac{L}{1+ae^{-bt}}$. In cell E3 we generate a prediction for 1983 sales with the formula

   $=\$B\$15/(1 + \$B\$18*EXP(-\$B\$17*C3))$.

Copying this formula to the range E4:E11 creates predictions for 1984-1991 sales.

Step 9: In the usual fashion we compute the absolute percentage error for each observation and the MAPE in cell F14.

Step 10: We now construct a one-way data table with table range E18:F44 to compute the value of L having the smallest MAPE. We enter trial values of L (15, 15.2, … 20) in the cell range F19:F44. Then we compute the MAPE in cell F18 with the formula

   $= F14$.

Selecting B15 (L) as the column input cell generates the MAPE for each value of L. We find L = 16 yields the smallest MAPE (3.5%). Substituting L = 16 in cell B15 yields a = 7.07and b = .535. Thus our best fitting Pearl curve is

$$Y = \frac{16}{1 + 7.07e^{-.535t}} .$$

We now try to fit a Gompertz curve to the phone data (see Figure 5.4).

Figure 5.4

	A	B	C	D	E	F
2	Year	Sales	ln[ln(L/y)]	Year	Prediction	Abs %age error
3	1983	2.2	0.884753	0	2.088130542	0.0508498
4	1984	3	0.747745	1	3.302131583	0.1007105
5	1985	4.2	0.574228	2	4.796990665	0.1421406
6	1986	6.5	0.291954	3	6.502915976	0.0004486
7	1987	8.8	0.035456	4	8.332490011	0.0531261
8	1988	11.1	-0.21828	5	10.19767708	0.0812904
9	1989	12.5	-0.37817	6	12.02210435	0.0382317
10	1990	13.8	-0.53414	7	13.74743105	0.0038093
11	1991	14.5	-0.62233	8	15.33473162	0.0575677
12						
13			**Upper Limit=24.8 million**			
14						
15					MAPE	0.0586861
16	L	24.8				
17	ln b	0.906068				
18	-k	-0.20482				
19	b	2.474574				

Step by Step

Step 1: **Enter the sales data in the range A3:B11.**

Step 2: **Enter the values of t (t = 0,1, ... 8) in the cell range C3:C11.**

Step 3: **Enter a trial value for L (17) in B16.**

Step 4: **Create the dependent variable** $Ln(Ln(\frac{L}{Y}))$ **in the cell range D3:D11.** To create this variable enter in cell C3 the formula

$= LN(LN(\$B\$16/B3))$.

Then copy this formula to the cell range C3:C11.

Step 5: **Compute our estimate of Ln b in cell B17 with the formula**

$=INTERCEPT(C3:C11, D3:D11)$.

Step 6: Compute our estimate of -k in cell B18 with the formula

$= SLOPE(C3:C11, D3:D11).$

Figure 5.5

Step 7: Compute our estimate of b in cell B19 with the formula

$=EXP(B17).$

Step 8: In the cell range E3:E11 we compute our predictions for Y using the relationship

$$Y = Le^{-be^{-kt}}.$$

In cell E3 we generate a prediction for 1983 sales with the formula

$= \$B\$16*EXP(-\$B\$19*EXP(\$B\$18*C3)).$

Copying this formula to the cell range E4:E11 generates predictions for 1984-1991 sales.

Step 9: In the usual fashion we compute the MAPE for the value of L in B15.

Step 10: We now construct a one-way data table in the cell range H7:I53 (see Figure 5.5) which can be used to find the value of L which minimizes MAPE. We begin by entering trial values of L (L = 23, 23.2, ..., 32) in the cell range E19:F44. Then compute the MAPE in cell F15 with the formula

$= F14.$

Choosing B16 as the column input cell computes the MAPE for different values of L. We find L = 24.8 minimizes MAPE (MAPE = 5.9%). This suggests that answering machines sales will level off at 24.8 million and future sales can be predicted with the equation

$$Y = 24.8e^{-2.474e^{-.2048t}}.$$

The best Pearl equation has a lower MAPE than the best Gompertz equation, so it seems like our best bet for forecasting future sales would be with the Pearl curve.

	H	I
6		MAPE
7	L	0.05869
8	23	0.05972
9	23.2	0.05959
10	23.4	0.05947
11	23.6	0.05934
12	23.8	0.05923
13	24	0.05911
14	24.2	0.059
15	24.4	0.05889
16	24.6	0.05879
17	24.8	0.05869
18	25	0.05874
19	25.2	0.05888
20	25.4	0.05903
21	25.6	0.05917
22	25.8	0.0593
23	26	0.05944
24	26.2	0.05957
25	26.4	0.0597
26	26.6	0.05983
27	26.8	0.05995
28	27	0.06008
29	27.2	0.0602
30	27.4	0.06031
31	27.6	0.06043
32	27.8	0.06055
33	28	0.06069
34	28.2	0.06085
35	28.4	0.06101
36	28.6	0.06116
37	28.8	0.06132
38	29	0.06147
39	29.2	0.06162
40	29.4	0.06176
41	29.6	0.06191
42	29.8	0.06205
43	30	0.06219
44	30.2	0.06256
45	30.4	0.063
46	30.6	0.06343
47	30.8	0.06386
48	31	0.06428
49	31.2	0.06469
50	31.4	0.06509

Remarks

As Charles Handy (1994) points out it is critical to find the point where the S-Shaped curve starts to flatten out. At this point to create growth in sales companies need to jump off the current S-shaped curve and find a "second curve" to generate new sales. A recent example of "looking for the second curve" was Microsoft's breakneck effort to revise Internet Explorer to compete with Netscape. Microsoft realized that the demand for personal computers was flattening out but the Internet was at the beginning stages of the S-Shaped curve.

As another example of the importance of the S-Shaped curve Amazon CEO Jeff Bezo bought two new businesses in August, 1998. (See the *New York Times,* August 5, 1998). When asked why, he replied "Our business is at an **inflection point**". Basically, this means that the growth in Amazon's primary business (sales of books) was flattening out and it was time to "jump" to the next S-shaped curve.

Reference

Handy, C., *Age of Paradox*, Harvard Business School Press, 1994.

Chapter 6: Using Multiple Regression to Forecast Auto Sales

Suppose you want to forecast quarterly auto sales (in thousands of cars). What are some variables that might influence auto sales?

- **Quarter of the year (January-March, April-June, July-September, October-December)**

- **Interest rates during previous quarter**

- **Unemployment rate during previous quarter**

- **Last quarter's GNP (billions of 1986 dollars)**

In the file *Auto.xls* we have tabulated all this data for the years 1979-1986 in columns A-F. See Figure 6.1.

Figure 6.1

	A	B	C	D	E	F
10	Year	Quarter	Sales	GNP	Unemp	Int
11	79	1	2709	2541	5.9	9.4
12						
13	Year	Quarter	Sales	GNP	Unemp	Int
14	79	2	2910	2640	5.7	9.4
15	79	3	2562	2595	5.9	9.7
16	79	4	2385	2701	6	11.9
17	80	1	2520	2785	6.2	13.4
18	80	2	2142	2509	7.3	9.6
19	80	3	2130	2570	7.7	9.2
20	80	4	2190	2667	7.4	13.6
21	81	1	2370	2878	7.4	14.4
22	81	2	2208	2835	7.4	15.3
23	81	3	2196	2897	7.4	15.1
24	81	4	1758	2744	8.3	11.8
25	82	1	1944	2582	8.8	12.8
26	82	2	2094	2613	9.4	12.4
27	82	3	1911	2529	10	9.3
28	82	4	2031	2544	10.7	7.9
29	83	1	2046	2633	10.4	7.8
30	83	2	2502	2878	10.1	8.4
31	83	3	2238	3051	9.4	9.1
32	83	4	2394	3274	8.5	8.8
33	84	1	2586	3594	7.9	9.2
34	84	2	2898	3774	7.5	9.8
35	84	3	2448	3861	7.5	10.3
36	84	4	2460	3919	7.2	8.8
37	85	1	2646	4040	7.4	8.2
38	85	2	2988	4133	7.3	7.5
39	85	3	2967	4303	7.1	7.1
40	85	4	2439	4393	7	7.2
41	86	1	2598	4560	7.1	8.9
42	86	2	3045	4587	7.1	7.7
43	86	3	3213	4716	6.9	7.4
44	86	4	2685	4796	6.8	7.4

To use regression in an effort to predict auto sales we begin by realizing that the quarter of the year is a **qualitative variable** which may take on 4 possible values.

We will model such qualitative variables by using **dummy variables**. We arbitrarily choose one value of the qualitative variable (say Quarter 4) to leave out and assign a dummy or indicator variable to each other quarter.

- Quarter 1 dummy = 1 if observation is January-March, =0 otherwise.

- Quarter 2 dummy = 1 if observation if April-June, = 0 otherwise.

- Quarter 3 dummy = 1 if observation is July-September, = 0 otherwise.

Note that an observation during Quarter 4 will be identified by the fact that all three dummy variables will equal 0.

Step by Step

To create these dummy variables we proceed as follows (see Figure 6.2):

Step 1: Create the Dummy Variable for Quarter 1 by entering the formula

=If(B14=1,1,0)

in G14 and copy it down to Row 44.

Step 2: Create the dummy variable for Quarter 2 by entering the formula

=If(B14=2,1,0)

in H14 and copy it down to Row 44.

Step 3: Create the dummy variable for Quarter 3 by entering the formula

=If(B14=3,1,0)

in I14 and copy it down to Row 44.

Step 4: A *lagged variable* is simply the value of an independent variable during a previous period. A one period lag means look at the value of the variable one period back, a two period lag means look at the value of the variable two periods back, etc. We create the one period lagged variables for GNP, Unemployment and interest rates for the second quarter of 1979 in J14:L14 by entering

= D11

in J14 and copying it to K14:L14.

Figure 6.2

	G	H	I	J	K	L
10	Q1	Q2	Q3	LagGNP	LagUnemp	LagInt
11	1	0	0			
12						
13	Q1	Q2	Q3	LagGNP	LagUnemp	LagInt
14	0	1	0	2541	5.9	9.4
15	0	0	1	2640	5.7	9.4
16	0	0	0	2595	5.9	9.7
17	1	0	0	2701	6	11.9
18	0	1	0	2785	6.2	13.4
19	0	0	1	2509	7.3	9.6
20	0	0	0	2570	7.7	9.2
21	1	0	0	2667	7.4	13.6
22	0	1	0	2878	7.4	14.4
23	0	0	1	2835	7.4	15.3
24	0	0	0	2897	7.4	15.1
25	1	0	0	2744	8.3	11.8
26	0	1	0	2582	8.8	12.8
27	0	0	1	2613	9.4	12.4
28	0	0	0	2529	10	9.3
29	1	0	0	2544	10.7	7.9
30	0	1	0	2633	10.4	7.8
31	0	0	1	2878	10.1	8.4
32	0	0	0	3051	9.4	9.1
33	1	0	0	3274	8.5	8.8
34	0	1	0	3594	7.9	9.2
35	0	0	1	3774	7.5	9.8
36	0	0	0	3861	7.5	10.3
37	1	0	0	3919	7.2	8.8
38	0	1	0	4040	7.4	8.2
39	0	0	1	4133	7.3	7.5
40	0	0	0	4303	7.1	7.1
41	1	0	0	4393	7	7.2
42	0	1	0	4560	7.1	8.9
43	0	0	1	4587	7.1	7.7
44	0	0	0	4716	6.9	7.4

Step 5: To create the lagged variables for all later quarters enter in cell J15 the formula

$$= D14$$

and copy it to the range J15:L44.

Step 6: We are now ready to run regression with column C (Sales) as our independent variable and Columns G-L as our dependent variables. We will use the years 1979-1984 to run the regression and then validate the regression on the years 1985-1986. We select the Excel *"Tools" "Data Analysis" "Regression"* command and fill in the dialog box as follows

INPUT Y RANGE: C14:C36

INPUT X RANGE: G14:L36

Check Residuals Box.

You will obtain the following output: (see Figures 6.3-6.5)

Figure 6.3

	A	B
3	SUMMARY OUTPUT	
4		
5	*Regression Statistics*	
6	Multiple R	0.858
7	R Square	73.5%
8	Adjusted R Square	63.6%
9	Standard Error	176.219
10	Observations	23

Figure 6.4

	A	B	C	D	E	F	G
17							
18		*Coefficients*	*Standard Error*	*t Stat*	*P-value*	*Lower 95%*	*Upper 95%*
19	Intercept	3181.770	454.514	7.000	0.0000	2218.245	4145.296
20	Q1	171.088	107.737	1.588	0.1318	-57.304	399.480
21	Q2	311.637	102.651	3.036	0.0079	94.027	529.247
22	Q3	75.972	101.977	0.745	0.4671	-140.209	292.154
23	LagGNP	0.242	0.095	2.540	0.0218	0.040	0.445
24	LagUnemp	-104.419	26.784	-3.899	0.0013	-161.200	-47.639
25	LagInt	-81.573	17.355	-4.700	0.0002	-118.364	-44.781

Figure 6.5

	A	B	C	D
29	RESIDUAL OUTPUT			
30				
31	*Observation*	*Predicted Sales*	*Residuals*	AbsError
32	1	2726.625173	183.3748272	183.37483
33	2	2535.847599	26.15240118	26.152401
34	3	2403.609215	-18.60921544	18.609215
35	4	2410.495597	109.5044028	109.5044
36	5	2428.167329	-286.1673287	286.16733
37	6	2320.700624	-190.7006242	190.70062
38	7	2250.379398	-60.37939779	60.379398
39	8	2117.391473	252.6085265	252.60853
40	9	2243.839635	-35.83963509	35.839635
41	10	1924.334279	271.6657215	271.66572
42	11	1879.708702	-121.7087025	121.7087
43	12	2188.9139	-244.9139002	244.9139
44	13	2156.402484	-62.40248352	62.402484
45	14	1898.231641	12.76835902	12.768359
46	15	1992.117018	38.88298179	38.882982
47	16	2207.950222	-161.9502221	161.95022
48	17	2409.560229	92.43977121	92.439771
49	18	2215.679257	22.32074265	22.320743
50	19	2197.644186	196.355814	196.35581
51	20	2541.248807	44.75119299	44.751193
52	21	2789.405151	108.5948489	108.59485
53	22	2590.2066	-142.2066002	142.2066
54	23	2494.54148	-34.54148007	34.54148
55				118.2104

Interpreting Regression Output

Here are the key things we learn from regression output:

R-SQ = .735 means our dependent variables explain 73.5% of sales variation. 26.5% is unexplained.

Standard Error = 176.22 means that 68% of our predictions should be accurate within one standard error (176.22) and 95% should be accurate within 2(176.22) = 352.44.

From Figure 6.4 we find that the equation used to predict quarterly sales is

$$Predicted\ Sales = 3181.77 + 171.09Q1 + 311.64Q2 + 75.97Q3 + .242LAGGNP$$

$$-104.42LagUnemp - 81.57LagInt.$$

All these variables have a significant effect on sales. We see this because all p-values are <= .15. How do we interpret the coefficients in this equation? *Ceteris Paribus* (this means after adjusting for the effects of all other independent variables in the equation) we can say that:

- During January-March car sales run 171,000 higher than October-December.

- During April-June car sales run 312,000 higher than October-December.

- During July-September car sales run 76,000 higher than October-December.

- A one billion-dollar increase in last quarter's GNP will yield 242 more car sales.

- A one-percentage point increase (say from 5% to 6%) in last quarter's unemployment rate will reduce car sales by 104,000.

- An one-percentage point increase (say from 6% to 7%) in last quarter's interest rate will reduce car sales by 82,000.

In Figure 6.5 we are given the residuals = actual sales - predicted sales for each observation. During no quarter were we off by more than 2 standard errors, so there are no outliers. Note our average absolute error (MAD) is 118.21.

Validation of the Regression

Does our regression forecast as well on data it has not seen as it does on data it has seen? To test this we make forecasts for our validation set (1985-1986). See Figure 6.6.

Figure 6.6

	E	F	G	H	I	J
	Year	Quarter	Actual	Prediction	AbsError	Prediction
31						
32	85	1	2646	2833.38	187.38	2833.3768
33	85	2	2988	3031.32	43.32	3031.322
34	85	3	2967	2885.75	81.25	2885.7487
35	85	4	2439	2904.51	465.51	2904.5066
36	86	1	2598	3099.70	501.70	3099.7002
37	86	2	3045	3131.62	86.62	3131.6231
38	86	3	3213	3000.39	212.61	3000.3922
39	86	4	2685	3001.05	316.05	3001.0522
40						
41				MAD	236.805	

To create these forecasts we use the Excel array function TREND. Simply highlight J32:J39 and type in J32 the following formula

=TREND(Data!C14:C36,Data!G14:L36,Data!G37:L44).

After hitting <Ctrl><Shift><Enter>(not <Enter>) you will obtain the correct forecasts. The TREND function has three arguments:

- First argument (C14:C36) is where dependent variable data used to fit regression is located.

- Second argument (G14:L36) is where independent variables used to fit regression is located.

- Third argument (G37:L44) is where independent variables used to make new forecasts are located.

We find the MAD (mean of absolute deviations) for these 8 data points to be 237, which is around double the MAD for the data used to fit the regression. Thus we should be cautious about the accuracy of this regression when it is applied to new data. Still, an average error of 237 is only about 8% of average sales for the periods, which is not too bad.

Chapter 7: Using Polynomial Regression to Resolve Nonlinearities

Recall in Chapters 3-5 we learned how to use the exponential, power, Gompertz, and Pearl curves to fit nonlinear relationships. Often a nonlinear relationship can be modeled by assuming that

$$y = \beta_0 + \beta_1 x + \beta_2 x^2 + \ldots \beta_n x^n . \ (7.1)$$

Usually we will use n = 2 or n = 3. If a scatterplot looks like part of a parabola we would use n = 2. If the scatterplot changes once from convex (slope increasing) to concave (slope decreasing) or vice versa, we would use n = 3. We can use the *"Polynomial"* option on *"Insert Trendline"* to fit (7.1) for n≤6. Alternatively, we can create columns for x^2, x^3, ... x^n and run a multiple regression with these (as well as x) as independent variables. Example 7.1 illustrates the idea.

Example 7.1 In Figure 7.1 we are given (file *Averagecost.xls*) the Output (in thousands of units produced per month) and Average Unit Cost of Production for Widgetco. Widgetco would like to determine how average unit costs depends on output.

Figure 7.1

	A	B	C
1	Output (thousands)	Output^2	Average Cost
2	80	6400	1.86
3	90	8100	1.63
4	75	5625	2.03
5	82	6724	1.77
6	96	9216	1.47
7	98	9604	1.51
8	110	12100	1.57
9	90	8100	1.63
10	96	9216	1.51
11	92	8464	1.61
12	84	7056	1.83
13	120	14400	1.85
14	60	3600	2.93
15	50	2500	3.78
16	75	5625	2.08
17	78	6084	1.85
18	68	4624	2.42
19	84	7056	1.66
20	64	4096	2.64

Solution

Before running any regressions, we construct a scatterplot with the range A1:A20 on the x-axis and the range C1:C20 on the y-axis. The resulting plot in Figure 7.2 shows that the relationship between output and average unit cost is clearly nonlinear.

Figure 7.2

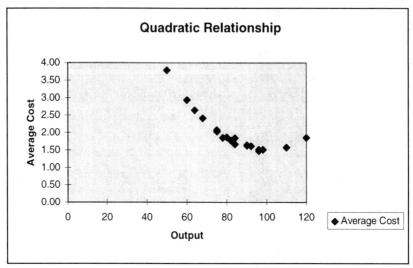

Despite this fact, we ran a simple linear regression (X-range A3:A20) and (Y-Range B3:C20) and obtained the output in Figure 7.3.

Figure 7.3

	A	B	C	D	E	F	G	H	I
1	SUMMARY OUTPUT								
2									
3	*Regression Statistics*								
4	Multiple R	0.80310382							
5	R Square	0.64497575							
6	Adjusted R Square	0.62409197							
7	Standard Error	0.36143304							
8	Observations	19							
9									
10	ANOVA								
11		*df*	*SS*	*MS*	*F*	*Significance F*			
12	Regression	1	4.034502485	4.035	30.8841	3.47455E-05			
13	Residual	17	2.220775296	0.131					
14	Total	18	6.255277782						
15									
16		*Coefficients*	*Standard Error*	*t Stat*	*P-value*	*Lower 95%*	*Upper 95%*	*Lower 95.0%*	*Upper 95.0%*
17	Intercept	4.31473629	0.428187554	10.08	1.4E-08	3.411338255	5.21813432	3.411338255	5.218134321
18	Output (thous	-0.02786198	0.005013545	-5.56	3.5E-05	-0.038439653	-0.0172843	-0.03843965	-0.017284314

We find 64% of variation in cost is explained by variation in output. Also output is highly significant (p-value = .0000347). Note, however, the coefficient of output is <0. This indicates that an increase in output will always decrease average cost. From Figure 7.2 it is apparent that for larger levels of output, an increase in output increases average cost. This leads us to believe that we need to fit a parabola! To do this we created a column of $(Output)^2$ in Column B by entering in B2 the formula

$= B2^2.$

Then we copied this formula to the range B2:B20. Next we ran a regression with the same Y-RANGE (C2:C20) and the X-RANGE (A2:B20). Figure 7.4 contains the result of this regression.

Figure 7.4

	A	B	C	D	E	F	G	H	I
1	SUMMARY OUTPUT								
2									
3	Regression Statistics								
4	Multiple R	0.99718253							
5	R Square	0.994372998							
6	Adjusted R Square	0.993669623							
7	Standard Error	0.04690313							
8	Observations	19							
9									
10	ANOVA								
11		df	SS	MS	F	Significance F			
12	Regression	2	6.220079323	3.110039662	1413.716306	1.00512E-18			
13	Residual	16	0.035198458	0.002199904					
14	Total	18	6.255277782						
15									
16		Coefficients	Standard Error	t Stat	P-value	Lower 95%	Upper 95%	Lower 95.0%	Upper 95.0%
17	Intercept	10.49257043	0.203723786	51.50390444	3.28763E-19	10.06069539	10.9244455	10.06069539	10.92444547
18	Output (thousands)	-0.17986306	0.004866115	-36.9623572	6.36352E-17	-0.190178764	-0.1695474	-0.19017876	-0.169547365
19	Output^2	0.000899104	2.85252E-05	31.51963717	7.87648E-16	0.000838634	0.00095958	0.000838634	0.000959575

Note that R^2 = .994, so that only .6% of all variation in average cost is now unexplained. and both OUTPUT and $OUTPUT^2$ are significant. Also notice that adding $OUTPUT^2$ as an independent variable dropped our standard error from $0.36 to $0.047. Clearly we have found a good equation. We can predict AVERAGE COST from the equation

$AVERAGE\ COST = .0009(OUTPUT)^2 - .1799(OUTPUT) + 10.49\ (7.1).$

95% of the time our forecasts will be accurate within 9 cents. Also note that AVERAGE COST tends to increase when monthly output increases beyond 100,000 units (see Figure 7.5). This is important information!

We could have obtained (7.1) by clicking on the points in Figure 7.2 until the points turn gold and using ADD TRENDLINE (POLYNOMIAL 2 OPTION). After checking Display R-SQ and Equation we obtained Figure 7.5.

Figure 7.5

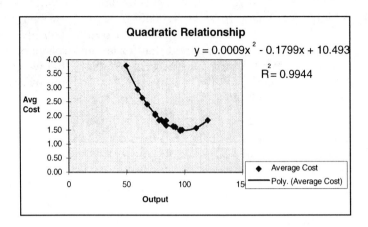

Chapter 8: The Multiplicative Model-Estimating Demand

In many economic situations the appropriate model to fit is the following generalization of the power model of Chapter 4.

$$Y = \beta_0 x_1^{\beta_1} x_2^{\beta_2} \ldots x_n^{\beta_n} \quad (8.1)$$

Here are three examples of where (8.1) is often useful:

Y	x_1
Demand for Product	Price of product i competing in market
Output produced by country	Amount used of input I
Total Operating Cost of a Company	Units produced of product I

To use regression to fit (8.1) we must take natural logs of both sides of (8.1) and obtain

$$Ln\ Y = Ln\ \beta_0 + \beta_1 Ln\ x_1 + \beta_2 Ln\ x_2 + \ldots \beta_n Ln\ x_n. \quad (8.2)$$

Note that to fit (8.2) we can run a regression with dependent variable LnY and independent variables $Ln\ x_1$, $Ln\ x_2$, ... $Ln\ x_n$. Then the Intercept of this regression will estimate $Ln\ \beta_0$. Thus

Intercept = Estimate of Ln β_0.

Taking e to both sides of this equation yields

$$e^{Intercept} = e^{LN\beta_0} = \beta_0.$$

Otherwise we estimate β_j to equal the coefficient of $Ln\ x_j$ in our estimate of (8.2).

The interpretation of β_j in (8.1) is the following:

- **A 1% increase in x_j will increase our prediction for Y by approximately β_j %.**

This interpretation will become clear in the following example.

Example 8.1   Figure 8.1 (*file Multiplicative.xls*) gives monthly sales (in thousands of days of therapy d.o.t.) for Wozac. You are also given the price per d.o.t. for Wozac and its chief competitor Zozo. Here you will:

a) **Determine an equation that can be used to predict monthly sales of Wozac on the basis of Wozac's and Zozo's price.**

b) **Interpret your prediction equation.**

c) **Predict monthly sales during a month in which Wozac charges $14.22 and Zozo charges $6.13 per d.o.t.** How accurate is this prediction likely to be?

Solution –
Part a)

We will try and fit both of the following models:

$$Model\ 1: SALES = \beta_0 + \beta_1(Wozac\ Price) + \beta_2(Zozo\ Price) + (error\ term)$$

$$Model\ 2: SALES = \beta_0(Wozac\ Price)^{\beta_1}(Zozo\ Price)^{\beta_2}(error\ term).$$

The error term for Model 1 has mean 0 while the error term for Model 2 has mean 1.

Figure 8.1

	A	B	C
		Wozac	Zozo
3	Sales	Price	Price
4	147	15	4.6
5	235	16	11.5
6	238	16.2	12.1
7	147	24.9	13.79
8	294	15.12	14.8
9	686	8.21	16.12
10	135	16.46	4.86
11	240	17.57	14.58
12	279	16.86	17.12
13	262	18.11	18.02
14		14.22	6.13

To determine which equation better fits the data, we can use the =TREND function to generate forecasts from Model 1 and our equation derived from (8.2) to generate forecasts for Model 2. Then we can choose the model with the smaller MAPE.

To obtain the predictions from Model 1 we select the cell range D4:D13 and array enter the formula

$= TREND(A4:A13, B4:C13, B4:C13).$

To obtain the predictions from Model 2 we proceed as follows:

To find our prediction equation we create columns for Ln Sales Ln Wozac and Ln Zozo in columns H-J (see Figure 8.2).

Step by Step

Step 1: Enter in cell H4 the formula

$$= LN(A4).$$

Step 2: Hit <Ctrl-C> and select the cell range H4:J13.

Step 3: Hit <Enter>.

Now we run a regression with Y-RANGE H4:H13 and X-Range I4:J13. The result is in Figure 8.3.

Figure 8.2

	H	I	J
3	Ln Sales	Ln Wozac	Ln Zozo
4	4.990433	2.70805	1.526056
5	5.459586	2.772589	2.442347
6	5.472271	2.785011	2.493205
7	4.990433	3.214868	2.623944
8	5.68358	2.716018	2.694627
9	6.530878	2.105353	2.780061
10	4.905275	2.800933	1.581038
11	5.480639	2.866193	2.679651
12	5.631212	2.824944	2.840247
13	5.568345	2.896464	2.891482

Figure 8.3

	D	E	F	G	H	I	J	K	L
16									
17	Regression Statistics								
18	Multiple R	0.99999721							
19	R Square	0.99999442							
20	Adjusted R Square	0.99999283	$e^{Intercept}$	2001					
21	Standard Error	0.00125814							
22	Observations	10							
23									
24	ANOVA								
25		df	SS	MS	F	Significance F			
26	Regression	2	1.985822646	0.993	627268	4.1034E-19			
27	Residual	7	1.10804E-05	2E-06					
28	Total	9	1.985833727						
29									
30		Coefficients	Standard Error	t Stat	P-value	Lower 95%	Upper 95%	Lower 95.0%	Upper 95.0%
31	Intercept	7.60134879	0.004775153	1592	1E-20	7.590057353	7.61264022	7.590057353	7.612640224
32	Ln Wozac	-1.30276387	0.001530699	-851	8.2E-19	-1.306383392	-1.2991443	-1.30638339	-1.299144341
33	Ln Zozo	0.6016963	0.000846607	710.7	2.9E-18	0.599694393	0.6036982	0.599694393	0.603698204

We find Ln Wozac and Ln Zozo both highly significant. Since $e^{\text{Intercept}} = e^{7.601349} = 2009.89$, our equation for predicting sales is

$$SALES = 2009.89(Wozac\ Price)^{-1.30276}(Zozo\ Price)^{.601696} \quad (8.3)$$

To make predictions for this equation enter into cell F4 the formula

=exp(7.601349)*B4^-1.30276*C4^.601696

and copy the formula to the cell range F5:F13.

After computing the MAPE for each model in the usual fashion we find Model 1 to have a MAPE of 19.7%while Model 2 has a MAPE of .099%(see Figure 8.4). Thus Model 2 (the multiplicative model) is preferred.

Figure 8.4

	A	B	C	D	E	F	G	H	I	J
1	Multiplicative Model					S_{pe}	0.001239324			
2				MAPE(Linea	0.196856	MAPE (Multiplicative)	0.00099146			
3	Sales	Wozac Price	Zozo Price	Linear Prediction	Abs%age Error Linear	Multiplicative Prediction	Abs % age Error Multiplicative	Ln Sales	Ln Wozac	Ln Zozo
4	147	15	4.6	165.033798	0.122679	147.176345	0.001199626	4.990433	2.70805	1.526056
5	235	16	11.5	257.392681	0.095288	234.8346755	0.000703509	5.459586	2.772589	2.442347
6	238	16.2	12.1	262.053549	0.101065	238.2449872	0.001029358	5.472271	2.785011	2.493205
7	147	24.9	13.79	32.5907029	0.778295	147.2253261	0.001532831	4.990433	3.214868	2.623944
8	294	15.12	14.8	342.06024	0.16347	294.2339807	0.000795853	5.68358	2.716018	2.694627
9	686	8.21	16.12	571.451005	0.166981	686.3109814	0.000453326	6.530878	2.105353	2.780061
10	135	16.46	4.86	126.108208	0.065865	134.7888897	0.00156378	4.905275	2.800933	1.581038
11	240	17.57	14.58	265.119238	0.104663	239.7801971	0.000915845	5.480639	2.866193	2.679651
12	279	16.86	17.12	331.261544	0.187317	278.6873372	0.001120655	5.631212	2.824944	2.840247
13	262	18.11	18.02	309.929035	0.182935	261.8428489	0.000599813	5.568345	2.896464	2.891482
14		14.22	6.13			187.5358344				

Solution– Part b)

We interpret (8.3) as indicating that a 1% increase in Wozac's price will reduce Wozac's demand by 1.3%. This is the same as saying the price elasticity of Wozac demand is 1.3. Also, a 1% increase in Zozo's price will increase Wozac's demand by .60%. To demonstrate this suppose we increase Wozac's price by 1% from a level x to 1.01x. (while keeping the Zozo price constant). Then Wozac's demand is now

$$\frac{2009.89(1.01x)^{-1.30}(Zozo)^{.60}}{2009.89x^{-1.30}(Zozo)^{.60}} = (1.01)^{-1.30} \approx 1 + .01(-1.30) = .987.$$

Here we have used the fact that for small x

$$(1 + x)^a \approx 1 + xa.$$

Thus a 1% increase in Wozac's price will reduce demand by 1.3%.

Solution –
Part c)
To predict Wozac sales when Wozac sells for $14.22 and Zozo sells for $6.13 we simply copy the formula from F13 to F14 and obtain a prediction of 187,536 d.o.t. Since we found the MAPE for the multiplicative model to equal .10%, we estimate $s_{pe} = 1.25(.10\%) = .124\%$. Thus we are 95% sure that the monthly demand for Wozac will be between

$187,071 = (1 - 2(.00124))*187,536$ and

$188,001 = (1 + 2(.00124)*187,536$ d.o.t.

Of course, in real-life we would never be this accurate.

Chapter 9: Using the Pivot Table Report and Regression to Analyze Market Efficiency

Using the Pivot Table Report

An important question in finance is whether or not the stock market is **efficient**. The market is efficient if knowledge of past changes in a stock's price tells us nothing about future changes in a stock's price. Let's see if daily price changes in IBM during 1994 are consistent with efficient markets (file *IBM.xls*).

Figure 9.1

	A	B	C	D
1	Date	Return	Down or Up today	Down or up yesterday
2	3-Jan-94	0.019912	Up	
3	4-Jan-94	0.023861	Up	Up
4	5-Jan-94	0.008475	Up	Up
5	6-Jan-94	-0.01681	Down	Up
6	7-Jan-94	0.00641	Up	Down
7	10-Jan-94	0.006369	Up	Up
8	11-Jan-94	-0.01055	Down	Up

We will say IBM goes "up" today if the return is greater than 0 and IBM goes "down" if the return is less than or equal to 0. We want to determine if knowing that IBM went up yesterday or down yesterday would help us determine whether IBM will go up or down today. Does it appear that knowing how IBM did yesterday will help us forecast how IBM does today?

Solution   Basically, we would like to know the fraction of the time IBM goes up today after going down yesterday and the fraction of the time IBM goes up today after going up yesterday. The Pivot Table Report is made to order for this type of situation. We proceed as follows:

Step by   **Step 1: In column C we determine if IBM went up or down today.** To see if IBM
Step   went up on January 3, 1994 enter in C2 the formula

$$=If(B2<=0,"Down","Up").$$

Copying this down to the bottom of Column C tells us for each day of 1994 whether IBM went Up or Down[1].

Step 2: In Column D we determine if IBM went Up or Down "yesterday". Begin by entering

$$=C2$$

in D3. Copying this formula down to the bottom of Column D tells us whether IBM went Up or Down for the day before the day corresponding to the same row in Column C.

Step 3: We want a breakdown of the percentage of times a Down is followed by an Up or Down and a breakdown of the percentage of the time an Up is followed by and Up or Down. Select *"Data" "Pivot Table Report"*. This brings up the Pivot Table Wizard.

Step 4: Click Next. Select A1:D253 as the range for the pivot table. (You need to have column headings in first row of range!)

Step 5: Click Next. Now drag *Down or Up Yesterday* to the Row Range and *Down or Up Today* to the Column Range. Drag either heading to the Data portion of the box (we just want a count). Your wizard will look as follows:

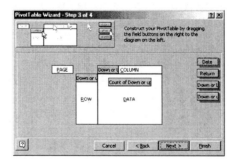

---

[1] An easy way to copy a formula down a long column is to obtain the cross-hair in the lower right hand corner and double click on the cell. This will copy the formula down to match the number of rows in the column to the left of the current column.

Click Finish and you will obtain the table in Figure 9.2. For example, consider the 135 days IBM went down. On 72 of those days IBM went down the next day and on 63 of those days IBM went up the next day.

Figure 9.2

	F	G	H	I
2	Count of Down or up yesterday	Down or Up today		
3	Down or up yesterday	Down	Up	Grand Total
4	Down	72	63	135
5	Up	64	52	116
6	(blank)			
7	Grand Total	136	115	251

Step 6: We would like to have the breakdowns in this Table displayed as a percentage. For example, after a Down 72/135 = 53% of the time IBM went Down and 63/135 = 47% of the time IBM went Up. To obtain this breakdown right-click anywhere in the data part of the Table (Columns G and H) and select Field and then Options. Then select Show Data as Percentage of Row. See the following dialog box.

You will obtain the following Pivot Table.

Figure 9.3

	F	G	H	I
2	Count of Down or up yesterday	Down or Up today		
3	Down or up yesterday	Down	Up	Grand Total
4	Down	53.33%	46.67%	100.00%
5	Up	55.17%	44.83%	100.00%
6	(blank)	#DIV/0!	#DIV/0!	#DIV/0!
7	Grand Total	54.18%	45.82%	100.00%

Figure 9.3 makes it clear that whether IBM went Down or up Yesterday, we have about the same chance of seeing IBM go up today. This is consistent with the efficient market hypothesis. Of course, this does not preclude us finding market inefficiencies with other PIVOT TABLE explorations. For example, if after a sequence Up Up we went Down 80% of the time and after a sequence Down Down we went up 80% of the time we would have found a market inefficiency!

Using Regression to Look for Market Inefficiencies

Let's look at our 1994 IBM data again. Can we use the return on IBM during the last five days to predict tomorrow's return? If the market is efficient, the answer is NO! To see if the last five days can be used to predict today's return we will run a regression. Our dependent variable will be "Today's Return" and our five independent variables will be the last five days of IBM returns. We will need to make five columns for our independent variables:

- Return One Trading Day Ago

- Return Two Trading Days Ago

- Return Three Trading Days Ago

- Return Four Trading Days Ago

- Return Five Trading Days Ago

When we are done things should look like

Figure 9.4

	A	B	C	D	E	F	G
1	Date	Today's return	One Day Ago	Two Days Ago	Three Days Ago	Four Days Ago	Five Days Ago
2	3-Jan-94	0.01991151					
3	4-Jan-94	0.02386117	0.0199115				
4	5-Jan-94	0.008474576	0.0238612	0.019912			
5	6-Jan-94	-0.01680672	0.0084746	0.023861	0.019912		
6	7-Jan-94	0.006410256	-0.0168067	0.008475	0.023861	0.019912	
7	10-Jan-94	0.006369427	0.0064103	-0.01681	0.008475	0.023861	0.01991
8	11-Jan-94	-0.01054852	0.0063694	0.00641	-0.01681	0.008475	0.02386
9	12-Jan-94	-0.00852879	-0.0105485	0.006369	0.00641	-0.016807	0.00847
10	13-Jan-94	0.01075269	-0.0085288	-0.01055	0.006369	0.00641	-0.01681
11	14-Jan-94	-0.00212766	0.0107527	-0.00853	-0.01055	0.006369	0.00641
12	17-Jan-94	-0.01918977	-0.0021277	0.010753	-0.00853	-0.010549	0.00637
13	18-Jan-94	-0.00652174	-0.0191898	-0.00213	0.010753	-0.008529	-0.01055
14	19-Jan-94	-0.01969365	-0.0065217	-0.01919	-0.00213	0.010753	-0.00853
15	20-Jan-94	-0.01339286	-0.0196937	-0.00652	-0.01919	-0.002128	0.01075
16	21-Jan-94	0	-0.0133929	-0.01969	-0.00652	-0.01919	-0.00213
17	24-Jan-94	0.06108597	0	-0.01339	-0.01969	-0.006522	-0.01919
18	25-Jan-94	-0.00639659	0.061086	0	-0.01339	-0.019694	-0.00652

Step 1: To create returns from one day ago in Column C enter

   $=B2$

in cell C3 and copy the formula down to the bottom of column C (use the double
click!)

Step 2: To create returns from two days ago in Column D enter

   $=B2$

in cell D4 and copy the formula down to the bottom of Column D.

**Step 3: Continue in this fashion and create returns from Three-Five Days Ago in
Columns E, F, and G, respectively.**

Step 4: We are now ready to run regression. Select *"Tools" "Data Analysis"* **and
select** *"Regression"*. See Figure 9.5.

Figure 9.5

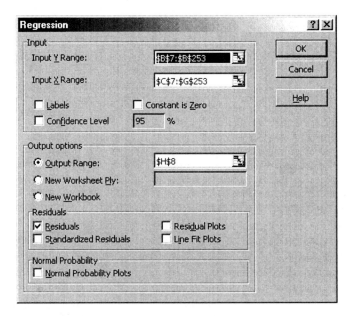

Step 5: Choose as your Y Range (dependent variable) B7:B253.

Step 6: Choose C7:G253 as our X Range.

**Step 7: Choose H8 as our Output range and Select Residuals Box to get errors for
each observation.**

We obtain the report in Figure 9.6:

Figure 9.6

	H	I	J	K	L	M	N	O	P
8	SUMMARY OUTPUT								
9									
10	*Regression Statistics*								
11	Multiple R	0.19481859							
12	R Square	0.03795428							
13	Adjusted R Square	0.01799483							
14	Standard Error	0.01886318							
15	Observations	247							
16									
17	ANOVA								
18		*df*	*SS*	*MS*	*F*	*Significance F*			
19	Regression	5	0.003383078	7E-04	1.90157	0.094735688			
20	Residual	241	0.085752516	4E-04					
21	Total	246	0.089135594						
22									
23		*Coefficients*	*Standard Error*	*t Stat*	*P-value*	*Lower 95%*	*Upper 95%*	*Lower 95.0%*	*Upper 95.0%*
24	Intercept	0.00128057	0.001216128	1.053	0.2934	-0.001115022	0.00367617	-0.00111502	0.003676171
25	1 day ago	-0.09216613	0.063999218	-1.44	0.15113	-0.218235396	0.03390314	-0.2182354	0.033903139
26	2 day ago	-0.07670237	0.064044219	-1.2	0.23223	-0.202860284	0.04945554	-0.20286028	0.049455542
27	3 day ago	0.00579105	0.0642966	0.09	0.92831	-0.120864017	0.13244612	-0.12086402	0.132446117
28	4 day ago	-0.08692299	0.063895633	-1.36	0.17498	-0.212788213	0.03894223	-0.21278821	0.038942226
29	5 day ago	0.11927379	0.063764137	1.871	0.06262	-0.006332403	0.24487998	-0.0063324	0.244879983

- The **R Square** value of .04 means that the last five days of returns explain only 4% of the variation in today's returns.

- Which independent variables are most helpful in predicting Today's Return? The P-value of .06 means the return from 5 days ago is the most useful for predicting Today's return on IBM. The question is will this relationship hold when tested on future data.

- In general any independent variable with a P-Value <= .15 is probably a useful predictor of the dependent variable.

- The **Standard Error** of .019 means that 68% of all predictions are accurate within 1.9%, 95% are accurate within 3.8% and 99.7% accurate within 5.7%.

- Looking at our forecast errors, we see they changed sign 129/247 = 52% of the time. **For any forecast method errors should change sign around half the time if the forecasts are good**. If forecast errors change sign much less than half the time it means there is further information to be extracted. Of course, this is not a sufficient condition for forecasts to be good.

- Our equation for forecasting today's IBM return would be

  Today's Return = .00128 -.092(1 day ago) -.077(2 days ago) + .006(3 days ago) - .087(4 days ago) + .119(5 days ago).

Using a Neural Network to Look for Patterns

A **neural network** such as the Excel add-in PREDICT (available from Neuralware) can be used to look for nonlinear patterns in data. The advantage of a neural network over regression is that it will usually find a pattern in data if one exists. The downside of a neural network is that, unlike regression, the network does not usually give us an explicit equation relating the dependent and independent variables. The upside of regression is, of course, that we are often given an equation relating the dependent variable to independent variables. For example, regression may state that Sales = 5*(advertising) - 2*(Price)^2 . The downside of regression is that it can only evaluate the pattern (such as a linear or exponential relationship) which we give to the computer. We used PREDICT to try and forecast Today's IBM Return from the last five days of IBM returns. We used only January-November as our **Training Set** and used December as our **Validation Set.** The good news is our MAPE for the Validation Set was no worse than for the Training Set. The Bad News is that the MAPE for multiple linear regression is just as good as PREDICT's MAPE. This means (given this set of independent variables) no subtle nonlinear pattern exists which can be used to make better forecasts than simple linear regression.

The January Effect

It is well known that stocks tend to do better in January than during other months. In the file *Dow.xls* we are given the monthly returns on the Dow for the years 1947-1992.

Figure 9.7

	A	B	C
2	Return	Month	Date
3	0.030892	Feb	Feb-47
4	-0.02688	Mar	Mar-47
5	-0.03045	Apr	Apr-47
6	-0.01524	May	May-47
7	0.030177	Jun	Jun-47
8	0.056169	Jul	Jul-47
9	-0.01874	Aug	Aug-47
10	-0.0181	Sep	Sep-47
11	0.028843	Oct	Oct-47
12	-0.00275	Nov	Nov-47
13	-0.01235	Dec	Dec-47
14	-0.0163	Jan	Jan-48

We can use a pivot table on this data to see if the Dow does better than expected in January.

Step by Step

Step 1: Position the cursor anywhere in columns A-C.

Step 2: Select *"Data"* *"Pivot Table Report"* and drag Month to the Row Box and Return to the Data Box.

Step 3: Double click on the Data Box to select AVERAGE OF RETURN. See the following wizard box.

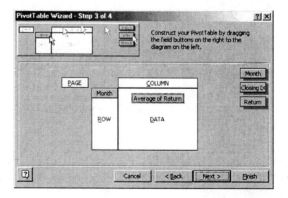

You will obtain the following pivot table.

Figure 9.8

	A	B
1	Average of Return	
2	Month Index	Total
3	Jan	0.019028894
4	Feb	0.005020048
5	Mar	0.009580402
6	Apr	0.012224413
7	May	0.00361093
8	Jun	0.00081518
9	Jul	0.005493552
10	Aug	0.004262214
11	Sep	-0.000152157
12	Oct	-0.00315117
13	Nov	0.003538478
14	Dec	0.010285213
15	Grand Total	0.005879666

For example, the average return on Dow during January was 1.9% while the average monthly return overall was .6%.

To see that January is a significantly better than average month compute in E13 the standard deviation of the 12 average monthly returns with the formula

=STDEV(B3:B14).

In E14 compute the mean of the 12 average monthly returns with the formula

=AVERAGE(B3:B14).

In E15 we compute the number of standard deviations by which January's average return exceeds an average month's with the formula:

=(B3-E14)/E13.

Figure 9.9

	D	E
12		
13	Stdev	0.006060173
14	Mean	0.005879666
15	January Standardized	2.169777457

The result of approximately 2.17 indicates that January's average is more than 2 standard deviations higher than an average month. The **January Effect** has yet to be satisfactorily explained.

Chapter 10: Testing Investment Strategies

Using Excel's If statements, it is easy to see if **technical trading rules** are worthwhile. Let's use the 1994 IBM data to compare the following strategy to buy and hold:

If the 5-day moving average exceeds the 20-day moving average, BUY. If the 5 day moving average is less than the 20-day moving average SELL.

Look at the sheet Pattern of *IBM.xls*.

Figure 10.1

	A	B	C	D	E	F	G	H	I
17	21-Jan-94	0	97.78761						
18	24-Jan-94	0.061086	103.7611				BH Profit		Profit
19	25-Jan-94	-0.0064	103.0973	Last 20	Last 5		31.16303		16.36813
20	26-Jan-94	-0.03219	99.77876			Buy?	Sell?	Own?	Profit
21	27-Jan-94	0.013304	101.1062			Yes	No	Yes	-101.106
22	28-Jan-94	0.010941	102.2124	102.2013	101.1062	No	Yes	No	102.2124
23	31-Jan-94	-0.02165	100	102.3119	101.9912	No	No	No	0
24	1-Feb-94	0	100	102.2124	101.2389	No	No	No	0
25	2-Feb-94	-0.00221	99.77876	101.9912	100.6195	No	No	No	0
26	3-Feb-94	-0.01109	98.67257	101.7146	100.6195	No	No	No	0
27	4-Feb-94	-0.06278	92.47788	101.4712	100.1327	No	No	No	0
28	7-Feb-94	0.043269	96.47932	100.885	98.18584	No	No	No	0
29	8-Feb-94	-0.01152	95.36781	100.4656	97.48171	No	No	No	0
30	9-Feb-94	-0.00932	94.4786	100.0459	96.55527	No	No	No	0
31	10-Feb-94	-0.00471	94.034	99.62602	95.49524	No	No	No	0

Step by Step

Step 1: In column D we compute the 20-day moving averages. Enter in D22 the formula

   =AVERAGE(C2:C21).

Copying this formula down to the bottom of the column computes the 20-day moving averages for the rest of the year.

Step 2: In column E we compute the 5-day moving averages. Enter in E22 the formula

   =AVERAGE(C17:C21).

Copying this formula to the bottom of Column E computes the 5-day moving averages.

Step 3: We assume that on 20th trading day (January 27) we bought the stock. To note this in F21 we enter "Yes" to indicate that we will buy a share. In G21 we enter "No" to indicate we have not sold a share that day. In H21 we enter a "Yes" to indicate that we now own a share. In I21 we compute our profit (negative) from buying the share by entering

$=-C21.$

Step 4: In column F (starting in Row 22) we see if we buy a share. Enter in F22 the formula

$=If(AND(H21="No",E22>D22),"Yes","No").$

This formula ensures that if we do not own a stock and the current 5-day average exceeds the current 20-day average we will BUY, otherwise we will not BUY.

Step 5: In Column G (starting in Row 22) we see if we sell a share. Enter in G22 the formula

$=If(AND(H21="Yes",E22<D22),"Yes","No").$

This formula ensures that we sell a stock if we own it and the current 5-day average is less than the current 20-day average.

Step 6: In Column H (starting in Row 22) we see if we own a share of stock. Enter in H22 the formula

$=If(F22="Yes","Yes",If(G22="Yes","No",If(AND(H21="Yes",F22="no",$

$G22="No"),"Yes","No"))).$

This formula ensures that:

- If we bought a share today we own it.

- Else if we sold a share we do not own it.

- Else if we owned the stock yesterday and did not buy or sell it we still own it.

- Otherwise we do not own the stock.

Step 7: In Column I we keep track of today's cash flow. In I22 enter the formula

$$=If(F22="Yes",-C22,If(G22="Yes",C22,0)).$$

This formula ensures that if we buy the stock we pay today's price for it and if we sell the stock we get today's price for it.

Step 8: By double-clicking on F22:I22 we copy these formulas down to the bottom of the spreadsheet.

Step 9: In cell I19 we compute our total profit ($16.36) with the formula

$$=SUM(I21:I254)+If(H254="Yes",C254,0).$$

This values our share of stock at its year-end value if we own the stock at the end of the year.

Remarks

Our strategy earned $16.37. Note that Buy and Hold did much better. Buy and Hold earned a profit of $31.16. Of course, we are ignoring transaction costs. Ignoring transaction costs works in favor of the Buy and Hold strategy.

Chapter 11: The Bass Model for Sales of a Product

It is of critical importance to be able to predict future sales of a product when the only available data is several months (or years) of sales. The **Bass Model** and its variants have been used to meet this challenge.

Model Description

Let:

$n(t)$ = *Product sales during period t.*

$N(t)$ = *Cumulative product sales during periods 1, 2, ... t.*

$\overline{N}$ = *Total number of customers in market; we assume that all of them eventually adopt the product.*

P = *Coefficient of innovation or external influence.*

Q = *Coefficient of imitation or internal influence.*

The Bass Model asserts that

$$n(t) = P(\overline{N} - N(t-1)) + \frac{QN(t-1)(\overline{N} - N(t-1))}{\overline{N}}$$

Thus the adopters at time t may be broken up into two components:

- A component tied to the number of people ($\overline{N}$ - N(t-1)) who have not yet adopted the product. This component is independent of the number of people (N(t-1)) who have already adopted the product. This explains why P is the coefficient of innovation or external influence.

- A component tied to the number of interactions between previous adopters (N(t-1)) and people who have yet to adopt ($\overline{N}$ - N(t-1)). This term represents the **diffusion** of the product through the market. This imitation or internal influence component reflects the fact that previous adopters tell non-adopters about the product and thereby generate new adoptions.

Estimating the Model

To estimate this model we must find values of P, Q, and $\overline{N}$ which accurately predict each period's sales (the n(t)). To estimate P, Q and $\overline{N}$ we will use the Solver. File *ColorTV.xls* contains 16 years of color TV sales (1964-1979). See Figure 11.1

Figure 11.1

	A	B	C	D	E	F	G
1					p	q	Nbar
2					0.055875	0.146583098	98.21177083
3		Color TV		SSE	74.22797		
4	t	n(t)	N(t)	Predicted	Sq Err		
5	0			0			
6	1	4.9	4.9	5.487541	0.345204		
7	2	4.3	9.2	5.896177	2.547782		
8	3	5.3	14.5	6.195732	0.802337		
9	4	10.9	25.4	6.489012	19.45681		
10	5	9.2	34.6	6.828623	5.62343		
11	6	2.5	37.1	6.83927	18.82926		
12	7	4.2	41.3	6.798507	6.752238		
13	8	8.3	49.6	6.688025	2.598462		
14	9	9.3	58.9	6.314844	8.911156		
15	10	6.2	65.1	5.652405	0.29986		
16	11	4.3	69.4	5.067348	0.588823		
17	12	2.8	72.2	4.594196	3.219138		
18	13	3.2	75.4	4.256425	1.116034		
19	14	3.5	78.9	3.841745	0.11679		
20	15	3.7	82.6	3.353189	0.120278		
21	16	4.5	87.1	2.796955	2.900364		

For example when t = 1 (1964) 4.9 million color TV's were sold. In 1965, 4.3 million color TV's were sold. To estimate P, Q and $\overline{N}$ we proceed as follows:

Step by Step

Step 1: Put trial values of P, Q, and $\overline{N}$ in E2:G2 and create RANGE NAMES for these cells.

Step 2: Using the trial values of P, Q, and $\overline{N}$ create predictions for 16 years of sales by copying from D6 to D7:D21 the formula

$=p*(Nbar-C5)+(q/Nbar)*C5*(Nbar-C5).$

Step 3: In E6:E21 we compute the squared error for each year by copying the formula

$=(B6-D6)^2$

from E6 to E7:E21.

Step 4: We compute the sum of squared errors for our predictions in cell E3 with the formula

=SUM(*E6:E21*).

Step 5: We now use Solver to determine values of p, q, and $\overline{N}$ that minimize SSE. Our Solver window follows.

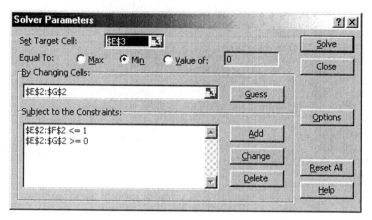

We minimize SSE (E3) by changing p, q and $\overline{N}$. All changing cells should be nonnegative. Solver found p = .056, q = .147, and $\overline{N}$ = 98.21.

How to Use the Bass Model

When we have several years of data, we can try and fit the Bass model and use our results to forecast sales for future years. This usually does not yield great forecasts.

A more useful approach is to look for a similar product that has already reached market maturity (for example a CD-ROM drive might be an analog for a digital camera). Then use the values of P and Q for the analogous product and an estimated value of $\overline{N}$ for the new product to forecast sales. Here are some sample values of P and Q. See Lilien and Randaswamy (1997) for a more complete list of Bass model parameters for other products.

Product	P	Q
Room air conditioner	.006	.185
Cable TV	.10	.06
Blender	.000	.26
VCR	.025	.603
CD player	.157	.00

Modifications of the Bass Model

Here are some modifications of the Bass model:

- Assume that $\overline{N}$ is growing over time. For example, if market size is growing 5% a year use $\overline{N}(t)=N(0)*1.05^t$ in Year t forecast and have Solver solve for N(0).

- Incorporate the effects of price and advertising on sales.

- Model the fact that customers return to the market and purchase product again. For example, if customers buy a product every 5 years you can adjust $\overline{N}(t)$ to include people who bought product 5 years ago.

For further discussion of the Bass model we refer the reader to Lilien and Randaswamy (1998).

Reference

Lilien, G. and Randaswamy, A., *Marketing Engineering*, Addison-Wesley, 1998.

Chapter 12: Fitting the Yield Curve

In order to analyze fixed income securities, it is vital to understand the **yield curve.** On January 2, 1993 the yield curve was as follows:

Duration	Spot Rate
.25	3.15%
.5	3.36%
1	3.7%
2	4.46%
3	4.94%
5	5.9%
7	6.29%
10	6.59%
30	7.32%

Essentially, the yield curve gives current **spot rates.** The **spot rate s_t** is the annual rate of interest for money held from time $t = 0$ (the present) to t years in future. Thus a \$100 30-year bond (paying no coupons and returning \$100 in 30 years) would sell for $100/(1.0732)^{30}$. The problem with the yield curve is that it only gives us a few spot rates. To price many fixed income securities it is important to be able to estimate spot rates for any time horizon, not just the points on the given yield curve. It is also important to understand the idea of a **forward rate**. The **forward rate** f_{t_1,t_2} between times t_1 and t_2 is the annual rate of interest charged **today** for borrowing money at t_1 and paid back at t_2. For example, we could find $f_{1,3}$ from

$$(1+s_3)^3 = (1+s_1)(1+f_{1,3})^2$$

or

$$(1.0494)^3 = (1.037)(1+f_{1,3})^2$$

$$1+f_{1,3} = \sqrt{\frac{1.0494^3}{1.037}}$$

or

$$f_{1,3} = 5.56\%.$$

We now show how to fit the yield curve and determine forward rates from our estimated yield curve. Our methodology is due to Haugen (1997).

Fitting the Yield Curve

An equation of the form $s(t) = (a_1 + a_2 t)e^{-a_3 t} + a_4$ does a great job of fitting the yield curve. We use the Excel Solver to fit this equation (see Figures 12.1 and 12.2 and *file Yield.xls*).

Figure 12.1

	A	B	C	D	E
1	Jan 2 1993				
2	a1	a2	a3	a4	
3	-0.04346536	-1.5E-05	0.213839	0.07263	
4					
5	t	Actual	Predict		
6	0.25	0.0315	0.031423	5.87E-09	
7	0.5	0.0336	0.033565	1.22E-09	
8	1	0.037	0.03752	2.71E-07	
9	2	0.0446	0.04427	1.09E-07	
10	3	0.0494	0.049722	1.04E-07	
11	5	0.059	0.057683	1.73E-06	
12	7	0.0629	0.062877	5.1E-10	
13	10	0.0659	0.06749	2.53E-06	
14	30	0.0732	0.072558	4.12E-07	
15				5.17E-06	

Figure 12.2

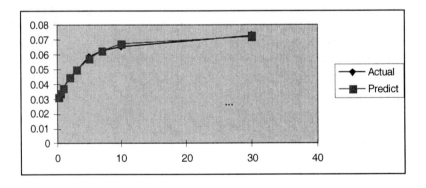

Step by Step

Step 1: Enter trial values of a_1-a_4 in A3:D3.

Step 2: Enter the actual yield curve data in A6:B14.

Step 3: Create predicted spot rates by entering the formula

=($A$3+$B$3*A6)*EXP(-A6*$C$3)+$D$3

in cell C6 and copy it to C7:C14.

These predictions are based on

$$s(t) = (a_1 + a_2 t)e^{-a_3 t} + a_4.$$

Step 4: In D6 through D14 compute the squared prediction error for each yield curve point by entering in D6 the formula

=(B6-C6)^2

and copying the formula to D7:D14.

Step 5: Determine the total squared error in our estimates in D15 by clicking on the summation icon.

Step 6: Invoke the Excel Solver and set the Solver up as follows:

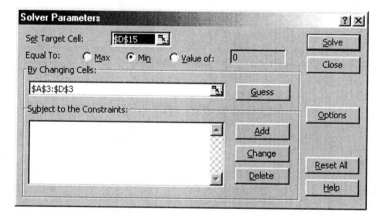

This chooses a_1-a_4 to minimize the sum of the squared errors. Note that the changing cells can be negative for this model. We will now predict spot rates with the formula

$$s(t) = (-.04 - .000015t)e^{-.2138t} + .07263$$

Note from Figure 12.2 our fit is quite good (it would be better if I had 15 year and 20 year points on curve).

Generating Implied Forward Rates

To illustrate the computation if forward rates implied by today's yield curve we use our predicted spot curve to generate implied forward rates at six- month intervals. See Figure 12.3.

To illustrate we will determine the implied forward rates $f_{.5,1}$, $f_{1,1.5}$, ...$f_{2,2.5}$.

Step by
Step

Step 1: In cell C18 generate $s_{.5}$ with the formula

=($A$3+$B$3*D18)*EXP(-D18*$C$3)+$D$3.

Copying this formula to the range C19:C22 generates all spot rates needed.

Step 2: We know that $s_{.5} = f_{0,.5}$ so we enter

=C18

in cell B18.

Step 3: To compute $f_{i,j}$ we note that

$$(1+s_j)^j = (1+s_i)^i (1+f_{i,j})^{j-i}$$

or

$$f_{i,j} = \left[\frac{(1+s_j)^j}{(1+s_i)^i} \right]^{1/((j-i)} - 1$$

Step 4: We now find $f_{.5,1}$ by entering in cell B19 the formula

=((1+C19)^D19/((1+C18)^D18))^(1/($D$19-$D$18))-1.

Copying this formula to B19:B22 generates the other forward rates.

Step 5: In cell F19 we compute the expected percentage increase in the forward rate at t = .5 over the forward rate at t= 0 with the formula

= B19/B18.

Copying this formula to F20:F22 gives us the expected percentage change in forward rates. Thus the yield curve estimates the July 93 forward six month rate to be 23.6% higher on average than Jan 93 forward six month rate etc. See Figure 12.3.

Generating Implied Forward Rates

Figure 12.3

	A	B	C	D	E	F
17	Predicted forwar	forward	spot	t	Period #	% age change
18	$f_{0,.5}$	0.033565	0.033565	0.5	1	
19	$f_{.5,1}$	0.041491	0.03752	1	2	1.236123579
20	$f_{1,1.5}$	0.048221	0.041075	1.5	3	1.16221663
21	$f_{1.5,2}$	0.053913	0.04427	2	4	1.118044117
22	$f_{2,2.5}$	0.058706	0.047141	2.5	5	1.088893642

If you believe the yield curve is a good predictor of future interest rates, then you can use the implied forward rates to simulate future interest rates. The problem, is however, that most of the time the implied forward rate turns out to be higher than the actual realized interest rate. For example, the actual one year rate two years from now tends to be higher than $f_{2,1}$ .We will address this problem in Chapter 53 by simulating movements in the entire yield curve.

Reference

Haugen, R. *Modern Investment Theory*, Prentice-Hall, 1997.

Chapter 13: Determining Monthly Loan Payments

Using the Excel =PMT function it is a simple matter to determine the monthly payment on a loan. The syntax of the =PMT function is as follows:

=PMT(rate, number of periods, principal).

Here

Rate = interest rate per period.

Number of periods = number of payments made.

Principal = Beginning unpaid balance.

Note that if periods are months, then the interest rate must be the monthly interest rate. For example, if we want to determine the monthly payment on a 60 month $25,000 loan at 1% interest per month we enter the formula

=PMT(.01,60,25000).

This formulas yields -$556.11. The negative sign indicates that we are making the payments.

It is instructive to use the Excel Solver to solve for the monthly payments. The key relationships are that for any Month t:

(Ending Month t balance) = (Ending Month t - 1 balance) -((Monthly Payment)(Month t interest)) (13.1)

and

(Month t interest) = (Beginning Month t balance)*(Monthly Interest rate). (13.2)

In the spreadsheet *mortgage.xls* we find the monthly payment. The key is to set up a monthly ledger that keeps track of the Beginning balance, Monthly payment, Monthly Interest, and Ending balance for each month. Figure 13.1 (with rows hidden) shows the details.

Figure 13.1

	A	B	C	D	E
1	**Determining monthly payments**				
2					
3	Length of loan	60			
4	Interest rate/month	$ 0.01			
5	Principal	$ 25,000.00			
6					
7	Monthly payment	($556.11)	=PMT(B4,B3,B5)		
8					
9	Payment?	$ 556.11			
10	Month	Beginning Balance	Payment	Interest	Ending Balance
11	1	$ 25,000.00	$ 556.11	$ 250.00	$ 24,693.89
12	2	$ 24,693.89	$ 556.11	$ 246.94	$ 24,384.72
13	3	$ 24,384.72	$ 556.11	$ 243.85	$ 24,072.45
14	4	$ 24,072.45	$ 556.11	$ 240.72	$ 23,757.07
15	5	$ 23,757.07	$ 556.11	$ 237.57	$ 23,438.53
16	6	$ 23,438.53	$ 556.11	$ 234.39	$ 23,116.80
17	7	$ 23,116.80	$ 556.11	$ 231.17	$ 22,791.86
18	8	$ 22,791.86	$ 556.11	$ 227.92	$ 22,463.66
19	9	$ 22,463.66	$ 556.11	$ 224.64	$ 22,132.19
20	10	$ 22,132.19	$ 556.11	$ 221.32	$ 21,797.40
21	11	$ 21,797.40	$ 556.11	$ 217.97	$ 21,459.26
22	12	$ 21,459.26	$ 556.11	$ 214.59	$ 21,117.74
23	13	$ 21,117.74	$ 556.11	$ 211.18	$ 20,772.81
67	57	$ 2,169.93	$ 556.11	$ 21.70	$ 1,635.51
68	58	$ 1,635.51	$ 556.11	$ 16.36	$ 1,095.76
69	59	$ 1,095.76	$ 556.11	$ 10.96	$ 550.61
70	60	$ 550.61	$ 556.11	$ 5.51	$ 0.00

Step By Step

Step 1: In B11 we enter the beginning balance ($25000).

Step 2: In B9 we enter a trial value for the monthly payment and in C11 we record the monthly payment for month 1 with the formula

=$B$9.

Step 3: In D11 we use (16.2) to compute the monthly interest paid during month 1 with the formula

=$B$4*B11.

Step 4: In E11 we use (16.1) to determine the month 1 ending balance with the formula

=B11-(C11-D11).

Step 5: In B12 we record Month 2's beginning balance (which equals Month 1's ending balance) with the formula

=E11.

Step 6: We now copy the formulas from C11:E11 to C12:E12. Then we copy the formulas from B12:E12 to B13:B70.

Using the Solver to Find the Monthly Payment

Our Solver model has no target cell. All we need to do is choose the changing cell B9 so that the ending Month 60 balance (cell E70) equals 0. All cells in the spreadsheet are linear functions of the changing cell, so we have a linear model. Our Solver window is as follows:

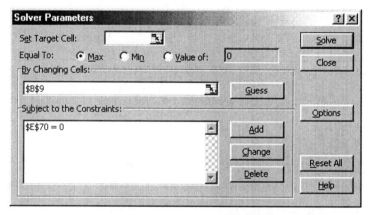

We find (in agreement with the =PMT function) that the monthly payment needed to pay off a $25,000 balance in 60 months is $556.11.

Chapter 14: Funding a Pension Liability

Suppose you are managing a pension fund and have a good idea of how much money you will need to pay out during each of the next n years. Today several bonds may be purchased to fund these pension liabilities. Given the bonds available for purchase today, what is the least amount of money that must be set aside today to ensure that payments from the bonds will meet the pension liabilities? The trick is to keep track of your cash balance after each liability payment is made and add a constraint that the cash balance after paying each liability is nonnegative. Here is an example:

Example 14.1

It is January 1, 2001 and you are managing the Fly-by-Night Pension fund. The following payments must be made on January 1 of each year.

Year	Payment
2001	$11,000
2002	$12,000
2003	$14,000
2004	$15,000
2005	$16,000
2006	$18,000
2007	$20,000
2008	$21,000
2009	$22.000
2010	$24,000
2011	$25,000
2012	$30,000
2013	$31,000
2014	$31,000
2015	$31,000

In order to finance these obligations, the following three bonds may be purchased on January 1, 2001 (all coupons are paid on January 1 of each year):

- Bond 1 costs $980 and pays $60 in 2002-2005 and $1060 in 2006.

- Bond 2 costs $970 and pays $65 in 2002-2011 and $1065 in 2012.

- Bond 3 costs $1050 and yields a $75 coupon in 2002-2014 and $1075 in 2015.

Payments from bonds are received in time to be used to meet pension liabilities. During each year we earn 4% interest on our cash. What is the minimum amount of money we need to set aside on January 1,2001 to ensure that we can meet all pension liabilities?

Solution   Our work is in file *pension.xls*. See Figure 14.1.

Figure 14.1

	A	B	C	D	E	F	G	H	I	J
1	Interest rate	0.04				Cash	Bond 1	Bond 2	Bond 3	
2						197768.40	73.69	77.21	28.84	
3						price	$ 980	$ 970	$ 1,050	
4	Date	Beginning balance	Interest received	Bond purchases	Liabilities	Coupons received	Bond 1 coupons	Bond 2 coupons	Bond 3 coupons	Ending balance
5	1/1/01	$ 197,768	$ -	$ 177,392	$ 11,000					$ 9,376
6	1/1/02	$ 9,376	375.05		$ 12,000	$ 11,603	$ 60	$ 65	$ 75	$ 9,354
7	1/1/03	$ 9,354	$ 374		$ 14,000	$ 11,603	$ 60	$ 65	$ 75	$ 7,332
8	1/1/04	$ 7,332	$ 293		$ 15,000	$ 11,603	$ 60	$ 65	$ 75	$ 4,228
9	1/1/05	$ 4,228	$ 169		$ 16,000	$ 11,603	$ 60	$ 65	$ 75	$ (0)
10	1/1/06	$ (0)	$ (0)		$ 18,000	$ 85,298	$ 1,060	$ 65	$ 75	$ 67,298
11	1/1/07	$ 67,298	$ 2,692		$ 20,000	$ 7,181		$ 65	$ 75	$ 57,171
12	1/1/08	$ 57,171	$ 2,287		$ 21,000	$ 7,181		$ 65	$ 75	$ 45,639
13	1/1/09	$ 45,639	$ 1,826		$ 22,000	$ 7,181		$ 65	$ 75	$ 32,646
14	1/1/10	$ 32,646	$ 1,306		$ 24,000	$ 7,181		$ 65	$ 75	$ 17,133
15	1/1/11	$ 17,133	$ 685		$ 25,000	$ 7,181		$ 65	$ 75	$ 0
16	1/1/12	$ 0	$ 0		$ 30,000	$ 84,390		$ 1,065	$ 75	$ 54,390
17	1/1/13	$ 54,390	$ 2,176		$ 31,000	$ 2,163			$ 75	$ 27,728
18	1/1/14	$ 27,728	$ 1,109		$ 31,000	$ 2,163			$ 75	$ 0
19	1/1/15	$ 0	$ 0		$ 31,000	$ 31,000			$ 1,075	$ 0

Step by Step

Step 1: Enter trial values for our changing cells (cash allocated on January 1, 2001 and number purchased of each bond) in F2:I2.

Step 2: In B5 we enter our beginning balance on January 1, 2001 by copying our allocated cash to B5 with the formula

=F2.

Step 3: In C5 we enter 0 because no interest is received until 2002.

Step 4: In D5 we compute the total amount of our bond purchases with the formula

$=SUMPRODUCT(G2:I2,G3:I3).$

Step 5: In E5:E19 we enter our pension liabilities.

Step 6: Columns F:I are used to keep track of received bond payments. Since bond payments do not begin until 2001, we leave F5:I5 blank. Columns G:I contain the annual payments received if one unit of each bond is bought.

Step 7: In cell J5 we compute our "ending" January 1, 2001 balance. This balance is computed after bond payments have been received and liabilities have been paid out.

$=B5+C5-D5-E5+F5.$

For each year:

(Ending balance) = (beginning balance) + (interest received on cash) - (bond purchases) -(liabilities paid out) + (bond payments received).

Step 8: In cell B6 we make our beginning January 1, 2002 balance equal our ending January 1, 2001 cash balance with the formula

$=J5.$

Step 9: In cell C6 we compute our interest on cash held during 2001 with the formula

$=\$B\$1*J5.$

Step 10: In cell F6 we compute our bond payments received on January 1, 2002 with the formula

$=SUMPRODUCT(\$G\$2:\$I\$2,G6:I6).$

Step 11: In cell J6 we compute our ending January 1, 2002 balance by copying the formula in J5 to J6.

By copying the formulas in B6, C6, F6, I6, and J6 down to row 19 we have completed our "ledger". We are now ready to invoke the Excel Solver.

Using the Excel Solver

Our Solver window looks as follows:

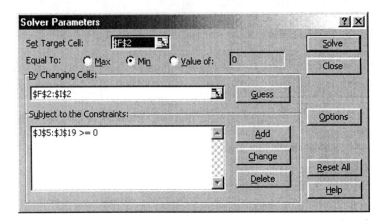

Our target cell (F2) is to minimize total cash allocated on January 1, 2001. Our changing cells are number of each bond purchased (G2:I2) and total cash allocated (F2). **Note that the target cell may also be a changing cell.** We have a linear model because changing cells are always multiplied by constants and added together. **We can ensure that all liability payments are met by adding constraints that require our ending cash positions on January 1, 2001-January 1, 2015 to be nonnegative(J5:J19>=0).** After checking the Linear model and Assume Nonnegative boxes in OPTIONS dialog box we obtain the optimal solution in Figure 14.1. Allocate $197,768.40 in cash and purchase 73.69 units of Bond 1, 77.21 units of Bond 2, and 28.84 units of Bond 3.

Remarks

The author has assigned this problem on exams and students often make the following error: they do not allow cash allocated to be a changing cell. This forces us to allocate cash which equals ($11,000) + (cost of bond purchases). This is not the optimal strategy (See Figure 14.2 and sheet Cash not changing cell of *pension.xls*). Suppose we restrict cash allocated to equal ($11,000) + (cost of bond purchases). Then from Figure 14.2 we find that we need to buy more bonds so we will receive enough coupons to make it through the early years. By allocating some money to cash today in excess of today's bond purchases the optimal solution in Figure 14.1 requires fewer bond purchases.

Figure 14.2

	A	B	C	D	E	F	G	H	I	J
1	Interest rate	0.04				Cash	Bond 1	Bond 2	Bond 3	
2						$221,128	54.48	64.92	89.30	
3						price	$ 980	$ 970	$ 1,050	
4	Date	Beginning balance	Interest received	Bond purchases	Liabilities	Coupons received	Bond 1 coupons	Bond 2 coupons	Bond 3 coupons	Ending balance
5	1/1/01	$ -	$ -	$ 210,128	$ 11,000					$ -
6	1/1/02	$ -	$ -		$ 12,000	$ 14,186	$ 60	$ 65	$ 75	$ 2,186
7	1/1/03	$ 2,186	$ 87		$ 14,000	$ 14,186	$ 60	$ 65	$ 75	$ 2,460
8	1/1/04	$ 2,460	$ 98		$ 15,000	$ 14,186	$ 60	$ 65	$ 75	$ 1,744
9	1/1/05	$ 1,744	$ 70		$ 16,000	$ 14,186	$ 60	$ 65	$ 75	$ (0)
10	1/1/06	$ (0)	$ (0)		$ 18,000	$ 68,666	$ 1,060	$ 65	$ 75	$ 50,666
11	1/1/07	$ 50,666	$ 2,027		$ 20,000	$ 10,917		$ 65	$ 75	$ 43,610
12	1/1/08	$ 43,610	$ 1,744		$ 21,000	$ 10,917		$ 65	$ 75	$ 35,272
13	1/1/09	$ 35,272	$ 1,411		$ 22,000	$ 10,917		$ 65	$ 75	$ 25,600
14	1/1/10	$ 25,600	$ 1,024		$ 24,000	$ 10,917		$ 65	$ 75	$ 13,541
15	1/1/11	$ 13,541	$ 542		$ 25,000	$ 10,917		$ 65	$ 75	$ (0)
16	1/1/12	$ (0)	$ (0)		$ 30,000	$ 75,837		$ 1,065	$ 75	$ 45,837
17	1/1/13	$ 45,837	$ 1,833		$ 31,000	$ 6,698			$ 75	$ 23,368
18	1/1/14	$ 23,368	$ 935		$ 31,000	$ 6,698			$ 75	$ (0)
19	1/1/15	$ (0)	$ (0)		$ 31,000	$ 95,998			$ 1,075	$ 64,998

Chapter 15: Multiperiod Capital Budgeting

Companies often have more worthwhile projects under consideration than their financial resources allow them to undertake. In this situation, the Excel Solver can be used to determine the combination of projects that will maximize the NPV added by the projects subject to the constraint that each year the money spent on the projects does not exceed the amount of available capital.

Example 15.1

A company has nine projects under consideration. The NPV added by each project and the capital required by each project during the next two years is given in Figure 15.1. All figures are in millions. For example, Project 1 will add $14 million in NPV and require expenditures of $12 million during year 1 and $3 million during year 2. $50 million is available for projects during year 1 and $20 million is available during year 2.

a) Assuming we may undertake a fraction of each project, how can we maximize NPV?

b) If we cannot undertake a fraction of a project, but must undertake all of a project or none of a project, how can we maximize NPV?

c) Suppose that if Project 4 is undertaken, then Project 5 must be undertaken. How can we maximize NPV?

Figure 15.1

	A	B	C	D	E	F	G	H	I	J
1	Project	1	2	3	4	5	6	7	8	9
2	Chosen	1	0	1	1	0	0.97	0.05	0	1
3	Year 1 Outflow	12	54	6	6	30	6	48	36	18
4	Year 2 Outflow	3	7	6	2	35	6	4	3	3
5	NPV	14	17	17	15	40	12	14	10	12
6										
7	Total NPV	70.27273								
8										
9	Period	Used		Available			NPV			NPV
10	1	50 <=		50		Year 1 Available	70.27		Year 2 Available	70.27
11	2	20 <=		20		45	68.33		15	60.95
12						46	68.89		16	62.82
13						47	69.44		17	64.68
14						48	70		18	66.55
15						49	70.14		19	68.41
16						50	70.27		20	70.27
17						51	70.41		21	71.38
18						52	70.55		22	72.35
19						53	70.68		23	73.11
20						54	70.82		24	73.78
21						55	70.95		25	74.44
22						56	71.09		26	75.11
23						57	71.23		27	75.78
24						58	71.36		28	76.44
25						59	71.5		29	77.11
26						60	71.64		30	77.78

Solution - Part a

Our target cell will be to maximize NPV. (*See file Capbudget.xls*). Our changing cells (constrained between 0 and 1) measure the fraction undertaken of each investment. Our constraints ensure that during year 1 and year 2 we spend no more money than we have available. We proceed as follows:

Step by Step

Step 1: In B2:J2 enter trial values for the fraction of each project undertaken.

Step 2: In B7 determine the NPV contributed by the chosen projects with the formula

$= SUMPRODUCT(B2:J2,B5:J5)$.

Note this formula implicitly assumes that undertaking, say half of a project yields half the NPV.

Step 3: In B10 and B11 we compute the money spent during each year by copying the formula

$$= SUMPRODUCT(B\$2:J\$2,B3:J3)$$

from B10 to B11. Again, we are implicitly assuming that undertaking, say, half of a project requires half the expenditures of the entire project.

Step 4: Set up the following Solver window and under options check the linear and assume non-negative boxes. The model is linear because each time a changing cell occurs in the target cell and/or constraints the changing cell is multiplied by a constant and we repeatedly add together terms of the form (changing cell)*(constant).

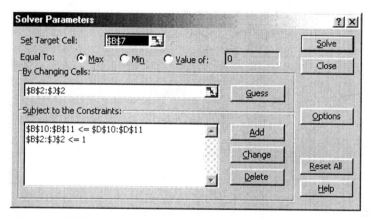

We maximize NPV (B7) by changing B2:J2 subject to the constraints that each changing cell is between 0 and 1 (B2:J2<=1) and financial resource constraints (B10:B11<=D10:D11). From Figure 15.1 we find that a maximum of $70.27 million in NPV can be added by undertaking all of Projects 1, 3, 4, and 9 as well as 97% of Project 6 and 5% of Project 7.

How Important Are the Resource Constraints?

A natural question is which is more important: the financial resource limitations during year 1 or year 2? To answer this question we use the Solver Table (see Winston and Albright (1999)) to resolve the problem for different amounts of capital available during each year. From Figure 15.2 we find that raising the amount of available year 1 funds by $1 million increases NPV by $130,000; while increasing the amount of available year 2 funds by $1 million increases NPV by $1.11 million. Therefore, year 2-fund availability is much more crucial than year 1 fund availability.

Figure 15.2

	F	G	H	I	J
9		NPV			NPV
	Year 1			Year 2	
10	Available	70.27		Available	70.27
11	45	68.33		15	60.95
12	46	68.89		16	62.82
13	47	69.44		17	64.68
14	48	70		18	66.55
15	49	70.14		19	68.41
16	50	70.27		20	70.27
17	51	70.41		21	71.38
18	52	70.55		22	72.35
19	53	70.68		23	73.11
20	54	70.82		24	73.78
21	55	70.95		25	74.44
22	56	71.09		26	75.11
23	57	71.23		27	75.78
24	58	71.36		28	76.44
25	59	71.5		29	77.11
26	60	71.64		30	77.78

**Solution -
Part b**

All we need to do is add a constraint to make the changing cells B2:J2 **binary** . This forces the changing cells to equal 0 or 1. We also set Tolerance on options to 0% to ensure that Solver finds an optimal solution. If we were to set Tolerance to say, 5%, Solver might stop when an integer solution was found that yielded an NPV within 5% of the solution to the problem without the binary constraints. We find the following optimal solution to the problem.

Figure 15.3

	A	B	C	D	E	F	G	H	I	J
1	Project	1	2	3	4	5	6	7	8	9
2	Chosen	1	0	1	1	0	1	0	0	1
3	Year 1 Outflow	12	54	6	6	30	6	48	36	18
4	Year 2 Outflow	3	7	6	2	35	6	4	3	3
5	NPV	14	17	17	15	40	12	14	10	12
6										
7	Total NPV	70								
8										
9	Period	Used		Available			NPV			NPV
10		1	48 <=	50		Year 1 Available	70		Year 2 Available	70
11		2	20 <=	25		45	58		15	58
12						46	58		16	58
13						47	58		17	58
14						48	70		18	58
15						49	70		19	58
16						50	70		20	70
17						51	70		21	70
18						52	70		22	70
19						53	70		23	70
20						54	70		24	70
21						55	70		25	70
22						56	70		26	70
23						57	70		27	70
24						58	70		28	70
25						59	70		29	70
26						60	70		30	70

Selecting Projects 1,3,4,6 and 9 maximizes NPV. Total NPV is $70 million. Note the constraint forbidding fractional projects has (for this problem) cost us very little money.

Running the Solver Table shows us that a small increase in available funds for each year does not improve NPV! This is because it takes a lot more money to do a **whole** project, and we are now forbidden from taking on a fractional project.

Solution - Part c

All we need to do is add the constraint that E2<=F2. This ensures that if we choose Project 4 (that is E2=1), then F2 must be 1 (which implies that Project 5 must be chosen). Note that if Project 4 is **not** chosen then E2 = 0, and the constraint E2<=F2 allows F2 to equal 0 or 1, as desired. The optimal solution is shown in Figure 15.4.

Figure 15.4

	A	B	C	D	E	F	G	H	I	J
1	Project	1	2	3	4	5	6	7	8	9
2	Chosen	1	0	1	-0	0	1	0	0	1
3	Year 1 Outflow	12	54	6	6	30	6	48	36	18
4	Year 2 Outflow	3	7	6	2	35	6	4	3	3
5	NPV	14	17	17	15	40	12	14	10	12
6										
7	Total NPV	55								
8										
9	Period	Used		Available						
10	1	42 <=		50						
11	2	18 <=		25						
12		If Project 4 then Project 5								
13		Pr 4		Pr 5						
14		-1.1E-13 <=		0						

Now Projects 1,3, 6 and 9 are chosen. Our NPV has dropped to $55 million. If Project 4 were chosen, we would have to choose Project 5, and this is infeasible. Therefore the lucrative Project 4 can no longer be chosen.

Reference

Winston, W. and Albright S.C., *Practical Management Science with Spreadsheets*, Duxbury Press, 2nd edition, 1999.

Chapter 16: Portfolio Optimization with Solver

Suppose we have a given set of investments under consideration. A **portfolio** is defined by the fraction of our capital that we place in each investment. How can we determine the minimum variance portfolio that yields a desired expected return? Harry Markowitz first answered this question in the 1950's. For his work he received the 1991 Nobel Prize in Economics. We begin by reviewing how to determine the mean and variance of a portfolio.

Finding the Mean and Variance of a Portfolio

Suppose n investments are under consideration and we know the mean annual return μ_i and standard deviation σ_i for each investment. Also suppose we know the correlation ρ_{ij} between the annual return on investments i and j. If we place a fraction x_j of our capital in investment j, then the mean and variance of the annual return on our portfolio may be found as follows:

$$Mean\ return = x_1\mu_1 + x_2\mu_2 + ...x_n\mu_n \quad (16.1)$$

$$Variance\ return = [x_1\sigma_1\ x_2\sigma_2...x_n\sigma_n]P[x_1\sigma_1\ x_2\sigma_2...x_n\sigma_n]^T \quad (16.2)$$

Here P is the matrix of correlations. The i-jth entry of P is the correlation between the annual return on investments i and j. Fortunately, Excel has a matrix multiplication (=MMULT) and transpose (=TRANSPOSE) function which can easily be used to determine the variance of a portfolio. In real life we never actually know the means, standard deviations, and correlations. Historical data is often used to estimate these parameters. Assuming we have monthly returns on each investment we estimate these parameters as follows (see Benninga (1997)).

Take Ln(1 + Return) for each month and each investment.

- Estimate μ_i by the average of Ln (1 + Return) for investment i.

- Estimate σ_i by the standard deviation of Ln(1 + Return) for investment i.

- Estimate ρ_{ij} by the correlation between Ln (1 + Return) for investment i and investment j.

In effect we are inputting into our portfolio model estimates of the continuously compounded rate of return on each investment. To estimate the mean and standard deviation of annual compounded returns proceed as follows:

$$Annual\ Mean\ Return = 12 * (monthly\ mean\ return)\ (16.3)$$

$$Standard\ deviation\ of\ Annual\ Return = \sqrt{12} * (standard\ deviation\ of\ monthly\ return)$$
(16.4).

We now use actual data to solve a portfolio optimization problem. Our target cell is to minimize the annual variance of the portfolio. Our changing cells will be the fraction of our capital placed in each investment. Our constraints will ensure that 100% of our capital is invested and that a desired expected annual return is obtained. If we constrain our weights to be nonnegative, then we get the variance-minimizing portfolio without short sales. If we allow our weights to be negative, we get the variance-minimizing solution with short sales.

Example 16.1 The file *portex2.xls* gives the monthly returns for IBM, GM, Dayton Hudson, and ARCO for the years 1990-1996. Determine a variance-minimizing portfolio that yields a compounded expected return of at least 8% annually.

Figure 16.1

	A	B	C	D	E	F	G	H	I
1					mean	0.006453	0.005738	0.007763	0.006053
2					sigma	0.080008	0.077854	0.074409	0.047225
3	Date	IBM	GM	DH	ARC	Ln(1+IBM)	LN(1+GM)	LN(1+DH)	Ln(1+ARC)
4	1/31/90	0.047809	-0.01479	-0.06287	-0.00786	0.046701	-0.0149	-0.06493	-0.007887
5	2/28/90	0.065501	0.096096	0.036981	0.038461	0.063445	0.091755	0.036314	0.03774
6	3/30/90	0.021661	0.022284	0.119919	0.015418	0.021429	0.022039	0.113256	0.015301
7	4/30/90	0.027091	-0.03542	-0.01815	-0.03579	0.02673	-0.03606	-0.01832	-0.036448
8	5/31/90	0.112018	0.115819	0.123179	0.075366	0.106176	0.109589	0.116163	0.072661
9	6/29/90	-0.02083	-0.02057	-0.03802	-0.00634	-0.02105	-0.02078	-0.03876	-0.006363
10	7/31/90	-0.05106	-0.021	-0.0378	0.101064	-0.05241	-0.02122	-0.03853	0.096277
11	8/31/90	-0.07547	-0.13137	-0.18457	0.052174	-0.07847	-0.14083	-0.20404	0.050858
12	9/28/90	0.044172	-0.08805	-0.07048	-0.00371	0.043224	-0.09217	-0.07309	-0.003714
13	10/31/90	-0.0094	0.013793	-0.09479	-0.03256	-0.00945	0.013699	-0.09958	-0.0331
14	11/30/90	0.089775	0.013605	0.145654	-0.00096	0.085971	0.013514	0.135976	-0.000962
15	12/31/90	-0.0055	-0.05822	0.052874	-0.03887	-0.00552	-0.05998	0.051523	-0.039648
16	1/31/91	0.121681	0.054545	0.144105	-0.03438	0.114828	0.05311	0.134623	-0.034983
17	2/28/91	0.025325	0.10069	0.047481	0.098429	0.02501	0.095937	0.046388	0.093881
18	3/28/91	-0.11553	-0.0443	0.025641	-0.02697	-0.12277	-0.04532	0.025318	-0.027346
19	4/30/91	-0.0955	-0.05298	0.069643	0.031683	-0.10037	-0.05444	0.067325	0.031192
20	5/31/91	0.042087	0.217483	0.073255	-0.03935	0.041226	0.196786	0.070696	-0.040142
21	6/28/91	-0.08481	-0.05507	-0.10625	-0.07273	-0.08862	-0.05665	-0.11233	-0.075506
22	7/31/91	0.042471	-0.02454	-0.03671	0.066449	0.041594	-0.02485	-0.0374	0.064334
23	8/30/91	-0.03126	-0.03396	0.139528	-0.01634	-0.03176	-0.03455	0.130614	-0.016478
24	9/30/91	0.069677	-0.01645	-0.0656	-0.02521	0.067357	-0.01658	-0.06785	-0.025533
25	10/31/91	-0.05187	-0.0602	-0.125	0.03125	-0.05326	-0.06209	-0.13353	0.030772
26	11/29/91	-0.04621	-0.11317	-0.09613	-0.13062	-0.04731	-0.1201	-0.10106	-0.139972
78	3/29/96	-0.09276	0.039024	0.141176	0.086758	-0.09735	0.038282	0.132059	0.083199
79	4/30/96	-0.03146	0.018779	0.125184	-0.0105	-0.03197	0.018605	0.117947	-0.01056
80	5/31/96	-0.00603	0.023502	0.07267	0.027601	-0.00605	0.02323	0.070151	0.027227
81	6/28/96	-0.0726	-0.04989	0.011029	-0.01149	-0.07537	-0.05117	0.010969	-0.011561
82	7/31/96	0.085859	-0.06921	-0.12	-0.01903	0.082371	-0.07172	-0.12783	-0.019211
83	8/30/96	0.067209	0.026154	0.145785	0.018319	0.065047	0.025818	0.13609	0.018153
84	9/30/96	0.088525	-0.03275	-0.04348	0.092077	0.084823	-0.03329	-0.04445	0.088081
85	10/31/96	0.036145	0.117188	0.049242	0.039216	0.035507	0.110815	0.048068	0.038466

Solution

We begin by estimating the mean and standard deviation of monthly returns for each stock. See Figure 16.1.

Step by Step

Step 1: In F4 determine Ln(1 + January, 1990 IBM return) with the formula

$$=LN(1+B4).$$

Copying this formula to F4:F85 computes Ln(1 + Monthly return) for all our data.

Step 2: Estimate the mean monthly return for IBM in cell F1 with the formula

$$=AVERAGE(F4:F85).$$

Estimate the standard deviation of the monthly returns for IBM in cell F2 with the formula

$$=STDEV(F4:F85).$$

Copying these formulas to G1:I2 yields the monthly mean and standard deviation estimates for each stock.

Step 3: To find the correlations invoke "Data Analysis" Tools" "Correlations" and select the range F3:I85 and check the labels box. You will obtain the following matrix of correlations (Excel only fills in only the lower portion of the matrix, so you need to manually copy some correlations).

	Ln(1+IBM)	LN(1+GM)	Ln(1+DH)	Ln(1+ARC)
Ln(1+IBM)	1	0.263435	0.038102	0.08685
LN(1+GM)	0.263435	1	0.038102	0.08685
Ln(1+DH)	0.038102	0.244003	1	0.095027
Ln(1+ARC	0.08685	0.089451	0.095027	1

Step 4: In sheet Analysis we have copied the correlation matrix and used (16.3) and (16.4) to compute the annualized mean and standard deviations. See Figure 16.2.

Figure 16.2

	A	B	C	D	E	F	G
1			Ln(1+IBM)	LN(1+GM)	Ln(1+DH)	Ln(1+ARC)	
2		mean month	0.006453	0.005738	0.007763	0.006053	
3		sigma month	0.080008	0.077854	0.074409	0.047225	
4		mean year	0.077442	0.068858	0.09315	0.072638	
5		sigma year	0.277155	0.269694	0.257762	0.163591	Total
6		weights	0.168031	0.054477	0.329605	0.447887	1
7		**Weight*Stdev**	0.04657	0.014692	0.08496	0.07327	
8							
9		**Correlations**					
10							
11				Ln(1+IBM)	LN(1+GM)	Ln(1+DH)	Ln(1+ARC)
12			Ln(1+IBM)	1	0.263435	0.038102	0.08685
13			LN(1+GM)	0.263435	1	0.038102	0.08685
14			Ln(1+DH)	0.038102	0.244003	1	0.095027
15			Ln(1+ARC	0.08685	0.089451	0.095027	1
16					Desired		
17		Port Mean	0.08	>=	0.08		
18		Port variance	0.017951				
19		Port sigma	0.133981				

We are now ready to set up our Solver model.

Step 5: In C6:F6 enter trial values for the "weights" or fraction of our money placed in each investment. In G6 total the weights with the formula

=SUM(C6:F6).

Step 6: In B17 use (16.1) to determine the expected annual return on the portfolio with the formula

=SUMPRODUCT(C6:F6,C4:F4).

Step 7: In C7:F7 we compute for each investment the product of the weight*standard deviation. This is needed to use (16.2) to compute the variance of the portfolio. Simply copy from C7 to D7:F7 the formula

=C6*C5.

Step 8: THE KEY STEP!! In C18 we use (16.2) to determine the annual variance of the portfolio return using (16.2) with the array formula

=MMULT(C7:F7,MMULT(D12:G15,TRANSPOSE(C7:F7))).

Finding the Mean and Variance of a Portfolio

You must hit *<Ctrl><Shift><Enter>* for this array formula to work. Note we close with three parentheses because one is needed to close the Transpose operation and one is needed to close each =MMULT function.

Step 9: Compute the standard deviation of the portfolio's annual return in C19 with the formula

   =SQRT(C18).

Step 10: Set up the Solver window for this problem.

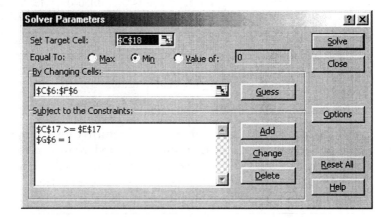

We minimize variance (C18). Our changing cells are C6:F6 (weights for each stock). Our first constraint (C17>=E17) ensures our expected return is at least 8%. Our last constraint (G6=1) ensures all money is invested. Since no short selling is allowed we constrain all our changing cells to be non-negative. We find the variance-minimizing portfolio yields an annual standard deviation of 13.4%, a mean return of 8%, and placed 17% in IBM, 5% in GM, 33% in Dayton Hudson and 45% in ARCO. Note that even though ARCO yielded the second lowest expected return, its low standard deviation caused us to place almost half our money in ARCO.

Finding the Efficient Frontier

Using the Solver Table (see Winston and Albright 1999) we solved the portfolio optimization problem for desired expected returns of 7%, 7.2%, ..., 8.8% and 9%. We obtained the following results:

Figure 16.3

	B	C	D	E	F	G	H
21			Sigma	IBM	GM	DH	ARCO
22	Sigma	Mean	0.133981	0.168031	0.054477	0.329605	0.447887
23	0.127455584	0.07	0.127456	0.143805	0.130405	0.186862	0.538928
24	0.127455584	0.072	0.127456	0.143805	0.130405	0.186862	0.538928
25	0.127455584	0.074	0.127456	0.143805	0.130405	0.186862	0.538928
26	0.127455584	0.076	0.127456	0.143805	0.130405	0.186862	0.538928
27	0.128520104	0.078	0.12852	0.153487	0.100061	0.243908	0.502544
28	0.133981429	0.08	0.133981	0.168031	0.054477	0.329605	0.447887
29	0.143577459	0.082	0.143577	0.182575	0.008893	0.415302	0.39323
30	0.156951949	0.084	0.156952	0.184031	0	0.510825	0.305144
31	0.173968838	0.086	0.173969	0.182316	0	0.608729	0.208955
32	0.19368939	0.088	0.193689	0.180601	0	0.706633	0.112766
33	0.215372324	0.09	0.215372	0.178885	0	0.804538	0.016577

Note an increase in required expected return causes an increase in portfolio standard deviation. Also, as desired expected return increases, our mix moves away from GM and ARCO towards IBM and Dayton Hudson. By plotting the portfolio standard deviation on the x -axis and the portfolio mean on the y-axis we obtain the following **efficient frontier**.

Figure 16.4

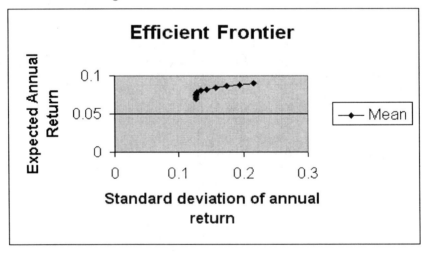

We will return to this problem in Chapter 18 and show how the genetic solver Evolver can be used to determine a portfolio mix that maximizes the probability of beating the S and P index.

      Finding the Efficient Frontier

The Scenario Approach to Portfolio Optimization

Instead of estimating a correlation matrix the following approach is often used:

1. Identify **scenarios** that encompass all events that may happen during the time period of interest. A probability must be assigned to each scenario.

2. For each scenario determine the return on each investment that will result if the scenario occurs.

3. Given a set of weights representing the fraction of the portfolio placed in each investment determine the return on the portfolio for each scenario.

4. Determine the mean and variance of the return on a given portfolio and use Solver to find the minimum variance portfolio yielding a desired expected return.

To illustrate the use of the scenario method we will assume that each of the 82 months of returns is a scenario. We will assume that each "scenario" has a 1/82 chance of occurring.

Our work is in the sheet scenario of *portex2.xls*. Our goal is to obtain a monthly expected return in excess of $.08/12 = .00667$.

Figure 16.5

	A	B	C	D	E	F	G	H
1	Scenario				mean return	0.006667	>=	0.006667
2					variance return	0.001494		
3					standard deviation	0.03865		
4	weights	0.177682	0.028966	0.322644	0.470707585	1		
5	Date	Ln(1+IBM)	LN(1+GM)	Ln(1+DH)	Ln(1+ARC)	Scenario return	Squared Deviation from mean	
6	1/31/90	0.046701	-0.0149	-0.06493	-0.007887364	-0.0168	0.000551	
7	2/28/90	0.063445	0.091755	0.036314	0.037740291	0.043412	0.00135	
8	3/30/90	0.021429	0.022039	0.113256	0.015300843	0.04819	0.001724	
9	4/30/90	0.02673	-0.03606	-0.01832	-0.036448033	-0.01936	0.000677	
10	5/31/90	0.106176	0.109589	0.116163	0.072660697	0.093721	0.007579	
11	6/29/90	-0.02105	-0.02078	-0.03876	-0.006362689	-0.01984	0.000703	
12	7/31/90	-0.05241	-0.02122	-0.03853	0.096276985	0.022958	0.000265	
13	8/31/90	-0.07847	-0.14083	-0.20404	0.050858405	-0.05992	0.004433	
14	9/28/90	0.043224	-0.09217	-0.07309	-0.003714028	-0.02032	0.000728	
15	10/31/90	-0.00945	0.013699	-0.09958	-0.033099908	-0.04899	0.003098	
16	11/30/90	0.085971	0.013514	0.135976	-0.000962002	0.059086	0.002748	
17	12/31/90	-0.00552	-0.05998	0.051523	-0.039648413	-0.00476	0.00013	
18	1/31/91	0.114828	0.05311	0.134623	-0.034983033	0.04891	0.001784	
19	2/28/91	0.02501	0.095937	0.046388	0.09388125	0.06638	0.003566	
84	7/31/96	0.082371	-0.07172	-0.12783	-0.019210852	-0.03773	0.001971	
85	8/30/96	0.065047	0.025818	0.13609	0.018153229	0.064759	0.003375	
86	9/30/96	0.084823	-0.03329	-0.04445	0.088081479	0.041226	0.001194	
87	10/31/96	0.035507	0.110815	0.048068	0.038466294	0.043134	0.00133	

Step 1: In B4:E4 enter trial weights for the fraction of our money placed in each investment. In F4 we compute the total fraction of our money invested with the formula

$=SUM(B4:E4)$.

Step 2: In F6:F87 we compute the return on the portfolio for each scenario by copying the formula

$=SUMPRODUCT(B6:E6,\$B\$4:\$E\$4)$

from F6 to F7:F87.

Step 3: Since each scenario is assumed equally likely, we can compute the mean return on our portfolio in F1 with the formula

$=AVERAGE(F6:F87)$.

Step 4: Recall that the variance of a random variable is the average squared deviation from the mean of the random variable. In G6:G87 we compute for each scenario the squared deviation of the portfolio return for that scenario from the mean return by copying from G6 to G7:G87 the formula

$=(F6-\$F\$1)^2$.

Step 5: In cell F2 compute the variance of the portfolio return with the formula

$=AVERAGE(G6:G87)$.

Step 6: In cell F3 compute the standard deviation of the portfolio return with the formula

$=SQRT(F2)$.

Step 7: Now use Solver to find the minimum variance portfolio yielding a monthly-expected return of at least .00067. Our Solver window

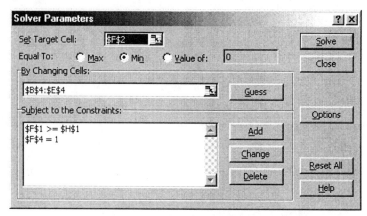

minimizes monthly portfolio variance (F2) by changing the fraction of our portfolio assigned to each investment (B4:E4). Our constraints ensure that all our money is invested (F4 =1) and an expected return of at least .00667 is obtained (F1>=H1). We check non-negative in the options box if short selling is not allowed. We find that we should place 17.8% in IBM, 2.9% in GM, 32.3% in Dayton Hudson, and 47.1% in ARCO. Our monthly standard deviation is 3.9%. This is equivalent to an annual (compounded) expected return of 12(.000667) =8% and annual standard deviation of $\sqrt{12}(.039) = 13.4\%$.

Remarks

In reality, the major use of the scenario approach is to look forward. An investment firm may identify, say, 10 possible scenarios (and their probabilities of occurrence) for the economy during the next year. For each scenario the investment firm then estimates the return on major asset classes (Japanese stocks, US stocks, bonds, gold, etc.). The model can now be used to determine the variance minimizing asset allocation that yields a desired expected return.

References

Benninga, S., *Financial Modeling*, MIT Press, 1997.

Winston, W., and Albright, S.C., *Practical Management Science with Spreadsheets*, Duxbury Press, 2nd edition, 1999.

The Scenario Approach to Portfolio Optimization

Chapter 17: An Introduction to Evolver-The Fixed Charge Problem

In previous chapters we used the Excel Solver to solve many interesting and important problems. Unfortunately, there are many interesting and important optimization problems for which the Solver is ill suited to find optimal solutions. Fortunately, however, **genetic algorithms** often perform well on optimization problems for which the Excel Solver performs poorly. The Excel add-in Evolver has a user interface similar to the Excel Solver and can easily be used to solve many optimization problems which cannot be solved with the Excel Solver. Before discussing genetic algorithms and Evolver let's look at the strengths and weaknesses of the Excel Solver.

Consider an optimization problem in which the target cell is a linear function of the changing cells, the left-hand and right-hand sides of each constraint are linear functions of the changing cells, and all changing cells may assume fractional values (e.g. changing cells are not required to be integers). For such problems (called **linear models)**, the Excel Solver is guaranteed to find (if one exists) an optimal solution. We have discussed some linear models in Chapters 13-15. The Excel Solver is an excellent tool to use for model solution for any optimization problem that can be set up as a linear model as long as the model does not exceed the size constraints (up to 200 changing cells and 200 constraints) of the Excel Solver[1]. Most larger linear models are difficult to handle in a spreadsheet format. Such larger models are often solved using a **modeling language** such as LINGO, GAMS or AMPLE. With a modeling language a user can generate, say 10,000 supply constraints for a transportation model with one line of computer code. This makes it easy to compactly represent and solve a large model.

It is important to note that if a spreadsheet uses =If, =ABS, =MAX, =MIN functions which depend on any of the model's changing cells, then the model is nonlinear and Solver may have great difficulty finding an optimal solution. If Solver starts with an initial solution near the problem's optimal solution, then Solver will usually find the correct answer. Unfortunately, we have no way of knowing whether or not an initial solution is near the problems' optimal solution.

An Introduction to Genetic Algorithms

In the early 1970's John Holland of the University of Michigan realized that many features of natural evolution (such as survival of the fittest and mutation) could be

---

[1] Solvers which handle problems involving thousands of changing cells may be purchased from Palisade Corporation (www.palisade.com)

used to help solve difficult optimization problems. Goldberg (1989), Davis (1991) and Holland (1975) are good references on genetic algorithms. Since his methods were based on behavior observed in nature, Holland coined the name **genetic algorithms** to describe his methods. Simply stated, genetic algorithms provide a method of intelligently searching an optimization problem's feasible region for an optimal solution. Biological terminology is used to describe the algorithm. For example, the target cell is called a **fitness function**. A specification of values for all changing cells is called a **chromosome.** For most problems, a genetic algorithm codes changing cells in binary notation. For example, 1001 represents $1(2^3) + 0(2^2) + 0(2^1) + 1(2^0) = 8 + 1 = 9$.

Here is a rough outline of how a GA (genetic algorithm) might work. To illustrate suppose we are trying to solve the following optimization problem:

Maximize $x^2 + y^2 - 3xy - 6x^2y$

Subject to $0 \leq x \leq 10$ and $0 \leq y \leq 10$.

In our discussion we assume our problem has no constraints except for lower and upper bounds on each changing cell. Later we discuss how GA's handle constraints.

Step by Step

Step 1: Randomly sample values of the changing cells between the lower and upper bounds to generate a set of (usually at least 50) chromosomes. The initial set of chromosomes is called the population. For example, two members of the population might be

Chromosome 1: $x = 1001$ and $y = 0000$ (or $x = 9$ and $y = 0$)

Chromosome 2: $x = 0100$ and $y = 0010$ (or $x = 4$ and $y = 2$).

The initial population is constructed by randomly choosing points from throughout the problem's feasible region.

Step 2: Generate a new generation of (hopefully improved) chromosomes. In the new generation chromosomes with a larger fitness function (in a max problem) have a greater chance of surviving to the next generation. In our example Chromosome 1 has a fitness value of 81 and Chromosome 2 has a fitness value of -196. Clearly, Chromosome 1 should have a larger chance of surviving to the next generation. The ideas of crossover and mutation are also used to generate chromosomes for the next generation.

- Crossover (fairly common) "splices" together two chromosomes at a pre-specified point. For example, if the Chromosomes 1 and 2 were combined by crossover and the crossover point is between the 2nd and 3rd digit, the resulting chromosomes would be

Chromosome 1': $x = 1000$ $y = 0010$

Chromosome 2': $x = 0101$ $y = 0000$.

An Introduction to Genetic Algorithms

- Mutation (very rare) randomly selects a digit and changes it (from 0 to 1 or 1 to 0). For example, if we chose to mutate the first digit of x in Chromosome 1, then Chromosome 1 would become x = 0001 y = 0000.

Step 3: At each generation the maximum fitness in the generation is recorded. If after many consecutive generations no improvement in the maximum fitness is observed, then the GA terminates.

How would a GA handle a constraint such as $x + y \leq 50$? Simply subtract (in a maximization problem), say $100*(x + y - 50)$ from the fitness function. Now any chromosome violating the constraint will have a low value of the fitness function (because $-100(x + y - 50)$ will greatly reduce the value of the new fitness function), This causes the GA to stay away from chromosomes which violate the constraint.

Strengths and Weaknesses of GA's

If you let a GA run long enough it is guaranteed to find the solution to any optimization problem. The problem is that the sun may supernova before the GA finds the optimal solution! In general, we never know how long we should run a GA. For the problems discussed in this chapter, an optimal solution was always found within 120 minutes. Therefore, we will usually tell Evolver to run for 120 minutes and report the best solution found. Again, we will not know if the best solution we have found is optimal, but it is usually a good solution in the sense that the best value of the fitness function we have obtained is close to the actual optimal value of the fitness function.

As a rule, GA's do very well in problems with few constraints (excluding bounds on changing cells, which are required by Evolver). **The complexity of the target cell does not bother a GA.** For example, GA's thrive on =MIN, =MAX, =If, =ABS functions in spreadsheets. This is the key advantage of GA's. Evolver usually does not perform as well, however, on problems having many constraints. Now it's time to see what Evolver can do!

Introduction to Evolver

We now show how Evolver can be used to solve optimization problems. To begin, we use Evolver to solve a **fixed charge problem.** A fixed charge problem involves the decision about which products should be produced by a company, and how many units of each product should be produced. If at least one unit of a product is produced, then the company incurs a fixed cost (often due to renting equipment), while if no units of a product are produced then no fixed cost is incurred. This cost structure makes the cost of producing x units of a product a nonlinear (actually discontinuous!!) function of the number of units produced. This causes Solver lots of grief, but we will see Evolver has no trouble with this problem. Let's solve the following example:

Example 17.1   Fruit Computer produces Pear and Apricot computers. Each computer uses the number of chips and hours of labor given in Figure 17.1 The sales price of each product is also given. If any Pear computers are produced, it costs $80,000 to rent needed equipment. If any Apricot computers are produced it costs $90,000 to rent needed equipment. 1200 hours of labor and 3000 chips are available. How can Fruit maximize profit?

Figure 17.1

	A	B	C	D	E
4		Labor Hours	Number of chips	Equipment Cost	Selling Price
5	Pear	1	2	$ 80,000.00	$ 400.00
6	Apricot	2	5	$ 90,000.00	$ 900.00

Solution   We have an optimization model in which our target cell is to maximize profit. Our changing cells will be the numbers of Pear and Apricot computers produced. We are constrained to use at most 1200 hours of labor and at most 3000 chips. Our work is in file *Fruit.xls* (see Figure 17.2)

Figure 17.2

	A	B	C	D	E	F	G
1							
2	Fruit						
3							
4		Labor Hours	Number of chips	Equipment Cost	Selling Price	Produced	Max produced
5	Pear	1	2	$ 80,000.00	$ 400.00	0	1200
6	Apricot	2	5	$ 90,000.00	$ 900.00	600	600
7							
8	Sales revenue	$540,000.00					
9	Equipment Cost	$ 90,000.00					
10	Profit	$450,000.00					
11		Used		Available			
12	Labor	1200 <=		1200			
13	Chips	3000 <=		3000			

Step 1: In cells F5:F6 we enter trial values for Pear and Apricot production.

Step 2: In cells G5:G6 we determine the maximum number of each type of computer that can be produced by copying from G5 to G6 the formula

$=MIN(\$D\$12/B5,\$D\$13/C5)$.

We need to compute the maximum number of each product that can be produced because Evolver requires upper (and lower) limits on each changing cell. For example, there is enough labor to produce 1200/1 = 1200 Pear computers and enough chips to produce 3000/2 = 1500 Pear computers so at most minimum (1200, 1500) = 1200 Pear computers can be produced.

Step 3: In cell B8 we compute sales revenue with the formula

$=SUMPRODUCT(F5:F6,E5:E6)$.

Sales revenue **is** a linear function of the changing cells.

Step 4: In cell B9 we compute the equipment cost with the formula

$=If(F5>0,D5,0)+If(F6>0,D6,0)$.

Unfortunately, equipment cost is a nonlinear function of each changing cell. Changing Pear production from 0 to 1 increases equipment costs by $80,000 while any subsequent increase in Pear computers produced results in **no** increase in equipment costs.

Step 5: In cell B10 we compute total profit with the formula

$=B8-B9$.

Step 6: In cells B12 and B13 we compute the labor and chip usage, respectively, with the formulas

$=SUMPRODUCT(B5:B6,F5:F6)$ *(labor usage)*

$=SUMPRODUCT(C5:C6,F5:F6)$ *(chip usage)*.

We are now ready to use Evolver! The Evolver toolbar looks as follows:

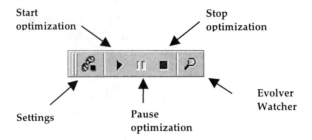

We will not use the Evolver Watcher icon (Evolver Watcher allows you to view Evolver's progress as it solves your problem). The functions of the other icons will be described as we proceed with our example.

Step by Step

Step 1: Click on the *"Settings"* icon. This allows you to set the cell you are optimizing, the adjustable cells (analogous to Solver changing cells), and constraints. You will see the following dialog box:

Step 2: Select cell B10 (profit) to maximize.

Step 3: Click *"Add"* and choose cells F5:F6 (production of each type of computer) as **Adjustable Cells.** This will bring up the following Adjustable Cells dialog box.

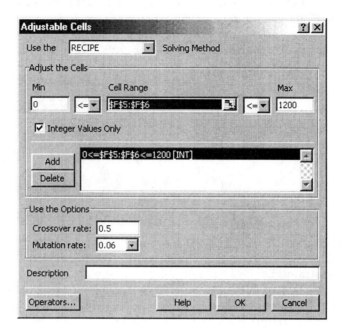

Evolver requires a lower and upper bound for each adjustable cell(the lower and upper bounds may be minus and plus infinity). These are called **range constraints.** From B8:D8 we find that the production of each computer cannot exceed 1200 units. Clearly we want to produce an integer number of each computer. We select the **Recipe** method, because this is analogous to using Solver to attack the problem. ' When the dust clears our dialog box will list the Recipe method, the bounds on the Adjustable cells, the crossover rate and mutation rate. Now click OK and you will return to the original dialog box.

Step 4: We now need to add the constraints that we use no more labor and clothing than is available (B12:B13<=D12:D13). Unfortunately, Evolver requires us to add these constraints one at a time. Under **Subject to Constraints** we click on *"Add"* and obtain the following dialog box.

Then we choose a Hard constraint and click on Excel formula and type B12<=D12(labor resource constraint). If you designate a constraint as a **Hard Constraint**, Evolver will not allow it to be violated. If we want to constrain a cell to be less than or equal to a number (not a cell) we would have selected Simple Range of Values and not Excel formula. We click OK and then enter constraint B13<=D13 (chip constraint). Now our dialog box looks as follows:

      Introduction to Evolver

Step 5: We now click on *"Options"* **and change the Stopping Criteria to 120 minutes.** This will allow Evolver to run for 120 minutes and keep the best answer found.

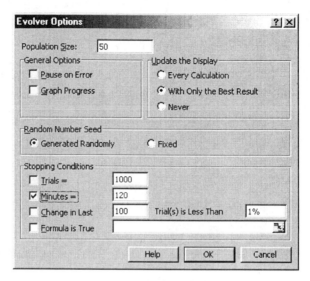

Step 6: We now click the *"Start Optimization"* **icon.** To stop Evolver click on the *"Stop"* icon. To pause Evolver click on the *"Pause"* icon. Quickly we found the optimal solution in Figure 17.2: produce 600 Apricot computers, no Pear computers, and earn a profit of $450,000.

References

Davis, M., *Handbook of Genetic Algorithms*, Van-Nostrand Reinhold, 1991.

Goldberg, D., *Genetic Algorithms in Search Optimization and Machine Learning*, Addison-Wesley, 1989.

Holland, J., *Adaptation in Natural and Artificial Systems*, University of Michigan Press, 1975.

Chapter 18: Using Evolver to Maximize the Chance of Beating the S and P Index

In Chapter 16 we used the Solver to determine a variance-minimizing portfolio which obtained a desired level of expected return. For many analysts, their primary goal is to maximize the probability of beating a benchmark, such as the Standard and Poor's (S and P) index. Unfortunately, this type of model requires an =If statement which gives Solver trouble. Solving this problem is easy, however, for Evolver.

Example 18.1 You are given monthly returns on Wal-Mart, Disney, and 3M. If you are only allowed to invest in Wal-Mart, Disney, and 3M, what investment strategy maximizes your chances of beating the S and P index?

Solution Our work is in the file *geneticport.xls*. See Figure 18.1.

Figure 18.1

	A	B	C	D	E	F	G
1						Total	
2	Weights	0.45285	0.192612	0.354538	1 =		1
3						%age beat S and P	0.644067797
4	DATE	WMT	DIS	3 M	S and P	Port return	Beat S and P?
5	2/28/90	0.032258	0.051621	0.034944	0.008539	0.036939804	1
6	3/30/90	0.075454	0.01484	0.015601	0.024255	0.042558955	1
7	4/30/90	0.050264	-0.00432	-0.02458	-0.02689	0.013216579	1
8	5/31/90	0.13602	0.167421	0.050142	0.091989	0.111621055	1
9	6/29/90	0.107672	-0.00581	0.048411	-0.00889	0.064803126	1
10	7/31/90	0.006012	-0.08172	0.04329	-0.00522	0.002331144	1
11	8/31/90	-0.09052	-0.12965	-0.12055	-0.09431	-0.108703614	0
12	9/28/90	-0.04386	-0.11477	-0.02063	-0.05118	-0.049284515	1
13	10/31/90	-0.01835	0.005738	0.024311	-0.0067	0.00141529	1
14	11/30/90	0.126168	0.09478	0.055385	0.059934	0.095026902	1
15	12/31/90	0.005311	0.018821	0.0519	0.024828	0.024430754	0
16	1/31/91	0.090909	0.067931	0	0.041518	0.054252478	1
17	2/28/91	0.07197	0.139723	0.007062	0.067281	0.062007579	0
18	3/28/91	0.096608	-0.03546	0.077475	0.022203	0.064386634	1
19	4/30/91	0.045161	-0.03109	-0.01706	0.000346	0.008413944	1
20	5/31/91	0.058642	0.0076	-0.06275	0.038577	0.005772553	0
21	6/28/91	-0.00192	-0.03879	-0.00108	-0.04789	-0.008727219	1
22	7/31/91	0.114035	0.084529	0.03741	0.044859	0.081185362	1
60	9/30/94	-0.05076	-0.06061	-0.06655	-0.0269	-0.05825396	0
61	10/31/94	0.005348	0.02129	0.041463	0.020834	0.021222788	1
62	11/30/94	-0.00883	0.101266	-0.01874	-0.0395	0.008864058	1
63	12/30/94	-0.08602	0.057471	0.05432	0.012299	-0.008626692	0

We will use 1990-1994 data and Evolver to find a strategy that maximizes our probability of beating the S and P during the years 1990-1994. Then we will **validate** our strategy by seeing how often the strategy found by Evolver beats the S and P during the years 1995-1996.

Step 1: In B2:D2 enter trial values for the fraction of our money invested in WMT, DIS, and 3M, respectively. For reasons that will soon be apparent, make these fractions add to 1.

Step 2: In F5:F87 compute the return on the portfolio during each month by copying from F5 to F6:F87 the formula

$=SUMPRODUCT(B5:D5,\$B\$2:\$D\$2)$.

Step 3: In G5:G87 determine if our portfolio beat the S and P during the current month by copying from G5 to G6:G87 the formula

$=If(F5>=E5,1,0)$.

This formula gives us a "1" during months in which we beat the S and P, and a "0" in months during which we do not beat the S and P.

Step 4: In cell G3 we compute the fraction of months in 1990-1994 for which our portfolio beat the S and P with the formula

$=SUM(G5:G63)/59$.

Step 5: We now set up Evolver to determine the fraction of our assets placed in WMT, DIS and 3M which maximizes the percentage of months in 1990-1994 for which our portfolio beats the S and P. The key is to choose the Budget method. If the Budget solution method is selected, then Evolver will ensure that the Adjustable cells always sum to the same value as they do initially. Since B2:D2 originally sum to one, Evolver will always make them sum to one. Our Evolver *Adjustable Cells* window looks as follows:

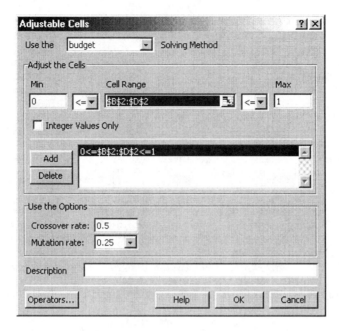

We ensure that between 0% and 100% of our money is placed in each stock. After selecting G3 as our cell to maximize we find from Figure 18.1 we find that we should invest 45.3% of our money in WMT, 19.3% in DIS and 35.4% in 3M. During 1990-1994 we beat the S and P 64.4% of the time.

lidation   In cell G86 we compute the fraction of the time our portfolio beats the S and P for the years 1995-1996 with the formula

$$= SUM(G64{:}G85)/22.$$

Unsurprisingly, we find from Figure 18.2 that "out of sample" we beat S and P only 59.1% of the time (worse than 64.4%). This is still pretty good! Virtually no investment strategy will do as well "out of sample" as it does "in sample", but we have come pretty close!

Figure 18.2

	A	B	C	D	E	F	G
64	01/31/95	0.076471	0.107609	0.061644	0.024278	0.077211559	1
65	02/28/95	0.038251	0.04914	0.025806	0.036074	0.03593648	0
66	03/31/95	0.081053	0.002342	0.014172	0.027329	0.042180206	1
67	04/28/95	-0.07317	0.036729	-0.04375	0.02796	-0.041571935	0
68	05/31/95	0.047368	0.002257	-0.01307	0.036312	0.017251064	0
69	06/30/95	0.077387	0	-0.02702	0.021279	0.025465039	1
70	07/31/95	-0.00467	0.057928	0.032037	0.031776	0.02039969	0
71	08/31/95	-0.07793	-0.04051	0.008869	-0.00032	-0.039951094	0
72	09/29/95	0.010204	0.02	0.157714	0.040097	0.064388829	1
73	10/31/95	-0.12626	0.005926	0.015296	-0.00498	-0.050613589	0
74	11/30/95	0.112139	0.043384	-0.02825	0.041049	0.049123152	1
75	12/29/95	-0.07292	-0.01929	0.016977	0.017444	-0.030717492	0
76	01/31/96	-0.08427	0.091295	-0.00768	0.032617	-0.023298958	0
77	02/29/96	0.042945	0.019455	0.017408	0.006934	0.029366701	1
78	03/29/96	0.084823	-0.02481	0.045171	0.007917	0.049648632	1
79	04/30/96	0.038043	-0.02763	0.010989	0.013431	0.015801735	1
80	05/31/96	0.08377	-0.02016	-0.02269	0.022853	0.02600686	1
81	06/28/96	-0.01729	0.034979	0.065231	0.002257	0.022032375	1
82	07/31/96	-0.05419	-0.11356	0.014545	-0.04575	-0.041254539	1
83	08/30/96	0.101146	0.024719	0.094982	0.018814	0.084239925	1
84	09/30/96	0	0.109649	0.102979	0.054203	0.057629718	1
85	10/31/96	0.004739	0.043241	-0.00896	0.026101	0.007299993	0
86					0	Out of sample	0.590909091

Chapter 19: A Portfolio Approach to Project Selection

The Markowitz approach to portfolio optimization may be applied when a company is trying to determine which R and D projects to pursue. The company chooses a desired level of expected return and picks the projects that minimize the variance of the return on the selected projects. Here is an example: *(file portprojects.xls)*

Example 19.1 Ten projects are under consideration at Eli Lilly. The cost (in billions), the annual mean return and standard deviation of the return are as follows:

Figure 19.1

	A	B	C	D
3	Project	Cost	Mean	Std Dev
4	1	3	0.2	0.22
5	2	2	0.18	0.18
6	3	1	0.14	0.13
7	4	4	0.16	0.15
8	5	2	0.14	0.14
9	6	1.8	0.12	0.12
10	7	3	0.18	0.15
11	8	4	0.19	0.16
12	9	5	0.09	0.1
13	10	6	0.11	0.12

The correlation of the returns between the projects is as follows:

Figure 19.2

	A	B	C	D	E	F	G	H	I	J	K
16	Correlations	1	2	3	4	5	6	7	8	9	10
17	1	1	0.4	0.5	0.6	0.3	0.2	0.4	0.3	0.5	0.2
18	2	0.4	1	0.3	0.6	0.5	0.4	0.2	0.3	0.25	0.32
19	3	0.5	0.3	1	0.2	0.4	0.5	0.3	0.28	0.18	0.1
20	4	0.6	0.6	0.2	1	0.5	0.4	0.35	0.25	0.18	0.17
21	5	0.3	0.5	0.4	0.5	1	0.3	0.2	0.34	0.4	0.26
22	6	0.2	0.4	0.5	0.4	0.3	1	0.35	0.3	0.28	0.2
23	7	0.4	0.2	0.3	0.35	0.2	0.35	1	0.18	0.26	0.19
24	8	0.3	0.3	0.28	0.25	0.34	0.3	0.18	1	0.32	0.19
25	9	0.5	0.25	0.18	0.18	0.4	0.28	0.26	0.32	1	0.18
26	10	0.2	0.32	0.1	0.17	0.26	0.2	0.19	0.19	0.18	1

Lilly desires an expected return of at least 15% on these projects. How can Lilly minimize the variance of the return on the chosen projects?

Step 1: In E4:E13 we place trial values of 0's and 1's. A 0 will indicate a project is not chosen and a 1 will indicate a project is chosen.

Figure 19.3

	E	F	G	H	I	J	K	L
3	Selected	Fraction in Project	Fraction*Std Dev					
4	0	0	0		Mean return	0.151	>=	0.15
5	0	0	0		Variance of return	0.007804		
6	1	0.05	0.0065		Std Dev of return	0.088337		
7	1	0.2	0.03					
8	1	0.1	0.014					
9	0	0	0					
10	1	0.15	0.0225					
11	1	0.2	0.032					
12	0	0	0					
13	1	0.3	0.036					
14								
15	6	>=	1					

Step 2: In F4:F13 we compute the fraction of our money invested in each project by copying from F4 to F4:F13 the formula

=(B4*E4)/SUMPRODUCT($B$4:$B$13,$E$4:$E$13).

Step 3: In G4:G13 we compute for each project

(Fraction invested in project)*(Standard deviation of project).

This will prepare us to compute the variance of the portfolio in J5. Simply copy from G4 to G4:G13 the formula

=F4*D4.

Step 4: In J4 we use (16.1) to compute the expected return on the portfolio with the formula

=SUMPRODUCT(C4:C13,F4:F13).

Step 5: In J5 use the =MMULT array function (and (16.2)) to compute the variance of the portfolio return with the formula

=MMULT(TRANSPOSE(G4:G13),MMULT(B17:K26,G4:G13)).

This formula uses (16.2) to compute the variance of the portfolio return.

Step 6: In J6 compute the standard deviation of the annual return on the selected projects with the formula

=SQRT(J5).

Step 7: In cell E15 we compute the total number of chosen projects with the formula

=SUM(E4:E13).

Step 8: We now use Solver to compute the minimum variance portfolio yielding a return of at least 15%. The Solver window is as follows:

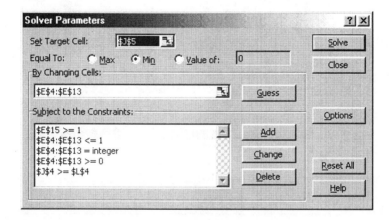

Note that the changing cells are constrained to be 0-1 integers and the constraint J4>=L4 ensures an expected return of at least 15%. We want to minimize variance (J5).

The answer obtained by Solver may depend on your starting solution. This is because the Fraction invested in a project is a highly nonlinear function of the changing cells. This causes our target cell (variance) to no longer be a convex function of the changing cells. Of course Solver has difficulty minimizing non-convex functions. The answer obtained by Solver is to select Projects 3, 4, 5, 7, 8 and 10 with a standard deviation of 8.8%! We note that if you set TOLERANCE = say, 5% you may not find the optimal solution because Solver will stop the first time it comes within 5% of the target cell value that would be obtained if fractional values of the changing cells were allowed. The constraint E15>=1 ensures that at least one project is chosen. **If we do not include this constraint then Solver may begin with the solution of choosing no projects, and this will cause F4:F13 to be undefined due to division by 0.**

Using Evolver to Select the Projects

Evolver is well suited to minimize a non-convex function of the target cells. Using the following Evolver window and choosing J5 as the cell to minimize we obtained the same answer as Solver : Projects 3, 4, 5, 7, 8 and 10 and found a standard deviation of 8.8%!

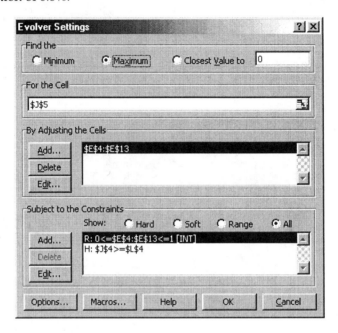

Chapter 20: Using AHP and Solver for Project Selection

Many times the selection of projects depends on objectives besides NPV. How can we select projects when multiple objectives are involved? Here is an easy way to do it. Our example is based on Liberatore's (1989) paper "A Decision Support System for R and D Project Selection". We assume the reader has some familiarity with the Analytic Hierarchy Process. See Section 7.4 of Winston and Albright (1997) for an introduction to the AHP. We proceed as follows:

- Determine the relevant objectives.

- For each project score the project on each objective on, say, a 1-4 scale with 1 = outstanding, 2 = above average, 3 = average, 4 = below average.

- Use AHP to determine the relative importance of the objectives.

- Use AHP to determine for each objective how much "better" a 1 is than a 2, 3, or 4, etc.

- For each project determine its resource usage (for example, cost and man hours needed).

- Now use a Solver model to select the projects which (subject to resource limitations) maximize the total benefit received.

This method factors in the relative importance of all objectives and how well each project scores on each objective.

AHP Analysis

Our work is in the file *AHPSolver.xls*. The relevant information on each of 9 projects is contained in Figure 20.1. Costs are in millions of dollars and man-hour usage is in thousands of hours.

Figure 20.1

	A	B	C	D	E	F	G	H
7	Score	Project	Cost	Manhours	NPV	Market Growth	Likelihood of TechnicalSuccess	Likelihood of FDA Approval
8	0.211	1	300	500	4	1	3	2
9	0.151	2	250	600	3	2	4	3
10	0.155	3	350	550	3	3	2	2
11	0.220	4	380	750	2	3	3	1
12	0.193	5	120	850	2	4	2	2
13	0.264	6	420	950	2	2	1	3
14	0.238	7	360	400	3	1	3	2
15	0.403	8	260	1100	1	2	2	4
16	0.423	9	180	1200	1	3	1	3
17		Available	1500	2500				

Next we construct pairwise comparison matrices that can be used to determine the weights for each objective and how each score of 1-4 "rates" on each objective.

Figure 20.2

	A	B	C	D	E
18	Objectives				
19		NPV	Market Growth	Likelihood of Technical Success	Likelihood of FDA Approval
20	NPV		1	2	4	5
21	Market Gr		0.5	1	2	2
22	Likelihood		0.25	0.5	1	1
23	Likelihood		0.2	0.5	1	1
24						
25						
26	NPV		1	2	3	4
27	1		1	3	5	7
28	2	0.333333333	1	2	3
29	3	0.2	0.5	1	2
30	4	0.142857143	0.333333	0.5	1
31						
32	Market G		1	2	3	4
33	1		1	2	4	6
34	2	0.5	1	2	3
35	3	0.25	0.5	1	1.5
36	4	0.166666667	0.333333	0.666667	1
37						
38	Likelihoo		1	2	3	4
39	1		1	3	5	8
40	2	0.333333333	1	2	4
41	3	0.2	0.5	1	2
42	4	0.125	0.25	0.5	1
43						
44	Likelihoo		1	2	3	4
45	1		1	2	4	7
46	2	0.5	1	2	4
47	3	0.25	0.5	1	2
48	4	0.142857143	0.25	0.5	1

Next we use Normalized matrices to determine the objective weights(see L20:L23 of Figure 20.4) and the relative scores for 1-4 on each objective (see Figure 20.3). For example, a project that is outstanding on NPV gets 58% of the NPV "value", a project that is above average on NPV gets 22% of the NPV "value", etc. The NPV objective is assigned 52% of the weight, the Market Growth objective is assigned 24% of the weight, etc.

Figure 20.3

			NPV	Market Growth	Likelihood of Technical Success	Likelihood of FDA Approval
1			NPV	Market Growth	Likelihood of Technical Success	Likelihood of FDA Approval
2	1	Outstanding	0.585994	0.521739	0.589041	0.523742
3	2	Above Average	0.217956	0.26087	0.228373	0.2708
4	3	Average	0.123565	0.130435	0.119212	0.1354
5	4	Below Average	0.072485	0.086957	0.063375	0.070058

We now compute the score of each project. To do this for Project 1 enter in Cell A8 the formula

$$=\$L\$20*VLOOKUP(E8,Lookup,3)+\$L\$21*VLOOKUP(F8,Lookup,4)+\$L\$22$$

$$*VLOOKUP(G8,Lookup,5)+\$L\$23*VLOOKUP(H8,Lookup,6).$$

"Lookup" is the range A2:F5 where objective weights and weights for ratings of 1-4 are located. Copying this formula to A9:A16 computes the scores for all projects.

Figure 20.4

	G	H	I	J	K	L
19	Normalized	NPV	Market Growth	Likelihood of Technical Success	Likelihood of FDA Approval	Weights
20	NPV	0.512821	0.5	0.5	0.555556	0.517094
21	Market Growth	0.25641	0.25	0.25	0.222222	0.244658
22	Likelihood of Technical Success	0.128205	0.125	0.125	0.111111	0.122329
23	Likelihood of FDA Approval	0.102564	0.125	0.125	0.111111	0.115919
24						
25						
26	NPV Norm	1	2	3	4	
27	1	0.596591	0.62069	0.588235	0.538462	0.585994
28	2	0.198864	0.206897	0.235294	0.230769	0.217956
29	3	0.119318	0.103448	0.117647	0.153846	0.123565
30	4	0.085227	0.068966	0.058824	0.076923	0.072485
31						
32	Mar Share Norm	1	2	3	4	
33	1	0.521739	0.521739	0.521739	0.521739	0.521739
34	2	0.26087	0.26087	0.26087	0.26087	0.26087
35	3	0.130435	0.130435	0.130435	0.130435	0.130435
36	4	0.086957	0.086957	0.086957	0.086957	0.086957
37						
38	Tech Success No	1	2	3	4	
39	1	0.603015	0.631579	0.588235	0.533333	0.589041
40	2	0.201005	0.210526	0.235294	0.266667	0.228373
41	3	0.120603	0.105263	0.117647	0.133333	0.119212
42	4	0.075377	0.052632	0.058824	0.066667	0.063375
43						
44	FDA Norm	1	2	3	4	
45	1	0.528302	0.533333	0.533333	0.5	0.523742
46	2	0.264151	0.266667	0.266667	0.285714	0.2708
47	3	0.132075	0.133333	0.133333	0.142857	0.1354
48	4	0.075472	0.066667	0.066667	0.071429	0.070058

Setting Up the Solver Model

We are now ready to set up the Solver model. See Figure 20.5. We assume 1500 million dollars and 2500 thousand man-hours are available.

Figure 20.5

	A	B	C	D	E
1	Score	Project	Cost	Manhours	Select?
2	0.211103015	1	300	500	0
3	0.151166485	2	250	600	0
4	0.155134037	3	350	550	0
5	0.219910222	4	380	750	0
6	0.193305731	5	120	850	0
7	0.264279717	6	420	950	1
8	0.237516213	7	360	400	1
9	0.402895774	8	260	1100	1
10	0.422678276	9	180	1200	0
11	2.257989469				
12	total benefit	Used	1040	2450	
13			<=	<=	
14		Available	1500	2500	
15					
16	Benefit				
17	0.904691703				
18	Percentage of Total	0.400662			

Step by Step

Step 1: In another sheet we paste the project scores to the cell range A2:A10.

Step 2: Paste the cost and man-hours to C2:D10.

Step 3: In E2:E10 we enter trial 0-1 changing cells for each project. A "1" indicates the project is chosen while a "0" indicates the project is not chosen.

Step 4: In C12 we compute total money spent(in millions) with the formula

$=SUMPRODUCT(\$E\$2:\$E\$10,C2:C10)$.

Copying this formula to D12 computes the total man-hours used. We have entered available money and man-hours in C14 and D14.

Step 5: In A17 we compute the total benefit earned by selected projects with the formula

$= SUMPRODUCT(A2:A10,E2:E10)$.

Step 6: We now create the following Solver window:

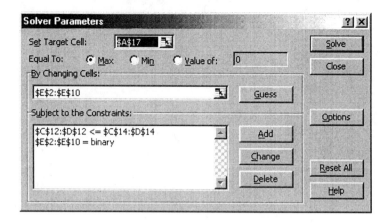

We choose to maximize benefit ($A$17) subject to the changing cells being the 0-1 project selection cells in E2:E10. The constraints C12:D12<=C14:D14 ensure that we do not use more resources than we have available.

By choosing Projects 6-8 our optimal solution "earns" .90 of 2.26 total benefit or 40% of the possible benefit.

Remarks

If desired, we could see how increasing man-hours or available money. For example, if we had 500 million more dollars simply change D14 to 3000 and solve the problem again. You will find that Project 1 has been added and 49% of total benefit has now been achieved.

References

Lieberatore, M., "A Decision Support System for R and D Project Selection", in *The Analytic Hierarchy Process: Applications and Studies,* Springer Verlag, 1989.

Winston, W. and Albright, S.C. *Practical Management Science with Spreadsheets,* Duxbury Press, 1997.

Chapter 21: Selecting Drivers for an ABC Costing System

Unbelievably, most companies do not know what it costs them to produce many of the products they sell. When you do not know what it costs to make a product, you cannot know if you are making a profit or loss on a product. In an ideal world, we determine the cost of producing a unit of a product by determining the resources used by the product and combining that information with the cost associated with each unit of a resource. Here is an example:

Example 21.1

Toolco produces two tools: Product 1 and Product 2. Figure 21.1 gives the amount of each resource (Material, Direct Labor Hours, Machine Hours, Setups, Orders, Time Handled, and Number of Part Numbers) needed to produce a unit of each product. For a recent month the total "cost pool" for each resource as well as the total amount used of each resource is given.

Figure 21.1

	A	B	C	D	E	F	G	H
2		Material	Direct Labor Hours	Machine Hours	Setups	Orders	Times Handled	No. of Part Numbers
3	Resource Usage							
4	Product 1	6	0.5	0.5	0.1	0.1	0.1	0.1
5	Product 2	6	0.5	0.5	0.03	0.03	0.03	0.01
6	Total Driver Cost	66	550	825	480	500	100	1000
7	Driver Availability	660	55	55	4	4	4	2
8	Driver Selected	1	-1.8E-11	0	0	9.41E-12	1.75E-12	1
9								

The resource pools are often called **cost drivers**. From Figure 21.1 we can compute the exact cost of one unit of each driver.

- Material unit cost $= 66/660 = \$.1$.

- Direct Labor hour unit cost $= 550/55 = \$10$.

- Machine hour unit cost $= 825/55 = \$15$.

- Setup unit cost $= 480/4 = \$120$.

- Order unit cost $= 500/4 = \$125$.

- Times handled unit cost $= 100/4 = \$25$.

- Number of part numbers unit cost $= 1000/2 = \$500$.

Now we can compute the exact cost of producing a unit of each product.

Unit cost for Product 1 = 6(.1) +.5(10) +.5(15) + .1(120) + .1(125) + .1(25) + .1(500) = $90.10.

Unit cost for Product 2=6(.1)+.5(10)+.5(15)+.03(120)+.03(125)+.03(25)+.01(500) = $26.20.

In reality, it is not possible to use this method to determine the cost of producing a unit of a product. The reason is it is virtually impossible to know for each product the amount of each resource needed to produce a unit of a product. The solution to this problem is to select a small subset (usually 2-4) of all cost drivers (called **cost pools**) and assign each cost driver to one of the chosen pools. Then (based on the drivers assigned to a selected pool) for each chosen pool compute a unit cost associated with that pool. Finally, cost out a product based on the amount the product uses of each selected cost pool. For example, suppose we select Machine hours and Times Handled as pools. Also assume we assign Material, Direct Labor Hours, Machine Hours, and Setups to Machine hours and assign Orders, Times Handled, and Number of Part Numbers to Time Handled. Then the unit cost associated with each cost pool is as follows:

$$Machine\ Hour\ Cost\ Pool\ Cost = \frac{66 + 550 + 825 + 480}{55} = \$34.93.$$

$$Times\ Handled\ Driver\ Cost\ Pool\ Cost = \frac{500 + 100 + 1000}{4} = \$400.$$

Then we can estimate the cost of each product as follows:

Estimated Product 1 Cost = .5*($34.93) + .1*($400) = $57.46.

Estimated Product 2 Cost = .5*($34.93) + .03*($400) = $29.46.

Of course, by choosing only 2 drivers we do not come out with the exact costs of producing each product. The benefit, however, is that we do not need to keep track of how many units of seven resources are consumed by each product; we need only keep track of how many units of two resources are consumed by each product.

Using Solver to Determine an Optimal Set of Drivers

Given we know how many drivers we are going to use, how can we determine the "best" set of cost pools? To illustrate, we will determine the "best" set of three pools. By "best" set of cost pools we mean the set of cost pools which minimizes the sum of our errors in estimating the cost of each product. Our work is in *file abc.xls*. See Figures 21.1 and 21.2. To set up our Solver model we need to define the following sets of changing cells:

- 0-1 changing cells to represent drivers selected as cost pools. See B8:H8. For example, if C8 = 1, then Direct Labor Hours is being selected as a cost pool.

- 0-1 changing cells to represent the assignment of each driver to a selected cost pool. See cells B11:H17. For example if D11 =1, then the cost pool for materials are assigned to the Machine Hour cost pool.

- Under and over changing cells (in E33:F34) which are used to determine the amount by which we have underestimated or overestimated the cost of each product.

Our target cell will be (in G35) our total absolute error in estimating the costs of all products. Our constraints will be

- Exactly three drivers are selected to be cost pools.

- Each driver is assigned to exactly one cost pool.

- If a driver is assigned to a cost pool, then that cost pool must have been selected. For example, if Times Handled is assigned to Machine Hours, then Machine hours must have been selected as a cost pool.

- For each product the following relationship must hold:

  (Estimated cost) + (Amount estimate is under actual cost) - (Amount estimated is over actual cost) = (Actual cost) (21.1)

These constraints ensure that the changing cells for cost over and under estimates will assume the proper values. Here is a step by step description of our solver model.

Figure 21.2

	A	B	C	D	E	F	G	H	I	J	K	L
1	ABC Accounting											
2		Material	Direct Labor Hours	Machine Hours	Setups	Orders	Times Handled	No. of Part Numbers				
3	Resource Usage											
4	Product 1	6	0.5	0.5	0.1	0.1	0.1	0.1				
5	Product 2	6	0.5	0.5	0.03	0.03	0.03	0.01				
6	Total Driver Cost	66	550	825	480	500	100	1000				
7	Driver Availability	660	55	55	4	4	4	2	Total Drivers			
8	Driver Selected	1	-1.8E-11	0	0	9.4E-12	1.75E-12	1	2	=	2	

	A	B	C	D	E	F	G	H	I	J	K	L
10	Driver Assignments	Material	Direct Labor Hours	Machine Hours	Setups	Orders	Times Handled	No. of Part Numbers	Driver Cost	Assigned		
11	Material	1	-8.7E-12	0	0	0	1.75E-12	0	66	1	=	1
12	Direct Labor Hours	1	-1.8E-11	0	0	9.4E-12	1.75E-12	0	550	1	=	1
13	Machine Hours	9.4E-12	-1.8E-11	0	0	-1.7E-12	1.05E-11	1	825	1	=	1
14	Setups	1	-1.8E-11	0	0	9.4E-12	0	0	480	1	=	1
15	Orders	-1E-06	-9.4E-12	0	0	0	-7E-12	1	500	1	=	1
16	Times Handled	9.4E-12	-9.4E-12	0	0	-1.7E-12	1.75E-12	1	100	1	=	1
17	No. of Part Numbers	1	0	0	0	0	1.75E-12	0	1000	1	=	1
18												
19	Lockbox Constraints	<=	<=	<=	<=	<=	<=	<=				
20		1	-1.8E-11	0	0	9.4E-12	1.75E-12	1				
21		1	-1.8E-11	0	0	9.4E-12	1.75E-12	1				
22		1	-1.8E-11	0	0	9.4E-12	1.75E-12	1				
23		1	-1.8E-11	0	0	9.4E-12	1.75E-12	1				
24		1	-1.8E-11	0	0	9.4E-12	1.75E-12	1				
25		1	-1.8E-11	0	0	9.4E-12	1.75E-12	1				
26		1	-1.8E-11	0	0	9.4E-12	1.75E-12	1				

	A	B	C	D	E	F	G	H
29	Exact Unit Driver Costs	Material	Direct Labor Hours	Machine Hours	Setups	Orders	Times Handled	No. of Part Numbers
30		0.1	10	15	120	125	25	500

	A	B	C	D	E	F	G	H
32		Exact Costs	Estimated Cost	Sq Error	Under	Over	Est+Under-Over	
33	Product 1	90.1	90.3045	0.04184	0	0.20454	90.1	
34	Product 2	26.2	26.1795	0.00042	0.02046	0	26.2	
35			SSE	0.04226	0.02046	0.20454	0.225001	Abs Err

	A	B	C	D	E	F	G	H
36	Estimated Unit Driver Costs	Material	Direct Labor Hours	Machine Hours	Setups	Orders	Times Handled	No. of Part Numbers
37		3.17576	-7.3E-10	0	0	2E-09	2.04E-09	712.5

Step by Step

Step 1: In A2:H7 enter resource usage as well as total cost and availability for each driver.

Step 2: In B8:H8 enter trial values (0 or 1) to indicate if a driver is selected as a cost pool. Then in I8 compute the total number of cost pools selected with the formula

=SUM(B8:H8).

Step 3: In B11:H17 enter trial values (0 or 1) to indicate how cost drivers are assigned to cost pools.

Step 4: In I11:I17 enter (by transposing B6:H6) the costs for each driver.

Step 5: In J11:J17 determine the number of cost pools to which each driver is assigned (later we constrain this to 1) by copying the formula

=SUM(B11:H11)

from J11 to J11:J17.

Step 6: In B20:H27 we set up constraints which will be used to ensure that a driver can be assigned only to a selected cost pool. In each of columns B-H we create 8 copies of row 8. To do this enter the formula

= B$8

in B20 and copy this formula to B20:H27. We later will enter the constraints

$B$11:$H$17<=$B$20:$H$27.

These constraints ensure that for i, j = 1, 2, ... 7

(0-1 changing cell for assigning driver i to cost pool j)<=(0-1 changing cell for selection of driver j as cost pool).

These constraints ensure that we cannot assign driver i to cost pool j unless we have selected driver j as a cost pool. Also, if no driver is assigned to cost pool j these constraints allow Solver to set equal to 0 the changing cell in row 8 which represents using driver j as a cost pool.

Step 7: In B30:H30 we compute the exact unit cost for each driver by dividing the total cost in the driver pool by the availability of the driver. To compute the exact unit driver cost copy the formula

=B6/B7

from B30 to B30:H30.

Step 8: In B33:B34 we compute the exact cost of producing each product by copying the formula

=SUMPRODUCT($B$30:$H$30,B4:H4)

from B33 to B34.

Step 9: In B37:H37 we compute (based on cost pool assignments) the "estimated" value for the unit cost of cost pool. Non-selected cost pools will be assigned a 0 cost. To compute the unit cost for each cost pool copy the formula

=SUMPRODUCT(B11:B17,$I$11:$I$17)/B7

from B37 to C37:H37. The SUMPRODUCT term computes the total cost associated with the drivers assigned to the cost pool. Dividing by the number of units available of the cost pool resource gives us a unit cost for each cost pool.

Step 10: In C33:C34 we compute the "estimated" (based on selected cost pools and driver assignments) unit cost of producing each product. To compute the estimated unit cost of producing each product copy the formula

=SUMPRODUCT($B$37:$H$37,B4:H4)

from C33 to C34.

Step 11: Enter trial values for the amount each product's unit cost is underestimated in E33:E34 and trial values for amount each product's unit cost is overestimated in F33:F34. In E35 and F35 create the total amount of underestimation and overestimation, respectively. In G35 add E35 and F35 to obtain the total estimation error.

Step 12: In G33 and G34 for each product we compute

(Estimated Cost) + (Underestimation) - (Overestimation).

For each product we set this quantity equal to the product's actual unit cost.

To do this copy the formula

=C33+E33-F33

from G33 to G34.

When we create Solver constraints G33:G34=B33:B34 (following (21.1)) we ensure that columns E and F do contain amount underestimated and amount overestimated, respectively.

Setting Up the Solver Window

Our Solver window looks as follows:

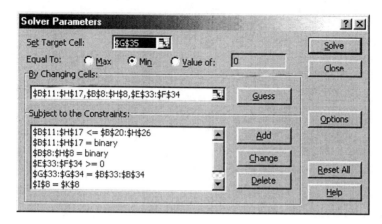

We minimize total estimation error (G35). Our changing cells are assignments of drivers to cost pools (B11:H17), selected drivers (B8:H8), and amount of underestimation and overestimation of unit cost for each product (E33:F34). Of course, B11:H17 and B8:H8 must be binary and E33:F34 must be non-negative (non-negativity box in options was checked). We have four types of constraints.

- I8=K8 ensures that three cost pools are selected.

- J11:J17=1 ensures that each driver is assigned to a cost pool.

- B11:H17<=B20:H26 ensures that if we assign a driver to a cost pool, then that cost pool is selected.

- G33:G34=B33:B34 ensures that columns E and F will yield our actual underestimation and overestimation errors.

When we solve this model we obtain the solution in Figure 21.2. Material, Time Handled, and Part Numbers are the selected cost pools. Material and Machine hours are assigned to Material. Setups, Orders and Number of Part Numbers are assigned to Time Handled. Direct Labor Hours and Times Handled are assigned to Number of Part Numbers. Each product's cost is estimated with 0 error.

Remarks

In D33:D35 we keep track of squared error for estimating each product and total squared error. In this case we want to minimize sum of squared errors, not sum of absolute errors.

Chapter 22: Pricing Models with Solver

An important business decision is the determination of the profit-maximizing price that should be charged for a product. Often demand for a product is modeled as a linear function of price

$$Demand = a - b(Price)$$

where a and b are constants. If the linear demand function is relevant, then profit from a product with a unit cost of c is given by

$$(Price - c)*(a - b(Price)).$$

This implies that profit is a concave function of price and Solver should find the profit-maximizing price. In this section we give two Solver models (based on Dolan and Simon, 1997) which can be used to determine optimal prices.

Our first model tackles the following problem: As exchange rates fluctuate, how should a US company change the overseas price of its product? To be more specific, suppose Eli Lilly is selling a drug in Germany. Their goal is to maximize their profit in $s, but when the drug is sold in Germany they receive marks. In order to maximize their dollar profit, how should the price in marks vary with the exchange rate? To illustrate the ideas involved consider the following example:

Example 22.1

The drug Taxoprol costs $60 to produce. Currently the exchange rate is .667 $/mark and we are charging 150 marks for Taxoprol. Current demand for Taxoprol is 100 units, and it is estimated that the elasticity for Taxoprol is 2.5. Assuming a linear demand curve, determine how the price (in marks) for Taxoprol should vary with the exchange rate.

Solution   We begin by determining the linear demand curve that relates demand to the price in marks. Currently demand is 100 and the price is 150 marks. Recall from economics that the price elasticity of a product is the percentage decrease in sales that will result from a 1% increase in price. Since price elasticity is 2.5, a 1% increase in price (to 151.5) will result in a 2.5% decrease in demand (to 100 - 2.5 = 97.5). In the file *Intprice.xls* (sheet Linear Demand) we entered these two points in B12:C13. We now find the slope and intercept of the demand curve.

$$Slope = \frac{97.5 - 100}{151.5 - 150} = -1.6667$$

(since demand is larger than one in absolute value, demand is elastic).

The slope is computed in D13 with formula

   =(B13 - B12)/(A13-A12).

Intercept = 100 + (-150)(-1.6667) = 350 .

The intercept is computed in D14 with the formula

   =B12 + (-A12)*(D13).

Thus *Demand = 350 – 1.6667(Price in Marks).*

Figure 22.1

	A	B	C	D	E	F	G	H	I	J	K
1	Price dependence										
2	on exchange rate										
3											
4	Current $/DM	0.666667	0.4	0.5	0.6	0.666667	0.7	0.8	0.9	1	
5	Unit Cost US $	60	60	60	60	60	60	60	60	60	
6	Current price DM	150	179.9999	164.9999	155	149.9999	147.8571	142.4999	138.3333	134.9999	
7	Current demand	100	50.00015	75.00013	91.66671	100.0001	103.5714	112.5001	119.4446	125.0001	
8	Current profit US$	4000	600	1687.5	3025	4000	4505.357	6075	7704.167	9375	36972.02
9	Elasticity	2.5	2.5	2.5	2.5	2.5	2.5	2.5	2.5	2.5	
10											
11	Price DM		demand								
12		150	100								
13		151.5	97.5	slope	-1.66667						
14	Demand = 350-(5/3)*price			intercept	350						

We can now compute (for a trial set of prices) our profit for exchange rates ranging from .4 $/mark/$ to 1 $/mark. Then we use Solver to find the set of prices maximizing the **sum** of these profits. This will ensure that we will have found a profit-maximizing price for a variety of exchange rates.

Step by Step

Step 1: Enter trial values for the exchange rate ($/mark) in the cell range B4:J4.

Step 2: In B5:J5 we enter the unit cost in dollars ($60).

Step 3: In B6:J6 we enter trial prices (in marks) for Taxoprol.

Step 4: Observe that demand for each exchange rate is given by

350 - 1.66667*(price in marks).

In cells B7:J7 we determine the demand for each exchange rate. In B7 we find the demand for the exchange rate of .6667 $/mark with the formula

= $D$14 + $D$13*B6.

Copying this formula to the range C7:J7 computes the demand for all other exchange rates.

Step 5: Observe that profit in dollars is given by

(($/mark)*price in marks - cost in dollars)*(demand).

In cells B8:J8 we compute the dollar profit (for the trial prices) for each exchange rate. In B8 we find the profit for our current exchange rate (.66667 $/mark) and current price (150 marks) with the formula

= (B4*B6 - B5)*B7.

Copying this formula to the cell range C8:J8 computes profits for all other exchange rates.

Step 6: In cell K8 we add up the profit for all exchange rates with the formula

= SUM(C8:J8).

Step 7: We now use the solver to determine the profit-maximizing price for each exchange rate. By changing the non-negative prices for each exchange rate (C6:J6) we can maximize the sum of the profits (K8). Since each price only impacts the profit for the exchange rate in its own column, this ensures that we find the profit-maximizing price for each exchange rate. For example, for .66667 $/mark optimal price is 150 marks. Note that if the mark drops in value by 25% to .5 $/mark we only raise the cost in marks by 10% ($\frac{165-150}{150}$ =.10). Due to the elastic demand, profit-maximization does not call for making the German customers absorb all of the loss in dollars due to depreciation of the mark. Our Solver window follows:

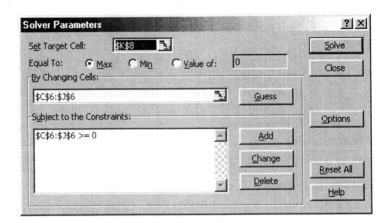

Tie-Ins and Pricing

Many products create tie-ins to other products. For example, if you own a Men's Clothing store you should realize that when a person buys a suit, he would probably also buy a shirt or tie. Failure to realize this will cause the store to price suits too high. The following example illustrates the idea.

Example 22.2

Suits cost the Men's Warehouse $320. Currently suits are being sold for $350 and 300 are being sold each year. The elasticity of the demand for men's suits is estimated to be 2.33. Each purchase of a suit leads to an average of 2 shirts and 1.5 ties being sold. Each shirt contributes $25 to profit and each tie contributes $15 to profit. Determine a profit-maximizing price for suits.

Solution

Let's first determine the profit-maximizing price if we ignore the tie-in profits. See Figure 22.2. Our work is the sheet Suits only of *Comprod.xls*. We assume linear demand and follow the procedure outlined in Example 22.1 to determine that the demand curve is

Suit demand = 999 – 1.997(price of suit).

Figure 22.2

	A	B	C	D	E	F
1	Pricing Complementary Products					
2		Suits		Cost	$ 320.00	
3		Price	Demand			
4		$ 350.00	300			
5		$ 353.50	293.01			
6					Elasticity	2.33
7		Slope	$ (1.997)			
8		Intercept	999.0			
9						
10		Suit Price	Demand	Profit		
11		410.1073	179.9571	$ 16,215.45		

We now compute our profit.

Step by
Step

Step 1: Enter a trial price for suits in B11.

Step 2: Compute the demand for suits in C11 with the formula

$$= C7*(B11) + C8.$$

Step 3: Compute our profit in D11 with the formula

$$= C11*(B11-E2).$$

Step 4: We now use the Solver to maximize profit.

We see we want to choose our non-negative suit price (B11) to maximize profit (D11).

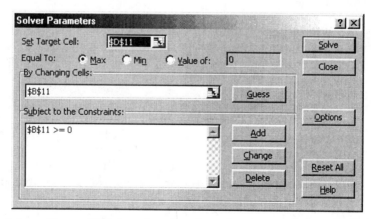

We find from Figure 22.2 that charging $410 for a suit attains a maximum profit of $16,215.

Pricing with a Tie-In

In the sheet Suits with Shirts and Ties we incorporate the profit earned from shirts and ties into our pricing model.

Figure 22.3

	A	B	C	D	E	F
1	Pricing Complementary Products					
2		Suits		Cost	$ 320.00	
3		Price	Demand			
4		$ 350.00	300			
5		$ 353.50	293.01			
6					Elasticity	2.33
7		Slope	$ (1.997)			
8		Intercept	$ 999.00			
9						
10		Suit Price	Demand	Profit		
11		373.8573	252.3536	13591.081		
12		Per Suit	Total	Unit Profit	Profit	
13	Shirts sold	2	504.7071	$ 25.00	$ 12,617.68	
14	Ties Sold	1.5	378.5304	$ 15.00	$ 5,677.96	
15				Total Profit	$ 31,886.71	

In rows 12-15 we add the profit earned by selling shirts and ties. For example, in E13 we compute profit from shirts with the formula

=B13*$C$11*D13.

This just computes (shirts per suit)*(suits demanded)*(profit per shirt). Copying this to cell E14 computes profits from ties. In cell E15 we compute total profit with the formula

= SUM(E13:E14) + D11.

We now change our target cell to E15 and find in Figure 22.3 that the maximum profit earned is $31,887. We charge $374 per suit. Note the large drop in the price of a suit when we consider tie-in sales.

Auto and appliance dealers who profit from maintenance contracts would probably greatly increase profits if they would factor the profits from the maintenance agreements into their determination of the price of their major product. Probably the ultimate "tie-in" reduction in price is the fact that many companies now give software away for free. They are hoping, of course, that the recipients of free software will later buy the "tie-in" good that is the upgrade!

Reference

Dolan R. and G. Simon, *Power Pricing*, Free Press, 1997.

Chapter 23: Nonlinear Pricing

Suppose we are a long distance phone carrier (let's use the name BTT). Clearly, most people value the first few minutes of long distance calls they purchase each month more than they value later minutes. How can we take advantage of this when pricing long distance calls? If we charge a single price for each long distance minute, then few people are going to make lots of long distance phone calls. This is because consumers attach less value to each additional minute phoned during a month. Alternatively, however, we can try the **two-part tariff approach**. The two-part tariff involves charging an "entry fee" to anybody who calls long distance and then a reduced price per minute used. For instance, if we are currently charging $1.10 per ten minutes of long distance calls, a reasonable two-part tariff might be an entry fee of $1.50 and a price of $0.50 for every ten minutes on the phone. This will give some customers an incentive to make more long distance calls. The following example shows how much a two-part tariff can increase profit. Since the total cost of purchasing n Ten-minute segments is no longer a linear function of n (it is now piecewise linear) we refer to the two-part tariff as a **nonlinear pricing** strategy.

Example 23.1

Four customers have been surveyed on the amount they are willing to pay for each 10 minutes of long distance calls made during a month. The relevant data is in Figure 23.1.

Figure 23.1

	A	B	C	D	E
1	BTT	Cust 1	Cust 2	Cust 3	Cust 4
2	1	1.236973	0.915758	1.271622	1.486487
3	2	1.025622	0.849361	1.107868	1.238578
4	3	0.887074	0.694547	0.96184	1.095671
5	4	0.798269	0.578962	0.8528	0.97373
6	5	0.772203	0.504336	0.732484	0.812574
7	6	0.658503	0.429462	0.631012	0.709801
8	7	0.592303	0.358183	0.509381	0.63302
9	8	0.508444	0.31825	0.449372	0.53419
10	9	0.421358	0.25983	0.387907	0.421402
11	10	0.350831	0.224386	0.32404	0.353971

For example, Customer 1 is willing to pay $1.24 for the first ten minutes of calls and only $0.66 for the sixth ten-minute group of calls. These four customers are considered representative of the market. The variable cost of producing ten minutes of long distance calls is $0.40. Determine a profit-maximizing single price and a profit maximizing two-part tariff.

Solution

Our work is in the file *Btt.xls*. For the single price problem, refer to the sheet Single Price. We assume that each customer will compare the value of buying n ten minute segments to the cost of buying n ten- minute segments (n = 1,2, …10) and will then purchase the number of ten -minute segments that yields the maximum "Consumer Surplus".

We first determine the value each customer associates with buying n ten-minute segments. Then we compute the Consumer Surplus = Value – Cost for each possible number of ten-minute segments purchased. Next we determine (using the Excel MATCH function) the number of ten-minute segments each customer will purchase. Finally, we determine our profit and use Evolver to find the profit-maximizing price.

Figure 23.2

	A	B	C	D	E	F	G	H	I	J
1	BTT	Cust 1	Cust 2	Cust 3	Cust 4		Cu Val 1	Cu Val 2	Cu Val 3	Cu Val 4
2	1	1.236973	0.915758	1.271622	1.486487	1	1.236973	0.915758	1.271622	1.486487
3	2	1.025622	0.849361	1.107868	1.238578	2	2.262595	1.765119	2.379491	2.725065
4	3	0.887074	0.694547	0.96184	1.095671	3	3.149669	2.459666	3.341331	3.820735
5	4	0.798269	0.578962	0.8528	0.97373	4	3.947939	3.038628	4.194131	4.794466
6	5	0.772203	0.504336	0.732484	0.812574	5	4.720142	3.542964	4.926615	5.60704
7	6	0.658503	0.429462	0.631012	0.709801	6	5.378645	3.972426	5.557627	6.316841
8	7	0.592303	0.358183	0.509381	0.63302	7	5.970948	4.330609	6.067008	6.949862
9	8	0.508444	0.31825	0.449372	0.53419	8	6.479392	4.648859	6.51638	7.484052
10	9	0.421358	0.25983	0.387907	0.421402	9	6.90075	4.908689	6.904287	7.905454
11	10	0.350831	0.224386	0.32404	0.353971	10	7.251581	5.133075	7.228327	8.259425
12					Cost		Surp 1	Surp 2	Surp 3	Surp 4
13					0.798058	1	0.438915	0.1177	0.473564	0.688428
14					1.596117	2	0.666479	0.169002	0.783374	1.128948
15		Price			2.394175	3	0.755494	0.065491	0.947156	1.42656
16		0.798058			3.192233	4	0.755705	-0.15361	1.001897	1.602232
17		cost			3.990292	5	0.72985	-0.44733	0.936323	1.616748
18		0.4			4.78835	6	0.590295	-0.81592	0.769277	1.528491
19					5.586409	7	0.38454	-1.2558	0.480599	1.363453
20					6.384467	8	0.094925	-1.73561	0.131913	1.099585
21					7.182525	9	-0.28178	-2.27384	-0.27824	0.722929
22					7.980584	10	-0.729	-2.84751	-0.75226	0.278842
23					Max surp		0.755705	0.169002	1.001897	1.616748
24					#bought		4	2	4	5
25					bought		15			
26					profit		5.970876			

Step by Step

Step 1: In G2:J11 we determine the cumulative value each customer associates with buying n Ten-minute segments (n = 1, 2, …10). In cell G2 we just recopy the amount Customer 1 is willing to pay for the first Ten-minute segment with the formula

= B2.

In cell G3 we compute the total amount Customer 1 is willing to pay for the first two Ten-minute segments with the formula

$$= G2 + B3.$$

Copying this formula to G4:G11 computes how much Customer 1 is willing to pay for 2,3, ... 10 Ten-minute segments. Copying G2:G11 to H2:J11 determines the total amount Customers 2-4 are willing to pay for buying 1,2, ... 10 Ten-minute segments.

Step 2: In cell B16 we enter a trial price for each Ten-minute segment.

Step 3: In E13:E22 we compute the total cost of purchasing in Ten-minute segments. In E13 we compute the cost of buying one Ten-minute segment with the formula

$$= F13*\$B\$16.$$

Copying this formula to the cell range E14:E22 computes the cost of buying 2,3,...10 Ten-minute segments.

Step 4: In G13:J22 we compute the Consumer Surplus each customer has for the proposed number of Ten-minute segments purchased. For Customer 1 buying one Ten-minute segment, the surplus is computed in G13 with the formula

$$= G2-\$E13.$$

Copying this formula to the cell range G13:J22 generates the Consumer Surpluses for all Customers and all possible numbers of Ten-minute segments purchased.

Step 5: In G23:J23 we determine the maximum Consumer Surplus for each customer. For Customer 1 the Maximum Consumer Surplus is computed in G23 with the formula

$$= MAX(G13:G22).$$

Copying this formula to the range H23:J23 computes the Maximum Consumer Surplus for Customers 2-4.

Step 6: Now the key step! In G24: J24 we compute the number of Ten-minute segments each customer will buy. The number of Ten-minute segments Customer 1 will buy is computed in G24 with the formula

$$= If(G23<0,0,MATCH(G23,G13:G22,0)).$$

If Customer 1 does not have any number of Ten-minute segments she values more than the purchase cost, she will buy no Ten-minute segments. Otherwise the MATCH function finds which number (with G13 being first and G22 being tenth) in

G13:G22 matches G23. Note: The "0" in the formula is needed to allow the MATCH function to work on an array which is not sorted from smallest to largest.

For example, from Figure 23.2 we see a "2" in H24, because the second number in H13:H22 matches the maximum Consumer surplus in H23. Copying this formula to H24:J24 computes the number of Ten-minute segments bought by each customer.

Step 7: In Cell G25 we compute the total number of candy bars bought with the formula

$= SUM(G24:J24).$

Step 8: In cell G26 we compute the total profit with the formula

$= (B16-B18)*G25.$

Step 9: We are now ready to use Evolver to find the profit-maximizing price. (See Figure 23.3)

Figure 23.3

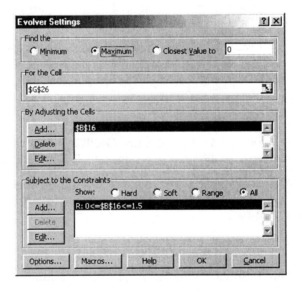

We simply choose to maximize profit (G26) by changing price (B16). We constrain price to be between $0 and $1.50 (this is because nobody is willing to pay $1.50 for a Ten-minute segment). From Figure 23.2 we find the optimal solution is to charge $0.798 per Ten-minute segment. We sell 15 Ten-minute segments and make a profit of $5.97.

Finding the Optimal Two-part Tariff

In *TPT.xls* we find the optimal Two-part Tariff (see Figure 23.4)

Figure 23.4

	A	B	C	D	E	F	G	H	I	J
1	BTT	Cust 1	Cust 2	Cust 3	Cust 4		Cu Val 1	Cu Val 2	Cu Val 3	Cu Val 4
2	1	1.237	0.916	1.272	1.486	1	1.237	0.916	1.272	1.486
3	2	1.026	0.849	1.108	1.239	2	2.263	1.765	2.379	2.725
4	3	0.887	0.695	0.962	1.096	3	3.150	2.460	3.341	3.821
5	4	0.798	0.579	0.853	0.974	4	3.948	3.039	4.194	4.794
6	5	0.772	0.504	0.732	0.813	5	4.720	3.543	4.927	5.607
7	6	0.659	0.429	0.631	0.710	6	5.379	3.972	5.558	6.317
8	7	0.592	0.358	0.509	0.633	7	5.971	4.331	6.067	6.950
9	8	0.508	0.318	0.449	0.534	8	6.479	4.649	6.516	7.484
10	9	0.421	0.260	0.388	0.421	9	6.901	4.909	6.904	7.905
11	10	0.351	0.224	0.324	0.354	10	7.252	5.133	7.228	8.259
12				Menthos	Cost	Menthos	Surp 1	Surp 2	Surp 3	Surp 4
13				1	3.962	1	-2.725	-3.047	-2.691	-2.476
14	fixed			2	4.329	2	-2.067	-2.564	-1.950	-1.604
15	fixed	unit price		3	4.696	3	-1.547	-2.237	-1.355	-0.876
16	3.595255	0.367068		4	5.064	4	-1.116	-2.025	-0.869	-0.269
17		cost		5	5.431	5	-0.710	-1.888	-0.504	0.176
18			0.4	6	5.798	6	-0.419	-1.825	-0.240	0.519
19				7	6.165	7	-0.194	-1.834	-0.098	0.785
20				8	6.532	8	-0.052	-1.883	-0.015	0.952
21				9	6.899	9	0.002	-1.990	0.005	1.007
22				10	7.266	10	-0.014	-2.133	-0.038	0.993
23						Max surp	0.002	-1.825	0.005	1.007
24						#bought	9.000	0.000	9.000	9.000
25						revnue	6.899	0.000	6.899	6.899
26						profit	9.897			

In cell A16 we enter a trial value for the Fixed Charge. The price per Ten-minute segment is in B16. Make the following changes to our spreadsheet:

Step by Step

Step 1: Change the purchase costs in E13:E22 to reflect the new pricing structure. In cell E13 compute the cost of buying one Ten-minute segment with the formula

$$= \$A\$16 + \$B\$16 * F13.$$

Copying this formula to the cell range E14:E22 computes the cost of buying 2,3, ... 10 Ten-minute segments .

Step 2: Compute the revenue collected from each customer in G25:J25. In G25 we determine the revenue received from Customer 1 with the formula

$$= If(G24 <= 0, 0, VLOOKUP(G24, \$D\$13:\$E\$22, 2)).$$

This formula ensures that no revenue is received if no Ten-minute segments are bought, and if any Ten-minute segments are bought we "lookup" the cost of buying that number of Ten-minute segments. Copying this formula to the range H25:J25 computes the revenue received from Customers 2-4.

Step 3: We now use Evolver to determine the optimal Two-part tariff. (See Figure 23.5)

We simply maximize profit (G26). Our Changing Cells are fixed charge and price per Ten-minute segment (A16 and B16). We constrain the fixed charge to be between $0 and $10 and constrain the price per Ten-minute segment to be between $0 and $1.50. We find from Figure 23.4 that the optimal two-part tariff consists of charging a $3.60 Entry Fee and $0.37 per Ten-minute segment. Our profit is now $9.90 (a 66% increase!).

Other Forms of Nonlinear Pricing

There are many other forms of nonlinear pricing:

- Just allow customers to buy one or six ten- minute segments.

- Charge one price for the first n ten-minute segments and another price each additional ten-minute segment purchased.

With Evolver it is easy to experiment with many nonlinear pricing schemes, and determine the profit earned by each of them. For example, if we allow only one or six ten-minute segments to be sold the interested reader can show we maximize profit at of $8.94 by charging $5.38 for six Ten-minute segments and virtually any price for a single ten-minute segment! Then we will sell three customers six ten-minute segments and make a profit of $17.14 - $7.20 = $8.94.

The best form of the charge one price for first n ten-minute segments and another price for remaining segments is to sell up to 4 ten-minute segments at $1.18 per ten-minute segment and $0.42 for each additional ten-minute segment.

Chapter 24: Price Bundling

Suppose you are a marketing manager for Microsoft and are trying to determine how to price Word and Excel. Families tend to value Word more than Excel while businesses tend to value Excel more than Word. Some groups may want to purchase both Word and Excel. How can we determine profit-maximizing prices for this situation? Microsoft has three strategies available.

- **No bundling:** With this strategy Microsoft charges a price for Word and a price for Excel. A consumer who wants to buy both Word and Excel will need to purchase Word and Excel separately.

- **Mixed bundling:** With this strategy Microsoft comes up with a price for Word, a price for Excel, **and a price for the "bundle" of software consisting of Word and Excel.**

- **Pure Bundling:** With this strategy Microsoft does not offer Word and Excel separately. All Microsoft offers is a **pure bundle** of Word and Excel.

The key in price bundling decisions is to divide the market into relatively homogeneous segments. Each segment is assumed to assign a value or **reservation price** to Word alone, Excel alone, and the Word-Excel bundle. A segment's **surplus** for a product is

(Reservation value for product) - (Price for product).

We assume all members of a segment will purchase the product that yields the maximum nonnegative surplus; if no product yields a nonnegative surplus the segment is assumed to purchase nothing. More realistic models for prediction of the number of members of a segment purchasing a product will be discussed in (Winston (1999)). Here is an example of how Evolver can be used to make the pricing decisions in bundling problems. Our example (but not the method of solution) is based on Schrage (1997).

Example 24.1

Figure 24.1 (*file officenb.xls*) gives the size of the four main markets for Word, Excel, and the Word-Excel bundle. Figure 24.1 also gives the reservation value for each segment-product combination.

Figure 24.1

	A	B	C	D	E
1	No bundling		Reservation prices		
2		Product			
3		Size	Excel Only	Word Only	Both
4	Business	70000	$ 450	$ 110	$ 530
5	Legal	50000	$ 75	$ 430	$ 480
6	Educational	60000	$ 290	$ 250	$ 410
7	Home	45000	$ 220	$ 380	$ 390

We assume the variable cost for each software product is $0.

a) For the no bundling case determine a profit-maximizing pricing policy.

b) For the mixed bundling case determine a profit-maximizing pricing policy.

c) For the pure bundling case determine a profit-maximizing pricing policy.

No Bundling Case

Solution

Figure 24.2 gives the setup for using Evolver to solve this problem. The key is to determine (for a given choice of Word and Excel price) the surplus for each segment-product combination. Then we use the Excel =MATCH function to determine the product (if any) bought by each segment. Finally, we determine the profit earned from each segment and use Evolver to maximize profit.

Figure 24.2

	A	B	C	D	E	F	G	H	I	J	K
1	No bundling		Reservation prices								
2		Product									
3		Size	Excel Only	Word Only	Both	Excel Surplus	Word Surplus	Both Surplus	Maximum Surplus	Product bought?	Profit
4	Business	70000	$ 450	$ 110	$ 530	$ 160	$ (270)	$ (140)	$ 160	1	$ 20,300,000
5	Legal	50000	$ 75	$ 430	$ 480	$ (215)	$ 50	$ (190)	$ 50	2	$ 19,000,000
6	Educational	60000	$ 290	$ 250	$ 410	$ -	$ (130)	$ (260)	$ -	1	$ 17,400,000
7	Home	45000	$ 220	$ 380	$ 390	$ (70)	$ -	$ (280)	$ -	2	$ 17,100,000
8	Price		$ 290	$ 380	$ 670					Total	$ 73,800,000

Step by Step

Step 1: In C8 and D8 enter trial prices for Excel and Word, respectively. Also, in E8 compute the price charged to a customer who buys both Word and Excel with the formula

=C8+D8.

Step 2: F4:H7 we compute the surplus for each segment-product combination, by copying the formula

=C4-$C$8

from F4 to F5:F7 we compute the surplus of each segment for Excel. By copying the formula

=D4-$D$8

from G4 to G5:G7 we compute the surplus of each segment for Word. By copying the formula

=E4-$C$8-$D$8

from H4 to H5:H7 we compute the surplus of each segment for the Word-Excel bundle. Recall that in the no bundling case a customer must purchase Word and Excel separately.

Step 3: In I4:I7 compute the maximum surplus for each segment by copying from I4 to I4:I7 the formula

$=MAX(F4:H4).$

Step 4: Now the key step! We determine the product (if any) purchased by each segment in J4:J7 by copying from J4 to J5:J7 the formula

$=If(I4<0,0,MATCH(I4,F4:H4,0)).$

If a segment views each product as having a negative surplus, then no products are purchased. Otherwise, the MATCH function finds the column number of the entry in the range F4:I4 which "matches" the number in I4. The last argument of the =MATCH function must be 0 for this to work. As an example, the maximum surplus for Business ($160) occurs for the first number in F4:H4, so the MATCH function enters a "1". In column K we use the product purchased (combined with the Excel =INDEX function) to determine the profit Microsoft earns from each segment.

Step 5: We compute Microsoft's profit from the Business segment in K4 with the formula

$=If(J4=0,0,B4*(INDEX(\$C\$4:\$E\$8,5,J4))).$

If the Business segment purchases no product, then no profit is earned from the segment. Otherwise, the =INDEX function finds the number in the fifth row and column # equal to J4 entry of the range C4:E8. This will be the price charged for the product purchased by the business segment. In Figure 24.2, the Business segment purchased the first product (Excel) for $290. Therefore Microsoft earns $290*70,000 = $20,300,000 from the Business segment. Copying this formula from K4 to K5:K7 yields the profit earned from each other segment. In K8 we determine the total profit earned with the formula

$= SUM(K4:K7.).$

Step 6: It is now a simple matter to set up Evolver to find the profit-maximizing prices. Our Settings window looks as follows:

We simply maximize profit (K8) by adjusting the Excel and Word prices (C8:D8). We have forced prices to be integers. Since no segment is willing to pay more than $500 we have limited each price to be at most $500.

As shown in Figure 24.2, we find that the maximum profit earned by Microsoft is $73,800,000. The profit-maximizing prices are $290 for Excel and $380 for Word. The Educational and Business segments purchase Excel while the Legal and Home segments purchase Word.

Mixed Bundling Case

Solution

If Microsoft chooses to sell Excel and Word separately **and** also sell the Excel-Word bundle how do we determine the profit-maximizing set of prices? Begin by copying the previous worksheet to a separate workbook (Evolver will not recognize more than one SETTING box in a single workbook). See Figure 24.3 and file *bundlemix.xls*.

Figure 24.3

	A	B	C	D	E	F	G	H	I	J	K
1	Mixed Bundling		Reservation prices								
2		Product									
3		Size	Excel Only	Word Only	Bundle	Excel Surplus	Word Surplus	Bundle Surplus	Maximum Surplus	Product bought?	Profit
4	Business	70000	$ 450	$ 110	$ 530	$ 69	$ (270)	$ 120	$ 120	3	$ 28,700,000
5	Legal	50000	$ 75	$ 430	$ 480	$ (306)	$ 50	$ 70	$ 70	3	$ 20,500,000
6	Educational	60000	$ 290	$ 250	$ 410	$ (91)	$ (130)	$ -	$ -	3	$ 24,600,000
7	Home	45000	$ 220	$ 380	$ 390	$ (161)	$ -	$ (20)	$ -	2	$ 17,100,000
8	Price		381	380	410					Total	$ 90,900,000

Step by Step

Step 1: In E8 enter a trial price for the Excel-Word bundle.

Step 2: In H4 change the formula for the Bundle surplus to

$=E4-\$E\$8.$

Step 3: Copying this formula to H5:H7 computes the Bundle surplus for each segment.

Now we change our Evolver settings to add the Bundle price as an Adjustable Cell. We raised the upper bound on each Adjustable cell to $530, because no segment will pay more than $530 for any product.

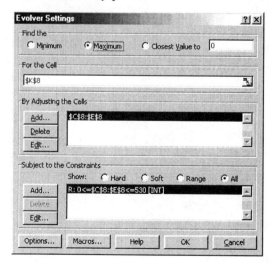

From Figure 24.3 we find that Microsoft can maximize its profit from mixed bundling by charging $381 for Excel, $380 for Word and $410 for the bundle. The maximum profit of $90,900,000 is attained by selling the Excel-Word bundle to the Business, Legal, and Educational segments, and Word to the Home segment. Actually, there are many values of the Excel price that will lead to maximum profit; any price for Excel which does not change the purchasing decisions of any segment will maintain profit maximization.

Pure Bundling Solution

If Microsoft just wants to sell an Excel-Word bundle we copy the sheet bundlemix.xls to a new workbook and proceed as follows: (see Figure 24.4 and file *bundlepure.xls*).

Figure 24.4

	A	B	C	D	E	F	G	H	I	J	K
1	Pure Bundling		Reservation prices								
2		Product									
3		Size	Excel Only	Word Only	Bundle	Excel Surplus	Word Surplus	Bundle Surplus	Maximum Surplus	Product bought?	Profit
4	Business	70000	$ 450	$ 110	$ 530	$ (750)	$ (1,090)	$ 140	$ 140	3	$ 27,300,000
5	Legal	50000	$ 75	$ 430	$ 480	$ (1,125)	$ (770)	$ 90	$ 90	3	$ 19,500,000
6	Educational	60000	$ 290	$ 250	$ 410	$ (910)	$ (950)	$ 20	$ 20	3	$ 23,400,000
7	Home	45000	$ 220	$ 380	$ 390	$ (980)	$ (820)	$ -	$ -	3	$ 17,550,000
8	Price		1200	1200	390					Total	$ 87,750,000

Step by Step

Step 1: We change the price of Excel and the price of Word to $1200. This effectively ensures that we are **only selling the Excel-Word bundle.**

Step 2: We change the Settings window so the only changing cell is the bundle price (E8). We find that a maximum profit of $87,750,000 can be earned by charging $390 for the bundle. This price ensures that all segments purchase the bundle.

Remarks

Bundling (either mixed or pure) produces more profit than no bundling because judicious setting of the bundle price entices market segments to buy more products than they would buy in the absence of bundling. Common applications of bundling include

- Phone companies may bundle call-waiting, voice mail and caller-ID features.

- Automobile companies often bundle popular options such as air conditioning, cassette players, and power windows.

- Computer mail order companies often bundle computers with printers, scanners, and monitors.

Dolan and Simon (1997) contains an outstanding discussion of bundling and other pricing issues.

Reference

Dolan R., and Simon, G., *Power Pricing*, Free Press, 1997.

Schrage, L., *Optimization Modeling with LINDO*, 1997.

Winston, W., *Step-by-Step Marketing Models with Excel and Palisade Add-Ins*, Palisades Publishing, 1999.

Chapter 25: Duration and Immunization Against Interest Rate Risk

A bond pays us money in the future. If interest rates increase, then money received in the future is less valuable. Therefore, bondholders are subject to interest rate risk. In this chapter we show to (approximately) price a bond off the current yield curve as the present value of its payments. Then we develop a measure, **quasi-modified duration,** of how sensitive a bond's value is to changes in interest rates. Finally, we show how "matching" the duration of a financial institution's assets and liabilities can greatly reduce the institution's interest rate risk. Our discussion is heavily based on Luenberger (1997).

Pricing Bonds

In Chapter 12 we showed how to fit the yield curve, so we could estimate the spot rate s_t that is relevant for payments received at time t. If a bond pays an amount c_t at time t (t = 0,1,2, ...n) the present value of the bond payments is as follows:

$$Present\,value = \sum_{t=1}^{t=n} (1+s_t)^{-t} c_t \ (25.1).$$

In the sheet Duration.xls of the file *duration.xls* we use (25.1) to price four streams of payments:

- Bond 1 pays $100 one year and two years from now and $1100 three years from now.

- Bond 2 pays $100 at the end of each of the next ten years, $1100 at the end of year 11, and $1200 at the end of Years 12 and 13.

- Bond 3 pays $100 at the end of Years 1-13, $1000 at the end of Year 14, and $1100 at the end of Year 15.

- We must make payments of $1630 at the end of each of the next 15 years to a pension fund.

Figure 25.1 and the sheet duration of workbook *duration.xls* show how to find the present value of these payment streams. We will assume the same yield curve used in Chapter 12.

Duration	Spot Rate
.25	3.15%
.5	3.36%
1	3.7%
2	4.46%
3	4.94%
5	5.9%
7	6.29%
10	6.59%
30	7.32%

Recall that our best fit to this yield curve was

$$s(t) = (-.04 - .000015t)e^{-.2138t} + .07263$$

Figure 25.1

	A	B	C	D	E	F	G	H	I	J
1	Year		Bond 1	Bond 2	Bond 3	Liability	Spot rate	Bond1*$(1+s_t)^t$	Bond2*$(1+s_t)^t$	Bond3*$(1+s_t)^t$	Liability*$(1+s_t)^t$

	A	B	C	D	E	F	G	H	I	J
2	1	100	100	100	1630	0.037521	96.38363313	96.38363313	96.38363313	1571.05322
3	2	100	100	100	1630	0.04427	91.7010515	91.7010515	91.7010515	1494.727139
4	3	1100	100	100	1630	0.049722	950.9762487	86.45238625	86.45238625	1409.173896
5	4	0	100	100	1630	0.054126	0	80.98972495	80.98972495	1320.132517
6	5	0	100	100	1630	0.057683	0	75.54780476	75.54780476	1231.429218
7	6		100	100	1630	0.060557	0	70.2743308	70.2743308	1145.471592
8	7		100	100	1630	0.062878	0	65.2554756	65.2554756	1063.664252
9	8		100	100	1630	0.064753	0	60.53556768	60.53556768	986.7297533
10	9		100	100	1630	0.066267	0	56.13149655	56.13149655	914.9433938
11	10		1100	100	1630	0.06749	0	572.4714426	52.04285842	848.2985923
12	11		1200	100	1630	0.068478	0	579.1067054	48.25889212	786.6199415
13	12		1200	100	1630	0.069276	0	537.1571712	44.7630976	729.6384909
14	13			100	1630	0.069921	0	0	41.53623137	677.0405713
15	14			1000	1630	0.070442	0	0	385.5819124	628.4985172
16	15			1100	1630	0.070863	0	0	393.9007191	583.6892474
17	a1		a2	a3	a4		Price	1139.060933	2372.00679	1649.355182	15391.11034
18	-0.04346536	-1.50E-05	0.2138	0.07263						

To price our four payment streams we proceed as follows:

Step 1: Enter in cells A18:D18 the four parameters characterizing our fitted yield curve. Then create range names $a1\_, a2\_, a3\_,$ and $a4\_$.

Step 2: In F2:F16 compute estimated spot rates for payments received at times 1, 2, ...15 by copying the formula

$$=(a1\_+a2\_*A2)*EXP(-a3\_*A2)+a4\_$$

from F2 to F2:F16. Note A2 is a cell address but a1_, a2_ , a3_ and a4_ are Range Names.

Step 3: In the cell range G2:J16 compute the present value of each year's payment by copying the formula

$$=B2*(1+\$F2)^{\wedge}-\$A2$$

from G2 to G2:J16.

Step 4: In G17:J17 compute the total present value of the payments for each stream by copying from G17 to H17:J17 the formula

$$=SUM(G2:G16).$$

We find the present values of the four streams to be: Bond 1: $1139.06, Bond 2: $2372.01, Bond 3: $1649.36, Liability Stream: $15,391.11.

Quasi-Modified Duration and Interest Rate Risk

As previously stated, increases in interest rates will reduce bond values and decreases in interest rates will increase bond values. The concept of **Quasi-modified duration** helps us measure how changes in interest rates change the present value of a bond's payment stream. Define

- s_t = current spot rate for t periods.

- c_t = bond payment at time t (t = 0, 1, ...n).

- PV = present value of bond payments with current yield curve.

The **Quasi-modified duration** D of the bond is defined by

$$D = \frac{1}{PV} \sum_{t=1}^{t=n} tc_t(1 + s_t)^{-(t+1)} \quad (25.2).$$

In a sense, D may be viewed as the time a "randomly chosen" dollar of present value is received. It can be shown (see page 93 of Luenberger) that if for a value of Δ near 0 all spot rates change to $s_t + \Delta$, then the approximate change in the present value of the payment stream is given by $-D*\Delta*PV$. For example, a bond with a current price of $1000 and a duration of 5 would decrease in value by around $5(.01)(1000) = \$50$ if the entire yield curve suddenly shifted upward by 1%. In Figure 25.2 and the sheet duration of workbook *duration.xls* we compute the duration for all four-payment streams.

Figure 25.2

	K	L	M	N
	$t*Bond1*(1+s_t)^{t-1}$	$t*Bond2*(1+s_t)^{t-1}$	$t*Bond3*(1+s_t)^{t-1}$	$t*Liability *(1+s_t)^{t-1}$
1				
2	92.89804736	92.89804736	92.89804736	1514.238
3	175.6270753	175.6270753	175.6270753	2862.721
4	2717.79432	247.0722109	247.0722109	4027.277
5	0	307.3246505	307.3246505	5009.392
6	0	357.1381326	357.1381326	5821.352
7	0	397.5704422	397.5704422	6480.398
8	0	429.7656571	429.7656571	7005.18
9	0	454.8329653	454.8329653	7413.777
10	0	473.7870651	473.7870651	7722.729
11	0	5362.779508	487.5254099	7946.664
12	0	5961.912298	496.8260248	8098.264
13	0	6028.26916	502.3557633	8188.399
14	0	0	504.6830046	8226.333
15	0	0	5042.914354	8219.95
16	0	0	5517.524945	8175.969
17	2.621738096	8.553507222	9.390242875	6.283669
18	durations			

Step 1: In K2:N16 compute the terms of the form $tc_t(1+s_t)^{-(t+1)}$ by copying from K2 to K2:N16 the formula

$$=\$A2*G2*(1+\$F2)\wedge{-1}.$$

Step 2: In K17:N17 compute the duration of each payment stream by copying from K17 to M17:N17 the formula

$$=SUM(K2:K16)/G17.$$

We find Bond 1 duration = 2.62, Bond 2 duration = 8.55, Bond 3 duration = 9.39, Liability payment stream duration = 6.28 years. We find that Bond 1 is the least sensitive of all four streams of payments to interest risks while Bond 3 is most sensitive to interest rate risk. This is unsurprising, because Bond 1 payments are received early and Bond 3 payments are received much later.

Immunization and Interest Rate Risk

Let's suppose Bonds 1-3 are available for purchase today and we want to buy a sufficient number of these bonds to cover our liability payments. Naturally, we do not want to take the chance that changes in interest rates could greatly reduce the values of our bonds (relative to the value of our liabilities) and leave us in the hole. This is exactly what happened to the Savings and Loans (S and L's) in the late 1970's. Most S and L's had assets in long-term mortgages of high duration and liabilities in short-term deposits. When interest rates skyrocketed in the late 1970's the value of long-term mortgages was greatly reduced while the value of short-term liabilities was not reduced very much. This led many S and L's to file for bankruptcy. To **immunize** against interest rate risk a financial institution can buy bonds that **match** their liability stream in present value and duration. Then changes in interest rates will have around the same affect on both assets and liabilities. This strategy is called **duration matching**.

Before showing an example of duration matching let's see what happens if we match present values and not durations. See the sheet mismatch of the file *duration.xls*. Suppose we wanted to cover our liabilities just by purchasing Bond 1 or just Bond 3. Then we could match the present value of our liabilities either by purchasing $15,391.11/$1139.06 = 13.51 units of Bond 1 or $15,391.11/$1649.36 = 9.33 units of Bond 3. We now show how changes in the yield curve will change Present Value of Bond 1 Purchases- Present Value of Liabilities and Present Value of Bond 3 Purchases - Present Value of Liabilities. (See Figure 25.3.)

Figure 25.3

	E	F	G	H	I	J	K	L
1	Liability	Spot rate	Bond1*(1+s_i)^-t	Bond2*(1+s_i)^-t	Bond3*(1+s_i)^-t	Liability*(1+s_i)^-t	Bond 1 PV	Bond 3 PV
2	1630	0.037520549	96.38363313	96.38363313	96.38363313	1571.05322	1302.346	899.4127818
3	1630	0.044270097	91.7010515	91.7010515	91.7010515	1494.727139	1239.074	855.7168385
4	1630	0.049722094	950.9762487	86.45238625	86.45238625	1409.173896	12849.69	806.7384335
5	1630	0.054125985	0	80.98972495	80.98972495	1320.132517	0	755.7631047
6	1630	0.057683258	0	75.54780476	75.54780476	1231.429218	0	704.9813234
7	1630	0.060556671	0	70.2743308	70.2743308	1145.471592	0	655.7714137
8	1630	0.062877691	0	65.2554756	65.2554756	1063.664252	0	608.9375024
9	1630	0.06475251	0	60.53556768	60.53556768	986.7297533	0	564.8932455
10	1630	0.066266908	0	56.13149655	56.13149655	914.9433938	0	523.7962486
11	1630	0.067490173	0	572.4714426	52.04285842	848.2985923	0	485.642744
12	1630	0.068478274	0	579.1067054	48.25889212	786.6199415	0	450.3323126
13	1630	0.069276418	0	537.1571712	44.7630976	729.6384909	0	417.710983
14	1630	0.069921125	0	0	41.53623137	677.0405713	0	387.5991824
15	1630	0.07044189	0	0	385.5819124	628.4985172	0	3598.093257
16	1630	0.070862542	0	0	393.9007191	583.6892474	0	3675.720971
17		Price	1139.060933	2372.00679	1649.355182	15391.11034	15391.11	15391.11034
18		bonds bought(formula)	13.51210448		9.331592435			
19		bonds bought (#)	13.51210448		9.331592435			
20	delta	0				Bond 3 PV - Liability PV	0	
21						Bond 1 Liability-PV	0	
22							Bond 3 PV - Liability PV	Bond 1 Liability-PV
23							0	0
24						-0.035	2349.134	-2536.073895
25						-0.03	1915.531	-2094.908336
26						-0.025	1519.319	-1683.030902
27						-0.02	1157.421	-1298.512659
28						-0.015	827.0178	-939.5606155
29						-0.01	525.5255	-604.5074026
30						-0.005	250.5765	-291.8017952
31						0	0	0
32						0.005	-228.1949	272.2423567
33						0.01	-435.8346	526.1776009
34						0.015	-624.5949	762.9727966
35						0.02	-796.0139	983.7159955
36						0.025	-951.5039	1189.421995
37						0.03	-1092.362	1381.037647
38						0.035	-1219.778	1559.446753
39						0.04	-1334.848	1725.47458

To begin we copied columns A-J of Duration worksheet to a new worksheet.

Step by Step

Step 1: In G17 and I17 we compute the units of Bond 1 or Bond 3 needed to be purchased to match the present value of our liabilities by copying from G17 to I17 the formula

$$=\$J\$17/G17.$$

We Paste>Special Value these numbers to G19 and I19.

Step 2: We define the range name delta for cell F20. This cell will signify the magnitude of the shift in the yield curve. We currently enter 0 in F20. Then we change the spot rate formula in F2 to

$$=(a1\_+a2\_*A2)*EXP(-a3\_*A2)+a4\_+delta.$$

and copy this formula to F3:F16. This induces a parallel shift of magnitude delta in yield curve at all points of time.

Step 3: In K2:L16 we compute the present value (with shifted yield curve) of each year's payment from our Bond 1 and Bond 3 purchases. In column K we compute the present value of the Bond 1 payments by copying from K2 to K2:K16 the formula

$$=\$G\$19*G2.$$

In column L we compute the present value of the Bond 3 payments by copying from L2 to L2:L16 the formula

$$=I2*\$I\$19.$$

Step 4: In K17:L17 we compute the NPV of our Bond 1 and Bond 3 purchases by copying from K17 to L17 the formula

$$=SUM(K2:K16).$$

Step 5: In cell K20 we compute the present value of our Bond 3 purchases less present value of Liabilities with the formula

$$=L17-J17.$$

In cell K21 we compute the present value of our Bond 1 purchases less the present value of the liabilities with the formula

$$=K17-J17.$$

Step 6: We input trial values for delta in J4:J39. We allow for a parallel shift in rates varying between a 3.5% decrease and a 4.5% increase. In cell L23 we keep track of the difference between Bond 1 NPV and Liability NPV and in cell K23 we keep track of the difference between Bond 3 NPV and Liability NPV. After selecting our table range to be J23:L39 and choosing Column Input cell delta our one-way data table shows us how the present value of our assets and liabilities varies with parallel shifts in the yield curve.

We find, for example, that if we have covered our liabilities with Bond 3 a decrease in interest rates helps us but an increase in interest rates bankrupts us! This is because Bond 3 has a higher duration than our liabilities so an increase in interest rates will reduce the value of our assets more than it reduces the value of our liabilities. Conversely, if we have covered our liabilities by purchasing Bond 1, then a decrease in interest rates bankrupts us while an increase in rates helps us. This is because Bond 1 has a lower duration than the liabilities, so a decrease in interest rates will increase the value of our assets by less than the corresponding increase in liability value.

Duration Matching

In the sheet immunized dur of *duration.xls* we have shown how to purchase a combination of Bonds 1-3 to immunize our interest rate risk. Note that if we purchase P_i \$s worth of Bond i (in present value) then the duration of our portfolio is given by

$$\frac{P_1 D_1 + P_2 D_2 + P_3 D_3}{P_1 + P_2 + P_3} \quad (25.3)$$

We can now (see Figure 25.4) use Solver to determine purchases of Bonds 1-3 that match the present value and duration of the liabilities.

Figure 25.4

	A	B	C	D	E	F
21		Buy				
22		Bond 1	Bond 2	Bond 3		
23		5.170513	4.0057	0		
24						
25						
26						
27	NPV bonds	15391.11	=	15391.1	NPV Liabilities	
28	Duration assets	6.283669		6.28367	Duration Liabilities	

Step by Step

Step 1: In B23:D23 enter trial values for the number of each bond purchased.

Step 2: In B27 compute the NPV of the purchased bonds with the formula

=SUMPRODUCT(B23:D23,G17:I17).

Step 3: In cell B28 compute the duration of the purchased bonds with the formula

=SUMPRODUCT(B23:D23,G17:I17,K17:M17)/J17.

Step 4: Set up the following Solver window

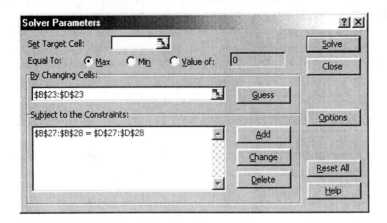

We choose the number of each bond to purchase (B23:D23) to ensure that present value (B27=D27) and duration (B28=D28) match. Under OPTIONS we check Linear and assume non-negative. Note that even though we divide by J17 in cell B28 we still have a linear model because J17 does not depend on our changing cells. There is no target cell in this model. There are an infinite number of possible solutions due to the fact that we have three changing cells and only two constraints. When we used Solver it found the solution 5.17 units of Bond 1 and 4.01 units of Bond 2.

Figure 25.5 shows that parallel shifts in the yield curve now have little effect on *the Value of our Assets - Value of Our Liabilities.*

	A	B	C	D	E	F	G	H	I	J
1	Year	Bond 1	Bond 2	Bond 3	Liability	Spot rate	PV Bond 1	PV Bond 2	PV Bond 3	PV Liabilities
2	1	100	100	100	1630	0.03752	498.35284	386.085	0	1571.05322
3	2	100	100	100	1630	0.04427	474.14149	367.328	0	1494.72714
4	3	1100	100	100	1630	0.04972	4917.0352	346.304	0	1409.1739
5	4	0	100	100	1630	0.05413	0	324.422	0	1320.13252
6	5	0	100	100	1630	0.05768	0	302.623	0	1231.42922
7	6		100	100	1630	0.06056	0	281.499	0	1145.47159
8	7		100	100	1630	0.06288	0	261.395	0	1063.66425
9	8		100	100	1630	0.06475	0	242.488	0	986.729753
10	9		100	100	1630	0.06627	0	224.847	0	914.943394
11	10		1100	100	1630	0.06749	0	2293.16	0	848.298592
12	11		1200	100	1630	0.06848	0	2319.74	0	786.619942
13	12		1200	100	1630	0.06928	0	2151.7	0	729.638491
14	13			100	1630	0.06992	0	0	0	677.040571
15	14			1000	1630	0.07044	0	0	0	628.498517
16	15			1100	1630	0.07086	0	0	0	583.689247
17	a1	a2	a3	a4		Price	5889.5295	9501.58	0	15391.1103
18	-0.043	-1.50E-05	0.213839	0.07263						
19						PV Bonds-PV Liabilities				
20	change	0				4.7E-08			Change	4.725E-08
21		Buy							-0.035	-13.8614168
22		Bond 1	Bond 2	Bond 3					-0.03	-9.49184232
23		5.170513	4.005714	0					-0.025	-6.14463866
24									-0.02	-3.66653508
25									-0.015	-1.92321835
26									-0.01	-0.79719888
27									-0.005	-0.18590774
28									0	4.725E-08
29									0.005	-0.16184173
30									0.01	-0.60416222
31									0.015	-1.26885201
32									0.02	-2.10589277
33									0.025	-3.07240394
34									0.03	-4.13179408
35									0.035	-5.25300554
36									0.04	-6.40984257

Figure 25.5

In B20 we define a range name shift representing the parallel shift in the yield curve. Then we incorporate that shift into the yield curve in column F. Columns G-J compute the present value of payments from each bond and liabilities. Cell F20 computes the Present Value of Assets - Present Value of Liabilities. This is the output cell for our one-way data table (table range I19:J36). The data table has a Column Input cell Shift. From the data table we find that parallel shifts in the yield curve ranging from -3.5% to +4.5% cause our assets to be worth, at most, $13.86 less than our liabilities. Duration matching has indeed immunized us against interest rate risk!

Remarks

The **convexity** of a bond measures the rate of change of its duration. Matching convexity of bond purchases to convexity of liabilities provides even more protection against interest rate risk. See Chapter 18 of Winston (1996) for a discussion of convexity.

Reference

Winston, W. *Simulation Modeling with @RISK*, Duxbury Press, 1996.

Luenberger, D., *Investment Science*, Oxford Press, 1997.

Chapter 26: Finding Arbitrage Opportunities

Often traders want to know if bond prices are inconsistent in a manner that will allow traders to make "infinite profits." If bond prices are such that a trade is possible which will make infinite profits we say that an **arbitrage opportunity** exists. The Excel Solver can easily be used to find an arbitrage opportunities or to show that one does not exist. We use two examples to illustrate the idea. Our work is in the file *Arbitrage.xls*.

Example 26.1

It is February 15, 2000. Three bonds are for sale. Each bond has a face value of $100. The coupon rates (paid semiannually), expiration dates, and prices are given in Table 26.1.

Table 26.1

Current Price	Expiration Date	Coupon Rate
$101.625 (Bond 1)	8-15-00	6.875
$101.5625 (Bond 2)	2-15-01	5.5
$103.80 (Bond 3)	2-15-01	7.75

Every six months starting six months from the current date and ending at the expiration date each bond pays .5*(coupon rate)*(Face value). At the expiration date the face value is paid. For example the second bond pays

- $2.75 on 8-15-00.

- $102.75 on 2-15-01.

Given the current price structure, is there a way to make an infinite amount of money? To answer this we look for an **arbitrage**. An arbitrage exists if there is a combination of bond sales and purchases today which yields

- A **positive** cash flow today.

- Non-negative cash flows at all future dates.

If such a strategy exists, then it is possible to make an infinite amount of money. For instance, if buying 10 of bond 1 today and selling 5 of bond 2 today yielded, say $1 today and nothing at all future dates, then we could make $k by purchasing 10k of bond 1 today and selling 5k of bond 2 today. We would also be able to cover all payments at future dates from money received on those dates. Clearly, bond prices at any point in time should be set so an arbitrage does not exist. Show that for the bonds in Table 26.1 an arbitrage opportunity exists. Hint: set up an LP which

---

maximizes today's cash flow subject to constraints that cash flow at each future date is nonnegative.

Solution Our spreadsheet is in sheet Arbitrage of file *Arbitrage.xls*. See Figure 26.1.

Figure 26.1

	A	B	C	D	E	F	G	H
1	Arbitrage							
2			Bond					
3			6 and 7/8	5 and 1/2	7 and 3/4			
4			1	2	3			
5		Price	101.625	101.5625	103.8			
6		8/15/00	103.4375	2.75	3.875		can make infinite profit	
7		2/15/01		102.75	103.875			
8			6 and 7/8	5 and 1/2	7 and 3/4			
9		Bought	0.10689	10.10949	0			
10		Sold	0	0	10			
11								
12		8/15/00 cash	0.107532	>=	0			
13		2/15/01 cash	9.75E-05	>=	0			
14		Profit	0.392226					

In C5:E5 we have entered the price of each bond and in C6:E7 we have entered the coupon payments from each bond. We now proceed as follows:

Step by Step

Step 1: Enter trial values for the number of each bond bought (in C9:E9) and the number of each bond sold (in C10:E10).

Step 2: In C12 compute our cash inflow on 8/15/2000. Note we pay out coupons on bonds sold and receive coupons from bonds purchased.

= SUMPRODUCT($C$9:$E$9,C6:E6)-SUMPRODUCT($C$10:$E$10,C6:E6).

Copying this formula to C13 computes our cash inflow on 2/15/01.

Step 3: In cell C14 compute our total profit earned today = (revenue from bond sales) - (cost of bond purchases) with the formula

= SUMPRODUCT($C$10:$E$10,C5:E5)-SUMPRODUCT($C$9:$E$9,C5:E5).

Step 4: We are now ready to use the Solver to determine if an arbitrage opportunity is possible. From our Solver window

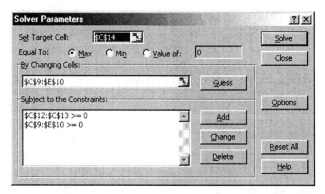

we see that our goal is to maximize our profit from today's bond transactions (in cell C14). Our changing cells (C9:E10) are the number bought and sold of each bond. Our constraint is that on each future date our receipts from bond coupons are at least as large as our bond coupon payments (C12:C13>=0). We also constrain the number bought and sold of each bond to be nonnegative. After checking the *"Assume Linear Model"* box under *"Options"* (because changing cells are always multiplied by constants and added together) we obtain the following message:

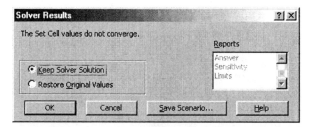

This indicates (when our goal is to maximize) that it is possible to make a profit larger than any given number. From Figure 26.1 it is easy to see how this is done. From Figure 26.1 we see that if we buy .10689 six and 7/8 bonds and 10.10949 five and 1/2 bonds and sell ten seven and 3/4 bonds our 8/15/00 position from coupons is .10753 and our 2/15/01 position from coupons is 0.0000975. Our profit today from these bond transactions is .392226. Consider any k>0. If we buy .10689k six and 7/8 bonds and 10.10949k five and 1/2 bonds and sell 10k seven and 3/4 bonds our 8/15/00 position from coupons is .10753k and our 2/15/01 position from coupons is 0.0000975k. Our profit today from these bond transactions is .392226k. Thus by choosing k arbitrarily large we can make a profit larger than any number, and still cover our coupon payments at all future dates. This demonstrates for the given set of bond prices and coupons an arbitrage exists. Of course, in reality if we trade to exploit the arbitrage opportunity prices will move quickly to eliminate the arbitrage opportunity.

An Example with No Arbitrage

Usually bonds are bought at an ask price and sold at a bid price. Consider the same three bonds listed above and suppose the ask and bid prices are given in Table 26.2

Table 26.2

	Ask Price	Bid Price
Bond 1	$101.6563	$101.5938
Bond 2	$101.5938	$101.5313
Bond 3	$103.7813	$103.7188

Show that in this case there is no arbitrage. See Figure 26.2 and sheet *No Arbitrage* of *Arbitrage.xls*.

Figure 26.2

	A	B	C	D	E	F	G	H
1	No Arbitrage							
2			Bond					
3			6 and 7/8	5 and 1/2	7 and 3/4			
4								
5			1	2	3			
6	Buy	Ask Price	101.6563	101.5938	103.7813			
7	Sell	Bid Price	101.5938	101.5313	103.7188			
8		8/15/00	103.4375	2.75	3.875		No way to make any money!!	
9		2/15/01		102.75	103.875			
10			6 and 7/8	5 and 1/2	7 and 3/4			
11		Bought	0	0	1.6156E-27			
12		Sold	3.72901E-29	0	0			
13								
14		8/15/00 cash	2.40321E-27	>=	0			
15		2/15/01 cash	1.67819E-25	>=	0			
16		Profit	-1.63879E-25					

Solution

Step by Step

Step 1: In cell C14 we compute (coupons received) - (coupons paid out) on 8/15/00 with the formula

=SUMPRODUCT($C$11:$E$11,C8:E8)-SUMPRODUCT($C$12:$E$12,C8:E8).

Step 2: In cell C15 we compute (coupons received) - (coupons paid out) on 2/15/01 with the formula

=SUMPRODUCT($C$11:$E$11,C9:E9)-SUMPRODUCT($C$12:$E$12,C9:E9).

Step 3: In cell C16 we compute our profit from today's transactions (revenue from bonds sold at bid price) - (cost of bonds bought at ask price) with the formula

=SUMPRODUCT($C$12:$E$12,C7:E7)-SUMPRODUCT($C$11:$E$11,C6:E6).

Step 4: We now set up our Solver window in an attempt to find an arbitrage:

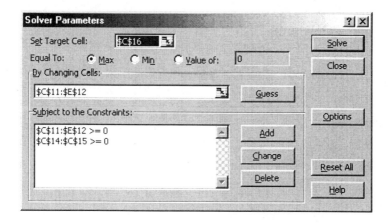

We try to maximize profit from today's bond transactions (C16). Our changing cells (C11:C12) are again the number bought and sold of each bond. We ensure that our net inflow from coupons at all future dates is nonnegative (C14:C15>=0) and the number bought and sold of each bond is nonnegative (C11:E12>=0). After checking the *"Assume Linear Model"* option we find the largest profit that can be made is -1.6388E-25. Therefore it is impossible to have a nonnegative net inflow at all future dates and make a profit on today's transactions. Therefore no arbitrage exists.

Remarks

If you want a more theoretical discussion of arbitrage and other important investment topics look at Pliska (1997).

Reference

Pliska, S., *Introduction to Mathematical Finance*, Blackwell, 1997.

Chapter 27: Introduction to @RISK - The Newsperson Problem

@RISK is used to model situations where we make decisions under uncertainty. Here is an easy example. See the Appendix for a more through discussion of @RISK.

Example 27.1

We need to determine how many Year 2000 nature calendars to order in August 1999. It costs $2.00 to order each calendar and we sell each calendar for $4.50. After January 1, 2000 leftover calendars are returned for $0.75. Our best guess is that the number of calendars demanded is governed by the following probabilities

Demand	Probability
100	.3
150	.2
200	.3
250	.15
300	.05

How many calendars should we order?

Solution

Our final result is in file *news.xls*. We proceed as follows:

Figure 27.1

	A	B	C	D	E	F	G
1	Order quantity		100		95% CI	Lower	339.6619641
2	Quantity demanded		150			Upper	360.3380359
3	Sales price		$4.50			Standard error	5.169017954
4	Salvage value		$0.75			demand	prob
5	Purchase price		$2.00			100	0.3
6						150	0.2
7	Full price revenue	$450.00				200	0.3
8	Salvage revenue	$0.00				250	0.15
9	Costs	$200.00				300	0.05
10	Profit	$250.00		1689.662033			

Step by Step

Step 1: Enter parameter values in C3:C5.

Step 2: It can be shown that ordering an amount equal to one of the possible demands for calendars always maximizes expected profit. Therefore in cell C1 enter the possible order quantities (100, 150, 200, 250, 300) with the formula

=RISKSimtable({100,150,200,250,300}).

On the first simulation @RISK will put 100 in this cell and run the desired number of iterations. On the second simulation @RISK will put 150 in this cell and run the desired number of iterations.

Step 3: @RISK to generate demand according to above probabilities. Type in C2 the formula

=RISKDiscrete(F5:F9,G5:G9).

This generates a demand for calendars of 100 30% of the time, 150 20% of the time, etc. This demand could also have been generated with the formula

=RISKDiscrete({100,150,200,250,300},{.3,.2,.3,.15,.05}).

Note in either format the demands are listed first followed by the probabilities. To see the spreadsheet recalculate when you hit F9 select Simulation Settings (3rd icon from left)

and choose *Method: Monte Carlo* from the *Sampling* tab *Standard Recalc* options. Approximately 30% of the time a demand of 100 will occur, around 20% of the time a demand of 150 will occur, etc.

Step 4: In cell B7 compute Full price revenue with formula

=C3*MIN(C1,C2).

This ensures that we sell at full-price the minimum of quantity ordered and quantity demanded.

Step 5: In B8 compute salvage revenue with formula

=C4*If(C1>C2,(C1-C2),0).

This ensures that number leftover is *(number ordered) - (number demanded)* (as long as that is >0).

Step 6: In B9 compute ordering costs with formula

= C1*C5.

Step 7: In cell B10 compute profit with formula

= B7 + B8 - B9.

Step 8: With cursor in B10 select B10 as an output cell by selecting the 4th icon from left.

Step 9: Select the Simulations Settings Icon (3rd from left)

and from the Iteration tab select 1000 iterations and 5 simulations. From Sampling Tab choose Latin Hypercube from the Sampling option (it is more accurate than Monte Carlo simulation). This will cause @RISK to recalculate demand and profit 1000 times for each of the five order quantities. **If you do not use a RISKSimTable leave simulations at 1.**

Step 10: To run the simulation select the 2nd icon from right.

@RISK will then send you to the Results menu. Then select Merge Simulations. This merges results for all five order quantities. You can go into the statistics portion of the results and copy the results to the clipboard and paste the results into your spreadsheet. First simulation is for 100 calendars ordered, 2nd simulation is for 150 calendars ordered, etc.

Figure 27.2

	B	C	D	E	F	G
16	Name	Profit	Profit	Profit	Profit	Profit
17	Description	Output (Sim#1)	Output (Sim#2)	Output (Sim#3)	Output (Sim#4)	Output (Sim#5)
18	Cell	B10	B10	B10	B10	B10
19	Minimum =	250	187.5	125	62.5	0
20	Maximum =	250	375	500	625	750
21	Mean =	250	318.75	350	325	271.875
22	Std Deviation	0	85.92329	163.4587	208.7912	225.5852
23	Variance =	0	7382.813	26718.75	43593.75	50888.67
24	Skewness =	0	-0.8728716	-0.3984589	3.48E-02	0.2898334
25	Kurtosis =	0	1.761905	1.432133	1.630593	2.072172
26	Errors Calcule	0	0	0	0	0
27	Mode =	250	375	500	62.5	0
28	5% Perc =	250	187.5	125	62.5	0
29	10% Perc =	250	187.5	125	62.5	0
30	15% Perc =	250	187.5	125	62.5	0
31	20% Perc =	250	187.5	125	62.5	0
32	25% Perc =	250	187.5	125	62.5	0
33	30% Perc =	250	375	312.5	250	187.5
34	35% Perc =	250	375	312.5	250	187.5
35	40% Perc =	250	375	312.5	250	187.5
36	45% Perc =	250	375	312.5	250	187.5
37	50% Perc =	250	375	312.5	250	187.5
38	55% Perc =	250	375	500	437.5	375
39	60% Perc =	250	375	500	437.5	375
40	65% Perc =	250	375	500	437.5	375
41	70% Perc =	250	375	500	437.5	375
42	75% Perc =	250	375	500	437.5	375
43	80% Perc =	250	375	500	437.5	375
44	85% Perc =	250	375	500	625	562.5
45	90% Perc =	250	375	500	625	562.5
46	95% Perc =	250	375	500	625	750

From Figure 27.2 we find that Average profit for 1000 trials when 200 calendars are ordered, for example, is $350.00. Standard deviation for 1000 trials is $163.46. It appears that ordering 200 calendars maximizes expected profit but a case can be made for ordering 150 calendars. For 10% less expected profit we can cut risk in half. The decision here depends on the store's aversion to risk.

Remarks

- The =RISKSimTable function uses the same set of random numbers to generate demand for each simulation. This means you can be sure that for each order quantity the profit keys off the same set of demands.

- You can return to the Results at any time by selecting the Results Icon.

- You can return to your worksheet from Results by selecting the Hide icon.

Finding Confidence Interval for Expected Profit

If we ran 1000 more trials @RISK would generate a different set of profits[1] and we would get a different estimate of average profit. So we do not learn average profit exactly from any simulation. How accurate is our estimate of average profit?

We can be 95% sure that average or expected profit for 200 calendars is between

(Mean Profit) ±2(Mean Standard Error).

Here:

Mean Standard Error = (Standard Deviation)/$\sqrt{iterations}$ =163.46/$\sqrt{1000}$)= 5.17.

Thus we are 95% sure expected profit is between

350 ± 2(163.46) /$\sqrt{1000}$ or $339.41 and $361.09.

If we wanted to be 95% sure we were accurate in estimating mean within $1 how many iterations are needed? The required number of iterations must satisfy

$2(163.46)/\sqrt{iterations}$ = 1 or iterations = 326.92^2 = 106,877!

We find that to achieve a precise estimate of expected profit requires many iterations!

If we desire a histogram of profits we may go up to Summary section of statistics and click on simulation #3. Selecting Graph will show a histogram.

---

[1] When the seed is set (from *Simulation Settings Sampling*) to 0, each time you run a simulation you will obtain different results. Other possible seed values are integers between 1 and 32,767. Whenever a non-zero seed is chosen the same values for the Input cells and Output cells will occur. For example, if we choose a seed value of , say, 10, then each time we run the simulation we will obtain **exactly the same results.**

Normal Demand

The assumption of discrete demand is unrealistic. Let's suppose demand is normal with a mean of 200 and standard deviation of 30. Then we are 68% sure demand is between 170 and 230, 95% sure demand is between 140 and 270, etc. To model normal demand simply change cell C2's formula to

=RISKNormal(200,30).

This implies, for example, by the well-known rule of thumb that 68% of the time demand will be between 170 and 230, 95% of the time demand will be between 140 and 260, and 99.7% of the time demand will be between 110 and 290.

Now any order quantity is reasonable, because demand may assume any value. We will still try the same set of order quantities, however. After running the simulation we obtain the following output:

Figure 27.3

	A	B	C	D	E	F
2	Name	Profit	Profit	Profit	Profit	Profit
3	Description	Output (Sim#1)	Output (Sim#2)	Output (Sim#3)	Output (Sim#4)	Output (Sim#5)
4	Cell	B10	B10	B10	B10	B10
5	Minimum =	235.9069	173.4069	110.9069	48.40687	-14.09313
6	Maximum =	250	375	500	625	750
7	Mean =	249.9859	372.7725	455.1196	435.2706	374.9961
8	Std Deviati	0.4454408	13.49851	65.67989	107.8357	112.4788
9	Variance =	0.1984175	182.2099	4313.848	11628.55	12651.47
10	Skewness =	-31.57532	-8.297598	-1.641624	-0.2265632	-2.53E-03
11	Kurtosis =	998.001	86.59334	5.415291	2.666282	2.990458
12	Errors Calcu	0	0	0	0	0
13	Mode =	250	375	500	625	384.8997
14	5% Perc =	250	375	314.5227	252.0227	189.5227
15	10% Perc =	250	375	355.2183	292.7183	230.2183
16	15% Perc =	250	375	383.788	321.288	258.1671
17	20% Perc =	250	375	405.0159	342.5159	280.0159
18	25% Perc =	250	375	423.7977	361.2977	298.7977
19	30% Perc =	250	375	441.2536	378.7536	315.795
20	35% Perc =	250	375	456.6783	394.1783	331.5533
21	40% Perc =	250	375	471.21	408.71	346.21
22	45% Perc =	250	375	485.6556	423.1556	360.6556
23	50% Perc =	250	375	499.7182	437.2182	374.7182
24	55% Perc =	250	375	500	451.4981	388.9981
25	60% Perc =	250	375	500	466.1211	403.2894
26	65% Perc =	250	375	500	480.7075	418.2075
27	70% Perc =	250	375	500	496.5688	433.6845
28	75% Perc =	250	375	500	513.3702	450.8702
29	80% Perc =	250	375	500	531.818	469.318
30	85% Perc =	250	375	500	554.44	491.3938
31	90% Perc =	250	375	500	581.2737	518.7737
32	95% Perc =	250	375	500	623.2046	559.4641
33	Target #1 (Value)=			400		
34	Target #1 (Perc%)=			18.70%		
35	Target #2 (Value)=			500		
36	Target #2 (Perc%)=			100%		
37	Target #3 (Value)=			453.4243164		
38	Target #3 (Perc%)=			34%		
39	Target #4 (Value)=			360		
40	Target #4 (Perc%)=			10.60%		

From Figure 27.3 we find that ordering 200 calendars yields a higher mean profit than 100, 150, 250, or 300 calendars. Plotting the expected profit for each order quantity yields the following graph:

Figure 27.4

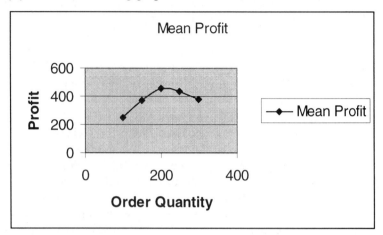

Under the assumption that profit is a unimodal function of order quantity (this is indeed correct), figure 27.4 tells us that expected profit is maximized by ordering between 150 and 250 calendars. Another =RISKSimTable (with values 160, 170, 180, 190, 200, 210, 220, 230, 240, 250) would help zero in on actual best order quantity (which turns out to be 213 calendars).

Remarks

If you are worried about the demand for calendars being a fraction you could change the formula in cell C2 to

$=Round(RISKNormal(200,30),0).$

This ensures that each demand generated by the =RISKNormal function is rounded to the nearest integer.

Target Functions

At the bottom of statistical output we may enter targets as values or percentages. Enter a value and @RISK tells you fraction of iterations for which output cell was less than or equal to target. For example, we entered 400 in D33 and found profit for ordering 200 calendars was less than or equal to $400 18.7% of time. We entered a 34% in D38 and found 34% of time profit was less than or equal to $453.42. In D36 we entered 99% and found 99% of time profit was less than or equal to $500. In D39 we entered $360 and found profit was less than or equal to $360 10.6% of time.

Histogram

Figure 27.5 is our histogram for expected profit when 200 calendars is ordered. To obtain a histogram for profit when 200 calendars are ordered go the Summary portion of the Results and select the third simulation (corresponding to 200 calendars). Then select Graph and right click to obtain Format. You may then choose a graph type from the following menu. After selecting histogram we obtain Figure 27.5. An area graph replaces bars with smooth areas. A fitted curve smooths out the variation in bar heights before creating an area graph.

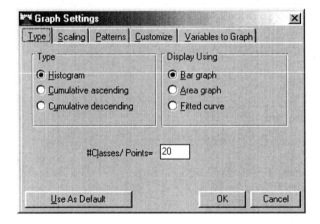

Figure 27.5

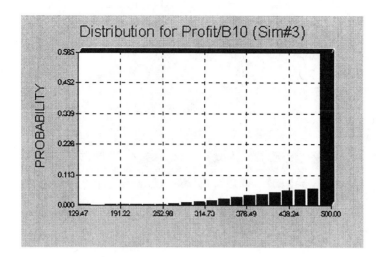

Distribution for Profit/B10 (Sim#3)

The big spike at 500 corresponds to any demand >=500.

If we right click on a selected graph and choose Format followed by Cumulative Ascending we obtain the following cumulative **ascending graph:**

Figure 27.6

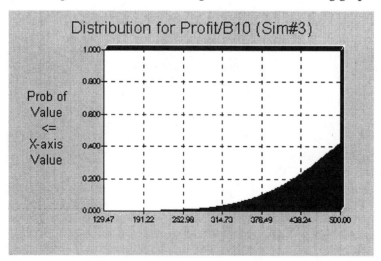

Distribution for Profit/B10 (Sim#3)

For instance, Figure 27.6 gives on (Y-axis) probability that profit is less than or equal to x-value. Thus there is around a 19% chance that profit is <=$400.

By right-clicking on the histogram or cumulative descending graph and selecting Format we can obtain a **cumulative descending graph.** In a cumulative descending graph the Y-coordinate is probability profit exceeds x -coordinate. For example, there is around an 81% probability that profit will exceed $400.

Figure 27.7

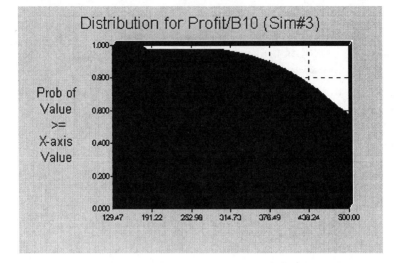

Distribution for Profit/B10 (Sim#3)

Chapter 28: Simulating a New Product The Hippo Example

When a company develops a new product, the profitability of the product is highly uncertain. Simulation is an excellent tool to estimate the average profitability and riskiness of new products. The following example illustrates how simulation can be used to evaluate a new product.

Example 28.1

ZooCo is thinking of marketing a new drug used to make hippos healthier. At the beginning of the current year there are 1,000,000 hippos that may use the product. Each hippo will use the drug (or a competitor's drug) at most once a year. The number of hippos is forecasted to grow by an average of 5% per year, and we are 95% sure that the number of hippos will grow each year by between 3% and 7%. We are not sure what use of the drug will be during year 1, but our worst case guess is 20% use, most likely use is 40% and best case use is 70%. In later years, we feel the fraction of hippos using our drug (or a competitor's) will remain the same, but in the year after a competitor enters, we lose 20% of our share for each competitor who enters. We will model Year 1 market use with a **triangular random variable**. See Figure 28.1. Basically, @RISK will generate Year 1 market use by making the likelihood of a given market use proportional to the height of the "triangle" in Figure 28.1. Thus a 40% Year 1 market use is most likely; a 30% market use occurs half as often as a Year 1 40% market use, etc. The maximum height of the triangle is 4, because that makes the total area under the triangle equal to one. Probability of market use being in a given range is equal to area in that range under the triangle. For example, the chance of a market use being at most 40% is .5*(4)*(.4-.2) =.4 or 40%.

Figure 28.1

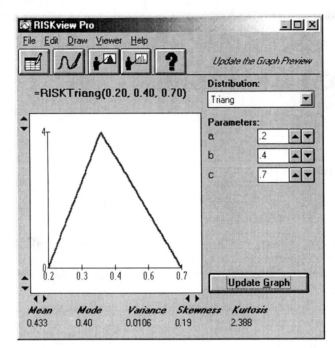

Figure 28.1

There are three potential entrants (in addition to ZooCo). At the beginning of each year each entrant who has not already entered the market has a 40% chance of entering the market. The year after a competitor enters, our market use drops by 20% for each competitor who entered. Thus if in Year 1 two competitors enter the market, in Year 2 our market use will be reduced by 40%. To model the number of entrants you can use the **binomial random variable** (in @RISK this requires us to use the =RISKBinomial function). The formula

$$= RISKBinomial\ (n, p)$$

generates n independent binomial trials (each a success or failure) having probability of success p and keeps track of the number of successes.

We consider a "success" to be a competitor entering the market. Then the formula

$$= RISKBinomial\ (2,.4)$$

will simulate the number of entrants during a year in which two competitors have yet to enter the market. Make sure that if all three entrants have entered, no more entrants may enter.

Each unit of the drug is sold for $2.20 and incurs a variable cost of $0.40. Profits are discounted by 10% (risk adjusted rate) annually. Find a 95% CI for risk-adjusted NPV of project. For now we ignore the fixed cost of developing the drug.

Recall that **risk-adjusted** NPV is expected discounted value of cash flows (discounted at risk-adjusted rate).

Solution

Our spreadsheet is in Figure 28.2 (*file hippo.xls*).

Figure 28.2

	A	B	C	D	E	F
1	Pigco					
2	Price	$ 2.20	Compet %age	0.2		
3	Unit Var Cost	$ 0.40	Year 1 Market S	1000000		
4	Interest Rate	0.1	Year 1 worst sha	0.2		
5	Entrant Prob	0.4	Year 1 most like	0.4		
6			Year 1 best shar	0.7		
7	Year	1	2	3	4	5
8	Market Size	1000000	1050000	1102500	1157625	1215506.25
9	Use per hippo of our drug	0.433333333	0.346666667	0.277333333	0.277333333	0.277333333
10	Competitors (beginning of year)	0	1	2	2	2
11	Entrants	1	1	0	0	0
12	Unit Sales	433333.3333	364000	305760	321048	337100.4
13	Revenues	$ 953,333	$ 800,800	$ 672,672	$ 706,306	$ 741,621
14	Costs	$ 173,333	$ 145,600	$ 122,304	$ 128,419	$ 134,840
15	Profits	$ 780,000	$ 655,200	$ 550,368	$ 577,886	$ 606,781
16						
17	NPV	$2,435,545				

Step by Step

Step 1: **In row 8 we determine the market size during each of the next five years.** In B8 we enter =D3. Assuming year to year growth in market size is normally distributed, the given information tells us that the number of pigs grows from year to year by a percentage which is a normal random variable having mean .05 and standard deviation of .01. This follows because 95% of the time a normal random variable is within 2 standard deviations of its mean. Therefore we may conclude 2σ = .02 or σ = .01.Thus in C8 we determine the Year 2 Market Size with the formula

=B8*RISKNormal(1.05,0.01).

Essentially, this formula ensures that each year there is a 68% chance that the size of the hippo market grows by between 4% and 6%, a 95% chance that the hippo market grows by between 3% and 7%, and a 99.7% chance that the hippo market grows by between 2% and 8%.

Copying this formula to D8:F8 generates the market size for Years 3-5.

Step 2: In row 9 we determine our market use/hippo for each year. Year 1 market use/hippo is computed in B9 with the formula

=RISKTriang (D4,D5,D6).

In C9:F9 we account for the fact that the year after entry, each entrant takes away 20% of our market share. Thus in C9 we compute our Year 2 Market use/hippo with the formula

= B9*(1-B11*$D$2).

Copying this formula to D9:F9 computes Years 3-5 market share.

Step 3: In Row 11 we determine the number of entrants during each year. If less than 3 competitors have entered, then each competitor who has not yet entered has a 40% chance of entering during the current year. If all three competitors have entered, then nobody can enter. In B11 we compute the number of Year 1 entrants with the formula

=If(B10<3, RISKBinomial(3-B10,$B$5),0).

Copying this to C11:F11 computes Years 2-5 entrants. If we do not use the =If statement then in a year after all 3 competitors have entered we will obtain an error message because =RISKBinomial cannot take 0 trials as the first argument.

Step 4: In Row 10 we compute the number of competitors present at the beginning of each Year by adding the number of new entrants to the number of competitors already present. In B10 we enter 0 and in C10 we enter

= B10 + B11.

Copying this formula to D10:F10 computes the number of competitors present at the beginning of each year.

Step 5: In row 12 we compute each year's unit sales = (use/hippo)*market size by copying the formula

= B8*B9

from B12 to C12:F12.

Step 6: In row 13 we compute our annual revenues by copying the formula

=$B$2*B12

from B13 to C13:F13.

Step 7: In row 14 we compute our annual variable costs by copying the formula

$$= \$B\$3*B12$$

from B14 to C14:F14.

Step 8: In row 15 we compute our annual profits by copying the formula

$$=B13-B14$$

from B15 to C15:F15.

Step 9: In B17 we compute the NPV of our 5-year profits with the formula

$$= NPV(B4,B15:F15).$$

Step 10: We now run a simulation with cell B17 (NPV) being our forecast cell. We used 500 trials. Our results follow.

Figure 28.3

	A	B
11	Name	NPV
12	Description	Output
13	Cell	B17
14	Minimum =	988749.5
15	Maximum =	4015476
16	Mean =	2301306
17	Std Deviation =	608755.1
18	Variance =	3.71E+11
19	Skewness =	0.4618648
20	Kurtosis =	2.776877
21	Errors Calculated =	0
22	Mode =	2283678
23	5% Perc =	1427195
24	10% Perc =	1571080
25	15% Perc =	1679758
26	20% Perc =	1766477
27	25% Perc =	1833494
28	30% Perc =	1922268
29	35% Perc =	2006219
30	40% Perc =	2072047
31	45% Perc =	2145033
32	50% Perc =	2214913
33	55% Perc =	2285939
34	60% Perc =	2413161
35	65% Perc =	2481320
36	70% Perc =	2593680
37	75% Perc =	2716010
38	80% Perc =	2834188
39	85% Perc =	2970997
40	90% Perc =	3132428
41	95% Perc =	3423116
42	Target #1 (Value)=	1312289.125
43	Target #1 (Perc%)=	2.50%
44	Target #2 (Value)=	3647925.25
45	Target #2 (Perc%)=	97.50%

Our point estimate of risk adjusted NPV is the sample mean of NPV's from simulation ($2,301,306). To find a 95% confidence interval for the mean in a simulation use fact that we are 95% sure actual mean NPV is between

(Sample Mean of NPV)±2*(Sample Standard deviation)/$\sqrt{n}$,

where n = number of iterations.

For example, we are 95% sure the mean NPV (or risk adjusted NPV) is between

2,301,306±2*(608755)/$\sqrt{500}$ or

$2,246,857 and $2,355,755.

Thus we are pretty sure risk adjusted NPV is between 2.25 and 2.35 million. Since 95% of the time we are accurate within $50,000 (which is 2% of sample mean) we feel comfortable that we have run enough iterations.

The **actual** discounted (at 10% rate) value of cash flows has much more variability than our confidence interval for risk-adjusted NPV would indicate. To show this look at the following histogram.

Figure 28.4

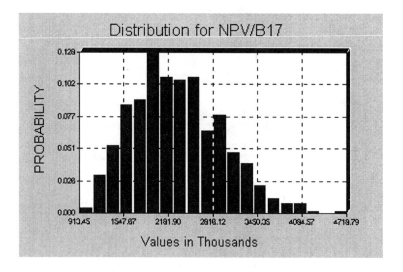

Note: If you are going to use distribution of NPV's as a tool to compare projects, then you must discount all the company's projects at the same rate (probably obtained from CAPM). Otherwise you will be double counting risk.

Tornado Graphs and Scenarios

A natural question is what factors have the most influence on the success of the project? Does market growth matter more than the timing of the entrance of competitors? Using @RISK Tornado graphs and Scenario Analysis we can easily answer questions such as:

a. What factors appear to have the most influence on the NPV earned by the drug?

b. When NPV is in the top 10%ile of all possible NPV, what seems to be going on?

Solution - Part a

Here we utilize a **Tornado Graph**. Make sure that in *"Simulation Settings"* you have checked *"Collect Distribution Samples"*. Then from the *"Results"* menu you obtain a Tornado graph by clicking on *"Sensitivity"* and then *"Graph"*. You have two options: A Regression Tornado Graph (See Figure 28.5) or a Correlation Tornado Graph (see Figure 28.6)

Figure 28.5

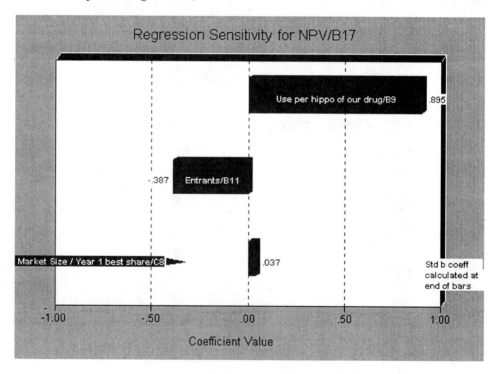

We find (ceteris paribus) from Regression Tornado Graph (obtained by checking *"Regression"* after choosing *"Graph"*) that

- A one standard deviation increase in Year 1 use increases NPV by .895 standard deviations.

- A one standard deviation increase in number of Year 1 entrants decreases NPV by .387 standard deviations.

- Not much else matters!

Basically, when running a Tornado Graph @RISK runs a regression where each iteration represents an observation. The dependent variable is the output cell (NPV) and the independent variables are each "random" @RISK function in the spreadsheet. Then the .895 coefficient for Year 1 use is the standardized, or beta weight coefficient of Year 1 Use in this regression.

Figure 28.6

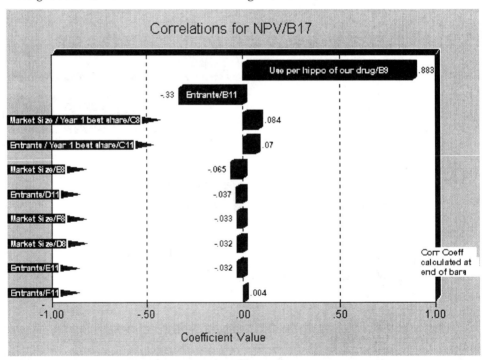

From Tornado Correlation Graph in Figure 28.6 (obtained by checking Correlation box on Graph) we find

- Year 1 use is most highly correlated (.88) with NPV

- Next is Year 1 Entrants (-.33)

- Rest of the random cells in the spreadsheet do not matter much!

These correlations are **rank correlations**; for example, for all iterations the values of Year 1 use are ranked, as are values of NPV. Then these **ranks** (not actual values) are correlated.

Solution - Part b

If you check *"Collect Distribution Samples"* under Settings you can obtain a **Scenario Analysis**. For a given scenario, such as all iterations where NPV is in top 10% of all iterations the Scenario Analysis identifies random variables whose values differ significantly from their median values.[1]

We find from Scenario Approach (see Figure 28.8) (click on Scenario and highlight the scenario of interest) that in the iterations yielding the top 10% of all NPV's the following variables differ significantly from their overall medians:

- Year 1 Use (median is .59, 1.61 sigma above average)

- Year 3 entrants (median is 0, 1.32 sigma below average)

To change the scenario settings just go to bottom of Statistics section of results. Figure 28.9 contains a listing of two Scenario settings (the bottom 25% of NPV's and Top 10% of NPV's) along with the random variables that differ significantly from their average values when the given scenario occurs. For example, for iterations in which the NPV is in the bottom 25% of all iterations, Year 1 Market Use averaged out to 31%.

Figure 28.8

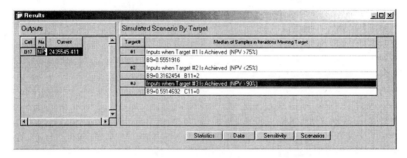

Figure 28.9

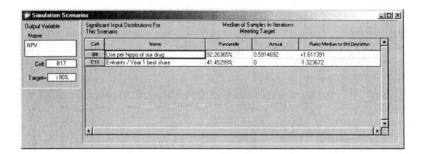

---

[1] @RISK will identify any random variable whose median value in iterations satisfying the scenario condition differs by more than .5 standard deviations from the median value of the random variable in all iterations.

Chapter 29: Using @RISK to Determine Plant Capacity

Again, we consider the Hippo problem (Example 28.1). How can @RISK be used to determine capacity level which maximizes expected NPV? Suppose it costs $3.50 to build one unit of annual capacity and $0.30 per year to operate one unit of capacity (whether or not we use the capacity to produce the drug). What capacity level maximizes risk adjusted NPV?

Solution   Our work is in Figure 29.1 (file *hippocap.xls*).

Figure 29.1

	A	B	C	D	E	F
1	**Pigco**		Capacity	100000	Unit op cost	0.3
2	Price	$ 2.20	Compet %age	0.2	Unit Building cos	3.5
3	Unit Var Cost	$ 0.40	Year 1 Market S	1000000		
4	Interest Rate	0.1	Year 1 worst sha	0.2		
5	Entrant Prob	0.4	Year 1 most like	0.4		
6			Year 1 best shar	0.7		
7	Year	1	2	3	4	5
8	Market Size	1000000	1050000	1102500	1157625	1215506.25
9	Market use per hippo	0.433333333	0.346666667	0.277333333	0.277333333	0.277333333
10	Competitors(beginning of year)	0	1	2	2	2
11	Entrants	1	1	0	0	0
12	Unit Sales	100000	100000	100000	100000	100000
13	Revenues	$ 220,000	$ 220,000	$ 220,000	$ 220,000	$ 220,000
14	Costs	$ 40,000	$ 40,000	$ 40,000	$ 40,000	$ 40,000
15	Building cost	$ 350,000				
16	Fixed op cost	$ 30,000	$ 30,000	$ 30,000	$ 30,000	$ 30,000
17	Profits	$ (200,000)	$ 150,000	$ 150,000	$ 150,000	$ 150,000
18						
19	NPV	$250,436				

We proceed as follows:

Step by Step

Step 1: Enter the cost information for capacity in F1 and F2.

Step 2: We will try capacity levels from 100,000 to 500,000, in increments of 50,000. We do this by using the =RISKSimTable function. In cell D1 we enter the formula

=RISKSimTable({100000,150000,200000,250000,300000,350000,400000,450000,500000}).

This ensures that our first simulation will use a capacity of 100,000 per year, our second simulation a capacity of 150,000 per year, etc.

Step 3: In row 12 we adjust unit sales to account for the fact that sales cannot exceed capacity. In cell B12 we compute Year 1 units sales with the formula

$$= MIN(\$D\$1,B8*B9).$$

Copying this formula across to F12 generates sales for Years 2-5.

Step 4: Insert two rows beneath row 14. In cell B15 compute building costs (incurred in year 1) with the formula

$$= \$F\$2*\$D\$1.$$

In cell B16 compute the fixed operating cost for Year 1 with the formula

$$=\$D\$1*\$F\$1.$$

Copying this formula to the range C16:F16 computes fixed operating costs for the remaining four years.

Step 5: Modify year 1 profits in B17 to account for building and fixed operating costs by entering the formula

$$=B13-B14-B15-B16.$$

Copying this formula to C17:F17 correctly computes the profits from the remaining years.

Step 6: Selecting our NPV (cell B19) as an output cell yields the following results:

Figure 29.2

	B	C	D	E	F	G	H	I	J	K
71	Capacity	100000	150000	200000	250000	300000	350000	400000	450000	500000
72	Minimum =	219263.3	85911.42	-48223.11	-248570.9	-464523.6	-680476.3	-896429.1	-1112382	-1328335
73	Maximum =	250436.2	375654.3	500872.4	626090.5	751308.6	876526.7	1001745	1126963	1252181
74	Mean =	250373.9	373182.9	477316.3	541867.3	552989.9	505917.4	407592.3	268525.3	99459.52
75	Std Deviation =	1392.699	16660.4	65496.81	144756.3	240162.2	336882.6	425744.8	499450.7	554519.7

We find that a capacity level of 300,000 maximizes risk-adjusted NPV.

Chapter 30: Utility Theory and Simulation

The best way to make a decision under uncertainty is to choose the decision that yields the largest expected utility. Again we consider the Hippo example (Example 28.1). We now assume that the 10% interest rate is the risk-free rate. To assess a decision-maker's utility function with respect to the NPV of the Hippo project we proceed as follows:

- Identify a worst possible outcome (say a negative NPV of $2,000,000) and assign it a utility of 0.

- Identify a best possible outcome (say an NPV of $10,000,000) and assign it a utility of 1.

- Ask yourself the following question: What amount (x) for certain makes you indifferent between receiving x and the following lottery: 50% chance at best and 50% chance at worst outcome. My answer was $1 million. If we let $U(x)$ be utility associated with NPV of x we now know that

  $U(1) = .5*U(10) + .5U(-2)$ or

  $U(1) = .5.$

- Now ask what amount y makes you indifferent between receiving y for certain and the following lottery: a 50% chance at 1 million NPV and a 50% chance at - 2 million NPV. Suppose your answer is -1.2 million. Then we know

  $U(-1.2) = .5U(-2) + .5U(1) = .25.$

  Thus $U(-1.2) = .25.$

- Now ask what NPV z makes you indifferent between receiving z for certain and the following lottery: 50% chance at 10 million and 50% chance at 1 million. Suppose your answer is 2.6 million. Then

  $U(2.6) = .5U(10) + .5U(1) = .75.$

Thus $U(2.6) = .75$. We now have five points on our **utility curve**.

X	U(x)
-2	0
-1.2	.25
1	.5
2.6	.75
10	1

Fitting the Utility Curve

In the sheet utility of file *Hippocap.xls* will fit a curve of the form $U(x) = ae^{-x/b} + c$ to the five points on our utility curve. This is the commonly used **exponential utility function**. This utility curve is often used to model **risk-averse** decision makers. A risk-averse decision maker always places a value on an uncertain situation which is smaller than the situation's expected value. For each capacity option we will find the **average utility of the earned NPV, and choose the capacity level that maximizes average utility.**

Figure 30.1

	A	B	C	D	E	F
1				a	b	c
2	u(x)=a*e^{-x/b}+c			-0.64313	4.172671	1.061115
3	x	actual	Predicted	Sq Err		
4	-2	0	0.022486	0.000506		
5	-1.2	0.25	0.20369	0.002145		
6	1	0.5	0.555036	0.003029		
7	2.6	0.75	0.716218	0.001141		
8	10	1	1.002569	6.6E-06		
9			SSE	0.006827		

Step by Step

Step 1: We begin by putting arbitrary values for a b and c in D2:F2 and assigning range names a, b, and c_ to those cells.

Step 2: Enter the five points on the curve in the range A3:B8.

Step 3: In C4 generate a predicted utility with the formula

$=a*EXP(-A4/b)+c\_.$

Copying this formula to the range C5:C8 generates predictions for the other 4 points on the curve.

Step 4: In column D we compute squared errors for each point on the utility curve by squaring the difference between actual and predicted utility. For the first point compute the squared error by entering

$=(B4-C4)^2$

in D4. Copying this formula to D5:D8 computes the squared error for the other four points on the utility curve. In D9 we compute the total squared error for all five points with the formula

$=SUM(D4:D8).$

Step 5: Now we use Solver to find the a, b and c that best fit the curve. Our Solver window follows:

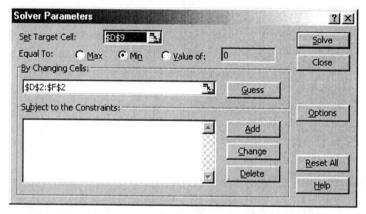

We simply choose a, b, and c to minimize the sum of squared errors (D9). We find our fitted utility curve to be

$$U(x) = -.643e^{-x/4.173} + 1.06.$$

The quality of our fitted utility curve can be seen in Figure 30.2.

Figure 30.2

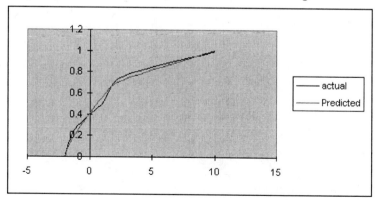

Simulating the Capacity Decision

We now choose the utility associated with profit to be our simulation output cell. In cell B20 we compute the profit associated with our (risk-free) NPV with the formula

$$=-0.643*EXP(-(B19/1000000)/4.173)+1.06.$$

We now make B20 our output cell and obtain the following result:

Figure 30.3

	A	B
18		
19	NPV	$250,436
20	Utility	0.45445356

Figure 30.4

B	C	D	E	F
34 Cell	Name	Minimum	Mean	Maximum
35 100000	Utility	0.4544536	0.4544536	0.4544536
36 150000	Utility	46.77%	0.4722686	0.4723541
37 200000	Utility	0.4560944	0.4872237	0.4897255
38 250000	Utility	0.4363675	0.4957014	0.5065834
39 300000	Utility	0.4106576	0.4949651	0.522943
40 350000	Utility	0.3761694	0.4872732	0.5388189
41 400000	Utility	0.3398495	0.4724004	0.5542255
42 450000	Utility	0.3016006	0.45112	0.5691767
43 500000	Utility	0.2613201	0.4250819	0.5836859

It appears that a capacity level of 250,000 maximizes expected utility. Note that a capacity level of 300,000 maximized expected NPV. The risk-averse nature of our utility function caused us to reduce capacity!

Finding the Certainty Equivalent of the Optimal Decision

We have found that expected utility is maximized with a capacity level of 250,000. A natural question is what NPV (received with certainty) would be just as desirable as the uncertain situation we face when we build 250,000 units of capacity? This is called the **certainty equivalent** of the uncertain situation. In the sheet Utility of the file *hippocap.xls* we found the certainty equivalent of the five years of drug production as follows (see Figure 29.5):

Step by Step
Step 1: Enter the expected utility of the simulation for 250,000 capacity in cell E21.

Step 2: Enter in F21 a trial value for the certainty equivalent.

Step 3: Compute in G21 the utility of the trial certainty equivalent with the formula

$$=a*EXP(-F21/b)+c\_.$$

Step 4: Go to Tools>Options>Calculations and change precision to .00000001. This will ensure that Goal Seek will accurately find the certainty equivalent.

Step 5: Set up Goal Seek to find the certainty equivalent (in F21) which makes G21 equal to the expected utility of 250,000 Capacity (.495701).

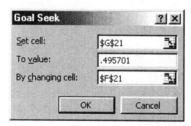

We find the certainty equivalent of 250,000 capacity to be $537,397. Note this is slightly less than the expected NPV of 250,000 capacity ($541,867). Since our utility function exhibits risk aversion, it is only natural that we value a capacity level of 250,000 at an amount less than its expected NPV.

Figure 30.5

	E	F	G
20	Expected Utility of best capacity level	x	u(x)
21	0.495701	0.537397	0.495701

Remarks

Another commonly used utility function is the **power function** $U(x) = a + bx^c$. When in doubt try the power and exponential function and select the utility function that yields the smaller SSE.

Chapter 31: Simulating Development of a New Drug

The pharmaceutical business deals with a very high degree of uncertainty. Over 90% of all products under development fail to come to market resulting in large losses. Products that do come to market (like Viagra and Prozac) can earn multibillion profits annually for 10-15 years (until their patent expires). @RISK is a natural tool to use in an effort to estimate whether a new product is worth developing.

Example 31.1

Eli Daisy wants to determine whether a new drug, Niagara, is worth developing. Before coming to market Niagara must go through the following stages of development:

- Initial R and D (Research and Development)

- Preclinical Testing

- Testing I (first phase of clinical trials)

- Testing II (2nd phase of clinical trials)

Only after all development stages succeed can the drug be sold. If the drug fails at any stage, then development is terminated. A success at any stage leads us to pursue the next stage. We want to determine the risk adjusted NPV from this drug (15% discount rate per year is used) and get an idea of the key drivers of the drug's profitability. We will use the triangular random variable for our modeling. For each stage we will model the cost, probability of success and time required to complete the stage with a triangular random variable. We will also model the profit earned from the drug with a triangular random variable. Our model is in the file *Drugsim.xls*. The inputs for our triangular random variables are given in Figure 31.1 (costs and revenues are in millions of dollars).

Figure 31.1

	B	C	D	E
3				
4	**initial r and d**		**testing I**	
5	cost	80	cost	476.66667
6	best	50	best	350
7	worst	120	worst	600
8	most likely	70	most likely	480
9	**time**	4.666667	**time**	4.3333333
10	best	3	best	3
11	worst	7	worst	6
12	most likely	4	most likely	4
13	**preclinical testing**		**testing II**	
14	cost	18.33333	cost	4566.6667
15	best	10	best	3500
16	worst	30	worst	6000
17	most likely	15	most likely	4200
18	**time**	1.5	**time**	4.3333333
19	best	0.5	best	3
20	worst	3	worst	6
21	most likely	1	most likely	4
22			**profit**	30666.667
23			best	60000
24			worst	14000
25			most likely	18000

	F	G	H	I	J	K
3						
4	**stage**	**succeed?**	Prob of success	worst	most likely	best
5	initial r and d	0	0.323333333	0.2	0.35	0.42
6	preclinical testing	0	0.466666667	0.3	0.5	0.6
7	testing I	1	0.5	0.4	0.5	0.6
8	testing II	1	0.853333333	0.7	0.9	0.96

For example, Preclinical testing will in the best case cost $10 million, worst case $30 million, and most likely case $15 million. In the best case Preclinical testing will require .5 years, most likely case 1 year, and worst case 3 years. In the best case scenario Preclinical testing has a .6 chance of success, in the most likely scenario Preclinical testing has a .5 chance of success, and in the worst case scenario Preclinical testing has a .3 chance of success. We are assuming these random variables are independent. For example, the independence assumption implies high development costs do not influence either chance of success or time needed to complete Preclinical trials. If you do not believe the independence assumption then you can model dependence with the =RISKCorrMat function (see Chapter 47). We now show how to determine the cash flows and NPV of the project.

Figure 31.2

	L	M	N	O
2	Interest rate	0.15		
3				
4	**stage**	Cash flow	Time	DCF
5	r and d	-80	0	-80
6	preclinical testing	0	4.666667	0
7	testing I	0	6.166667	0
8	testing II	0	10.5	0
9	Profit!	0	14.83333	0
10	Total DCF			-80

Step by Step

Step 1: In C5 we compute the actual cost of Initial R and D by entering the formula

=*RISKTriang(C6,C8,C7).*

Copying this formula to C9, C14, C18, E5, E9, E14, and E18 generates costs and duration of other stages of the drug development process.

Also, in H5:H8 we generate the probability of success for each stage by copying from H5 to H6:H8 the formula

=*RISKTriang(I5,J5,K5).*

Step 2: In G5:G8 we determine, assuming we have gotten to a stage, whether a given stage will succeed. To do this simply copy the formula

=*RISKBinomial(1,H5)*

from G5 to G5:G8.

Step 3: In M5:M9 we determine all possible cash flows. Even if R and D fails, we must pay for it, so in M5 we compute R and D cash flow with formula

= *C5.*

We incur Preclinical testing costs if and only if R and D is successful. Therefore in M6 we compute cash flows from Preclinical testing with the formula

=*If(G5=1,-C14,0).*

We incur Testing I cost if and only if R and D and Preclinical trials both succeed. Therefore in M7 we compute cash flows from Testing I cost with the formula

=*If(G5*G6=1,-E5,0).*

We incur Testing II cost if and only if R and D, Preclinical trials, and Testing I all succeed. Therefore in M8 we compute cash flows from Testing II cost with the formula

$= If(G5*G6*G7=1,-E14,0).$

Finally, we earn profit if and only if all stages of the project succeed. Therefore in M9 we compute profit from drug (excluding development costs) with the formula

$= If(G5*G6*G7*G8=1,E22,0).$

Step 4: In N5:N9 we compute the time at which the cash flows in M5:M9 are received. Simply enter the following formulas

Cell	Formula
N	=0
N6	=N5 + C9
N7	=N6 + C18
N8	=N7 + E9
N9	=N8 + E18

For example, Profit will be earned at (Time when Testing I is completed) +(Time to Complete Testing II).

Step 5: In O5:O9 we compute the discounted value of each cash flow by copying the formula

$=M5/(1+\$M\$2)\wedge N5$

from O5 to O6:O9.

Step 6: In Cell O10 we compute the total NPV of the project with the formula

$=SUM(O5:O9).$

Step 7: We select Cell O10 as our output cell and run 900 iterations. Since we desire tornado graphs, we go into *"Simulation Settings"* and check *"Collect Distribution Samples"*. We obtain the output in Figure 31.3:

Figure 31.3

	D	E	F	G
36	Name	Total DCF / DCF		
37	Description	Output		
38	Cell	O10		
39	Minimum =	-1580.556		
40	Maximum =	6623.446	95% CI	
41	Mean =	72.80399	Lower	19.66381
42	Std Deviatic	797.1027	Upper	125.94417
43	Variance =	635372.6		
44	Skewness =	4.592729		
45	Kurtosis =	26.55617		
46	Errors Calc	0		
47	Mode =	-68.77261		
48	5% Perc =	-289.2545		
49	10% Perc =	-115.693		
50	15% Perc =	-106.549		
51	20% Perc =	-100.4727		
52	25% Perc =	-96.12266		
53	30% Perc =	-91.62334		
54	35% Perc =	-88.46071		
55	40% Perc =	-85.80322		
56	45% Perc =	-83.22971		
57	50% Perc =	-80.78676		
58	55% Perc =	-78.2244		
59	60% Perc =	-75.7506		
60	65% Perc =	-73.49867		
61	70% Perc =	-71.2056		
62	75% Perc =	-68.6027		
63	80% Perc =	-65.65778		
64	85% Perc =	-62.54356		
65	90% Perc =	-57.80053		
66	95% Perc =	1427.246		

Thus we are 95% sure that the expected NPV from the drug (often called the risk-adjusted NPV) is between $20 and $125 million. The large width of this interval indicates that many more iterations are needed to obtain an accurate estimate of the project's risk adjusted NPV. Note that over 90% time the drug has negative NPV. By the way, the probability of a project yielding a return exceeding the risk-adjusted rate is equal to the probability that the NPV (at risk adjusted rate) is positive.

Interpreting the Tornado Graphs

The regression tornado graph (Figure 31.4) tells us the following:

Figure 31.4

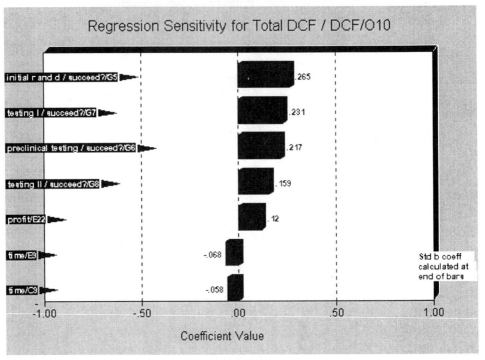

After adjusting for all other random cells in the spreadsheet (*ceteris paribus)*

- A one standard deviation increase in initial R and D success results in a .265 standard deviation increase in NPV.

- A one standard deviation increase in Testing I success results in a .231 standard deviation increase in NPV.

- A one standard deviation increase in Preclinical testing success results in a .217 standard deviation increase in NPV.

- A one standard deviation increase in Testing II success results in a .159 standard deviation increase in NPV.

- A one standard deviation in profit results in a .12 standard deviation increase in NPV.

- A one standard deviation increase in Testing I time results in a .068 standard deviation decrease in NPV.

- A one standard deviation increase in Initial R and D time results in a .058 standard deviation decrease in NPV.

Admittedly it is difficult to interpret a "one standard deviation increase" for a random variable that is always 0 or 1, but that is all @RISK gives us.

Alternatively, we can look at the correlation Tornado graph. For a given random cell in the spreadsheet @RISK ranks the values of this cell for each iteration (the largest value receives a rank of 1, the smallest value a rank of 900). @ RISK then ranks the NPV values for each iteration, and finds the correlation between the ranks of the random cell and NPV. For example, the correlation tornado graph in Figure 31.5 tells us

Figure 31.5

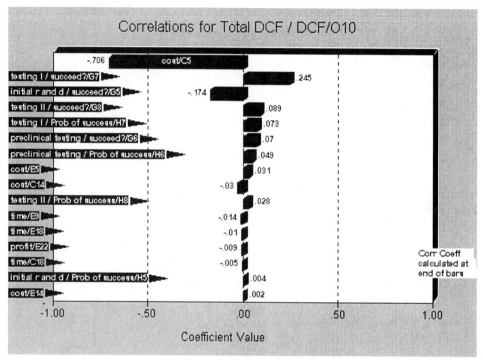

- There is a -.706 correlation between ranking of R and D cost and ranking of project NPV's. This is not surprising, because we always incur R and D cost and for many projects this will be the complete cost.

- There is a .245 correlation between rank of Testing I success and rank of project NPV. This is not surprising, because most of our "good iterations" will involve a success in Test I.

- There is a -.174 correlation between ranking of R and D success and project NPV. This surprising result occurs because many projects that succeed with R and D will fail before completion of the drug thereby incurring large costs and earning no profits. Thus many iterations that have a "1" in G5 will rank very low in NPV.

Chapter 32: Using Simulation to Model an Acquisition

Suppose we are considering purchasing a firm. The cash flows from the firm are highly uncertain. Future cash flows depend on many uncertain parameters such as Sales growth, Gross margin, SG and A expenses, Variations in Working Capital, Litigation Liability, and Terminal Value of firm. As the following example will show, simulation is well suited to modeling the uncertainty involved in a potential acquisition. Our example is based on Razaire (1995).

Example 32.1

We are considering buying a small chain (Cleanco) of dry cleaners. Cleanco is asking $20 million. Current data on Cleanco is as follows:

- Annual sales revenue: $40 million

- Annual cost of goods sold: $28 million

- S G and A annual costs: $10 million

- Working Capital: $4 million

- Tax rate: 34%

We have decided the appropriate discount factor for a discounted cash flow analysis is 12%. We are going to project cash flows out seven years and then use future growth rates from that point to access a terminal value. Should we purchase Cleanco?

Here is our assessment of the uncertainty involved in factors impacting future cash flows:

Sales Growth

- During each of Years 1 and 2 there is a 70% chance growth will be between 3% and 6% and a 30% chance that growth will be between 0% and 3%.

- During Year 3 there is a 40% chance that growth will be between 3% and 6% and a 60% chance that sales will range between a decline of 3% and an increase of 3%.

- During Years 4-7 there is a 10% chance that growth will be between 6% and 12%. There is a 40% chance that growth will be between 3% and 6%. There is a 50% chance that sales will range between a decline of 3% and increase of 3%.

Gross Margin

- If sales decline there is a 60% chance sales margin will be between 29% and 32%; a 30% chance sales margin will be between 32% and 34%; a 10% chance sales margin will be between 34% and 36%.

- If sales growth is positive there is a 15% chance that margin will be between 29% and 32% of sales; a 50% chance that margin will be between 32% and 34%; a 35% chance that margin will be between 34% and 36%.

This reflects the fact that higher prices are more likely when Cleanco does well.

SG&A Expenses

- There is a 30% chance that the change in SG&A expense will range from a decline of -2% to an increase of 1%.

- There is a 50% chance that SG&A growth will be between 1% and 4%.

- There is a 20% chance that SG&A growth will be between 4% and 7%.

Variations in Working Capital

- If sales growth is positive the change in working capital will equal 15% of sales growth.

- If sales growth is negative there is a 40% chance that the change in working capital will equal 15% of sale growth and a 60% chance that the change in working capital will be between 10%-15% of the change in sales.

Litigation Liability

- During Year 2 there is a 5% chance of a liability cost that will range between 2 and 3 million dollars.

- If there is no liability cost incurred during Year 2, then during Year 3 there is a 5% chance of a liability cost that will range between 2 and 3 million dollars. If Year 2 liability cost is greater than 0, there can be no Year 3 liability cost.

Terminal Value

- After Year 7 there is a 15% chance the growth rate of free cash flow will be between 0% and 3%; a 60% chance the growth rate of free cash flow will be between 3% and 6%; a 25% chance the growth rate of cash flow will be between 6% and 9%.

Modeling the Cash Flows

During each year Sales Growth, Gross Margin, SG&A expense, Variation in Working Capital, Litigation Liability, and Terminal Value is governed by one of two or three scenarios. We will use a random number between 0 and 1 (generated by the Excel=Rand() function) to generate the scenario which occurs. Then conditional on the scenario that occurs, we model the value of the relevant financial quantity with the *RISKUniform* function. For example, if a liability occurs we model the size of the liability with the function

=RISKUniform(2,3).

This will make any liability value between $2 million and $3 million equally likely.

Our spreadsheet is in *mergerdcg.xls*. See Figure 32.1.

Figure 32.1

	A	B	C	D	E	F	G	H	I	J
1	discount rate	0.12								
2	Tax rate	0.34								
3	Year	0	1	2	3	4	5	6	7	
4	Sales scenario rand#		0.824	0.039	0.850	0.591	0.118	0.009	0.395	
5	Sales growth		0.015	0.045	0.000	0.000	0.045	0.090	0.045	
6	Sales revenue	40	40.600	42.427	42.427	42.427	44.336	48.326	50.501	
7	Sales up or down		up	up	down	down	up	up	up	
8	Gross Margin Scen		2	2	2	2	2	2	2	
9	Gross Margin		0.325	0.325	0.325	0.325	0.325	0.325	0.325	
10	COGS	28	27.405	28.638	28.638	28.638	29.927	32.620	34.088	
11	rand# for SGandA growth		0.799	0.286	0.459	0.656	0.184	0.611	0.807	
12	Sgand A growth		0.025	-0.005	0.025	0.025	-0.005	0.025	0.055	
13	SGandA	10	10.250	10.199	10.454	10.715	10.661	10.928	11.529	
14	WC	4	4.090	4.364	4.364	4.364	4.650	5.249	5.575	
15	rand# for CWC		0.474	0.164	0.819	0.663	0.295	0.596	0.335	
16	CWC		0.090	0.274	0.000	0.000	0.286	0.599	0.326	
17	rand# for litigation			0.429	0.256					
18	Litigation cost	0	0.000	0.000	0.000	0.000	0.000	0.000	0.000	
19	EBT	2	2.945	3.590	3.335	3.074	3.748	4.778	4.884	
20	Tax	0.68	1.001	1.221	1.134	1.045	1.274	1.625	1.660	
21	NI	1.32	1.944	2.369	2.201	2.029	2.474	3.154	3.223	
22										
23	Cash Flow									
24	Revenue	40.000	40.600	42.427	42.427	42.427	44.336	48.326	50.501	
25	Costs	38.000	37.655	38.837	39.092	39.353	40.588	43.548	45.617	
26	Taxes	0.680	1.001	1.221	1.134	1.045	1.274	1.625	1.660	
27	CWC	0.000	0.090	0.274	0.000	0.000	0.286	0.599	0.326	Term Value
28	FCF	1.320	1.854	2.095	2.201	2.029	2.187	2.555	2.897	45.210
29	NPV	28.287								
30	terminal growth rate rand#	0.659								
31	terminal growth rate	0.045								

We proceed as follows:

Step 1: In C4:I4 generate a random number which defines the Sales Growth scenario for each year by copying =RAND() from C4 to C4:I4.

Step 2: In C5 compute the Year 1 sales growth with the formula

=If(C4<=0.7,RISKUniform(0.03,0.06), RISKUniform(0,0.03)).

Note this formula gives us (as desired) a 70% chance that Year 1 sales growth is between 3% and 6% and a 30% chance that Year 1 sales growth is between 0% and 3%.

Copying this formula to D5 computes Year 2 sales growth. In E5 compute Year 3 Sales Growth with the formula

=If(E4<=0.4, RISKUniform(0.03,0.06), RISKUniform(-0.03,0.03)).

In F5:I5 compute Year 4-7 Sales Growth by copying the formula

=If(F4<=0.1, RISKUniform(0.06,0.12),If(F4<=0.5, RISKUniform(0.03,0.06), RISKUniform(-0.03,0.03)))

from F5 to F5:I5.

Step 3: In C6:I6 we use the Sales Growth rates determined in Step 1 to generate Sales Revenue for years 1-7. Simply copy the formula

=B6*(1+C5)

from C6 to C6:I6.

Step 4: In C7:I7 we record whether Sales went up or down during the current year. We need this information to help us determine the Gross Margin %age for the year. Just copy the formula

=If(C5>0,"up","down")

from C7 to C7:I7.

Step 5: In C8:I8 we generate the scenario (1,2 or 3) which governs Gross Margin. Scenario 1 constrains margin to be between 29%-32%; Scenario 2 constrains margin to be between 32%-34%; Scenario 3 constrains margin to be between 34%-36%. Note that when Sales Growth is positive Scenario 3 is more likely and Scenario 1 is less likely. This is consistent with the ability to charge higher prices when a company's product sells well. We generate the Gross Margin scenario for each year by copying the formula

=If(C7="down",RISKDiscrete({1,2,3},{0.6,0.3,0.1}), RISKDiscrete ({1,2,3},{0.15,0.5,0.35}))

from C8 to C8:I8. Then we generate the actual Gross Margin by copying the formula

=RISKUniform(VLOOKUP(C8,$K$10:$M$12,2),VLOOKUP(C8,$K$10:$M$12,3))

from C9 to C9:I9. The lookup tables key off Figure 32.2.

Figure 32.2

	K	L	M
9	GrossMargin	lower	upper
10	1	0.29	0.31
11	2	0.31	0.34
12	3	0.34	0.36

This works because whether Sales Growth is positive or negative, each scenario yields the same range of sales. The sign of Sales Growth does, however, affect the likelihood of each scenario.

Step 6: In C10:I10 we compute the actual Cost of Goods Sold by copying the formula

=(1-C9)*C6

from C10 to C10:I10.

Step 7: In C11:I11 we enter the =RAND() function to create a random number for each year that will be used to generate SG&A growth in row 12.

Step 8: In C12:I12 we generate the change in SG&A costs by copying the formula

=If(C11<0.3,RISKUniform(-0.02,0.01),If(C11<0.8, RISKUniform(0.01,0.04),RISKUniform(0.04,0.07)))

from C12 to C12:I12.

Step 9: In row 13 we compute the SG&A expense for each year by copying the formula

=B13*(1+C12)

from C13 to C13:I13.

Step 10: In C15:I15 we enter =RAND() in each cell to generate the random numbers used to create the change in working capital during each year.

Step 11: In C16:I16 we determine the change in working capital during each year by copying the formula

=If(C7="up",0.15*(C6-B6),If(C15<=0.6,RISKUniform(0.1,0.15)*(C6-B6),0.15*(C6-B6)))

from C16 to C16:I16. Note that for each scenario the change in working capital is a fraction of the sales change.

Step 12: In C14:I14 we compute the working capital for each year by copying the formula

=B14+C16

from C16 to C16:I16.

Step 13: In D17 and E17 we enter =RAND(). These random numbers will be used to generate Litigation costs during Years 2 and 3.

Step 14: In D18 generate Year 2 Litigation Costs with the formula

$=If(D17<=0.95,0,RISKUniform(2,3))$.

In E18 generate Year 3 Litigation Costs with the formula

$=If(D17>0,0,If(E17<=0.95,0,RISKUniform(2,3)))$.

This formula ensures that if any Litigation Costs occur during Year 2, none can occur during Year 3.

Step 15: We compute Earnings Before Taxes (revenues - cost of good sold - SG&A - Litigation Costs) in C19:I19 by copying the formula

$=C6-C10-C13-C18$

from C19 to D19:I19.

Step 16: In C20:I20 we compute each year's taxes by copying the formula

$=\$B\$2*C19$

from C20 to C20:I20.

Step 17: In C21:I21 we compute each year's net income by copying the formula

$=C19-C20$

from C21 to C21:I21.

Step 18: In rows 24-27 we recopy the revenues, costs, taxes, and change in working capital for each year. Then in C28:I28 we use the relationship that

Free cash flow = revenue - costs - taxes - change in working capital

to compute free cash flow for each year. Just copy the formula

$=C24-C25-C26-C27$

from C28 to C28:I28.

Step 19: In B30 we enter =RAND() to compute a random number which is used to generate (in cell B31) the growth rate (g) of cash flows in all years after Year 7 with the formula

=If(B30<0.15,RISKUniform(0,0.03),If(B30<0.75,RISKUniform(0.03,0.06),RISKUnif orm(0.06,0.09)).

Step 20: Assume that cash flow during every year after year 7 grow at a rate g and cash flows are discounted at a rate r. Then in Year 7 $s the NPV of all cash flows from Year 8 onward is given by

$$\frac{year\,8\,cash\,flow}{r-g}$$

Since year 8 cash flow = (1+ g)*(year 7 cash flow), we may write (in Year 8 $s) the NPV of all cash flows earned from Year 8 onward is given by

$$\frac{(Year\,7\,Cash\,Flow)*(1+g)*(1+r)}{r-g}.$$

Therefore in J28 we compute the Terminal Value of the Firm in Year 8 $s with the formula

=I28*(1+B1)*(1+B31)/(B1-B31).

Step 21: In cell B29 we compute the NPV of the cash flows from the company with the formula

=NPV(B1,C28:J28).

Step 22: After running 900 iterations with cell B29 as the output cell we obtain the results in Figure 32.3.

Figure 32.3

	D	E
31		
32	Name	NPV
33	Description	Output
34	Cell	B29
35	Minimum =	-3.0257
36	Maximum =	88.5944
37	Mean =	29.0341
38	Std Deviation =	11.7756
39	Variance =	138.664
40	Skewness =	0.92568
41	Kurtosis =	4.59335
42	Errors Calculated =	0
43	Mode =	27.2708
44	5% Perc =	12.7067
45	10% Perc =	16.3977
46	15% Perc =	17.68
47	20% Perc =	19.4888
48	25% Perc =	20.8675
49	30% Perc =	22.104
50	35% Perc =	23.8178
51	40% Perc =	24.7953
52	45% Perc =	26.1692
53	50% Perc =	27.3083
54	55% Perc =	28.9561
55	60% Perc =	30.2741
56	65% Perc =	31.3871
57	70% Perc =	33.2982
58	75% Perc =	35.3341
59	80% Perc =	37.12
60	85% Perc =	40.1553
61	90% Perc =	43.9936
62	95% Perc =	50.9096
63	Filter Minimum =	
64	Filter Maximum =	
65	Type (1 or 2) =	
66	# Values Filtered =	0
67	Scenario #1 =	>75%
68	Scenario #2 =	<25%
69	Scenario #3 =	>90%
70	Target #1 (Value)=	20
71	Target #1 (Perc%)=	21.90%

Thus our best estimate of the (risk-adjusted) NPV of the company is $29.03 million. Using the Target command we find there is around a 78% chance that the cash flows of the company (when discounted at 12%) will exceed $20 million in NPV. The distribution of the NPV of Cleanco's cash flows (when discounted at 12%) is pictured in Figure 32.4.

Figure 32.4

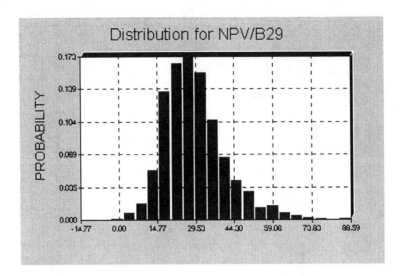

This analysis suggests that a $20 million purchase price is a good deal!

Reference

Razaire, C. "How to Figure Odds in Forecasting Acquisition Results," *Mergers and Acquisitions Magazine*, November-December 1995, pages 6-11.

Chapter 33: Simulating Pro Forma Financial Statements

A company's future profitability, borrowing, and many other quantities are all highly uncertain quantities. It seems natural to run a simulation to obtain a range of values on future profitability and borrowing. We illustrate how to create a simulation of a Pro Forma financial statement (based on actual data) for Home Depot.

The Income Statement

Each year we keep track of the following quantities:

- Revenue

- Non-interest expenses(excluding depreciation)

- Depreciation

- Earnings before interest and taxes (EBIT) = Revenue – Non-interest expenses

- Interest

- Earnings before taxes = EBIT – Interest

- Taxes = Tax Rate*(Earnings before taxes)

- Net Income = Earnings before Taxes – Taxes

Sources and Uses of Funds (Statement of Cash Flows)

We keep track of the following sources and uses of funds:

Sources
- Operating Cash Flow = Net Income + Depreciation

- Borrowing(more on this later)

- Stock Issues(a corporate decision)

- Total Sources (sum of the above)

Uses
- Increase in Net Working Capital from Previous Year

- Investment(Needed to increase Fixed Assets)

- Dividends

- Total Uses (sum of the above)

Balance Sheet

On the balance sheet we keep track of

Assets
- Net Working capital = current assets – current liabilities
- Fixed Assets
- Total Assets (represents total of all assets less value of current liabilities)

Liabilities
- Debt
- Book Equity
- Total Liabilities (represents all liabilities except for current liabilities)

Column B of Figure 33.1 displays the relevant data for Home Depot in 1995 (source is 1997 S and P 500 guide). All numbers are in millions of dollars. Note that in 1995 *Sources = Uses* and *Assets = Liabilities* as they must!

Figure 33.1

	A	B	C	D	E
2	**Income Statement**	1995	1996	Copied	@RISK
3	Revenue	12477	16843.95	1.35	1.3526
4	Noninterest Expenses(exc dep)	11313	15454.64	0.917519	0.908
5	Depreciation	130	182.2529		
6	EBIT	1034	1207.053		
7	Interest	54.065	139.9389	0.064331	0.062
8	Earnings before Taxes	979.935	1067.114		
9	Tax	372.3753	406.3367	0.380781	0.377
10	Net Income	607.5597	660.7772		
11					
12	**Sources and Uses of Funds**				
13	**Sources**				
14	Net Income	607.5597	660.7772		
15	Depreciation	130	182.2529	0.037994	0.0346
16	Operating Cash Flow	737.5597	843.0302		
17	Borrowing	111	1192.296		
18	Stock Issues	628.44	300		
19	Total Sources	1477	2335.326		
20	**Uses**				
21	Increase in Net Working Capital	300	868.7209		
22	Investment	1101	1379.14		
23	Dividends	76	87.46444	0.132366	0.0942
24	Total Uses	1477	2335.326		
25					
26	**Balance Sheet**				
27	**Assets**				
28	Net Working Capital	1119	1987.721	0.118008	0.099
29	Fixed Assets	3600	4796.887	0.284784	0.2709
30	Total Assets	4719	6784.608		
31	**Liabilities**				
32	Debt	983	2175.296		
33	Book equity	3736	4609.313		
34	Total Liabilities	4719	6784.608		

The Dynamics of the Model

The trick is to link year t with the next year (year $t + 1$). Here are the key relationships. (based on Brealey and Myers 1997). In what follows a_1-a_8 are constants which can be estimated for each company based on past data. We will make them =RISKNormal functions to model the fact that each constant may differ in different years! This drives the randomness of the model.

1) Year t+1 Revenue = a_1*(Year t Revenue)

2) Year t + 1 Non Interest Expenses(excluding depreciation) = a_2*(Year t + 1 Revenue)

3) Year t + 1 Interest = a_3*(Year t + 1 Debt)

4) Year t+1 Tax = a_4*(Year t + 1 Earnings before taxes)

5) Year t+1 Depreciation = a_5*(Year t + 1 Fixed Assets)

6) Year t + 1 Dividends = a_6*(Year t + 1 Net Income)

7) Year t + 1 NWC = a_7*(Year t + 1 Revenue)

8) Year t + 1 Fixed Assets = a_8*(Year t + 1 Revenue)

9) EBIT Year $t + 1$ = (Revenue year $t + 1$) − (Noninterest expenses excluding depreciation year $t + 1$) −(Year $t + 1$ Depreciation)

10) Earnings Before Taxes Year $t + 1$ = (EBIT Year $t + 1$)-(Interest Year $t + 1$)

11) Net Income Year $t + 1$= (Earnings Before Taxes Year $t + 1$) − (Taxes Year $t + 1$)

12) Operating Cash Flow year $t + 1$ = (Net Income Year $t + 1$) + (Depreciation Year $t + 1$)

13) Borrowing Year $t + 1$ = (Increase in NWC Year $t + 1$) +(Investment Year $t + 1$) +(Dividends year $t + 1$) − (Net Income Year $t + 1$) − (Depreciation Year $t + 1$) −(Stock Issue Year $t + 1$)

14) Stock Issue Year $t + 1$ is defined by the company or us. It could even involve an = If statement.

15) Total Sources Year $t + 1$ = (Year $t + 1$ Operating Cash Flow) +(Year $t + 1$ Borrowing) + (Year $t + 1$ Stock Issue)

16) Increase in NWC Year $t + 1$ = (NWC Year $t + 1$) − (NWC Year t)

17) Investment Year $t + 1$ = (FA year $t + 1$) − (FA Year t) +(Depreciation Year $t + 1$)

18) Total Uses Year $t + 1$ = (Increase in NWC Year $t + 1$) + (Investment Year $t + 1$) + (Dividends Year $t + 1$)

19) Total Assets Year $t + 1$ = (NWC Year $t + 1$) + (Fixed Assets Year $t + 1$)

20) Debt Year $t + 1$ = (Debt Year t) + (Borrowing Year $t + 1$)

21) Book Equity Year $t + 1$ = (Book Equity Year t) + (Net Income Year $t + 1$) −(Dividends Year $t + 1$) + (Stock Issue Year $t + 1$)

22) Total Liabilities Year $t + 1$ = (Debt Year $t + 1$) + (Book Equity Year $t + 1$)

Equation 13 ensures that Sources and Uses of funds are equal. A little algebra shows that this ensures that *Assets = Liabilities*.

Estimation of Model Parameters

We will soon see that parameters a_1-a_8 drive the model. Figure 33.2 shows our work in estimating the mean and standard deviation of these parameters:

Figure 33.2

	A	B	C	D
1	Analysis of revenue growth			
2				
3	Year	Revenue	%age growth	
4	1990	2760		
5	1991	3815	38.22463768	
6	1992	5137	34.65268676	
7	1993	7148	39.14736227	
8	1994	9239	29.25293788	
9	1995	12477	35.04708302	
10		mean	35.26494152	
11		st dev	3.885855704	
12	Noninterest Expenses			
13	Year	Revenue	COGS	%AGE
14	1990	2760	2538.5	91.97464
15	1991	3815	3449.6	90.42202
16	1992	5137	4664.7	90.80592
17	1993	7148	6457.4	90.33856
18	1994	9239	8371.1	90.60613
19	1995	12477	11313	90.67083
20			mean	90.80302
21			st dev	0.598302
22	Tax rate analysis			
23		1990	39	
24		1991	37	
25		1992	37	
26		1993	37	
27		1994	38	
28		1995	38	
29	Mean	37.6666667		
30	St dev	0.81649658		
31				
32	Depreciation Analysis	Fixed Assets	Depreciation	%age
33		1990	552	20.5	3.713768
34		1991	926	34.4	3.714903
35		1992	1352	52.3	3.868343
36		1993	2370	65.6	2.767932
37		1994	2734	85.9	3.141917
38		1995	3645	130	3.566529
39			Mean	3.462232
40			Stdev	0.421324

	A	B	C	D
41	Interest Expense Analysis			
42	Year	Expense	LT Debt	Percentage
43	1990	18.3	303	6.039604
44	1991	31.1	531	5.856874
45	1992	24	271	8.856089
46	1993	48.6	844	5.758294
47	1994	44.6	882	5.056689
48	1995	53.5	983	5.442523
49		Mean		6.168345
50		St dev		1.361491

	E	F	G	H	I
2	Dividend Analysis				
3	Year	Div/Share	EPS	%age paid out	
4	1990	0.02	0.32	6.25	
5	1991	0.04	0.45	8.8888889	
6	1992	0.05	0.6	8.3333333	
7	1993	0.08	0.82	9.7560976	
8	1994	0.12	1.01	11.881188	
9	1995	0.15	1.32	11.363636	
10	mean	9.41219			
11	st dev	2.07169			
12	Net WC Analysis				
13	Year	Revenue	WC	WC/Rev	
14	1990	2760	276	10	2538.5
15	1991	3815	301	7.8899083	3449.6
16	1992	5137	624	12.147168	4664.7
17	1993	7148	807	11.289871	6457.4
18	1994	9239	994	10.75874	8371.1
19	1995	12477	919	7.3655526	11313
20	mean	9.90854			
21	st dev	1.90748			
22	Fixed Assets Analysis				
23	Year	Revenue	FA	FA/Rev	
24	1990	2760	552	20	
25	1991	3815	926	24.272608	
26	1992	5137	1352	26.318863	
27	1993	7148	2370	33.156128	
28	1994	9239	2734	29.591947	
29	1995	12477	3645	29.213753	
30	mean	27.0922			
31	st dev	4.61234			

As an example, consider a_1. This parameter measures the year to year growth in revenue. For 1991-1995 we found the average growth in revenue to be 35.26% and the standard deviation to be 3.89%. Thus we can model year to year revenue growth as

=RISKNormal(.3526,.0388).

As another example, a_7 is just the ratio of NWC/Revenue. We found on average that NWC is 9. 91% of Revenue with a standard deviation of 1.91%. Therefore we model a_7 as

=RISKNormal(.0991, .0191).

Setting Up the Spreadsheet

In Column C of Figure 33.1 we now operationalize our model to compute a 1996 Pro Forma for Home Depot. Originally we put our estimated mean values for a_1-a_8 in column D and the appropriate **RISKNormal** functions in column E. You will soon see why we cannot put the **RISKNormal** functions directly in column C.

Step by Step

Step 1: In C3 use (1) to compute 1996 revenue with the formula

=B3*D3.

Step 2: In C4 use (2) to compute 1996 Noninterest expenses excluding depreciation with the formula

=C3*D4.

We enter depreciation in C5 with the formula

= C15.

Step 3: In C6 use (9) to compute 1996 EBIT with the formula

= C3 – C4-C5.

Step 4: In C7 use (3) to compute 1996 interest with the formula

=D7*C32.

Step 5: In C8 use (10) to compute 1996 Earnings Before Taxes with the formula

= C6 – C7.

Step 6: In C9 compute 1996 Taxes with (4) using the formula

= C8*D9.

Step 7: In C10 use (11) to determine 1996 Net Income with the formula

= C8 – C9.

Step 8: In C14 just recopy 1996 Net Income with the formula

= C10.

Step 9: In C15 use (5) to compute 1996 Depreciation with the formula

= D15*C29.

Step 10: In C16 compute 1996 Operating Cash Flow from (12) with the formula

$= C14 + C15.$

Step 11: In C17 use (13) to compute 1996 Borrowing with the formula

$=C28-B28+C22+C23-C15-C10-C18.$

Step 12: In C18 type in a number for stock issues. We chose $300 million.

Step 13: In C19 use (15) to compute 1996 Sources of Funds with the formula

$= SUM(C16:C18).$

Step 14: In C21 use (16) to compute the 1996 increase in NWC with the formula

$= C28 - B28.$

Step 15: In C22 use (17) to compute 1996 Investment with the formula

$= C15 + C29 - B29.$

Step 16: In C23 use (6) to compute 1996 Dividends with the formula

$= D23*C10.$

Step 17: In C24 use (18) to compute 1996 Total Fund Uses with the formula

$= SUM(C21:C23).$

Step 18: In C28 use (7) to compute 1996 NWC with the formula

$= D28*C3.$

Step 19: In C29 use (8) to compute 1996 Fixed Assets with the formula

$= D29*C3.$

Step 20: In C30 compute 1996 Total Assets as

$=C28 + C29.$

Step 21: In C33 use (20) to compute 1996 Debt with the formula

$= B32 + C17.$

Step 22:   In C33 use (21) to compute 1996 Book Equity with the formula

  $= B33+C14-C23+C18.$

Step 23:   In C34 compute 1996 Total Liabilities as

  $= C32 + C33.$

This spreadsheet has many **circular references**. For example, net income influences borrowing, borrowing influences debt, debt influences interest, and interest influences net income. Fortunately, if you choose *"Tools" "Options" "Calculation" Automatic"* and check *"Iterations"* and put in, say 1000, then Excel can resolve your circular references. The proof that it works is that 1996 Assets = 1996 Liabilities and 1996 Uses = 1996 Sources!

Running the Simulation

After putting the @RISK functions for a_1-a_8 in column E we are ready to run our simulation. Here are the formulas

Cell	Quantity	Formula
E3	Revenue Growth %age (a_1)	=RISKNormal(1.3526,0.0388)
E4	Noninterest expenses/revenue	=RISKNormal(0.908,0.006)
E7	Interest/Debt (a_3)	=RISKNormal(0.062,0.0136)
E9	Tax/EBT (a_4)	=RISKNormal(0.377,0.0081)
E15	Depreciation/Fixed Assets (a_5)	=RISKNormal(0.0346,0.0042)
E23	Dividends/net Income (a_6)	=RISKNormal(0.0942,0.0207)
E28	NWC/Revenue (a_7)	=RISKNormal(0.099,0.019)
E29	FA/Revenue (a_8)	=RISKNormal(0.2709,0.046)

We will simply keep track of 1996 Net Income (actual was 733 million!). **We cannot put the =RISKNormal functions in column C because Excel will recalculate them as it tries to resolve the circularities. This will not allow Excel to resolve circular references because after each iteration the new RISKNormal values force Excel to start from scratch.** To get around this problem we use a **Macro** to copy the numbers generated by @RISK in column E to column D. Then we tell @RISK to run this Macro before recalculating the spreadsheet. To do this proceed as follows:

Step by Step

Step 1: Select *"Tools" "Macro" "Record New Macro"*. We chose the name MACRO2. The Macro Recorder is now turned on. The recorder serves as a tape recorder to record your keystrokes until you hit the stop button.

Step 2: Select the cell range E3:E29.

Step 3: Edit>Copy> Paste Special Values this range to D3:D29.

Step 4: Click on the Stop Recording button.

Step 5: Play back the macro a few times to see what it is doing. Just select *"Tools" "Macro" "Macros" "Macro2"* and you will see the numbers generated by @RISK are pasted to column D (as numbers, not formulas!). Then they feed into column C and Excel can resolve the circularities!

Step 6: Go to the @RISK simulation settings and click on MACRO and fill in the dialog box as follows:

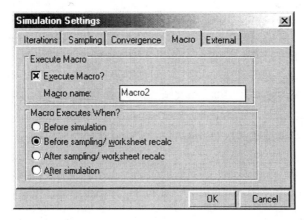

This will ensure that before each time the value of an output cell is tabulated new values of a_1-a_8 will be generated.

Step 7: We now select 1996 Net Income (C10) as our output cell. 1000 iterations of @RISK yielded the results in Figure 33.3:

Figure 33.3

	F	G
10	Cell	C10
11	Minimum =	545.4294
12	Maximum =	1051.677
13	Mean =	810.9655
14	Std Deviation =	85.23196
15	Variance =	7264.488
16	Skewness =	-8.96E-02
17	Kurtosis =	3.135224
18	Errors Calculated =	0
19	Mode =	805.9567
20	5% Perc =	665.9233
21	10% Perc =	701.6457
22	15% Perc =	721.3383
23	20% Perc =	742.3972
24	25% Perc =	756.118
25	30% Perc =	770.418
26	35% Perc =	782.8461
27	40% Perc =	794.1696
28	45% Perc =	804.1207
29	50% Perc =	811.8783
30	55% Perc =	820.97
31	60% Perc =	830.6593
32	65% Perc =	842.0099
33	70% Perc =	850.6343
34	75% Perc =	865.6616
35	80% Perc =	881.0942
36	85% Perc =	897.8645
37	90% Perc =	920.2802
38	95% Perc =	952.0782

We see that on average we expect Home Depot's 1996 Net Income to be 811 million. They actually made 733 million, which was in between the 15th and 20th percentile of what we expected.

Remarks

- Clearly we can go ahead as many years as we like. Just do not blindly expect past revenue growth assumptions to hold. Think about where company is on S-shaped curve of growth that most companies follow.

- Also if the industry is expected to become more competitive, do not blindly expect margins (as factored into a_2) to remain the same.

- The model gives you flexibility to build in (with If statements) future assumptions about the industry and firm behavior (e.g. stock issuing policy).

- We could even build in correlations between a_1-a_8 with the =RISKCorrmat function (see Chapter 47 for a discussion of the =RISKCorrmat function). If you build in correlations, however you must generate, say 1000 rows each of which contains correlated values of a_1-a_8. Then choose one of these rows to generate values of a_1-a_8 for spreadsheet by using =RISKDUniform function to pick a row. Then use a lookup table to place values from the chosen row in range E3:E29.

- Tax rate should probably depend on actual EBIT through a Lookup Table.

- Instead of assuming that, say revenue growth follows a normal random variable we could simply use the =RISKDUniform function to take the given growth rates as equally likely scenarios of future growth. For example, for revenue growth we would enter in cell E3 the formula

  $= RISKDUniform(\{1.3822,1.3465,1.3914,1.2925,1.3504\})$.

Reference

Brealey, R. and Myers, S., Principles *of Corporate Finance*, Prentice-Hall, 1997.

Chapter 34: The Value of a Customer

In making marketing decisions it is very important to take a long-term view. Improvements in customer service, for example, may not pay off in the short-term. If we look at the long-term value of a customer, however, a small increase in customer retention resulting from improved customer service may greatly increase a company's profit.

The book *The Loyalty Effect* (Reichheld (1996)) contains a great discussion of how the value of a customer depends on the probability that a customer will leave your business. Here is an example.

Example 34.1

Reichheld (1996) has obtained data in Figure 34.1 on how the average profitability of a credit card customer depends on how many years they have had a credit card.

Figure 34.1

Length of Time a Customer has been with Us	Average Profit
1	-40
2	66
3	72
4	79
5	87
6	92
7	96
8	99
9	103
10	106
11	111
12	116
13	120
14	124
15	130
16	137
17	142
18	148
19	155
>=20	161

Let's assume that the standard deviation of the profit earned by a customer during a year equals 10% of the absolute value of the mean profit.

Assuming a 30-year horizon, estimate the NPV you receive from a customer (if the discount rate is 15%) for the following retention rates:

80%, 85%, 90%, 95%, 99%.

For instance, a 90% retention rate means that during any year there is a 10% chance the customer will cancel their credit card.

- Why do you think going from a 90% to 95% retention rate results in a much greater increase in NPV than going from an 85% to a 90% retention rate?

Assume that if a customer quits during Year i, you receive Year i Profit but no profit from Years i+1 or later.

Solution

Our solution is in the file *Loyalty.xls* (see Figure 34.2). We will value a customer through 30 years.

Figure 34.2

	A	B	C	D	E	F
1	The Loyalty Effect					
2		Retention Rate	0.8			
3		Interest rate	0.15	NPV	$473.66	
4	Year	Mean Profit(if still here)	Quits?	Still Here?	Actual Profit	Random #
5	1	$ (40.00)	No	Yes	-40	0.47923904
6	2	$ 66.00	No	Yes	66	0.81797428
7	3	$ 72.00	No	Yes	72	0.53674141
8	4	$ 79.00	No	Yes	79	0.54875063
9	5	$ 87.00	No	Yes	87	0.49121947
10	6	$ 92.00	No	Yes	92	0.47771621
11	7	$ 96.00	No	Yes	96	0.86220834
12	8	$ 99.00	No	Yes	99	0.95943354
13	9	$ 103.00	No	Yes	103	0.80809969
14	10	$ 106.00	No	Yes	106	0.55833421
15	11	$ 111.00	No	Yes	111	0.61160465
16	12	$ 116.00	No	Yes	116	0.78059891
17	13	$ 120.00	No	Yes	120	0.47323968
18	14	$ 124.00	No	Yes	124	0.8981959
19	15	$ 130.00	No	Yes	130	0.3932867
20	16	$ 137.00	No	Yes	137	0.67999259
21	17	$ 142.00	No	Yes	142	0.41855261
22	18	$ 148.00	No	Yes	148	0.81649287
23	19	$ 155.00	No	Yes	155	0.98776179
24	20	$ 161	Yes	Yes	161	0.01984046
25	21	$ 161	Yes	No	0	0.06444544
26	22	$ 161	Yes	No	0	0.13003331
27	23	$ 161	No	No	0	0.26845113
28	24	$ 161	No	No	0	0.66984261
29	25	$ 161	No	No	0	0.73559044
30	26	$ 161	No	No	0	0.44501153
31	27	$ 161	No	No	0	0.66960333
32	28	$ 161	No	No	0	0.38563218
33	29	$ 161	No	No	0	0.50501292
34	30	$ 161	No	No	0	0.94319515

The key to our spreadsheet is to figure out the average profit earned per customer. To do this we need to determine the year in which a customer leaves (we do this in column C). Then in column E we can compute the profit the customer contributes each year.

Step 1: In cell C2 we enter the various retention probabilities with the formula

   =RiskSimTable({.8,.85,.9,.95,.99}).

Step 2: In the range C5:C34 we determine for each year whether or not the customer quits. A "quit" will occur during each year with a probability equal to

   1 – (number in C2).

We begin by entering random numbers between 0 and 1 in column F by copying the formula

   =RAND()

from F5 to F5:F34.

Whether or not somebody quits during the first year is determined in C5 with the formula

   =If(F5<=1-$C$2,"Yes","No").

Copying this formula to C5:C34 determines for each year whether or not a customer quits. Note: we may see more than one "quit" in this column, but in column D we make sure than once somebody quits, they are gone for good.

Step 3: In D5:D34 we determine whether or not the customer is still with us. Our assumption is that even if she quits during Year 1, we earn the profit from the customer. Thus we enter a

   = "Yes"

in D5. In later years we note that if a customer will no longer be with us if she is already recorded as having left or she left during the last year. This logic is utilized for Year 2 in D6 with the following formula.

   =If(D5="No","No",If(C5="Yes","No","Yes")).

Copying this formula to D6:D34 determines if we earn the profit for the current year.

Step 4: In E5:E34 we compute the actual profit earned during each of the next 30 years. If the customer has already left, no profit is earned; otherwise profit earned is normally distributed with a mean equal to the number given and a standard deviation equal to .1*(absolute value of mean profit for the year). To begin in E5 we compute the actual profit for Year 1 with the formula

$=If(D5="Yes",RISKNormal(B5,0.1*ABS(B5)),0).$

Copying this formula to E6:E34 computes the actual profit for years 2-30.

Step 5: In E3 we compute the NPV of all earned profits with the formula

$NPV(C3,E5:E34).$

Step 6: We now ran @RISK (300 iterations, 5 simulations) and obtained the results in Figure 34.3

Figure 34.3

	G	H	I	J	K
23	Retention %age		Min	Mean	Max
24	0.8	NPV	-41.4107	115.8807	486.308
25	0.85	NPV	-44.1777	169.3962	526.9057
26	0.9	NPV	-43.8234	233.1386	557.4472
27	0.95	NPV	-39.2289	334.9144	554.2653
28	0.99	NPV	-42.1936	477.7418	562.5447

In Figure 34.4 we graph average profit as a function of retention probaiblity.

Figure 34.4

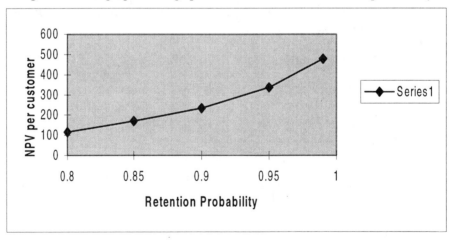

252

Note the increasing slope of Figure 34.4. This means, for example, that going to a 95% retention from a 90% retention is much more beneficial than going from an 85% retention to 90%. To see why this is the case note that if you retain a fraction p of your customers, the average customer stays with you for $\dfrac{1}{1-p}$ years.

Thus we see that going from 90% to 95% ensures that a customer will remain an average of 1/.05 = 20 years instead of 10 years while going from 85% to 90% ensures that a customer will remain an average of 1/.1 = 10 years instead of an average of 1/.15 = 6.7 years. This explains the large increase in profitability associated with a seemingly small increase in the retention rate.

Reference

Reichfeld, F. *The Loyalty Effect* ,Harvard Business School Press, 1996.

Chapter 35: The RISKGeneral Function

What if a continuous random variable such as market share does not appear to follow a normal or triangular distribution? We can model it with the =RISKGeneral function.

Example 35.1

Suppose that a market share of between 0 and 60% is possible. A 45% share is most likely. There are five market-share levels for which we feel comfortable about comparing their relative likelihoods (see Figure 35.1)

Figure 35.1

Market Share	Relative Likelihood
10%	1
20%	6
45%	8
50%	7
55%	6

Thus a market share of 45% is 8 times as likely as 10%; 20% and 55% are equally likely, etc. Note this cannot be triangular because then 20% would be (20/45) as likely as peak of 45% and 20% is .75 as likely as 45%. See Figure 35.2 and file *riskgeneral.xls* for our analysis.

To model market share enter the formula (see Figure 35.2)

=*RISKGeneral(0,60,{10,20,45,50,55},{1,6,8,7,6})*.

The syntax of *RISKGeneral* is as follows:

- Begin with the smallest and largest possible values.

- Then enclose in {} the numbers for which you feel you can compare relative likelihoods.

- Finally enclose in {} the relative likelihoods of the numbers you have previously listed.

Running this in @RISK yields the output in Figure 35.3.

Figure 35.2

	B	C	D	E	F
1	EXAMPLE OF				
2	RISKGENERAL				
3	DISTRIBUTION				
4					
5			Minimum	0	
6			Maximum	60	
7			Specified Points		
8			10	1	
9			20	6	
10			45	8	
11			50	7	
12			55	6	
13	35.75 =RISKGENERAL(0,60,{10,20,45,50,55},{1,6,8,7,6})				

Figure 35.3

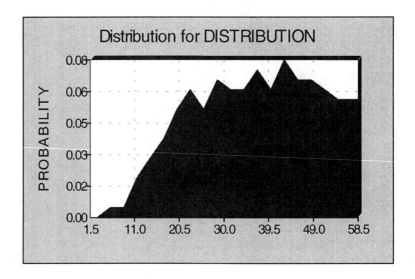

Distribution for DISTRIBUTION

Note 20 is 6/8 as likely as 45; 10 is 1/8 as likely as 45, 50 is 7/8 as likely as 45, 55 is 6/8 as likely as 45, etc. In between the given points, the density function changes at a linear rate. Thus 30 would have a likelihood of

$$6 + \frac{(30-20)*(8-6)}{(45-20)} = 6.8$$

Basically what @RISK has done is as follows: Consider the curve constructed by connecting (with straight lines) the points (0, 0), (10,1), … (55,6), (60,0). @RISK rescaled the height of this curve so the area under it equals 1, and then randomly selects points based on the height of the curve. Thus a share around 45 is 8/6 as likely as a share around 20, etc. Figure 35.4 illustrates this idea.

Figure 35.4

	C	D
29	Share	Likelihood
30	0	0
31	10	1
32	20	6
33	45	8
34	50	7
35	55	6
36	60	0

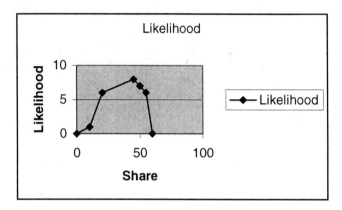

Remarks

For the spreadsheet in Figure 35.2 the syntax

=*RISKGeneral(0,60,D8:D12,E8:E12)*

is also acceptable.

Chapter 36: Using Data to Obtain Inputs for New Product Simulations

Many companies use subjective estimates to obtain inputs to a new product simulation. For example, market size may be subjectively modeled as a triangular random variable, with the marketing department coming to a consensus on best, worst, and most likely scenarios. In many situations, however, past data may be used to obtain estimates of key variables such as share, price, volume, and costs. We now discuss how past data on similar products or projects can be used to model share, price, volume and cost uncertainty. The utility of each of our models will depend on the type of data you have available.

The Scenario Approach to Modeling Volume Uncertainty

When trying to model volume of sales for a new product in the auto and drug industries it is common to look for similar products that were sold in the past. For past products we often have knowledge of the following:

* Accuracy of forecasts for Year 1 sales volume

* Data on how sales change after the first year

To illustrate suppose we have the data on Actual and Forecasted Year 1 Sales for seven similar products given in Figure 36.1. See file *Volume.xls*

Figure 36.1

	B	C	D	E	F
				Unbiased	%age
3	Actual	Forecasted	Actual/Forecasted	forecast	error
4	80000	44396	1.801964141	60516.733	1.32195
5	100000	99209	1.007973067	135233.01	0.73946
6	120000	94808	1.265715973	129233.95	0.92855
7	150000	96813	1.549378699	131966.99	1.13665
8	180000	172862	1.041293055	235630.31	0.76391
9	200000	108770	1.8387423	148265.72	1.34893
10	55000	53052	1.036718691	72315.832	0.76055
11		mean	1.363112275	stdev	0.26775

For example, For Product 1 actual Year 1 sales were 80,000 and our forecast for Year 1 was 44,396. The percentage change in sales from year to year for these products is given in Figure 36.2.

Figure 36.2

	A	B	C	D	E	F	G	H	I	J
13	Scenario	Year 2	Year 3	Year 4	Year 5	Year 6	Year 7	Year 8	Year 9	Year 10
14	1	1.43	1.33	0.93	0.75	0.57	0.40	0.37	0.38	0.24
15	2	1.39	1.13	0.96	0.59	0.49	0.45	0.46	0.40	0.24
16	3	1.30	1.38	0.98	0.84	0.80	0.65	0.57	0.48	0.35
17	4	1.47	1.49	1.36	1.15	1.20	1.15	0.93	0.99	0.71
18	5	1.23	1.06	0.73	0.45	0.39	0.31	0.28	0.23	0.15
19	6	1.26	1.22	1.08	0.79	0.77	0.70	0.60	0.60	0.49
20	7	1.30	1.02	0.84	0.62	0.45	0.32	0.27	0.24	0.22

For Example, for Product 1 sales went up 43% during the second year, up 33% during the third year, etc.

Suppose we forecast Year 1 sales to be 90,000 units. How can we model the uncertain volume in product sales?

Step 1: From cell D11 (formula = AVERAGE(D4:D10)) of Figure 36.1 we see that past forecasts for Year 1 sales of similar products have underforecasted actual sales by 36.3%.

Step 2: Therefore we can create unbiased forecasts in Column E by copying the formula

   $=\$D\$11*C4$

from E4 to E5:E10.

Step 3: In column F we compute the percentage error (measured as a percentage of our unbiased forecast) of our unbiased forecasts. In cell F4 we compute the percentage error for Product 1 with the formula

   $=B4/E4.$

Copying this formula from F4 to F5:F10 generates %age errors for other products.

Step 4: In cell F11 we compute the standard deviation (26.7%) of these percentage errors with the formula

   $= STDEV(F4:F10).$

We are now ready to model 10 years of sales for the new product. To generate Year 1 sales we model year 1 sales to be normally distributed with a mean of 1.36*90,000 and a standard deviation of .267*(90,000*1.363). To model sales for Years 2-10 we use @RISK to randomly choose one of the seven volume change patterns (or **scenarios**) from Figure 36.2. Then we use the chosen scenario to generate sales growth for Years 2-10.

Step 5: In cell G4 we choose a scenario with the formula

=RISKDUniform(A14:A20).

This formula gives us a 1/7 chance of choosing each scenario.

Step 6: In H4 we generate Year 1 sales with the formula

=RISKNormal(I1*D11,(I1*D11)*F11).

This implies

mean year 1 sales = (Biased forecast)(Factor to correct for bias)

and

(Standard deviation year 1 sales) = (Unbiased forecast for year 1 sales)
*(Standard deviation of errors as percentage of unbiased forecast).

Step 7: In cell I4 we generate Year 2 sales with the formula

=H4*VLOOKUP($G$4,$A$14:$J$20,I3).

This formula takes Year 1 generated sales and multiplies it by the Year 2 growth factor for the chosen scenario. Copying this formula to I4:Q4 generates sales for Years 2-10. See Figure 36.3.

Figure 36.3

	G	H	I	J	K	L	M	N	O	P	Q
1	Year 1 Forecast		90000								
2		Year									
3	Scenario		1	2	3	4	5	6	7	8	9	10
4		4	122680.1	180768	270167	366359.3	420470	503211.7	579399.3	540064.4	532508.7	376477.4

Modeling Market Share's Response to Competition

If we have a good idea about when competition to our product will enter the market, we should use this information in our simulation of future market share. To do this we need an index that measures strength of our competitive products. This index would probably be derived from conjoint analysis (see Winston (1999)). Let's suppose our index is 1 and in the market when a product was introduced (Quarter 0) a competitor of strength 2 was present. During Quarter 4 a competitor of strength .7 entered and during Quarter 8 a competitor of strength 1.5 entered. Define the **long-run market share** for our product to equal

$$\frac{our\ strength}{total\ strength\ of\ companies\ in\ market}$$

Thus during Quarter 0 our long-run share is 33.33%; during Quarter 4 our long-run share drops to $1/3.7 = 27\%$; during Quarter 8 our long-run share drops to $1/5.2 = 19\%$.

Powell (1997) proposed to model market share as follows. Let S(t) = quarter t market share. Then we assume that for some c between 0 and 1.

$$S(t + 1) = cS(t) + (1 - c)(Long\text{-}run\text{-}Share\ at\ time\ t\ ).\ (36.1)$$

Given data from a past product we may find the value of c that best estimates the evolution of market share. Then (36.1) (with an error term) may be used to model evolution of market share. Note that (36.1) says that if Long-run share remains constant, then market share "slides" towards" long-run share at a rate proportional to the difference between current and long-run-share. To see this rewrite (36.1) as

$$S(t + 1) = S(t) + (1 - c)(Long\text{-}run\text{-}Share - S(t)).\ (36.2)$$

Here is an example of how to use (36.1) to model market share. See file *Share.xls*.

Example 36.1

Suppose for the product described above we are given in column D the three years of market shares given in Figure 36.4. In Column F we are given the total strength of competitors in the market. Use this data to estimate c.

Solution

To estimate c we proceed as follows: we have given C5 the range name c_ and entered a trial value for C in C5.

Step by Step

Step 1: In column E we compute Long-Run-Share (L(t)) by copying the formula

=1/(1+F8)

from E8 to E9:E20.

Figure 36.4

	C	D	E	F	G	H	I	J	K
5		c	0.604475						
6		S(0)	0.4		SSE	0.05207			
7	Quarter	S(t)	L(t)	Competitor's Strength	Biased Forecasted S(t)	Sq Error	%age error biased forecast	Unbiased Forecast	%age error unbiased forecast
8	0	0.34	0.333333	2					
9	1	0.39	0.333333	2	0.3373632	0.00277	1.1560243	0.355446	1.097212
10	2	0.44	0.333333	2	0.3675869	0.00524	1.1969959	0.38729	1.136099
11	3	0.46	0.333333	2	0.3978106	0.00387	1.1563291	0.419134	1.097501
12	4	0.36	0.27027	2.7	0.4099001	0.00249	0.8782627	0.431872	0.833581
13	5	0.3	0.27027	2.7	0.3245096	0.0006	0.9244718	0.341904	0.877439
14	6	0.44	0.27027	2.7	0.2882411	0.02303	1.5264997	0.303691	1.448839
15	7	0.4	0.27027	2.7	0.3728676	0.00074	1.0727669	0.392854	1.01819
16	8	0.28	0.192308	4.2	0.3486886	0.00472	0.8030087	0.367379	0.762156
17	9	0.28	0.192308	4.2	0.2453155	0.0012	1.1413875	0.258465	1.083319
18	10	0.24	0.192308	4.2	0.2453155	2.8E-05	0.9783321	0.258465	0.92856
19	11	0.14	0.192308	4.2	0.2211365	0.00658	0.6330932	0.23299	0.600885
20	12	0.188978	0.192308	4.2	0.160689	0.0008	1.1760511	0.169302	1.11622
21						mean %e	1.0536019		1
22						st dev %	0.2298247		0.218132

Step 2: In column G we use (36.1) to forecast S(t). In G9 we forecast S(1) with the formula

=c_*D8+(1-c_)*E8.

Copying this formula to G9:G21 computes forecasts for other quarters.

Step 3: In H9:H20 we compute the squared error for each forecast by entering in H9 the formula

=(G9-D9)^2.

Then we copy this formula to H10:H20 to generate other squared errors.

Step 4: **To find the value of c which best forecasts market shares for the 12 quarters we use the following Solver window to minimize the sum of squared errors (computed in H6 with the formula**

$$= SUM(H9:H20)).$$

We find c = .605 minimizes SSE.

Figure 36.5

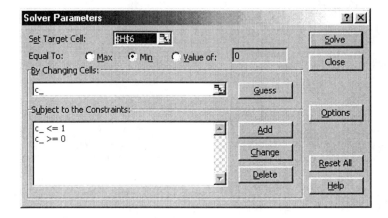

Step 5: **In column I we compute the %age error of our forecasts.** We will then build these errors into our simulation. In I9 we compute the percentage error for Quarter 1 with the formula

$$=D9/G9.$$

Copying this formula to I10:I20 computes the percentage error for each quarter's forecast. In I21 we average these errors and find our forecasts to be on the average 5% too low.

Step 6: **In J9:J20 we create unbiased forecasts by copying from J9:J20 the formula**

$$=\$I\$21*G9.$$

Step 7: **In K9:K20 we compute the percentage errors for the unbiased forecasts with the formula**

$$=D9/J9.$$

Step 8: **In K22 we compute the percentage standard deviation of our unbiased forecasts (21.8%) with the formula**

$$=STDEV(K9:K20).$$

Simulating Market Share for a New Product

Let's suppose we are ready to enter the market with a new product. Currently a competitor with strength 1 is in the market. In Quarter 1 a competitor with strength .5 will enter the market. In Quarter 2 a competitor with strength .4 will enter the market. In Quarter 4 a competitor of strength .9 will enter the market. Let's simulate 8 Quarters of market share. Our best guess is that our initial market share will be 40%.

Figure 36.6

	C	D	E	F	G
23	New product				
24	Quarter	S(t)	L(t)	Competitor's Strength	Forecasted S(t)
25	0	0.4	0.333333	2	
26	1	0.393659	0.285714	2.5	0.393659011
27	2	0.369776	0.25641	2.9	0.369776483
28	3	0.342355	0.25641	2.9	0.342354524
29	4	0.32489	0.208333	3.8	0.324890146
30	5	0.293733	0.208333	3.8	0.293732593
31	6	0.273889	0.208333	3.8	0.273889106
32	7	0.261251	0.208333	3.8	0.261251272
33	8	0.253203	0.208333	3.8	0.253202543

Step by Step

Step 1: Compute L(t) in Column E by copying the formula

=1/(1+F25)

from E25 to E26:E33.

Step 2: In Column G we create unbiased forecasts for each quarter's share by copying the formula

=$I$21*(c_*D25+(1-c_)*E25)

from G26 to G27:G33.

Step 3: To generate our simulated market shares copy the formula

=RISKNormal(G26,$K$22*G26)

from D26 to D27:D33.

We have now incorporated the effect of competition into our simulation of future market shares. Of course, we could simulate the time that a competitor enters as well as the strength of the competitor.

Remarks

Instead of (36.1) a more accurate forecast of long-run-share may be obtained by finding the value of α which makes

$$\frac{(our\ strength)^{\alpha}}{\sum_{all\ companies}(strength\ of\ company)^{\alpha}}$$

best fit each company's observed market share.

Modeling Price Uncertainty

Often changes in a product's price over time are highly uncertain. For most products the following is true:

- Increased competition results in price drops.

- As time goes on the price of a product (in real terms) drops.

Equation (36.3) (Again due to Powell (1997)) below incorporates both of these facts. See the file *Price.xls*. Let

$P(t)$ = Product price at time t (in real \$s)

$N(t)$ = Number of competitors at time t

$P(0)$ = Product price at time 0 (in real \$s)

$P(t) = P(0)*(1 + a)^{-t}(N(t))^{-b}$ (36.3)

To estimate (36.3) divide both sides of (36.3) by P(0) and take logarithms. This yields (36.4)

$Ln\ (P(t)/P(0)) = -t*Ln(1+a)-bLn(N(t)).$ (36.4)

Therefore to estimate (36.3) we can run a regression with no intercept using

- Dependent variable Ln(P(t)/P(0)).

- Independent variables t and Ln(N(t)).

The coefficient of t in the regression will estimate -Ln(1+a). Thus

(coefficient of t) = -Ln(1+a) or

(estimate of a) = $e^{-(coefficient\ of\ t)}-1$.

The coefficient of Ln(N(t)) in the regression estimates -b so

(Estimate of b) = -(coefficient of Ln(N(t))).

Figure 36.7

	A	B	C	D	E	F	G	H	I	J
1	Anderson Model		{1}	P(t)=P(0)*(1+a)^ -t(N(t)^ -b						
2	Powell			P(t)= Year t price (in constant dollars)				Model Year t Price as		
3	Interfaces June 1997			N(t)= # of competitors during year t				risk.normal(Forecast,.08*Forecast)		
4		5.00	P(0)	Ln (P(t)/P(0))= -t*LN(1+a)-b*Ln(N(t))						
5		Year	P(t)	N(t)	t	Ln(N(t))	Ln((P(t)/P(0))	Forecasted P(t)	%age error	
6		1	4.190855	1	1	0	-0.17653311	4.134418257	0.01365	
7		2	3.3422	1	2	0	-0.402808552	3.418682865	-0.02237	
8		3	1.553393	2	3	0.693147	-1.168996646	1.579957927	-0.01681	
9		4	1.1209	2	4	0.693147	-1.495306009	1.30644138	-0.14202	
10		5	0.839128	3	5	1.098612	-1.784830284	0.768668447	0.091664	
11		6	0.575366	3	6	1.098612	-2.162186159	0.635599372	-0.09477	
12		7	0.576222	3	7	1.098612	-2.160700676	0.52556673	0.096382	
13		8	0.637646	2	8	0.693147	-2.059410137	0.610755729	0.044028	
14		9	0.905764	1	9	0	-1.708414281	0.903586333	0.00241	
15		10	0.73557	1	10	0	-1.916547118	0.747160766	-0.01551	
16										
17								stdev %age err	0.074393	
18								mean % err	-0.00434	

We now show how to estimate (36.3). We build in the percentage errors from our forecasts based on (36.3) to simulate future product prices. See Figure 36.7 and file *price.xls*.

Estimating (36.3)

We are given the data in Columns C and D of Figure 36.7. Also, the Year 0 price is $5. For example, during Year 2 the price (in real $s) was $3.34 and one competitor was present.

Step by Step

Step 1: In Column F create Ln(N(t)) by copying from F6 to F7:F15 the formula

$=LN(D6).$

Step 2: In Column G create Ln(P(t)/P(0)) by copying from G6 to G7:G15 the formula

$=LN(C6/\$B\$4).$

Step 3: Run a regression with Y Range: G5:G15 and X Range: E5:F15. After checking labels and Constant Equals 0 box we obtain the following results:

Figure 36.8

	A	B	C	D	E	F
19		SUMMARY OUTPUT				
20		Regression Statistics				
21		Multiple R	0.994201			
22		R Square	0.988437			
23		Adjusted R	0.861991			
24		Standard E	0.081105			
25		Observatio	10			
26						
27		ANOVA				
28			df	SS	MS	F
29		Regression	2	4.4982595	2.24913	341.9191
30		Residual	8	0.0526237	0.006578	
31		Total	10	4.5508832		
32						
33			Coefficient	Standard Erro	t Stat	P-value
34		Intercept	0	#N/A	#N/A	#N/A
35	-LN(1+a)	t	-0.19009	0.0056623	-33.5713	6.77E-10
36	-b	Ln(N(t))	-0.83931	0.0493804	-16.9968	1.46E-07
37						
38			b	0.8393107		
39			a	0.20936		

The R-SQ of .99 indicates an excellent fit. In D38 we estimate b with the formula

=-C36

and in D39 we estimate a with the formula

=EXP(-C35)-1.

We then named D38 and D39 b and a respectively.

By the way, these coefficients may be interpreted as follows:

- Each year prices drop by (.21/1.21).

- A 1% increase in competitors results in a .84% decrease in product price.

Step 4: In H6: H15 we create our forecasted prices for Years 1-10 by copying from H6 to H7:H15 the formula

=$B$4*(1+a)^(-E6)*D6^(-b).

Step 5: In column I we determine the %age error for each forecast by copying the formula

=(C6-H6)/H6

from I6 to I7:I15.

Step 6: We now compute in I17 the standard deviation of our percentage errors with the formula

=STDEV(I6:I15)

and the mean of our percentage errors in I18 with the formula

=AVERAGE(I6:I15).

We find our forecast errors have about an 7.4% standard deviation and are essentially unbiased.

Simulating the Price of a New Product

Let's consider a new product currently priced at $10. The number of competitors during the next six years is expected to be as follows:

Figure 36.9

	H	I	J	K	L	M
17	stdev %age err	0.074393				
18	mean % err	-0.00434				
19						
20		P(0)	10.00			
21		Year	Competitors	Price	Mean	St dev
22		1	1	8.268837	8.268837	0.615142
23		2	3	2.719167	2.719167	0.202286
24		3	5	1.464469	1.464469	0.108946
25		4	2	2.612883	2.612883	0.19438
26		5	1	3.865646	3.865646	0.287576
27		6	1	3.196439	3.196439	0.237792

Simulate the (real) price of the product for the next six years.

Solution

We compute the mean and standard deviation for each Year's price in columns L and M.

Step by Step

Step 1: In L22 we compute the mean for Year 1 price with the formula

=$J$20*(1+a)^-I22*(J22)^(-b).

Copying this formula to the range L23:L27 computes the mean for Years 2-6 prices.

Step 2: In M22 we compute the standard deviation for Year 1 price with the formula

=$I$17*L22.

Copying this to the range M23:M27 computes the price standard deviation for Years 2-6.

Step 3: We can now generate prices for Years 1-6 by copying the formula

=RISKNormal(L22,M22)

from K22 to K23:K27.

Remarks

With this method the Year 2 price does not "know" if the error term for Year 1 was large or small. A better approach to use with this model might be to be to assume (36.3) gives an exact price. Then the randomness in price estimates for later years is solely due to the entrance of competitors.

Modeling Statistical Relationships with One Independent Variable

Suppose we want to model the dependence of a variable (Y) on a single independent variable (X). We proceed as follows:

Step by Step

Step 1: We try and find the straight line, power, and exponential curve that best fit the data. The easiest way to do this is to plot the points with Excel and use the Trend Curve feature.

- Straight line is curve of form $Y = a + bX$

- Power function is of form $Y = ax^b$

- Exponential function is of form $Y = ae^{bX}$

Step 2: For each curve and each data point compute the percentage error

$$\frac{Actual\ value\ of\ Y - Predicted\ value\ of\ Y}{Predicted\ value\ of\ Y}$$

Step 3: For each curve compute Mean Absolute Percentage Error (MAPE) by averaging the absolute percentage errors.

Step 4: Choose the curve that yields the lowest MAPE as the best fit.

Step 5: Assuming that at least one of the three curves appears to have some predictive value (check plot for this, or look at p-value from regression; it should be <=.15) model the uncertainty associated with the relationship between X and Y as follows:

- If straight line is best fit then model Y as

    =RISKNormal(Prediction, Standard deviation of actual (not percentage) errors).

- If power or exponential curve is best fit then model Y as

    = RISKNormal (Prediction, Prediction*(Standard Deviation of Percentage Errors)).

Here are some illustrations of this method.

Example 36.2

For a new product we are not sure of the cost of building capacity, but we believe that costs will run around 50% more (in real terms) than for the drug Zozac. Here is some data on the costs incurred when capacity was built for Zozac.

Capacity(000's)	Cost(000's)
20	156
50	350
80	490
110	654
140	760
160	890

For example, when 110,000 units of capacity for Zozac were built, the cost was $654,000 (in today's dollars). How would you model the (uncertain) cost of building capacity for the new product?

Solution

See Figures (36.10)-(36.15) and the file *Capacity.xls*. To begin we plot the best-fitting straight line, power and exponential curves. To do this use Chart Wizard (X-Y option 1) and click on points till they turn Gold. Next choose desired curve from Add Trendline and select R-SQ and equation option. We obtain the following charts (see Figures 36.10-36.12).

Figure 36.10

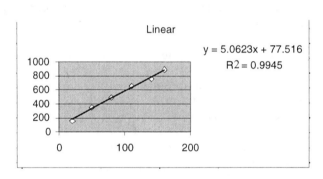

Linear

$y = 5.0623x + 77.516$
$R2 = 0.9945$

Figure 36.11

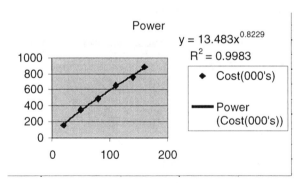

Power

$y = 13.483x^{0.8229}$
$R^2 = 0.9983$

♦ Cost(000's)

━ Power (Cost(000's))

Figure
36.12

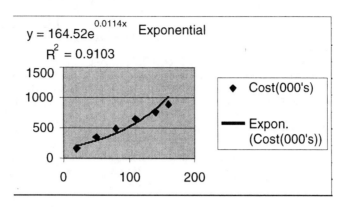

Step 1: In C3:E8 (see Figure 36.13) we compute the predictions for each curve. In C3:C8 we compute the straight line predictions by copying from C3 to C3:C8 the formula

$$=5.0623*A3+77.516.$$

In D3:D8 we compute the power curve prediction by copying from D3 to D3:D8 the formula

$$=13.483*A3^0.8229.$$

In E3:E8 we compute the exponential curve predictions by copying from E3 to E3:E8 the formula

$$=164.52*EXP(0.01114*A3).$$

Figure
36.13

	A	B	C	D	E
1	Capacity Cost Modeling				
2	Capacity(0	Cost(000's)	Linear Prediction	Power Prediction	Exponential Prediction
3	20	156	178.762	158.6369	205.5793608
4	50	350	330.631	337.1855	287.1578726
5	80	490	482.5	496.4086	401.1085718
6	110	654	634.369	645.132	560.2774701
7	140	760	786.238	786.7474	782.6081654
8	160	890	887.484	878.1261	977.9241819

Step 2: In F3:H8 we use

$$\frac{Actual\ value\ of\ Y - Predicted\ value\ of\ Y}{Predicted\ value\ of\ Y}$$

to compute the %age error for each model. See Figure 36.14.

Figure 36.14

	F	G	H	I	J	K
2	%age Error Linear	%age Error Power	%age Error Exponential	APE Linear	APE Power	APE Exponential
3	-0.12733	-0.01662	-0.241169	0.127331	0.016622	0.24116896
4	0.058582	0.038004	0.21884174	0.058582	0.038004	0.21884174
5	0.015544	-0.01291	0.22161438	0.015544	0.01291	0.22161438
6	0.030946	0.013746	0.16727878	0.030946	0.013746	0.16727878
7	-0.03337	-0.034	-0.0288882	0.033372	0.033997	0.02888823
8	0.002835	0.013522	-0.089909	0.002835	0.013522	0.089909
9	St dev	0.026132		0.044768	0.021467	0.16128351
10				MAPE		

To do this simply copy the formula

$$=(\$B3-C3)/C3$$

from F3 to F3:H8.

Step 3: In I3:K9 we compute the MAPE for each equation. We begin by computing the absolute percentage error for each point and each curve by copying the formula

$$=ABS(F3)$$

from I3:K8.

Next we compute the MAPE for each equation by copying the formula

$$=AVERAGE(I3:I8)$$

from I9:K9.

Step 4: We find the power curve (see J9) has the lowest MAPE. Therefore we will model cost of adding capacity with a power curve. By entering in G9 the formula

$$=STDEV(G3:G8)$$

we find the standard deviation of the percentage errors for the power curve to equal 2.6%. We now model the cost of adding capacity for the new product with the formula

$$=1.5*RISKNormal(13.483*(Capacity)^{\wedge}.8229,.026*13.483*(Capacity)^{\wedge}.8229).$$

This says our best guess for the cost of adding capacity has a mean equal to the power curve forecast and a standard deviation equal to 2.6% of our forecast.

Example 36.3

We are bidding against a competitor for a construction project and want to model her bid. In the past her bid has been closely related to our (estimated) cost of completing the project. Here is some past data (*see file Biddata.xls*).

Figure 36.15

	A	B	C	D	E	F
1	(All numbers in 000's)					
2	Our cost	Comp1 bid	Linear prediction	Power prediction	Exponential prediction	Actual Linear Error
3	10	13	13.1027	13.35697	16.3795084	-0.1027
4	14	20	19.0587	19.07213	19.5315493	0.9413
5	16	22	22.0367	21.96795	21.3282198	-0.0367
6	18	25	25.0147	24.88511	23.2901627	-0.0147
7	30	44	42.8827	42.73548	39.4893521	1.1173
8	25	34	35.4377	35.23444	31.6909474	-1.4377
9	38	56	54.7947	54.88668	56.1502464	1.2053
10	44	63	63.7287	64.10133	73.114819	-0.7287
11	24	33	33.9487	33.74424	30.3267775	-0.9487
12					stdev	0.94189151

Figures 36.16-36.18 give the best fitting linear, power and exponential curves:

Figure 36.16

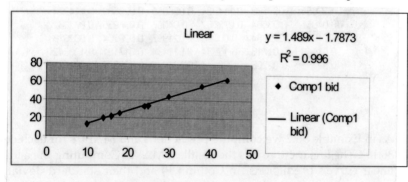

Linear

$y = 1.489x - 1.7873$

$R^2 = 0.996$

Figure 36.17

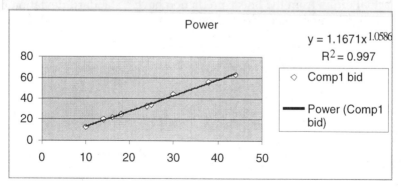

Power

$y = 1.1671x^{1.0586}$

$R^2 = 0.997$

Figure
36.18

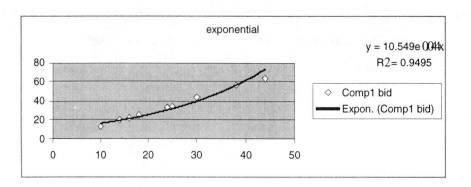

Figure
36.19

	G	H	I	J	K	L
2	Linear %age error	Power %age error	Exponential %age error	Linear abs %age error	Power abs %age error	Exponential %age error
3	-0.00784	-0.02673	-0.20633	0.007838	0.026726	0.206325
4	0.04939	0.048651	0.023984	0.04939	0.048651	0.023984
5	-0.00167	0.001459	0.031497	0.001665	0.001459	0.031497
6	-0.00059	0.004617	0.073415	0.000588	0.004617	0.073415
7	0.026055	0.029589	0.114224	0.026055	0.029589	0.114224
8	-0.04057	-0.03504	0.072862	0.04057	0.035035	0.072862
9	0.021997	0.020284	-0.00268	0.021997	0.020284	0.002676
10	-0.01143	-0.01718	-0.13834	0.011434	0.017181	0.138342
11	-0.02795	-0.02206	0.088147	0.027945	0.022055	0.088147
12				0.020831	0.022844	0.083497
13				MAPE		

As in Example 36.2 we compute predictions and MAPE's for each curve (See Figure 36.19). The linear curve has the smallest MAPE. Computing the actual errors for the linear curve's predictions (in Column F) and their standard deviation we find the actual errors from the linear prediction have a standard deviation of .94. Therefore we model our competitor's bid as

=RISKNormal(1.489*(Our cost) - 1.7893, .94).

Example 36.4

For other similar products, the year after the first competitor comes in has resulted in a significant price drop. Figure 36.20 contains data on this situation.

Figure 36.20

	B	C	D
		Share drop	Price drop
3	Year competitor enters	next year	next year
4	1	35	22
5	1	33	21
6	2	20	17
7	3	15	15
8	3	13	19
9	4	14	24
10	5	10	15
11	6	9	22
12	5	11	25
13	4	13	17
14		Mean	19.7
15		Std Dev	3.622461

For example, for the first product a competitor entered in Year 1 and during Year 2 a 22% price drop was observed (this was after allowing for a normal inflationary increase of 5% during any year). Model the effect on price the year after the first competitor enters the market. *See file Pricedata.xls.*

Solution

Figures (36.21)-(36.23) give the best fitting linear, power, and exponential curves.

Figure 36.21

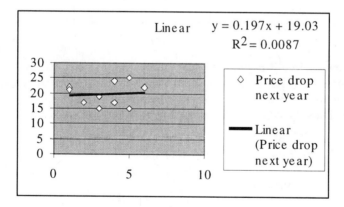

Figure 36.22

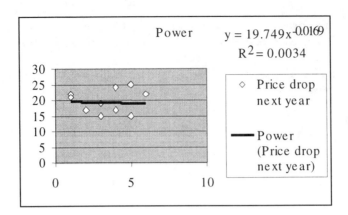

Figure 36.23

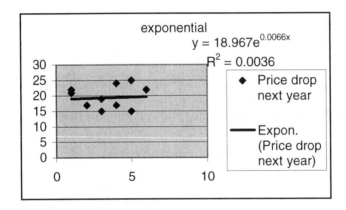

The extremely low R-SQ values imply that the Year of Entry has little or no effect on the price drop the year after the first competitor comes in. Therefore we model price drop as a RISKNormal using the mean and standard deviation found in D14 and D15. Thus if a competitor enters during Year t we would model Year t + 1 price with the formula

=1.05*(Year t Price)*RISKNormal(.803,.0366).

Note: .803 = 1 - .197.

Modeling Relationships Involving More than One Independent Variable

Now suppose we believe that Y can be predicted based on n independent variables, $X_1, X_2, \ldots X_n$. How do we build such a relationship into a simulation? Here are two commonly used relationships:

- **Multiple Linear regression model**

$$Y = a + b_1 X_1 + b_2 X_2 + \ldots b_n X_n + (error\ term)$$

- **Multiplicative Model**

$$Y = \beta_0 x_1^{\beta_1} x_2^{\beta_2} \ldots x_n^{\beta_n} * (error\ term)$$

To fit the Multiple Linear Regression Model use Data Analysis>Tools> Regression. Make sure your final equation has all variables significant (P-values<=.15).

To fit the Multiplicative Model note the model implies that

$$(36.4)\ LN\ Y = LN\ B_0 + B_1\ (Ln\ X_1) + B_2(Ln\ X_2) + \ldots B_n(Ln\ X_n) + (error\ term)$$

To estimate the original Multiplicative Model run a regression with independent variables $Ln\ X_1, Ln\ X_2, \ldots Ln\ X_n$ and dependent variable Ln Y. After making sure all independent variables remaining in your equation are significant, estimate the original value of $B_0, B_1, \ldots B_N$ as follows:

- Estimate B_0 by $e^{Estimate\ of\ Ln\ \beta_0}$.

- Estimate B_1 (i =1,2, …n) as coefficient of $Ln\ X_1$ in (36.4).

Next we create predictions for each model and choose the model with the smaller MAPE.

We model the error term as follows:

- If we selected the Multiple Linear Regression Model, find the standard deviation of the actual errors and model the forecast as

  =RISKNormal(Prediction, standard deviation of errors).

- If we selected the Multiplicative Model find the standard deviation of the percentage errors and model the forecast as

  =RISKNormal(Prediction, Prediction*(standard deviation of percentage errors).

Here is an example of a relationship with more than one independent variable.

Example 36.5 Our crack market research team always conducts market research prior to a product launch. They choose a random sample of potential customers and ask

Customers to state their purchase intentions on a 1-7 scale.

- A "1" means you definitely would buy the product.

- A "3" means you probably would buy the product.

- A "5" means you probably would not buy the product.

- A "7" means you definitely would not buy the product.

Figure 36.24 contains some past data on Year 1 %age from similar products.

Figure 36.24

	A	B	C	D	E	F	G	H
2	Market share	1	2	3	4	5	6	7
3	47	40	15	10	8	12	10	5
4	35	32	17	6	12	12	13	8
5	30	16	14	20	8	19	16	7
6	23	14	17	13	13	14	15	14
7	20	14	15	9	8	17	17	20
8	33	20	17	10	12	12	13	16
9	23	16	12	13	15	14	24	6
10	28	15	14	14	16	12	15	14
11	34	22	18	10	15	14	10	11
12	24	15	18	11	15	16	19	6
13	27	17	13	9	13	20	12	16
14	24	11	10	20	13	13	16	17
15	23	11	16	14	11	15	12	21
16	23	15	10	11	19	16	11	18
17	22	10	15	5	19	20	18	13
18	32	18	17	17	10	8	14	16
19	34	22	18	5	12	14	17	12
20	23	20	10	5	10	10	30	15
21	20	18	12	3	12	8	32	15
22	19	16	14	1	14	4	34	17
23	18	7	14	6	14	8	34	17
24	19	7	14	6	14	8	34	17
25	35	19	22	10	10	8	14	17
26	25	17	14	6	14	8	24	17

For example, the last product had a 25% market %age during Year 1 and

- 17% of all sampled customers gave it a "1".

- 14% of all sampled customers gave it a "2".

- 6% of all sampled customers gave it a "3".

- 14% of all sampled customers gave it a "4".

- 8% of all sampled customers gave it a "5".

- 24% of all sampled customers gave it a "6".

- 17% of all sampled customers gave it a "7".

See file *%agedata.xls*. Model market %age for a new product that scored as follows:

- 30% of all sampled customers gave it a "1".

- 20% of all sampled customers gave it a "2".

- 15% of all sampled customers gave it a "3".

- 20% of all sampled customers gave it a "4".

- 5% of all sampled customers gave it a "5".

- 5% of all sampled customers gave it a "6".

- 5% of all sampled customers gave it a "7".

See file Marksharedata.xls.

Solution

First we fit a linear regression to the data. We run a regression with X-Range being B2:G26 and Y-RANGE being A2:A26. **We needed to drop a column because for each product all responses add to 100%, and this cause Excel to be unable to run the Regression.**[1] Most logically, we dropped people responding a "7", because they are unlikely to buy. After checking the label box we obtain the following results in Figure 36.25:

Figure 36.25

	A	B	C	D	E
15					
16		Coefficients	Standard Error	t Stat	P-value
17	Intercept	4.32913167	12.27878909	0.35257	0.728744
18	1	0.74121262	0.128004284	5.79053	2.17E-05
19	2	0.60539201	0.247952279	2.441567	0.025853
20	3	0.35033449	0.186205329	1.881442	0.077151
21	4	0.09721781	0.240655482	0.403971	0.691271
22	5	-0.11303292	0.193248165	-0.58491	0.566291
23	6	-0.13543285	0.163045348	-0.83065	0.417688

---

[1] If there is a linear relationship between the independent variables which holds in a regression for all observations then Excel cannot estimate a regression equation. In our example, if we do not delete one of the independent variable we know that for each observation all the independent variables will add to one. This is a linear relationship that requires us to drop at least one independent variable.

Since 4, 5, and 6 are insignificant (p-values>.15), we dropped those columns and ran the regression again. The results are in Figure 36.26.

Figure 36.26

	A	B	C	D	E
1	SUMMARY OUTPUT				
2					
3	Regression Statistics				
4	Multiple R	0.94092688			
5	R Square	0.8853434			
6	Adjusted R Square	0.86814491			
7	Standard Error	2.54403736			
8	Observations	24			
9					
10	ANOVA				
11		df	SS	MS	F
12	Regression	3	999.5158117	333.1719	51.47797
13	Residual	20	129.4425217	6.472126	
14	Total	23	1128.958333		
15					
16		Coefficients	Standard Error	t Stat	P-value
17	Intercept	-1.51729102	3.05598836	-0.4965	0.624956
18	1	0.78807251	0.076633634	10.28364	1.97E-09
19	2	0.70575667	0.187353579	3.766977	0.001212
20	3	0.43367409	0.107160831	4.046946	0.00063

Here all variables appear to be significant (p-values<=.15) (except for the intercept). Then we removed the intercept and obtained the following results:

Figure 36.27

	A	B	C	D	E
1	SUMMARY OUTPUT				
2					
3	Regression Statistics				
4	Multiple R	0.94017562			
5	R Square	0.8839302			
6	Adjusted R Square	0.82525689			
7	Standard Error	2.4979798			
8	Observations	24			
9					
10	ANOVA				
11		df	SS	MS	F
12	Regression	3	997.9203685	332.6401228	53.3085399
13	Residual	21	131.0379649	6.239903089	
14	Total	24	1128.958333		
15					
16		Coefficients	Standard Error	t Stat	P-value
17	Intercept	0	#N/A	#N/A	#N/A
18	1	0.77845206	0.072801208	10.69284539	5.9197E-10
19	2	0.63088212	0.109158752	5.779491881	9.7651E-06
20	3	0.41339838	0.09728079	4.24953769	0.00035777

Now all variables are significant (p-values<=.15) and we will forecast Year 1 Market %age for a New Product as

$$.778*(\% \; age \; "1") + .630*(\%age \; "2") + .413*(\%age \; "3").$$

Next we try and fit the Multiplicative Model. We create columns for Ln %age, Ln "1", Ln "2", ... "Ln 6" and run a regression with dependent variable Ln %age and independent variables Ln "1", Ln "2", ... "Ln 6".

Step by Step

Step 1: In cell A28 compute Ln %age for first observation with formula

$=LN(A3).$

Copying this formula from A28 to A28:G51 yields the logarithm of the dependent and independent variables. See Figure 36.28.

Figure 36.28

	A	B	C	D	E	F	G
27	Ln Share	Ln "1"	Ln "2"	Ln "3"	Ln "4"	Ln "5"	Ln "6"
28	3.850147602	3.688879	2.70805	2.302585	2.079442	2.484907	2.302585
29	3.555348061	3.465736	2.833213	1.791759	2.484907	2.484907	2.564949
30	3.401197382	2.772589	2.639057	2.995732	2.079442	2.944439	2.772589
31	3.135494216	2.639057	2.833213	2.564949	2.564949	2.639057	2.70805
32	2.995732274	2.639057	2.70805	2.197225	2.079442	2.833213	2.833213
33	3.496507561	2.995732	2.833213	2.302585	2.484907	2.484907	2.564949
34	3.135494216	2.772589	2.484907	2.564949	2.70805	2.639057	3.178054
35	3.33220451	2.70805	2.639057	2.639057	2.772589	2.484907	2.70805
36	3.526360525	3.091042	2.890372	2.302585	2.70805	2.639057	2.302585
37	3.17805383	2.70805	2.890372	2.397895	2.70805	2.772589	2.944439
38	3.295836866	2.833213	2.564949	2.197225	2.564949	2.995732	2.484907
39	3.17805383	2.397895	2.302585	2.995732	2.564949	2.564949	2.772589
40	3.135494216	2.397895	2.772589	2.639057	2.397895	2.70805	2.484907
41	3.135494216	2.70805	2.302585	2.397895	2.944439	2.772589	2.397895
42	3.091042453	2.302585	2.70805	1.609438	2.944439	2.995732	2.890372
43	3.465735903	2.890372	2.833213	2.833213	2.302585	2.079442	2.639057
44	3.526360525	3.091042	2.890372	1.609438	2.484907	2.639057	2.833213
45	3.135494216	2.995732	2.302585	1.609438	2.302585	2.302585	3.401197
46	2.995732274	2.890372	2.484907	1.098612	2.484907	2.079442	3.465736
47	2.944438979	2.772589	2.639057	0	2.639057	1.386294	3.526361
48	2.890371758	1.94591	2.639057	1.791759	2.639057	2.079442	3.526361
49	2.944438979	1.94591	2.639057	1.791759	2.639057	2.079442	3.526361
50	3.555348061	2.944439	3.091042	2.302585	2.302585	2.079442	2.639057
51	3.218875825	2.833213	2.639057	1.791759	2.639057	2.079442	3.178054

Step 2: We now run a regression with X RANGE B27:G51 and Y-RANGE A27:A51. From the following results we find only Ln "1", Ln "2" and Ln "3" to be significant. We now drop the insignificant variables and obtain the results in Figure 36.29:

Figure 36.29

	A	B	C	D	E
15					
16		Coefficients	Standard Error	t Stat	P-value
17	Intercept	0.80757577	0.311608303	2.591638	0.017439
18	Ln "1"	0.45581116	0.057187778	7.97043	1.23E-07
19	Ln "2"	0.33803992	0.112563909	3.003093	0.007027
20	Ln "3"	0.13272057	0.033426045	3.970573	0.000754

All variables are significant (p-values<=.15) and our multiplicative model for predicting %age is

$$\%age = e^{.807576}*(\%age\ "1")^{.455811}*(\%age\ "2")^{.33804}*(\%age\ "3")^{.132721}.$$

Step 3: We now compute predictions for each model in columns I and J. We create the predictions for our linear regression model in I3:I26 by copying from I3: to I4:I26 the formula

$$=0.778*B3+0.63*C3+0.413*D3.$$

We create the predictions for our Multiplicative Model in J3:J26 by copying from J3 to J3:J26 the formula

$$=EXP(0.807576)*B3^{\wedge}0.455811*C3^{\wedge}0.33804*D3^{\wedge}0.13272.$$

As before we now compute the percentage errors and MAPE for each forecast method. We find the multiplicative model has a slightly lower MAPE. See below. In L1 we found the standard deviation of the percentage errors for the multiplicative model to be 9.6% of the forecast.

Therefore, we would model Year 1 Market %age for a new product as

$$=RISKNormal(e^{.807576}*(\%age\ "1")^{.455811}*(\%age\ "2")^{.33804}*(\%age\ "3")^{.132721},$$
$$.096*e^{.807576}*(\%age\ "1")^{.455811}*(\%age\ "2")^{.33804}*(\%age\ "3")^{.132721}).$$

Of course, the MAPE for the linear model is very close to the MAPE for the multiplicative model so in the interest of simplicity we might model Year 1 Market %age as

$$=RISKNormal(.778*(\%\ age\ "1") + .630*(\%age\ "2") + .413*(\%age\ "3"), 2.39)$$

where in O27 we computed the standard deviation of the errors (2.39) associated with the linear model.

Figure
36.30

	I	J	K	L	M	N	O
1			stdev	0.095826204	0.079950077	0.07646131	MAPE
2	Linear prediction	Multiplicative Prediction	Linear %age Error	Multiplicative %age Error	Abs Linear %age Error	Multiplicative %age Error	Actual Linear Error
3	44.7	40.8553802	0.051454	0.150399281	0.051454139	0.15039928	2.3
4	38.084	35.97556993	-0.08098	-0.027117567	0.080978889	0.02711757	-3.084
5	29.528	28.81960719	0.015985	0.040957977	0.015984828	0.04095798	0.472
6	26.971	27.34816526	-0.14723	-0.158992942	0.147232212	0.15899294	-3.971
7	24.059	24.9664892	-0.16871	-0.198926215	0.168710254	0.19892621	-4.059
8	30.4	31.07502862	0.085526	0.061945925	0.085526316	0.06194592	2.6
9	25.377	25.83610483	-0.09367	-0.109772926	0.093667494	0.10977293	-2.377
10	26.272	26.69030358	0.065773	0.049070121	0.065773447	0.04907012	1.728
11	32.586	33.08797148	0.043393	0.027563748	0.043392868	0.02756375	1.414
12	27.553	28.14155748	-0.12895	-0.147168737	0.128951475	0.14716874	-3.553
13	25.133	25.98862992	0.074285	0.038915868	0.074284805	0.03891587	1.867
14	23.118	21.6829338	0.038152	0.106861287	0.038152089	0.10686129	0.882
15	24.42	24.2415296	-0.05815	-0.051214986	0.058149058	0.05121499	-1.42
16	22.513	23.07043652	0.021632	-0.003053107	0.021631946	0.00305311	0.487
17	19.295	19.80937109	0.140192	0.110585485	0.14019176	0.11058549	2.705
18	31.735	31.77899664	0.00835	0.006954385	0.008350402	0.00695438	0.265
19	30.521	30.17985443	0.113987	0.126579324	0.113987091	0.12657932	3.479
20	23.925	23.68959204	-0.03866	-0.029109494	0.038662487	0.02910949	-0.925
21	22.803	22.44002078	-0.12292	-0.108735228	0.122922422	0.10873523	-2.803
22	21.681	19.36484634	-0.12366	-0.018840652	0.123656658	0.01884065	-2.681
23	16.744	16.85174646	0.075012	0.068138548	0.075011945	0.06813855	1.256
24	16.744	16.85174646	0.134735	0.127479578	0.13473483	0.12747958	2.256
25	32.772	33.12144847	0.067985	0.056717071	0.067984865	0.05671707	2.228
26	24.524	25.25178524	0.01941	-0.009970988	0.019409558	0.00997099	0.476
27						stdev	2.386961

Simulating Sales of a New Product with the Bass Model

A common marketing procedure is to fit the Bass model of product diffusion (see Chapter 11) to products considered similar to the new product under consideration. Then the likely total size of the market (Nbar) is estimated by other methods. Next, we may use the methods discussed earlier in this chapter to build a simulation model for Nbar. Finally, we randomly choose (with =RISKDUniform) Bass parameters p and q from a similar product. Then we can simulate the sales path of the product. Here is an example:

Example 36.5

We want to simulate the first six years of sales for a new hair dryer. We have fit the Bass model to five similar products and obtained the parameters in Figure 36.31.

Figure 36.31

	G	H	I
4	Bass #	p	q
5	1	0.04	0.53
6	2	0.01	0.19
7	3	0.04	0.01
8	4	0.26	0.04
9	5	0.11	0.24

For five similar products predicted market size and actual market size are given in Figure 36.32.

Figure 36.32

	A	B	C	D	E
4	Predicted market size	Actual Market Size	Actual/forecasted	Unbiased Forecast	%age error
5	400000	380000	0.95	375333.3	1.012433
6	500000	460000	0.92	469166.7	0.980462
7	300000	295000	0.983333333	281500	1.047957
8	800000	720000	0.9	750666.7	0.959147
9		mean	0.938333333	stdev	0.038752
10				mean	1

Total market size for the new hair dryer is predicted to be 200,000. Use this information to simulate six years of sales for the new hair dryer.

Solution   As we did earlier in the chapter we evaluate the forecast for total market size for bias. We find actual sales average to be 93.8% of predicted sales. After adjusting for bias, we find that actual sales have a standard deviation of around 3.9% of predicted sales. Therefore in cell B13 we simulate total market size with the formula

$$=RISKNormal(A13*C9,E9*A13*C9)).$$

This will be the value of Nbar used to predict sales with Bass model. Recall the Bass model works as follows:

Let

$n(t)$ = Product sales during period t.

$N(t)$ = Cumulative product sales during periods 1, 2, ... t.

$\overline{N}$ = Total number of customers in market; we assume that all of them eventually adopt the product.

P = Coefficient of innovation or external influence.

Q = Coefficient of imitation or internal influence.

The Bass Model asserts that

$$n(t) = P(\overline{N} - N(t-1)) + \frac{QN(t-1)(\overline{N} - N(t-1))}{\overline{N}}$$

To simulate six years of sales we proceed as follows: We have used range names Nbar, p and q, for cells B13, D13, and E13 respectively.

Step by   **Step 1:** In C13 randomly choose a similar product that will be used to generate
Step   **Bass parameters with the formula**

$$=RISKDUNIfORM(G5:G9).$$

Step 2: In D13 and E13 use =VLOOKUP to lookup the p and q for the selected product

$=VLOOKUP(\$C\$13,Bass,2).$ *(in cell D13)*

$=VLOOKUP(\$C\$13,Bass,3)$ *(in cell E13).*

We have used the range name Bass for G5:I9, where the p and q values for similar products are located.

**Figure
36.33**

	A	B	C	D	E
12	Forecast	Nbar	Bass #	p	q
13	200000	187666.6667	3	0.04	0.01
14		**Simulated sales N(t)**		n(t)	Nbar-N(t)
15		Year 0	0		187666.7
16		Year 1	7506.666667	7506.667	180160
17		Year 2	14785.13067	7278.464	172881.5
18		Year 3	21836.5951	7051.464	165830.1
19		Year 4	28662.75519	6826.16	159003.9
20		Year 5	35265.76193	6603.007	152400.9
21		Year 6	41648.18537	6382.423	146018.5
22			Six year cum	41648.19	

Step 3: In cell C15 note that N(0) = 0 and in cell E15 note that Nbar - N(0) simply equals Nbar (cell B13).

Step 4: In D16 use the Bass model to compute Year 1 sales with the formula

$=p*E15+q*C15*E15/(Nbar).$

Step 5: In cell C16 compute N(1) = (Sales through Year 0) + (Year 1 Sales) with the formula

$=C15+D16.$

Step 6: In cell E16 compute Nbar - N(1) with the formula

$=Nbar-C16.$

Step 7: Copying the formulas from C16:E16 to C17:C21 generates sales for Years 2-6. In cell D22 we compute total sales through six years with the formula

$=C21 \ or \ =SUM(D16:D21).$

After running 1000 iterations with Output cell D22 we obtain output in Figure 36.34.

Figure 36.34

	J	K
15	Name	Six year cum / n(t)
16	Description	Output
17	Cell	D22
18	Minimum =	15828.38
19	Maximum =	178399.1
20	Mean =	92292.75
21	Std Deviation =	54437.52
22	Variance =	2.96E+09
23	Skewness =	-0.1866238
24	Kurtosis =	1.459278
25	Errors Calculated =	0
26	Mode =	17380.84
27	5% Perc =	16836.63
28	10% Perc =	17356.23
29	15% Perc =	17776.55
30	20% Perc =	18821.81
31	25% Perc =	40681.81
32	30% Perc =	41755.46
33	35% Perc =	42683.07
34	40% Perc =	46520.74
35	45% Perc =	106439.8
36	50% Perc =	110043.8
37	55% Perc =	113367.9
38	60% Perc =	119241
39	65% Perc =	128686.8
40	70% Perc =	131487.6
41	75% Perc =	135313.6
42	80% Perc =	143475.1
43	85% Perc =	156935.8
44	90% Perc =	160364.7
45	95% Perc =	164378.3
46	Filter Minimum =	
47	Filter Maximum =	
48	Type (1 or 2) =	
49	# Values Filtered =	0
50	Scenario #1 =	>75%
51	Scenario #2 =	<25%
52	Scenario #3 =	>90%

We learn, for example, that during the first six years an average of 92,293 hair dryers will be sold. There is a 5% chance that sales will be less than 16,837 and a 5% chance that sales will exceed 164,378.

References

Powell, S., "From Intelligent Consumer to Active Modeler, Two MBA Success Stories", *Interfaces*, Vol. 26 No. 2, June 1997, pages 88-98.

Winston, W., *Marketing Models with Excel and Palisade Add-Ins*, Palisade Corporation, 1999.

Chapter 37: Obtaining a Distribution of IRR's

If the cash flows associated with a project are random, then the IRR (Internal rate of return) of the project is also random. In this case the distribution of IRR's may be of interest. In Excel you can often obtain the IRR (if there is a single IRR of the project) with the function

    = IRR(range of cash flows).

The problem is that unless you give Excel a starting "guess" near the actual IRR of the project, it may not obtain the IRR of the project. The syntax used to obtain IRR with a starting guess is as follows:

    = IRR(range of cash flows, guess).

As shown in Figure 37.1 for a guess of 100% IRR, Excel could not find an IRR. This is indicated by the #NUM message in L16.

Figure 37.1

	A	B	C	D	E	F
1	Price		2.2 Comp %age		0.2 **New Product Simulation**	
2	Unit Var Cost	0.4				
3	Interest rate	0.15				
4	Year	1	2	3	4	5
5	Market Size	1000000	1062435.53	1118982.47	1182647.573	1246520.132
6	Market Share	0.373809829	0.14952393	0.14952393	0.149523932	0.149523932
7	Competitors (beginning of year)	0	3	3	3	3
8	Entrants	3	0	0	0	0
9	Unit Sales	373809.8294	158859.537	167314.658	176834.115	186384.5912
10	Revenues	822381.6247	349490.981	368092.248	389035.053	410046.1006
11	Variable costs	149523.9318	63543.8148	66925.8633	70733.646	74553.83647
12	Fixed Costs	1800000			1200000	
13	Profits	-1127142.31	285947.167	301166.385	-881698.593	335492.2641

	C	D	E	F	L	M	N	O	P
15	-0.8	-0.6	-0.4	-0.2	1	Max	Min		
16	-57%	-57%	#NUM!	#NUM!	#NUM!			max-min	irr
17	-57%	-57% Error	Error		Error	-57%	-57%	0%	-57%

The problem in using @RISK to find a distribution of IRR's for a project is that we do not know which guess will yield the IRR. The following example shows how to address this problem. The trick is to determine the largest and smallest IRR's obtained for a wide range of guesses. If these numbers are equal, then we have found the IRR; otherwise we are in a multiple IRR situation. The problem is that if any guess yields a #NUM message (because an IRR cannot be found) the =MAX and =MIN functions will mess up. To remedy this we create a row in which the =COUNT function is used to replace any #NUM message by the text string error. Then the MAX and MIN functions will work!

Example 37.1

Consider the HIPPO problem (Example 28.1) but assume that during Year 1 a fixed cost of $1,800,000 is incurred and during Year 4 a fixed cost of $1,200,000 is incurred. Let's find the distribution of IRR's for this project. Our work is in file *IRR.xls*.

Step by Step

Step 1: In C15:L15 enter guesses for IRR ranging from -80%, -60%, ... 80%, 100%.

Step 2: In C16:L16 compute the IRR corresponding to each guess by copying the formula

$$=IRR(\$B\$13:\$F\$13,C15)$$

from C16 to C16:L16.

Step 3: In C17:L17 we keep any numerical values from row 16 and replace any #NUM value by the text string error. To do this copy the formula

$$=If(COUNT(C16)=1,C16,"Error")$$

from C16:L16. The COUNT function equals 1 if and only if a number appears in the row 16 cell above the current cell, so this formula keeps any IRR we have found and replaces any #NUM value with the text error.

Step 4: In cell M17 we compute the largest IRR found with the formula

$$=MAX(C17:L17).$$

Step 5: In cell N17 we compute the smallest IRR found with the formula

$$=MIN(C17:L17).$$

Step 6: In cell O17 we compute the difference between the largest and smallest IRR found with the formula

$$=M17 - N17.$$

Step 7: In cell P17 we compute the IRR found by Excel with the formula

$$= If(O17<=0.001,M17,"error").$$

If the largest and smallest IRR's found are equal, then we record the common value; otherwise there is no single IRR and we enter the text string error.

Step 8: After selecting cell P17 as our output cell we obtain @RISK output in Figure 37.2.

Figure 37.2

	T	U
117	Name	irr
118	Description	Output
119	Cell	P17
120	Minimum =	-0.7918435
121	Maximum =	2.05957
122	Mean =	1.27E-02
123	Std Deviation =	0.4769704
124	Variance =	0.2275008
125	Skewness =	0.7413931
126	Kurtosis =	3.403636
127	Errors Calculated =	0
128	Mode =	0.2627913
129	5% Perc =	-0.6550735
130	10% Perc =	-0.5577239
131	15% Perc =	-0.4826237
132	20% Perc =	-0.4104706
133	25% Perc =	-0.3509495
134	30% Perc =	-0.2951939
135	35% Perc =	-0.2276816
136	40% Perc =	-0.1665352
137	45% Perc =	-0.1122724
138	50% Perc =	-5.99E-02
139	55% Perc =	1.26E-03
140	60% Perc =	6.24E-02
141	65% Perc =	0.1458257
142	70% Perc =	0.2363454
143	75% Perc =	0.3113391
144	80% Perc =	0.3907341
145	85% Perc =	0.5183617
146	90% Perc =	0.6903509
147	95% Perc =	0.9166622
148	Filter Minimum =	
149	Filter Maximum =	
150	Type (1 or 2) =	
151	# Values Filtered =	0
152	Scenario #1 =	>75%
153	Scenario #2 =	<25%
154	Scenario #3 =	>90%

Thus we obtain an average IRR of 1.27%. If our "hurdle rate " is 15%, for example, this output demonstrates that this project has a chance between 30% and 35% of beating the hurdle rate. Note that no errors were recorded, so each iteration of @RISK yielded a unique IRR. Figure 37.3 gives a histogram of IRR's.

Figure 37.3

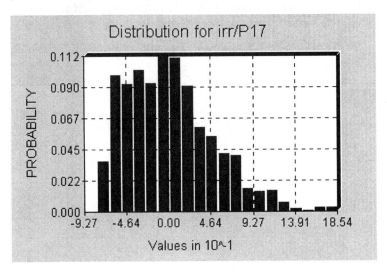

Remarks

When cash flows exhibit at most a single change in sign, a unique IRR is assured. Since Years 1 and 4 can both yield negative cash flows, we cannot be certain that a unique IRR will always exist for this project. All our iterations, however, have yielded a unique IRR.

Chapter 38: Using PrecisionTree to Analyze Decision Trees

Palisade Corporation's add-in PrecisionTree can be used to determine optimal decisions for financial problems that can be set up as **decision trees**. PrecisionTree also allows for extensive sensitivity analysis which can be used to determine how optimal decisions and profits depend on inputs to the problem. PrecisionTree can also be used to set up **influence diagrams** that can be used to solve problems involving decision making under uncertainty. We now show by example how PrecisionTree can be used to analyze (with decision trees) problems involving decision making under uncertainty. See Clemen (1996) for a discussion of decision trees and influence diagrams. We confine our discussion to decision trees.

Example 38.1

Drugco is trying to determine the appropriate capacity level for a new drug Niagara. At present Drugco believes there are two possible scenarios for Niagara.

- Annual demand will be low (500,000 units per year).

- Annual demand will be high (1,000,000 units per year).

At present Drugco believes the low demand scenario has a 70% chance of occurring and the high demand scenario has a 30% chance of occurring. Drugco needs to build capacity before the level of demand is known, but after the first year of sales Drugco will know whether the high or low demand scenario will occur. Current sales price of Niagara is $8 per unit with a unit production cost of $4. After the first year's demand is known Drugco can, if desired, expand capacity to 1,000,000 or contract capacity to 500,000. Relevant cost information is as follows.

- Cost of building one unit of annual production capacity at beginning of Year 1 is $10.

- Cost of building one unit of capacity at beginning of Year 2 is $18.

- Annual cost of maintaining one unit of annual capacity is $1.20.

- Cost of reducing annual capacity by one unit is $2.

- Unit sales price, unit variable cost, and annual cost of maintaining a unit of capacity are assumed to grow (due to inflation) at 5% per year.

Sales revenue and variable costs occur at the end of each year. All capacity costs occur at the beginning of a year.

Our goal is to maximize expected discounted profit over an infinite horizon. The interest rate is 15%. What strategy should Drugco follow?

Before setting up a decision tree we need to review the following result from basic finance: If we receive a cash flow of $c one year from now, cash flows are growing at a rate g% per year , and cash flows are discounted at interest rate r, then the NPV (in time 0 dollars) of all cash flows is given by

$$\frac{c}{r-g} \quad (38.1).$$

Solution   Our work is in file *captree.xls*. Figure 38.1 contains the inputs into our tree and Figure 38.2 contains the tree.

Figure 38.1

	A	B	C	D	E
1	**Possible demands**	**Name**	Size	Name	Probability
2	Low	Lowd	500000	Lowp	0.7
3	High	Highd	1000000		0.3
4					
5	**Unit building cost capacity**				
6	Now	capnow	10		
7	Next year	capnext	18	sales	Capacity costs
8				unit cost	beginning of Year
9	Capacity operating cost	capoc	1.2	end of yr.	
10	This year's sales price	prnow	8		
11	This year's unit cost	costnow	4		
12	unit cost to reduce capacity	capred	2		
13	interest rate	r_	0.15		
14	inflation rate	I	0.05		
15					
16	year 1 profit/unit of sales	Year1pr	3.47826087		
17	year 2 onward profit/unit of sales	Yeargte2pr	36.5217391		
18	cost of 1 unit capacity year 2 on	Yeargte2cap	12.6		

We will utilize the range names listed in Figure 38.1. In PrecisionTree you enter for each decision node the payoff associated with that node. A payoff must also be entered for each branch emanating from a chance or event fork. To determine these payoffs it will be helpful to compute the following quantitities:

- NPV of profit earned for each unit of Niagara sold during Year 1. This is computed in cell C16 with the formula

  =(prnow-costnow)/(1+r_).

Note that we divide by $1/((1+r\_)$ because costs and revenues are received at the end of each year.

- NPV earned if one unit of Niagara is sold during Year 2, Year 3, ... This is computed in cell C17 with the formula

  =(1/(1+r_))*(prnow-costnow)*(1+I)/(r_-I).

Note that at time 2 a unit sold yields a profit of (prnow-costnow)*(1+I). Note that unit profit is increasing at a rate I per year. Then the formula in C17   follows because from (38.1) the NPV (in Year 1 $s) of the profit earned from selling one unit during Years 2, … is *(prnow-costnow)*(1+I)/(r_-I)*. Discounting this back to the present yields the formula in B17.

- NPV of the cost incurred in operating one unit of capacity during Years 2, 3, … . This is computed in C18 with the formula

    =capoc*(1+I)/(r_-I).

This follows from (38.1) because capacity operating costs are incurred at the beginning of the year, they grow at rate I, and at time 1 a cost of *capoc*(1+I)* is incurred.

Using PrecisionTree

We are now ready to use PrecisionTree. The key to PrecisionTree is using the Node Settings to create decision or chance forks. For decision forks the payoff for a decision is entered in the cell under the branch corresponding to the decision. For each branch of a chance fork the probability of the branch is entered to the right of the branch and the payoff associated with the branch is entered in the cell below the branch. PrecisionTree automatically finds the path of decisions maximizing expected value. Let's see how to set up Example 38.1 in PrecisionTree.

Our tree is in Figure 38.2 and file *CH38tree.xls*.

Figure38.2

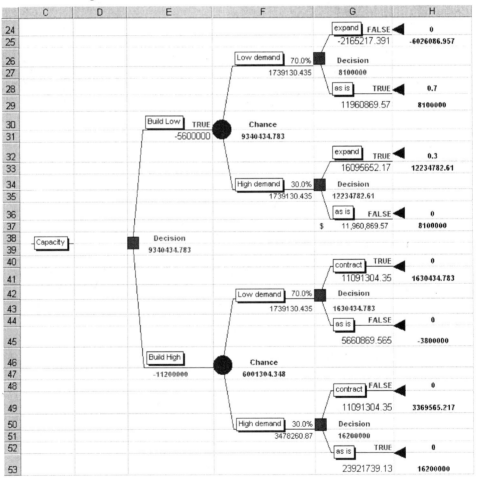

Step 1: Click on the New Tree icon and select cell C38 for the beginning of the tree. Click on the place in the spreadsheet where the tree is named (tree#1, tree#2, etc.) and from the Tree Settings dialog box name the tree Capacity and Click OK. To delete a tree click on Delete Tree from the Tree Settings dialog box.

New Tree
Icon

End Node

Tree
Settings
Dialog Box

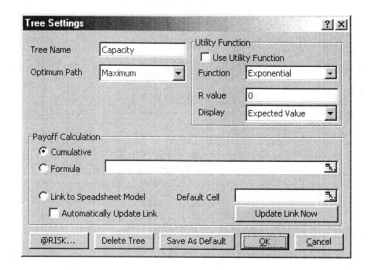

Step 2: Click on the End Node to reveal the Node Settings dialog box.

***Node
Settings
Dialog Box***

Clicking on the Decision Fork Icon let's you create a Decision Fork. Clicking on the Chance Fork Icon let's you create a Chance Fork. Since we begin with a decision fork (Low Capacity of 500,000 or High Capacity of 1,000,000) we click on the Decision Fork icon and indicate the number of branches in the decision fork (2). After clicking OK we click on a branch and we see the Branch Settings dialog box from which we can name a branch (Build Low). Clicking on the other branch we can use the Branch Settings dialog box to name the branch Build High.

Decision Fork Icon   ***Chance Fork Icon***

***Branch
Settings
Dialog Box***

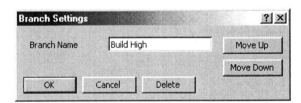

Step 3: Now we enter the payoffs for the Low Capacity and High Capacity decisions. This will just equal cost of building the capacity and operating the capacity for one year. In E31 we compute the "payoff" (negative since it is a cost) associated with Low Capacity with the formula

$$=-Lowd*capnow-Lowd*capoc.$$

Similarly, in E47 we compute the payoff associated with High Capacity with the formula

$$=-Highd*capnow-Highd*capoc.$$

Step 4: Next we create a chance fork following Build Low based on whether Year 1 demand is High (1,000,000) or Low. Click on the triangle following Build Low to bring up the Node Settings dialog box. Select the Chance Fork Icon and choose 2 branches. From the Branch Settings Dialog Box name these branches Low Demand and High Demand. In cell F26 we enter the probability of low demand with the formula

$$=Lowp.$$

In cell F27 compute the payoff associated (during Year 1) with Building Low and Low Demand with the formula

$$=Lowd*Year1pr.$$

This follows because each unit sold in Year 1 (and Lowd are sold) earns an NPV of Year1pr.

Now go to the High Demand branch (following Build Low) and enter the probability of High Demand in cell F35 with the formula

$$=1-Lowp.$$

Since we are following Build Low we can only meet 500,000 units of demand, so the fact that demand is high does not change profit. Therefore the payoff from this branch is computed in F35 with the formula

$$=F27.$$

Step 5: Now we create a decision fork with two branches following Low demand and Build Low. The two branches correspond to Expand or As Is. To do this click on the triangle after Build Low and Low Demand and choose the Decision fork icon. From Branch Settings name the branches Expand and As Is. For the Expand decision enter the payoff in cell G25 with the formula

$$=Yeargte2pr*Lowd-(Highd-Lowd)*capnext/(1+r\_)-Yeargte2cap*Highd.$$

The term *Yeargte2pr*Lowd* gives the NPV of all sales from Year 2 and later. The term -*(Highd-Lowd)*capnext/(1+r_)* gives the cost of expanding capacity. The term -*Yeargte2cap*Highd* gives the NPV of operating capacity from Year 2 and later.

For the As Is decision enter the payoff in cell G29 with the formula

   =Yeargte2pr*Lowd-Lowd*Yeargte2cap.

Step 6: Now we create a decision fork with two branches following High demand and Build Low. The two branches correspond to Expand or As Is. To do this click on the triangle after Build Low and High Demand and choose the Decision fork icon. From Branch Settings name the branches Expand and As Is. For the Expand decision enter the payoff in cell G33 with the formula

   =Yeargte2pr*Highd-(Highd-Lowd)*capnext/(1+r_)-Yeargte2cap*Highd.

The term *Yeargte2pr*Highd* gives the NPV of all sales from Year 2 and later. The term -*(Highd-Lowd)*capnext/(1+r_)* gives the cost of expanding capacity. The term -*Yeargte2cap*Highd* gives the NPV of operating capacity from Year 2 and later.

For the As Is decision enter the payoff in cell G37 with the formula

   =G29.

This follows because if we leave capacity As Is after Build Low then our profit from Year 2 onward is the same for Low Demand as for High Demand.

Step 7: Next we create a chance fork following Build High based on whether Year 1 demand is High (1,000,000) or Low. Click on the triangle following Build High to bring up the Node Settings dialog box. Select the Chance Fork Icon and choose 2 branches. From the Branch Settings Dialog Box name these branches Low Demand and High Demand. In cell F42 we enter the probability of low demand with the formula

   =Lowp.

In cell F43 compute the payoff associated (during Year 1) with Building High and Low Demand with the formula

   =F27.

Now go to the High Demand branch (following Build High) and enter the probability of High Demand in cell F50 with the formula

   =1-Lowp.

Since we are following Build High we can meet 1,000,000 units of demand, so the fact that demand is high leads to the following expression for profit being placed in cell F51

$= Highd*Year1pr.$

Step 8: Now we create a decision fork with two branches following Low demand and Build High. The two branches correspond to Contract or As Is. To do this click on the triangle after Build High and Low Demand and choose the Decision fork icon. From Branch Settings name the branches Contract and As Is. For the Contract decision enter the payoff in cell G41 with the formula

$=Yeargte2pr*Lowd-Lowd*Yeargte2cap-(Highd-Lowd)*capred/(1+r\_).$

The term *Yeargte2pr*Lowd* gives the NPV of all sales from Year 2 and later. The term -*(Highd-Lowd)*capredt/(1+r_)* gives the cost of contracting capacity. The term -*Yeargte2cap*Lowd* gives the NPV of operating capacity from Year 2 and later.

For the As Is decision enter the payoff in cell G45 with the formula

$=Yeargte2pr*Lowd-Highd*Yeargte2cap.$

This follows because from Year 2 onward we will sell Lowd per year and operate Highd units of capacity from Year 2 onward.

Step 9: Now we create a decision fork with two branches following High demand and Build High. The two branches correspond to Contract or As Is. To do this click on the triangle after Build High and High Demand and choose the Decision fork icon. From Branch Settings name the branches Contract and As Is. For the Contract decision enter the payoff in cell G49 with the formula

$=Yeargte2pr*Lowd-Lowd*Yeargte2cap-(Highd-Lowd)*capred/(1+r\_).$

The term *Yeargte2pr*Lowd* gives the NPV of all sales from Year 2 and later. The term -*(Highd-Lowd)*capred/(1+r_)* gives the cost of reducing capacity. The term -*Yeargte2cap*Lowd* gives the NPV of operating capacity from Year 2 and later.

For the As Is decision enter the payoff in cell G53 with the formula

$=Yeargte2pr*Highd-Highd*Yeargte2cap.$

This follows because if we leave capacity As Is after Build High then we sell Highd units per year from Year 2 onward and we operate Highd units of capacity per year from Year 2 onward.

Step 10: The tree is now complete. PrecisionTree has automatically found our optimal strategy by working backward through the tree. The decision path maximizing our expected NPV is found by following the True found on branches from decision forks. Thus our optimal strategy is to Build Low and if Year 1 demand is Low leave capacity as is; if Year 1 demand is high Expand. If the optimal strategy is followed an expected NPV of $9,340,435 will be received.

Meaning of Numbers Computed by PrecisionTree

For each ending branch of a decision tree, PrecisionTree computes two numbers: the probability that the branch will occur if an optimal strategy is followed and the total payoff received if the path leading to that terminal branch occurs. For example, the branch defined by the path Build Low, Low Demand, Capacity as is will occur 70% of the time and lead to an NPV of $8.1 million (the sum of the NPV's in cells E31, F27, and G29. For each chance and decision fork PrecisionTree gives you the expected payoff that will be received if that fork is reached. For example, if we Build Low an expected NPV of $9,340,435 will be received. If we Build Low and Low Demand occurs, our expected NPV (obtained by As Is) is $8.1 million. Observe that if we choose to initially Build High our expected NPV is $6.001 million.

Remarks

- From Node Settings box it is possible to copy nodes and then paste them elsewhere in the tree. This would make it easier, for example to create all the Expand and As Is branches.

- PrecisionTree allows you (through the Tree Settings dialog box) to maximize expected utility instead of expected value.

Sensitivity Analysis

It is natural to wonder how changes in various input parameters change both Drugco's optimal decision strategy and Drugco's expected NPV. PrecisionTree makes this type of sensitivity analysis an easy matter. To illustrate suppose we want to know how changes in E2 (probability of low demand), C7 (unit cost of building capacity next year), and C3 (the level of high demand) change Drugco's optimal strategy and expected NPV. More specifically, suppose we believe these parameters might reasonably vary between the following limits:

- Probability of low demand (E2) might vary between .1 and .9.

- Unit cost of building capacity next year (C7) might vary between $11 and $28.

- The level of high demand (C3) may vary between 600,000 and 2,000,000.

To perform sensitivity analysis click on the sensitivity analysis icon.

You will then see the Sensitivity Analysis dialog box.

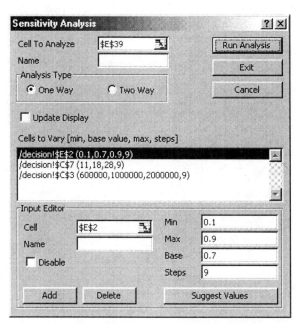

If you are interested in looking at sensitivity of the maximum NPV to changes in problem input select the cell containing the tree's NPV (E39) as the Cell to Analyze.

You will also find out how the optimal decision associated with the root of the tree varies. If you want to find out how another decision varies, select the cell containing the expected NPV for the decision fork of interest. From the Input Editor we select the cells we want to vary, the cell's minimum value, the cell's maximum value, a base value from which to measure percentage changes in expected NPV, and the number of equally spaced steps between the minimum and maximum value at which the cell will be evaluated. For example, for cell E2 (probability of Low Demand) we told PrecisionTree to let the probability of Low Demand vary between .1 and .9 using 9 steps and to use .7 (the current value) as a base level. After selecting Run Analysis we will obtain three types of charts (*see sheets in Captree.xls*).

- A **tornado graph**, which measures the percentage change in expected NPV from the base value (calculated with all inputs at their base levels) as each input parameter is varied from its lowest to highest levels.

- A set of **sensitivity graphs** which shows how the optimal decision and expected NPV for the cell to analyze change as each input parameter varies between its minimum and maximum values.

- A **spider graph** that shows how the expected NPV associated with the Cell to Analyze varies with changes in the selected input parameters.

Tornado Graph

The tornado graph is given in Figure 38.3. Again we define the **base NPV** as the expected NPV when all input parameters assume their base values.

Figure 38.3

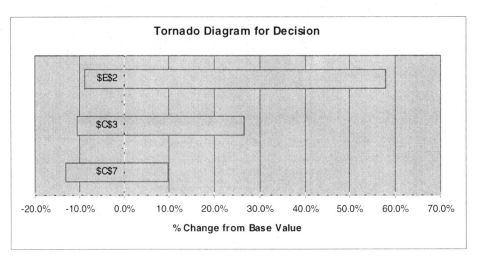

From Figure 38.3 we find that

- As the probability of low demand (E2) varies from .1 to .9, expected NPV changes from 9% below to 59% above the base NPV.

- As the level of high demand (C3) varies from 600,000 to 2,000,000, expected NPV changes from 11% below to 27% above the base NPV.

- As the unit cost (C7) of adding capacity varies between $11 and $28 expected NPV changes from 13% below to 10% above the base NPV.

Sensitivity Graph

To illustrate the interpretation of the **Sensitivity Graph,** we look at the sensitivity graphs for cell E2 (probability of low demand). See Figures 38.4 and 38.5.

Figure 38.4

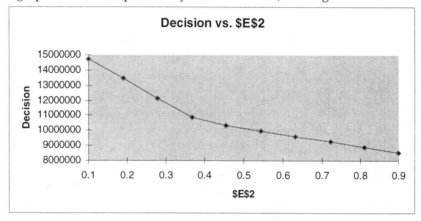

Figure 38.5

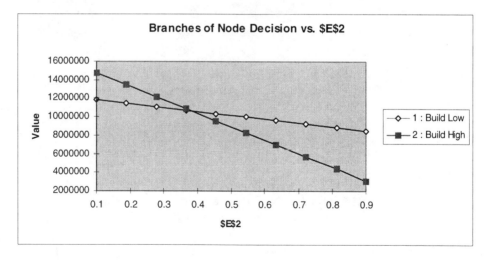

From Figure 38.4 we see that if probability of low demand is less than .3667, an increase in the probability of low demand decreases expected NPV with the slope of the decrease being about $14.6 million. If probability of low demand is greater than .3667, an increase in the probability of low demand decreases expected NPV but at a smaller rate (slope of the decrease being about $4.2 million). From Figure 38.5 we find that if the probability of low demand is less than .3667 Build High is the correct decision while if probability of low demand exceeds .3667 Build Low is the correct decision.

Spider Graph

Figure 38.6 shows the Spider Graph for our chosen inputs.

Figure 38.6

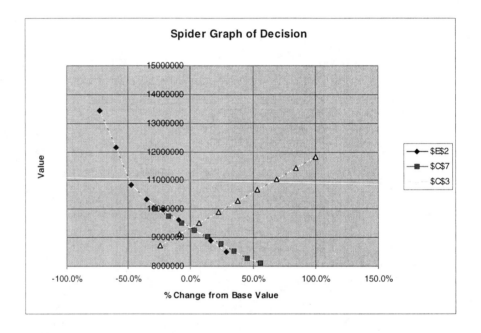

We find that as the level of high demand (C3) increases expected NPV increases in a linear fashion. As the probability of low demand (E2) increases, expected NPV decreases in a piecewise linear fashion. As the unit cost of adding capacity increases (C7), expected NPV decreases in a linear fashion.

Reference

Clemen, R., *Making Hard Decisions*, Duxbury Press, 1996.

Chapter 39: Combining TopRank and @RISK for Simulation Analysis

Simulation in the business world is often used to analyze the profitability of a new product. The profitability of a new product is highly uncertain because it depends on many highly uncertain quantities. The author has worked with several companies (including General Motors and Eli Lilly) that begin the analysis of a new product by determining the uncertain quantities that might affect the profitability of a new product. Suppose for a new drug (code name Orange) the following uncertain quantities may affect profitability of the drug:

- Initial cost incurred in developing the product

- Salvage value obtained from equipment after production of product has stopped

- Number of years (Life) for which product sells

- Discount rate used to discount cash flows from the product

- Annual fixed cost incurred during years in which product is manufactured

- Unit price for the product

- Years after product is developed until revenue is earned

- Percentage of demand for product which is lost to competition

- Unit cost of producing product

- Initial demand for product during first year it is sold

- Annual percentage growth in demand

We refer to these uncertain quantities as **input variables.**

A natural question is how changes in the input variables will affect a quantity of interest, called an **output variable.** In our problem the NPV of Orange will be the output variable. We will use the Palisade Excel add-in TopRank to answer this question. To begin such a sensitivity analysis many companies (such as GM and Eli Lilly) begin by identifying for each input variable.

- A base case (the most likely value of the variable)

- Lowest possible value of the variable

- Highest possible value of the variable

For our new product analysis (*see file Tor.xls*) suppose we have identified the following base, high and low possibilities for each uncertain input which impacts product profitability:

Figure 39.1

	A	B	C	D	E
1		Low	Base	High	Actual Value
2	Development Cost	90%	120000	150%	120000
3	Salvage	0%	20000	150%	20000
4	Life	50%	12	200%	12
5	Discount rate	60%	0.1	200%	0.1
6	Annual Fixed Cost	80%	6000	125%	6000
7	Price	60%	5	125%	5
8	Years till revenue	50%	2	300%	2
9	sales Lost to Comp	0%	0.2	200%	0.2
10	Unit cost	0%	2	150%	2
11	**Initial demand**	30%	20000	120%	20000
12	Annual demand growth	50%	0.1	120%	0.1

For example, the most likely product price is $5 with the lowest possible product price being $3.00 and the highest possible product price being $6.25. A natural question is the following: When an input changes between its lowest and highest values, by how much does the output of interest (in this case project NPV) fluctuate about its base value? To answer this question we need to create a **Tornado Graph.** A tornado graph shows for each input variable (such as price, life of project, etc.) how the output variable (in this case product NPV) is affected as each input variable changes from its lowest to highest possible value and each other variable remains at its base value. Before creating a tornado graph we need to answer the following question: if the actual values of the input variables are given in E2:E12, how can we determine the NPV of the project? We proceed as follows (many years of the spreadsheet have been hidden):

Step 1: In B14 and B15 we determine the time at which the drug begins to earn revenue and the time at which we stop earning revenue. To simplify our spreadsheet, we round the life of the project and starting date of revenue to the nearest integer. In B14 we determine the number of years until revenue starts to be earned with the formula

=ROUND(E8,0).

If B14 contains a "2" for instance, revenue is earned starting with year 3.

In B15 we compute the last year in which revenue is earned with the formula

=B14+ROUND(E4,0).

Step 2: In cell B17 we compute the development cost of the project (assume incurred in Year 0) with the formula

= E2.

Step 3: In B18:AF18 we determine if the project is earning revenue. Note the project is earning revenue if and only if the project has begun and is not yet finished. By copying the formula

=If(AND(B16>$B$14,B16<=$B$15),"Yes","No")

from B18 to C18:AF18 we enter a Yes during a year in which revenue is earned and a No during a year for which revenue is not earned.

Step 4: In C19:AF19 we compute the fixed cost during each year by copying from C19 to D19:AF19 the formula

=If(C18="Yes",$E$6,0).

Note these formulas insure that a fixed cost is incurred only for years in which product is being sold.

Step 5: In C20:AF20 we compute the demand for each year by copying from C20 to D20:AF20 the formula

=If(AND(B18="No",C18="Yes"),$E11,If(C18="Yes",(1+$E$12)*B20,0)).

This ensures that during the first year the product is sold demand is generated from E11, and during other years in which the product is sold demand grows by the annual rate given in E12.

Step 6: In C21:AF21 we keep track of the product price (from E7) by copying the formula

=$E$7

from C21 to D21:AF21.

Step 7: In C22:AF22 we keep track of the revenue earned each year by copying from C22 to D22:AF22 the formula

=C20*C21*(1-$E$9).

This accounts for the fraction of demand lost to competition (given in E9).

Step 8: In C23:AF23 we compute the unit cost (from E10) for each year by copying from C23 to D23:AF23 the formula

=$E$10.

Step 9: In C24:AF24 we compute the total variable cost for each year by copying from C24 to D24:AF24 the formula

=C23*C20*(1-$E$9).

Again, the term (1-$E$9) keeps track of demand lost to competition.

Step 10: In C25:AF25 we compute the salvage value received by copying from C25 to D25:AF25 the formula

=If(AND(B18="No",C18="Yes"),$E$3,0).

This formula ensures salvage value (given in E3) is received during the year after the project stops.

Step 11: In B26:AF26 we compute the profit earned each year by copying from B26 to C26:AF26 the formula

=B22-B24-B19-B17+B25.

Step 12: Finally in B28 we compute the NPV of the project (assuming all cash flows occur at end of year) with the formula

=NPV(E5,B26:AF26).

Constructing a Tornado Graph

TopRank makes it easy to create a Tornado Graph. The key function used in TopRank is the =RISKVary function. A RISKVary function should be entered into the spreadsheet for every input.

Here are some illustrations of the syntax of the =RISKVary function.

=RISKVary(base, minimum, maximum, range type, #Steps, distribution)

- Base is simply the base case for the input variable.

- Range Type is optional. If omitted or equal to 0, then Minimum and Maximum must indicate the percentage departure of the Minimum and Maximum value of the input from the base. If Range Type =1, then Minimum and Maximum must represent the actual amount by which the Minimum and Maximum value differ from the base case. If Range Type = 2 then the Minimum and Maximum must be entered as their actual values.

- #Steps lets you choose the number of equally spaced points between Minimum and Maximum for which TopRank evaluates the output function. #Steps is optional and if omitted the default (usually 4) number of Steps is used. For example, if 4 steps are used for Salvage Value TopRank will evaluate product NPV by holding each other input at its base level and letting Salvage Value equal $0, $10,000, $20,000 and $30,000. The default may be changed by accessing Steps through the Settings Icon.

Settings Icon

- Distribution setting is optional and we will ignore it. Distribution lets you choose the spacing of the points at which output is evaluated by using percentiles of an @RISK distribution.

We can now use TopRank to generate a Tornado Graph. We will use 8 steps. We will place our *=RISKVary* functions in E2:E12.

Figure 39.2

	A	B	C	D	E	P	Q	AF
1		Low	Base	High	Actual Value			
2	Development Cost	90%	120000	150%	120000			
3	Salvage	0%	20000	150%	20000			
4	Life	50%	12	200%	12			
5	Discount rate	60%	0.1	200%	0.1			
6	Annual Fixed Cost	80%	6000	125%	6000			
7	Price	60%	5	125%	5			
8	Years till revenue	50%	2	300%	2			
9	sales Lost to Comp	0%	0.2	200%	0.2			
10	Unit cost	0%	2	150%	2			
11	**Initial demand**	30%	20000	120%	20000			
12	Annual demand growth	50%	0.1	120%	0.1			
13								
14	Revenue begins	2						
15	Revenue ends	14						
16	Year	0	1	2	3	14	15	30
17	Development Cost	120000						
18	project going	No	No	No	Yes	Yes	No	No
19	fixed cost		0	0	6000	6000	0	0
20	unit demand		0	0	20000	57062.33412	0	0
21	price		$ 5.00	$ 5.00	$ 5.00	$ 5.00	$ 5.00	$ 5.00
22	revenue		$ -	$ -	$ 80,000.00	$228,249.34	$ -	$ -
23	unit cost		$ 2.00	$ 2.00	$ 2.00	$ 2.00	$ 2.00	$ 2.00
24	total variable cost		$ -	$ -	$ 32,000.00	$ 91,299.73	$ -	$ -
25	salvage value		$ -	$ -	$ -	$ -	$20,000.00	$ -
26	profit	-120000	0	0	42000	130949.6019	20000	0
27								
28	NPV of profit	$257,962.06						

Step 1: Enter in E2 the formula

$=RiskVary(C2,B2*C2,C2*D2,2,8)$.

Note that since we chose RANGE TYPE =2 we entered the **actual values** for the minimum and maximum development cost. We could have also entered in E2

$=RISKVary(C2,100*B2-100,100*D2-100,0,8)$

or

$=RISKVary(C2,(1-B2)*C2,(D2-1)*C2,1,8)$.

Step 2: Simply copy the formula in E2 to E3:E12.

Step 3: Click the Select Output cell icon. and select the cell B28 containing the project's NPV.

Select Output Cell Icon

To check selected output cells or to delete or rename an output cell click on the List Inputs and Outputs Icon.

List Inputs and Outputs Icon

Step 4: Click on the Settings Icon. Then select the Auto-ID tab and uncheck (if it is checked) the Automatically Insert Autovary Functions. If you do not do this TopRank will insert many =RISKAutovary functions into your spreadsheet. These will clutter your graphs in TopRank and @RISK.

Step 5: Clicking on the Run What-If Analysis Icon runs the What-If Analysis. For each of the inputs TopRank is computing project NPV for the 8 equally spaced values of the INPUTS between input's minimum and maximum value. Of course, each other input is held at its base value. At any time you can switch to the results of the What-If analysis by clicking on the Results icon.

Run What-If Icon

Results Icon

You may return to your spreadsheet any time by clicking on Hide icon.

Hide Icon

Step 6: Now select the Graph icon and choose Tornado Graph.

***Graph Icon
and Dialog
Box***

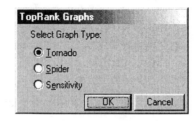

You will find your Tornado graph contains references to columns B and D. This is because TopRank searches for any spreadsheet cell which influences the output and the Minimum and Maximum values for each input do influence the input values used in the Tornado graph. To eliminate these cells from the Tornado graph select your graph and right click the Mouse. Then choose the Format option and Variables To Graph. Holding down the Control key, you may now select the input variables you want to include in your Tornado graph. Simply select E2:E12. You will obtain the following Tornado graph:

Note: In Office 97 to paste a TopRank (or @RISK) graph into your worksheet you must first save it as a bitmap (suffix.bmp) file and then choose Insert Picture From File. With earlier versions of Excel you may simply copy your graph to the Clipboard and paste it into your worksheet.

Figure 39.4

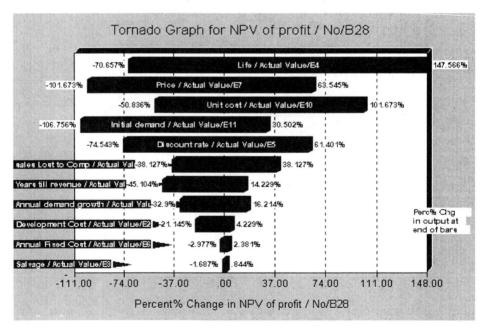

We see there is a "bar" for each input variable and the widest bars are on top, giving the appearance of a Tornado. The right-hand number on a bar is the percentage by which the product NPV increases over the base case when the input assumes its maximum value. Similarly, the left-hand number on a bar is the percentage by which the product NPV decreases from the base case when the input assumes its minimum value. For example, given the ranges within which our inputs can reasonably vary, the number of years for which the product sells appears to be the most important single driver of product NPV. If the Life of the product is 6 years, then our NPV is 71% less than the base case;' if the Life of the Product is 24 years, then our NPV is 148% higher than the base case. Once we drop below discount rate there appears to be a substantial drop-off in the width of the bars. The moral learned from the tornado graph is that the 5 key drivers of NPV are (in descending order):

- Number of years (Life) for which product sells.

- Product price.

- Product unit cost.

- Initial product demand.

- Discount rate.

Clearly, if we going to simulate product NPV we need to spend a lot of time accurately accessing the distributions of Life, Unit Price, Unit Cost, and Initial demand. The discount rate used in a typical new product analysis is usually a corporate rate of 10%-15% per year and is obtained from the CAPM (Capital Asset Pricing Model). Riskier projects should be discounted at a higher rate than the corporate rate and less risky projects should be discounted at a lower rate than the corporate rate.

Our tornado graph also indicates that Annual Fixed Cost and Salvage Value have virtually no effect on NPV. Therefore, little effort should be spent trying to accurately estimate their values.

Spider Graphs and Sensitivity Graphs

Spider plots and Sensitivity Graphs are used less frequently than tornado graphs, but they still provide useful information. A **Spider Graph** shows for each input how the output (product NPV) varies when the input varies between its minimum and maximum value. To avoid clutter at most five inputs should be graphed on a spider plot. With this in mind we choose Spider from the Graph Menu. After selecting (with Format Variables to Graph option) the five most significant inputs (as determined from the Tornado Graph we obtain the Spider Graph in Figure 39.5. From Figure 39.5 we learn (unsurprisingly) that changes in Unit Price, Unit Cost and Initial demand result in linear changes in Product NPV. Also, a 1% increase in Unit Price results in a larger percentage increase in NPV than does a 1% percentage increase in initial demand. As the discount rate increases, product NPV decreases, but the rate of decrease slows; after a while increases the discount rate cannot knock NPV down much further. Increases in Product life appear to increase product NPV in a complex, nonlinear fashion.

Figure 39.5

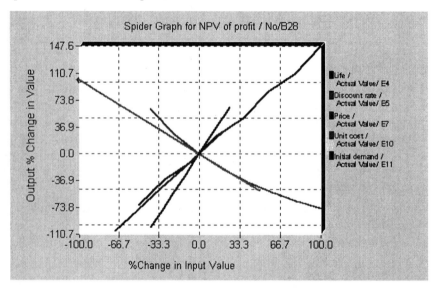

For clarity you may want to display a graph of how the output changes as a function of a single input. To do so simply click on go to Input and Output List icon and select the desired input. Then click on Graph and choose Sensitivity graph. As an example, the sensitivity graph for price is displayed in Figure 39.6.

Inputs and Outputs Icon

Figure 39.6

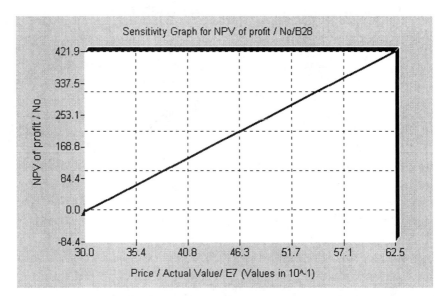

Note that the scale for both axis of the sensitivity graph is in actual values, not percentages.

Running an @RISK Simulation

Our initial sensitivity analysis with TopRank has shown us that the five key drivers of NPV are Number of years (Life) for which product sells, Product price, Product unit cost, Initial product demand, and Discount rate. Suppose we want to get an idea about the distribution of NPV earned from Orange. To obtain a distribution of the NPV earned from Orange we will model our first four key drivers of NPV as **triangular variables.** For instance we will determine life of project by entering in E4 the formula

$=RISKTriang(6,12,24).$

This will ensure that the life of the drug Orange is modeled according to the following random variable:

Figure 39.7

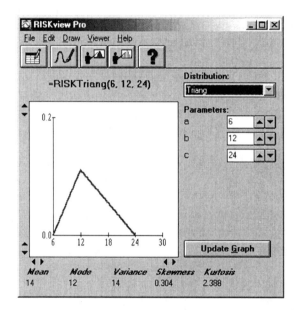

The likelihood of a particular value of life is proportional to the height of the triangle. Thus a product life of 12 years is twice as likely as a life of 9 years, etc.

The use of a triangular random variable is common at many companies such as General Motors and Eli Lilly. The triangular random variable is often used because, unlike the normal random variable, the triangular random variable makes no assumption that the distribution of the uncertain quantity is symmetric about its mean or most likely value. At GM the use of a triangular random variable to model uncertain quantities in analysis of different products grew directly out of deterministic tornado graph analysis.

In a similar fashion we model in E7 price with the formula

=RISKTriang(3,5,6.25).

In E10 we model unit cost with the formula

=RISKTriang(0,2,3).

In E11 we model initial demand with the formula

=RISKTriang(6000,20000,24000).

We model various discount rates in E5 with a RISKSimTable function.

=RISKSimTable({0.06,0.1,0.15,0.2}).

This allows us to try a discount rate appropriate for a less risky project (.06) a project of average risk (.10), or a project of higher risk (.15 or .20).

All other inputs are assumed to equal their base values. Our output cell (B28) is NPV. After changing the simulation settings to 400 iterations and 4 simulations we obtain the following results:

Figure 39.8

	A	B	C	D	E
34	Discount factor	0.06	0.1	0.15	0.2
35	Minimum =	-82537.88	-88121.06	-91432.89	-92662.52
36	Maximum =	2169776	1234136	661014.9	380520.4
37	Mean =	291244.1	161403.3	69685.92	18541.41
38	Std Deviation =	252710	157381	96335.91	64389.63

Thus we see that if the project is deemed be less risky than the company's typical project (justifying a 6% discount rate) our simulation indicates the project has a mean NPV (often called the **risk-adjusted project NPV**) of $291,244. If the project is so risky that it deserves a 20% discount rate, our simulation indicates the risk-adjusted project NPV is only $18,541. Even if the project is extremely risky, it is still worth doing because it has a positive risk-adjusted NPV. Our 95% confidence interval for risk-adjusted NPV would be $12,231-$24,852 (see cells E64 and E65 of simulation spreadsheet).

Figure 39.9

	A	B	C	D	E	P
63	95% CI for RA NPV	6%	10%	15%	20%	Discount rate
64	Lower	266478.52	145980	60245.00082	12231.22626	
65	Upper	316009.68	176826.6	79126.83918	24851.59374	

Tornado Graphs and @RISK

@RISK can also be used to construct Tornado Graphs. The interpretation of @RISK tornado graphs is different, however, from the interpretation of a TopRank Tornado Graph. To obtain an @RISK Tornado graph make sure that under *"Simulations Settings" "Sampling"* the *"Collect Distribution Samples"* box is checked. Then simply click Sensitivity and then Graph from the Results menu. Next highlight either Regression or Correlation Graph. For a 6% discount rate, our tornado graphs are displayed in Figures 39.10 and 39.11:

Figure 39.10- Correlation Tornado Graph

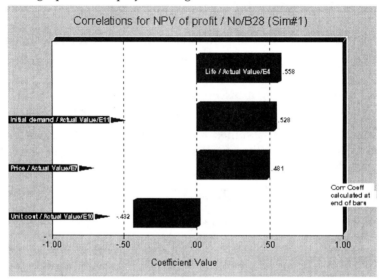

Figure 39.11- Regression Tornado Graph

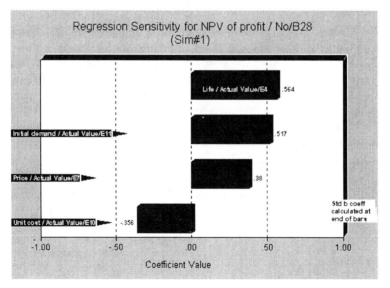

The regression tornado graph is interpreted as follows: @RISK takes all 400 iterations as observations and runs a regression with the dependent variable being project NPV and the independent variables being every cell in spreadsheet containing an @RISK random variable. Then the coefficient for each random cell in the spreadsheet is (after adjusting for the influence of all other random cells in the spreadsheet) the number of standard deviations by which the output cell will increase when the random cell is increased by one standard deviation. Thus from the regression tornado graph we find (after adjusting for the effect of all other random cells in the spreadsheet) that:

- A one standard deviation increase in the life of the product will increase NPV by .56 standard deviations.

- A one standard deviation increase in the initial demand for the product will increase NPV by .52 standard deviations.

- A one standard deviation increase in the price of the product will increase NPV by .38 standard deviations.

- A one standard deviation increase in the unit cost will decrease NPV by .36 standard deviations.

The correlation tornado graph gives the **rank order** correlation of each random cell in the spreadsheet with the output cell (NPV). Thus the correlation tornado graph tells us

- The number of years the product sells for has a rank order .56 correlation with NPV.

- The initial demand for the product has a .53 rank order correlation with NPV.

- The price of the product has .48 rank order correlation with NPV.

- The unit cost of the product has a -.43 rank order correlation with NPV.

The rank order correlation between an input and output is computed by ranking the values of the output cells from smallest to largest, ranking the values of the input cells from smallest to largest, and correlating the input and output ranks, instead of the actual input and output values.

Chapter 40: The Risk Neutral Approach to Option Pricing

A **European option** on a stock gives the owner of the option the right to buy (if the option is a **call option**) or sell (if the option is a **put option**) one share of stock for a particular price (**the exercise price**) on a particular date (the **exercise date**). An **American option** allows you buy or sell the stock at any date between the present and the exercise date.

Options are usually priced by arbitrage arguments. For example, suppose 3 months from now a stock will sell for either $18 (bad state) or $22 (good state). The stock currently sells for $20 and we own a 3-month European call option with an exercise price of $21. The risk free rate is 12% per year. Three months from now the option is worth $1 (in good state) or $0 (in bad state). If we create a portfolio that is long .25 shares of stock and short 1 call we will show that in both Good and Bad states this portfolio yields $4.50.

State	Portfolio Value
Good	.25($22) −(1)($1) = $4.50.
Bad	.25($18) −(1)($0) = $4.50.

Note that in the Good state the option is worth $1 because we can exercise the option and buy the stock for $20 and immediately sell the stock for $21. In the Bad state the option is worthless because there is no benefit to be gained by buying the stock for $20 when the current price is $18!.

Since this portfolio yields $4.50 for certain three months from now its value today must equal the NPV (discounted at the risk-free rate) of $4.50 received three months from now. This is just

$4.5e^{-.25(.12)}$ =$4.37. *This implies that*

.25(today's stock price) − (today's option price) = $4.37 or

5 − (today's option price) = $4.37 or

(today's option price) = $0.63.

This pricing approach is called **arbitrage pricing**. The argument works independent of a person's risk preferences. Therefore we may use the following approach to price derivatives;

1) In a world where everyone is risk neutral arbitrage pricing is valid.

2) In a risk neutral world all assets must grow on average at risk free rate.

3) In a risk neutral world any asset (including an option) is worth the expected value of its discounted cash flows.

4) Set up a risk neutral world in which all stocks grow at risk free rate and use @RISK (or binomial tree; see Chapters 56-58) to determine expected discounted cash flows from option.

5) **Since the arbitrage pricing method gives the correct price in all worlds it yields the correct price in a risk neutral world. Therefore if we use the above method to find a derivative's price in a risk neutral world we have found the right price for our complicated non risk-neutral world!**

It is important to note that actual growth rate of a stock is irrelevant to pricing a derivative. Information about a stock's future growth rate is imbedded in today's stock price.

Example of Risk Neutral Approach

Let's find the call option value of $0.63 using the risk neutral approach. Let p be probability (in the risk neutral world) that in 3 months stock price is $22. Then 1 – p is probability that stock price 3 months from now is $18. If stock grows on average at risk free rate we must have

$$p(\$22) + (1-p)(\$18) = 20 * e^{(.25)(.12)} = \$20.61 \text{ or}$$

$$4p = 2.61$$

$$or$$

$$p = .65.$$

Now value option as expected discounted value of its cash flows:

$$e^{-.25(.12)}(.65(\$1) + .35(\$0)) = \$0.63.$$

For further discussion of the risk neutral approach we refer the reader to Hull (1997).

Reference

Hull, J. *Options Futures and Derivative Securities*, Prentice-Hall, 1997.

Chapter 41: The Lognormal Model of Stock Prices

The Lognormal model for asset value (or stock price) assumes that in a small time

$$Standard\ Deviation = \sigma S \sqrt{\Delta t}$$

Δt the stock price changes by an amount that is normally distributed with

$$Mean = \mu S \Delta t$$

Here S = current stock price.

μ may be thought of as the instantaneous rate of return on the stock. By the way, this model leads to really "jumpy" changes in stock prices (like real life). This is because during a small period of time the standard deviation of the stock's movement will greatly exceed the mean of a stock's movement. This follows because for small Δt, $\sqrt{\Delta t}$ will be much larger than Δt.

In a small time Δt the natural logarithm (Ln (S)) of the current stock price will change (by Ito's Lemma, see Hull (1997)) by an amount that is normally distributed with

$$Mean = (\mu - .5\sigma^2)\Delta t$$

$$Standard\ Deviation = \sigma \sqrt{\Delta t}$$

Let S_t = stock price at time t. In Chapter 11 of Hull (1997) it is shown that at time t Ln S_t is normally distributed with

$$Mean = Ln\ S_0 + (\mu - .5\sigma^2)\ t\ and$$

$$Standard\ Deviation = \sigma \sqrt{t}$$

We refer to $(\mu - .5\sigma^2)$ as the **continuously compounded rate of return** on the stock. Note the continuously compounded rate of return on S is less than instantaneous return. Since Ln S_t follows a normal random variable we say that S_t is a **Lognormal random variable.**

To simulate S_t we get Ln (S_t) by entering in @RISK the formula

$$= LN(S_0) + (\mu - .5\sigma^2)t + \sigma \sqrt{t} RISKNORMAL(0,1)$$

Therefore to get S_t we must take the antilog of this equation and get

---

$$S_t = S_0 e^{(\mu - .5\sigma^2)t + \sigma\sqrt{t}RISKNORMAL(0,1)} \quad (41.1).$$

Risk Neutral Valuation

To apply the risk neutral valuation approach of Chapter 40 we assume the asset grows at instantaneous rate r. **Then the value of a derivative is simply the expected discounted (at risk free rate) value of cash flows.** We will often apply this approach. We can estimate volatility by implied volatility (see Chapter 42) or historical volatility (see below).

Historical Estimation of Mean and Volatility of Stock Return

If we average values of

$$Ln\frac{S_t}{S_{t-1}}$$

we obtain an estimate of $(\mu - .5\sigma^2)$.

If we take the standard deviation of

$$Ln\frac{S_t}{S_{t-1}}$$

we obtain an estimate of σ.

Using monthly returns of Dell Computer for 1988-1996 we may estimate μ and σ. See the file *Dell.xls*.

We begin by estimating σ and μ for a monthly lognormal process. Then our estimate of σ for an annual lognormal process is just $\sqrt{12}$ *(monthly estimate of σ)* and our estimate of μ for an annual lognormal process is just *12*(monthly estimate of μ)*.

Step by Step

Step 1: Note that for any month $\dfrac{S_{t+1}}{S_t} = (1 + Month\,t\ Return)$. Therefore in C6:C107 we compute for each month $Ln\dfrac{S_{t+1}}{S_t}$ by copying from C6 to C7:C107 the formula

=LN(1+B6).

Step 2: In C2 we estimate $\mu - .5\sigma^2$ **with the formula**

=AVERAGE(C6:C107).

Figure 41.1

	A	B	C	D	E	F
1		estimate of	monthly			
2		mu-.5*sigma^2	0.03457215			
3		sigma	0.16092853			
4	DATE	Dell	Ln(1+Dell)			
5	6/30/88				monthly estimate	
6	7/29/88	0.106667	0.101352795		sigma	0.160929
7	8/31/88	-0.228916	-0.259957962		mu	0.047521
8	9/30/88	0.28125	0.247836164		annual estimate	
9	10/31/88	0.158537	0.147158002		sigma	0.557473
10	11/30/88	-0.0842105	-0.087968744		mu	0.570254
11	12/30/88	-0.0804598	-0.083881516			
12	1/31/89	-0.05	-0.051293294			
13	2/28/89	-0.171053	-0.187599058			
14	3/31/89	-0.0952381	-0.100083464			
15	4/28/89	0.105263	0.100083316			
16	5/31/89	0.0793651	0.076372998			
17	6/30/89	-0.0735294	-0.076372966			
18	7/31/89	-0.142857	-0.154150513			
19	8/31/89	0.037037	0.036367608			
20	9/29/89	0.0178571	0.017699535			
21	10/31/89	-0.157895	-0.171850569			
22	11/30/89	-0.0416667	-0.042559649			
23	12/29/89	-0.0434783	-0.044451803			
24	1/31/90	-0.159091	-0.173271829			
25	2/28/90	0.351351	0.301104833			
26	3/30/90	0.22	0.198850859			
27	4/30/90	0.114754	0.108633753			
99	4/30/96	0.369403	0.314374878			
100	5/31/96	0.207084	0.188207534			
101	6/28/96	-0.0812641	-0.084756576			
102	7/31/96	0.0909091	0.087011385			
103	8/30/96	0.209459	0.190173152			
104	9/30/96	0.158287	0.14694219			
105	10/31/96	0.0466238	0.045569555			
106	11/29/96	0.248848	0.222221526			
107	12/31/96	0.0455105	0.044505283			

Step 3: In C3 we estimate σ with the formula

=STDEV(C6:C107).

Step 4: In cell F7 we find our estimate of μ for a monthly lognormal process with the formula

=C2+0.5*F6^2.

Thus for the monthly lognormal we estimate for Dell Computer that μ = .0475 and σ = .161.

Step 5: In cells F9 and F10 we find our annualized estimates of μ and σ with the formulas

$=12*F7$ *(for μ)*

$=SQRT(12)*F6.$ *(for σ).*

Our annualized estimates are μ = 57.0% and σ = 55.7%.

Finding Mean and Variance of a Lognormal Random Variable

It is important to point out that μ is not actually the mean of a Lognormal random variable and σ is not really the standard deviation. Assume a stock follows a Lognormal random variable with parameters μ and σ. Let S = current price of stock (which is known) and S_t = Price of stock at time t (unknown). Then (see page 310 of Luenberger (1997)) the mean and variance of S_t are as follows:

$$Mean\ of\ S_t = Se^{\mu t}$$

$$Variance\ of\ S_t = S^2 e^{2\mu t}(e^{\sigma^2 t} - 1).$$

The file *Lognormal.xls* contains a template to determine the mean and variance of a stock price at any future time. See Figure 41.2.

Figure 41.2

	A	B	C	D
1	Confidence interval for stock price			
2				
3	S=current price	20		
4	t=time	1		
5	mu	0.2		
6	sigma	0.4		
7	alpha	0.95		
8				
9	Mean for ln S(T)	3.115732	Mean S(T)	24.42806
10	Sigma for ln S(T)	0.4	var S(T)	103.5391
11				
12	CI			
13	Lower(for ln S(T))	2.331748		
14	Upper (for ln S(T))	3.899717		
15	Lower for S(T)	10.29592		
16	Upper for S(T)	49.38846		

For example, consider a Stock currently selling for $20 following a lognormal with $\mu = .20$ and $\sigma = .40$. The mean stock price one year from now is $24.43 with a standard deviation of $10.18.

Confidence Intervals for a Lognormal Random Variable

The file *Lognormal.xls* computes a confidence interval for a future stock price. If you want a 95% Confidence interval enter .95 for alpha, etc. From Figure 41.2 we find that for a stock currently selling for $20 with $\mu = .20$ and $\sigma = .40$, we are 95% sure that the price of the stock one year from now will be between $10.30 and $49.39.

Remarks

There is a lot of evidence that changes in stock prices have "fatter tails" than a Lognormal random variable. Despite this evidence, the Lognormal random variable is still widely used to model changes in stock prices. For foreign exchange rates, however, the recent Asian financial crisis demonstrated that sudden jumps in exchange rates are fairly common. Sudden jumps in exchange rates or stock prices can be modeled with a **jump diffusion** process which combines a "jump process" with a Lognormal process. It is usually assumed that the number of jumps per unit time follows a Poisson random variable and the size of each jump (as a percentage of the current price) follows a normal distribution. See Chapter 19 of Hull (1997) for a brief discussion of the jump diffusion process.

Reference

Hull, J. *Options Futures and Derivative Securities*, Prentice-Hall, 1997.

Finding Mean and Variance of a Lognormal Random Variable

Chapter 42: Pricing European Puts and Calls by Simulation

Even though European puts and calls can easily be priced by the Black-Scholes (BS) formula, it is instructive to use Monte Carlo simulation to price European options. The file *option.xls* contains a template that gives the BS price for a European put or call.

Of course, the key input into pricing an option is the stock's **volatility.** This is just the value of σ in the lognormal representation of the stock's price. In Chapter 41 we showed how historical data could be used to estimate σ. **Implied volatility** is a more commonly used method for estimating a stock's volatility. Given the price of an option, the stock's implied volatility is the value of σ which makes the BS price for the option match the actual price. In a sense the volatility estimate is "implied" by the actual option price. We now show how to use Goal Seek to find an implied volatility. We note that the risk free rate input to the BS formula should be the continuously compounded rate, or Ln(1+ current 90 day T-Bill Rate).

Example 42.1

On June 30, 1998 Dell Computer sold for $94. A European put with an exercise price of $80 expiring on November 22, 1998 was selling for $5.25. The current 90 day T-Bill rate is 5.5%. What is the implied volatility of Dell computer?

Solution

Our work is in the file *option.xls*. See Figure 42.1

Figure 42.1

	A	B	C	D	E	F
1	Black-Schole's Option Pricing Problem					
2	Using the Option Price to Find the Implied Volatility					
3						
4	Input data					
5	Stock price	$94			today	6/30/98
6	Exercise price	$80			expire	11/22/98
7	Duration	0.39726				
8	Interest rate	5.35%				
9						
10	Implied volatility (stdev)	53.27%				
11						
12	Call price	Actual		Predicted		
13			=	$21.06		
14	Put price	$5.25		$5.25		
15						
16						
17	Other quantities for option price					
18	d1	0.715534		N(d1)	0.76286	
19	d2	0.37981		N(d2)	0.647957	

Step 1: Enter the duration of the option (145/365) years in B7, the current Stock and exercise prices in B5 and B6, and in B8 the risk free rate Ln(1+.055).

Step 2: Now use Goal Seek (see below) to change the volatility until the predicted BS price for a put matches actual price.

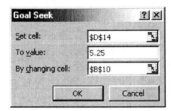

We change volatility (B10) until predicted put price (D14) equals $5.25 (actual put price). From Figure 42.1 we obtain a 53.27% annual volatility. Interestingly enough, in Chapter 40 historical data indicated 55.7% volatility.

Remarks

If you want Excel to figure out the duration of the option enter the current date and expiration dates with the DateValue function and subtract them. To do this we entered in cell G5 the formula =DateValue("6/30/98") and in cell G6 the formula =DateValue("11/22/98"). See Figure 42.2. Note that the DateValue function yields the number of days the date is after January 1, 1900.

Figure 42.2

	E	F	G
5	today	6/30/98	35976
6	expire	11/22/98	36121
7			145.00

Using Simulation to Price the Put

Now we will use Monte Carlo Simulation to price the put. We begin by entering relevant parameters in cells B2:B4 of sheet Dell Sim in file *Option.xls*. Recall from Chapter 40 that a fair price for the put is the **expected discounted value of the put's cash flows in a risk neutral world.** In a risk neutral world, the stock will grow at the risk free rate. Therefore we will use (41.1) with μ = risk free rate to price the put. We have used the following range names:

$r\_$ = *the risk free rate*

p = *the current stock price*

v = *volatility*

d = *duration*

x = *exercise price*

We proceed as follows:

Figure 42.3

	A	B	C	D	E
1	Pricing Put by Simulation				
2	Current stock price	$ 94.00		95% CI	
3	Risk free rate	0.053541		Lower Limit	5.09071778
4	Duration	0.39726		Upper Limit	5.46908822
5	volatility	53.265%			
6	Exercise price	$ 80.00			
7	Stock price at expiration	90.75913		Name	
8	Put cash flows at expiration	0		Description	
9	Discounted value of put cash flows	0		Cell	

Step by Step

Step 1: In cell B7 we use (41.1) to generate Dell's price at the expiration date with the formula

$=p*EXP((r\_-0.5*v^2)*d+RISKNormal(0,1)*v*SQRT(d))$.

Step 2: In cell B8 we compute the cash flows from the put. Recall a put pays nothing if Dell's price on the expiration date exceeds $80; otherwise the put pays $80 (Dell price at expiration).

$=If(B7>x,0,x-B7)$.

Step 3: In cell B9 we compute the expected discounted value of the put's cash flows with the formula

$=EXP(-r\_*d)*B8$.

Step 4: We select B9 as our output cell and ran 10,000 iterations from Figure 42.4.

Our best estimate of the put price is $5.28. We are 95% sure that the put price is between $5.09 and $5.47 (see cells E3 and E4). After 10,000 iterations why have we not come closer to the price of the put? The reason is that this put only pays off on very **extreme results** (Dell's price dropping a lot). It takes many iterations to accurately represent extreme values of a Lognormal random variable.

Figure 42.4

	D	E	F
2	95% CI		
3	Lower Limit	5.09071778	
4	Upper Limit	5.46908822	
5			
6			
7		Name	Discounted value of put cash flows
8		Description	Output
9		Cell	B9
10		Minimum =	0
11		Maximum =	57.99311
12		Mean =	5.279903
13		Std Deviation =	9.459261
14		Variance =	89.47761
15		Skewness =	1.900912
16		Kurtosis =	5.931631
17		Errors Calculated =	0
18		Mode =	0
19		5% Perc =	0
20		10% Perc =	0
21		15% Perc =	0
22		20% Perc =	0
23		25% Perc =	0
24		30% Perc =	0
25		35% Perc =	0
26		40% Perc =	0
27		45% Perc =	0
28		50% Perc =	0
29		55% Perc =	0
30		60% Perc =	0
31		65% Perc =	0.2465744
32		70% Perc =	3.815132
33		75% Perc =	7.46743
34		80% Perc =	11.33537
35		85% Perc =	15.56934
36		90% Perc =	20.52942
37		95% Perc =	27.15265

Remarks

If the stock pays dividends at a rate q% per year, then in a risk neutral world the stock price must grow at a rate r – q. Therefore, for stocks that pay dividends at a rate of q% per year, we should price their options by using (41.1) with r - q replacing r.

Chapter 43: Pricing Exotic Options

While a fairly simple closed form formula exists to price European puts and calls, it is much more difficult to come up with a closed form formula to price so-called **exotic options.** Here are some examples of exotic options:

- **As you like it** options-Owner decides if option is a put or call (see Chapter 44).

- **Knockout** options-These options terminate if stock price reaches a certain value. Otherwise, a knockout option is treated as a normal put or call.

- **Lookback** option-In a lookback option the exercise price is determined (for a call) by the minimum price observed before expiration or (for a put) by the maximum price observed before expiration.

- **Bermuda** option-Exercise option is restricted to specific dates.

- **Asian** option-The payoff from the option depends on the average value of the stock price during the option's duration. The average may be used as either a strike price or be substituted for the stock's final price. The average is sometimes computed as an arithmetic mean and sometimes as a geometric average (the n'th root of the product of the stock's price at the end of each of n weeks).

There are many other exotic options, but they all share the property that the payoff from the option depends on the entire path of the stock price during the option's duration, not just the stock's price at expiration. To illustrate how Monte Carlo Simulation and the risk neutral approach can be used to price exotic options we show how to price a knockout put.

Example 43.1

Let's reconsider the put on Dell discussed in Chapter 42. Suppose you are confident that Dell will not fall below $60 during the next 21 weeks, but you are worried about it falling to a price of between $60 and $80. The put priced in Chapter 42 is pretty expensive, so you opt to buy a put which gets "knocked out" if Dell's price drops below $60 during the next 21 weeks. What is a fair price for this put? Of course, if Dell drops below $60, you are in trouble, but as we will see the knockout put will be much cheaper. For simplicity we are assuming a 21-week duration rather than a 145 day put.

Solution   Our work is in the file *Knockout.xls*. See Figure 43.1 We begin by defining the following range names:

- S= current price

- X =exercise price

- K = knockout value for put

- R = risk-free rate

- V = volatility

We will approximate the path of Dell's price by looking at the price at the end of each week.

Figure 43.1

	A	B
1		
2	Knockout put	
3	Today's price	$ 94.00
4	Duration(weeks)	21
5	Exercise price	$ 80.00
6	Knockout value	$ 60.00
7	riskfree rate	0.053541
8	volatility	0.53265
9	Week	Price
10	0	$ 94.00
11	1	93.84049
12	2	93.68124
13	3	93.52227
14	4	93.36356
15	5	93.20513
16	6	93.04696
17	7	92.88906
28	18	91.16978
29	19	91.01506
30	20	90.86061
31	21	90.70643
32	Min price	$ 90.71
33	Option payoff	0
34	Discounted value of option payoff	0

Step by Step

Step 1: We enter today's price in cell B10 and generate Dell's price in a week in cell B11 with the formula (based on (41.1))

$$=B10*EXP((r\_-0.5*v\char94 2)*(1/52)+RISKNormal(0,1)*SQRT(1/52)*v).$$

Again we assume the stock grows at the **risk-free rate**.

Step 2: Copying this formula to B11:B31 generates Dell's price at the end of each week.

Step 3: In cell B32 we compute the lowest price of Dell during the option's duration with the formula

$$=MIN(B10:B31).$$

Step 4: In cell B33 we compute the payoff from the option with the formula

$$=If(B32<k,0,If(B31>x,0,x-B31)).$$

This ensures the put is knocked out if Dell price ever drops below $60. If price of Dell at expiration exceeds $80 there is no value to the put. Otherwise the put *pays (Exercise Price) - (Stock Price at Expiration).*

Step 5: We compute the discounted value of the option's payoffs in B34 with the formula

$$=EXP(-r\_*(B4/52))*B33.$$

Step 6: We select B34 as our output cell and after running 10,000 iterations obtain the following output:

Figure 43.2

	C	D	E	F	G	H
3	95% CI					
4	Lower	1.429149	Name	Discounted value of option payoff / Price		
5	Upper	1.583197	Description	Output		
6			Cell	B34		
7			Minimum =	0		
8			Maximum =	19.57092		
9			Mean =	1.506173		
10			Std Deviation =	3.851216		
11			Variance =	14.83186		
12			Skewness =	2.754046		
13			Kurtosis =	9.835486		
14			Errors Calculated =	0		
15			Mode =	0		
16			5% Perc =	0		
17			10% Perc –	0		
28			65% Perc =	0		
29			70% Perc =	0		
30			75% Perc =	0		
31			80% Perc =	0		
32			85% Perc =	2.951085		
33			90% Perc =	6.718378		
34			95% Perc =	11.73514		

Our best estimate of the price of the knockout put is $1.51 and we are 95% sure a fair price is between $1.43 and $1.58. Note the knockout allows us to protect ourselves against a moderate drop in Dell price much cheaper than an ordinary put, but a catastrophic drop in Dell's price will be a real wipe out!

Chapter 44: Pricing an "As You Like It" Option

We will now learn how to price an "As You Like It" option. Here is an example.

Example 44.1   On January 1, 1996 a stock sells for $44. On April 1,1996 you observe the price of the stock and have the choice of obtaining a put or call option with an expiration date of January 1, 1997 and an exercise price of $42. Suppose the stock grows at 15% per year with an annual volatility of 20%. The risk-free rate is currently 10%. Run 400 iterations. From your simulation, find a 95% Confidence interval for the value of the option.

Solution   For this problem, we will need to create a template that computes the Black-Scholes formula for pricing a call or put option.

Recall that if

S = *Current Stock Price*

X = *Exercise price*

T = *Duration of option (in years)*

σ = *Annual volatility*

Then Call Price = $SN(d_1) - Xe^{-rT}N(d_2)$

and by Put-Call Parity,

Put Price = $Xe^{-rT}N(-d_2) - SN(-d_1)$, *where*

$$d_1 = \frac{ln(S/X) + (r + \sigma^2/2)T}{\sigma T^{.5}}$$

$$d_2 = d_1 - \sigma T^{.5}.$$

To set up a template note that N(y) is the cumulative function for the standard normal. That is, N(y) = Probability that the standard normal is ≤y. Thus *N(0)* = *.50, N(1)* = *.84,* etc. The Excel function =*NormsDist(y)* will compute the cumulative standard normal. The file *Likeit.xls* contains our work. See Figure 44.1.

Figure 44.1

	A	B	C	D	E
2	**As You Like It**				
3	Stock Price on 1//196	43.00		d1	0.770939
4	Stock Price on 4/1/96	43.87		d2	0.597734
5	Strike Price	42.00		N(d1)	0.779628
6	Volatility	0.20		N(-d1)	0.220372
7	Variance	0.04		N(d2)	0.724991
8	Time to expiration	0.75		N(-d2)	0.275009
9	Risk-free Rate	0.10			
10					
11	Value of CALL on 4/1/96	5.95			
12	Value of PUT on on 4/1/96	1.05			
13	Choose the highest one on 4/1/96	5.95			
14	Discounted to 1/1/96	5.80			

By risk neutral pricing, we let stock grow at risk free rate. Then on April 1, 1996 we choose the option with more value, and discount its value back to January 1, 1996!

We proceed as follows:

Step 1: In B3:B9 we input the relevant parameters.

Step 2: In E3 we compute d_1 with the formula

$$=(LN(B4/B5)+((B9+0.5*B7)*B8))/SQRT(B7*B8).$$

Step 3: In E4 we compute d_2 with the formula

$$=E3-SQRT(B7*B8).$$

Step 4: In E5:E8 we compute $N(d_1)$, $N(-d_1)$, $N(d_2)$, and $N(-d_2)$. For example, in E5 we compute $N(d_1)$ with the formula

$$= NormsDist(E3).$$

Step 5: In B4 we compute the April 1, 1996 stock price (assuming stock grows at risk free rate) with the formula

$$=B3*EXP((B9-0.5*B7)*0.25+B6*RISKNormal(0,1)*0.25^0.5).$$

Chapter 45: Finding Value at Risk (VAR) of a Portfolio

Anybody who owns a portfolio of investments knows there is a great deal of uncertainty about the future worth of the portfolio. Recently the concept of **value at risk (VAR)** has been used to help describe a portfolio's uncertainty. Simply stated, **value at risk** of a portfolio at a future point in time is usually considered to be the fifth percentile of the loss in the portfolio's value at that point in time. In short, there is considered to be only one chance in 20 that the portfolio's loss will exceed the VAR. To illustrate the idea suppose a portfolio today is worth $100. We simulate the portfolio's value one year from now and find there is a 5% chance that the portfolio's value will be $80 or less. Then the portfolio's VAR is $20 or 20%. The following example shows how @RISK can be used to measure VAR The example also demonstrates how buying puts can greatly reduce the risk, or **hedge**, a long position in a stock.

Example 45.1

Let's suppose we own one share of Dell computer on June 30, 1998. The current price is $94. From historical data (see Chapter 41) we have estimated that the growth of the price of Dell stock can be modeled as a Lognormal random variable with $\mu = 57\%$ and $\sigma = 55.7\%$. To hedge the risk involved in owning Dell we are considering buying (for $5.25) a European put on Dell with exercise price $80 and expiration date November 22, 1998. Here you will:

a) Compute the VAR on November 22, 1998 if we own Dell computer and do not buy a put.

b) Compute the VAR on November 22, 1998 if we own Dell computer and buy the put.

Solution   The key idea is to realize that **in valuing the put we let Dell price grow at the risk-free rate, but when doing a VAR calculation we should let Dell price grow at the rate at which we expect it to grow.** Our work is in file *var.xls*. See Figure 45.1.

Figure 45.1

	A	B	C
2	**Stress Testing Dell**	Range Name	
3	Current price	S	$ 94.00
4	Put exercise price	x	$ 80.00
5	put duration	d	0.39726
6	risk free rate	r_	0.053541
7	actual growth rate	g	0.57
8	volatility	v	0.557
9	put price	p	$ 5.25
10			
11	Dell price at expiration	110.8422852	
12	put value at expiration	0	
13			
14	% age Gain without put	17.9%	
15	%age Gain with put	11.7%	

We have created range names as indicated in Figure 45.1.

Step by Step   **Step 1: In cell B11 we generate Dell's price on November 22, 1998 with the formula**

$$=S*EXP((g-0.5*v^2)*d+RISKNormal(0,1)*v*SQRT(d)).$$

Step 2: In cell B12 we compute the payments from the put at expiration with the formula

$$=If(B11>x,0,x-B11).$$

Step 3: The percentage gain on our portfolio if we just own Dell is given by

$$\frac{Ending\ DellPrice - Beginning\ Dell\ Price}{Beginning\ Dell\ Price}.$$

In B14 we compute the percentage gain on our portfolio if we do not buy a put with the formula

$$=(B11-S)/S.$$

Step 4: The percentage gain on our portfolio if we own Dell and a put is

$$\frac{Ending\ Dell\ Price + Cash\ Flows\ from\ Put - Beginning\ Dell\ Price - Put\ Price}{Beginning\ Dell\ Price + Put\ Price}.$$

In cell B15 we compute the percentage gain on our portfolio if we buy the put with the formula

$$=((B12+B11)-(S+p))/(S+p).$$

Step 5: After selecting B14 and B15 as output cells and running 1600 iterations we obtained the @RISK output in Figure 45.2.

Figure 45.2

	D	E	F
13	Name	% age Gain without put / p	%age Gain with put / p
14	Description	Output	Output
15	Cell	B14	B15
16	Minimum =	-0.6363322	-0.1939547
17	Maximum =	3.042318	2.828493
18	Mean =	0.2542094	0.2109912
19	Std Deviation =	0.4544247	0.402881
20	Variance =	0.2065018	0.1623131
21	Skewness =	1.133957	1.465861
22	Kurtosis =	5.305563	6.118122
23	Errors Calculated =	0	0
24	Mode =	0.1333048	-0.1939547
25	5% Perc =	-0.339354	-0.1939547
26	10% Perc =	-0.2480843	-0.1939547
27	15% Perc =	-0.1808263	-0.1939547
28	20% Perc =	-0.122943	-0.1693365
29	25% Perc =	-7.00E-02	-0.1191809
30	30% Perc =	-1.95E-02	-7.04E-02
31	35% Perc =	2.95E-02	-2.50E-02
32	40% Perc =	0.0784621	2.14E-02
33	45% Perc =	0.1277232	6.81E-02
34	50% Perc =	0.1790788	0.1167094
35	55% Perc =	0.2323373	0.1673023
36	60% Perc =	0.2883818	0.2212769
37	65% Perc =	0.349322	0.2779473
38	70% Perc =	0.4169043	0.3419547
39	75% Perc =	0.4937013	0.4146894
40	80% Perc =	0.5836527	0.4998827
41	85% Perc =	0.6958588	0.6080295
42	90% Perc =	0.8485417	0.75076
43	95% Perc =	1.09956	0.9885007

We find our VAR if we do not buy the put to be 33.9% of our invested cash while if we buy the put our VAR drops to 19.4% of the invested cash. The reason for this is, of course, that if Dell stock drops below $80, every one dollar decrease in the value of Dell is countered by a one dollar increase in the value of the put. Also note that if we do not buy the put, Dell (despite its high growth rate) might lose up to 64% of its value.

The following histograms give the distribution of the percentage gain on our portfolio with and without the put.

Figure 45.3

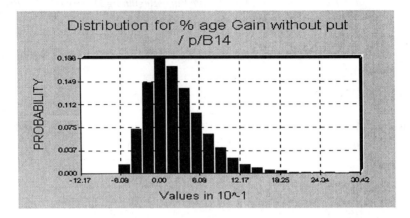

Figure 45.4

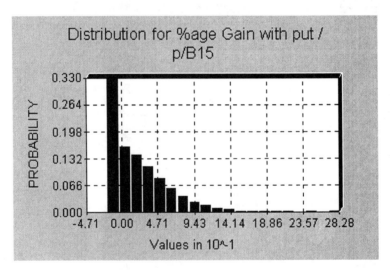

From Figures 45.3 and 45.4 we see that there is a much greater chance of a big loss if we do not buy the put. Note, however, that our average return without the put is 25.4% while our average return with the put is 21.1%. In effect, buying the put is a form of **portfolio insurance**, and we must pay for this insurance.

Chapter 46: Finding Confidence Intervals for Percentiles

In the last chapter we wanted to estimate the 5th percentile of a random variable (the return on Dell or the return on Dell plus the put). We need to understand that each time @RISK runs a simulation it will give us a different 5 %ile. Can we get a confidence interval for the 5 %ile (or any other percentile)? All we need to use is the file *Percentile.xls*.

Figure 46.1

	A	B
1	Confidence	
2	Interval	
3	for	
4	a Percentile	
5		
6	Sample Size	1600
7	Level of Confidence	0.95
8	Desired percentile	0.05
9	Lower Limit(percentile)	0.039321
10	Upper Limit(percentile)	0.060679

Suppose we run 1600 trials (as we did in Chapter 45) and want an interval in which we are 95% sure the 5 %ile lies. Simply enter the number of trials (1600) in B6; the desired percentile (.05) in B8 and the desired level of confidence (.95) in B7. Our spreadsheet reports that we are 95% sure that the 5 %ile is between the 3.93 %ile and 6.07%ile. These %iles can be obtained with the Target command.

Remarks

For further discussion of the theory behind the confidence intervals for percentiles see Morgan and Hendrion (1990).

Reference

Morgan, G. and Hendrion, M., *Uncertainty*, Cambridge University Press, 1990.

Chapter 47: Doing VAR and Pricing Options Involving Correlated Stocks

We can easily do VAR calculations and price options involving correlated stocks.

To model the correlations between investments we use the RISKCorrmat function. Here is an illustration to get us started.

Example 47.1

Suppose we have invested 25% of our portfolio in four different stocks. The annual return on each stock is assumed to follow a Lognormal random variable with the given value of μ and σ for each stock as well as the following correlations:

Figure 47.1

	A	B	C	D	E
9		Mu	Sigma	New Price	
10	Stock 1	0.15	0.2	1.13882838	
11	Stock 2	0.1	0.12	1.09724226	
12	Stock 3	0.25	0.4	1.18530485	
13	Stock 4	0.16	0.2	1.1502738	
14					
15	Correlation Matrix				
16		Stock 1	Stock 2	Stock 3	Stock 4
17	Stock 1	1	0.8	0.7	0.6
18	Stock 2	0.8	1	0.75	0.55
19	Stock 3	0.7	0.75	1	0.65
20	Stock 4	0.6	0.55	0.65	1

What is the probability that during the next year my portfolio will lose money? What is the VAR?

Solution   See file *corrinv.xls*. The trick is to ensure that the stock prices a year from now are correlated.

Figure 47.2

	A	B	C	D	E
4	Fraction in		Current Price		
5	Stock 1	0.25	$ 1.00		
6	Stock 2	0.25	$ 1.00		
7	Stock 3	0.25	$ 1.00		
8	Stock 4	0.25	$ 1.00		
9		Mu	Sigma	New Price	
10	Stock 1	0.15	0.2	1.13882838	
11	Stock 2	0.1	0.12	1.09724226	
12	Stock 3	0.25	0.4	1.18530485	
13	Stock 4	0.16	0.2	1.1502738	
14					
15	Correlation Matrix				
16		Stock 1	Stock 2	Stock 3	Stock 4
17	Stock 1	1	0.8	0.7	0.6
18	Stock 2	0.8	1	0.75	0.55
19	Stock 3	0.7	0.75	1	0.65
20	Stock 4	0.6	0.55	0.65	1
21					
22	New Value	1.142912			
23	Portfolio return	0.142912			

Step by Step

Step 1: To generate Stock 1 price a year from now enter into D10 the formula

$=RISKCorrmat(\$B\$17:\$E\$20,1)+EXP((B10-0.5*C10\text{^}2)+C10*RISKNormal(0,1)).$

This ensures that Stock 1's price one Year from now will be correlated with Stocks 2-4 according to Column 1 of the numbers in B17:E20. Note that *EXP((B10-0.5*C10^2)+C10*RISKNormal(0,1))* would generate the Stock 1 Price in absence of correlations.

In D11 generate Stock 2 price a year from now with formula

$=RISKCorrmat(\$B\$17:\$E\$20,2)+EXP((B11-0.5*C11\text{^}2)+C11*RISKNormal(0,1)).$

In D12 generate Stock 3 Price a Year from now with formula

$=RISKCorrmat(\$B\$17:\$E\$20,3)+EXP((B12-0.5*C12\text{^}2)+C12*RISKNormal(0,1)).$

In D13 generate Stock 4 price a year from now with the formula

$=RISKCorrmat(\$B\$17:\$E\$20,4)+EXP((B13-0.5*C13\text{^}2)+C13*RISKNormal(0,1)).$

Step 2: In B22 we now compute the value of our portfolio one year from now with the formula

=SUMPRODUCT(B5:B8,D10:D13).

In B23 we now compute the return on our portfolio with the formula

=(B22/1)-1.

We now run an @RISK simulation with output cell B23. After using the Target function we find that during the next year there is a 23.5% chance of losing money on this portfolio. See the output below. Also there is a 5% chance we will lose 16.8% or more so VAR is 16.8%.

Figure 47.2

	G	H
26	Minimum =	-0.377644
27	Maximum =	1.329535
28	Mean =	0.191561
29	Std Deviation =	0.2537631
30	Variance =	0.0643957
31	Skewness =	0.7555982
32	Kurtosis =	3.937907
33	Errors Calculated =	0
34	Mode =	0.1702891
35	5% Perc =	-0.1677546
36	10% Perc =	-0.1052121
37	15% Perc =	-0.0598706
38	20% Perc =	-2.70E-02
39	25% Perc =	1.25E-02
40	30% Perc =	4.10E-02
41	35% Perc =	7.21E-02
42	40% Perc =	0.1022982
43	45% Perc =	0.1345115
44	50% Perc =	0.1686599
45	55% Perc =	0.1893861
46	60% Perc =	0.2237442
47	65% Perc =	0.2562818
48	70% Perc =	0.2946385
49	75% Perc =	0.3343091
50	80% Perc =	0.3856383
51	85% Perc =	0.447285
52	90% Perc =	0.5196691
53	95% Perc =	0.6608666
54	Target #1 (Value)=	0
55	Target #1 (Perc%)=	23.52%

Pricing Options on Correlated Stocks

The risk neutral approach can be used to price options involving correlated investments.

Example 47.2

Let's suppose that currently Stock 1 sells for $14, Stock 2 sells for $16, Stock 3 for $18 and Stock 4 for $20. We have bought a European option of six months duration. If after six months Stock 1 sells for $17 or more we have the right to buy, if desired, one share of any or all of Stocks 1-4. What is this option worth?

Solution

We simply use risk neutral pricing and assume each stock grows at the risk-free rate. Then the expected discounted value of our cash flows yields the option's value. Our work is in the file *corropt.xls*. See Figure 47.3.

Figure 47.3

	A	B	C	D	E	F	G
1							
2		Stock 1	Stock 2	Stock 3	Stock 4		
3	Std. Dev	0.2	0.12	0.4	0.2		
4	Current Price	14	16	18	20		
5	Exercise Price	20	20	20	20		
6	Cutoff Price	17					
7	Riskfreerate	0.08					
8	Duration	0.5					
9	Correlation matrix						
10		1	0.8	0.7	0.6		
11		0.8	1	0.75	0.55		
12		0.7	0.75	1	0.65		
13		0.6	0.55	0.65	1		
14		Stock 1	Stock 2	Stock 3	Stock 4		
15	Price 6 months later	14.42636	16.59313	18	20.609091	total cashflow	discounted cash flow
16	Cash flows	0	0	0	0	0	0
17	Any Value?	0					

Step by Step

Step 1: In Rows 2-13 we enter all relevant information.

Step 2: In B15:E15 we generate the six month price for Stocks 1-4. In B15 we generate Stock 1's price in six months with the formula

$$=RISKCorrmat(\$B\$10:\$E\$13,1)+B4*EXP((\$B\$7$$
$$-0.5*B3\wedge2)*\$B\$8+B3*RISKNormal(0,1)*\$B\$8\wedge0.5).$$

This ensures that the Stock 1 price is correlated with Stocks 1-4 according to B10:B13 and grows according to Lognormal growth with a mean equal to the risk-free rate and an annual standard deviation of 20%.

In a similar fashion we generate Stock 2-4 prices six months hence in C15:E15.

Step 3: In B17 we check if Stock 1 sells for at least $17 six months from now, because if it does not, the option has no value. The formula

=If(B15>=$B$6,1,0)

puts a "1" in B17 if Stock 1 sells for >=$17, and a "0" otherwise.

Step 4: In B16:E16 we compute the cash flow from the option to buy each individual stock. In B16 we compute the cash flow associated with the option to buy Stock 1 with the formula

=$B$17*MAX(B15-B5,0).

Note that if Stock 1 sells for less than $17, this will yield a value of $0, as desired. Copying this formula to B16:E16 computes the value of the option of buying Stocks 2-4.

Step 5: Clicking on the Summation icon in F16 computes the total cash flow from the option.

Step 6: In G16 we compute the discounted cash flow from the option with the formula.

=EXP(-$B$7*$B$8)*F16.

Step 7: We now run a simulation with output cell G16. The results are in Figure 47.4.

Figure 47.4

	A	B	C	D	E
28	Summary Statistics				
29					
30	Cell	Name	Minimum	Mean	Maximum
31					
32	G16	Cash flows	0	1.243215	22.01244
33	B15	(Input) Pric	-2.7585	-1.52E-03	2.471639
34	C15	(Input) Pric	-3.12701	-2.83E-03	2.653772
35	D15	(Input) Pric	-2.4937	2.82E-05	2.395635
36	E15	(Input) Pric	-2.38781	1.35E-03	2.709884

We find a fair price for the option to be $1.24!

Remarks

Suppose we do not believe that @RISK is correlating the stock prices correctly. How could we check? The key is to extract the data from the simulation and use the Excel Data Analysis Correlations tool to check the correlations between the stock prices. To ensure that @RISK collects the stock priceswhen we simulate *corrinv.xls* we need to go to *Simulations Settings* and check the *Collect Distribution Samples Box*. Then choose D10:D13 as output cells. Next from the Results menu we click on the *Data* button and paste our data into our workbook. The worksheet data (range G7:G406 of sheet Data, see Figure 47.7) shows the actual stock prices generated by @RISK. Using Data Analysis Tools Correlation yields the correlations in Figure 47.5 for the range G7:G406.

Figure 47.5-
Correlations
from
Simulation
Data

	J	K	L	M	N
7	Correlation from Data Analysis Tools Regression				
8		D10	D11	D12	D13
9	D10	1			
10	D11	0.8041	1		
11	D12	0.667746	0.712702	1	
12	D13	0.57483	0.542758	0.601922	1

Note how closely the observed correlations match our original correlations.

Figure 47.6 -
Given
Correlations

	A	B	C	D	E
15	Correlation Matrix				
16		Stock 1	Stock 2	Stock 3	Stock 4
17	Stock 1	1	0.8	0.7	0.6
18	Stock 2	0.8	1	0.75	0.55
19	Stock 3	0.7	0.75	1	0.65
20	Stock 4	0.6	0.55	0.65	1

Figure 47.7 –
Correlation
Data

	C	D	E	F	G
6	Iteration	D10	D11	D12	D13
7	1	0.8629699	9.36E-01	1.088142	1.151188
8	2	1.233416	1.141332	1.095051	0.8641179
9	3	1.06303	0.9831284	0.9699233	1.269036
10	4	1.031748	1.050323	1.060856	1.167135
11	5	0.9079968	0.8337644	0.5353328	0.9401368
12	6	1.521341	1.221263	2.142355	1.46E+00
13	7	1.072593	1.025428	1.042641	1.253548
14	8	1.278855	1.17E+00	1.720478	1.42E+00
15	9	1.142791	1.059054	0.6783471	0.9563865
16	10	1.773506	1.375328	3.907997	2.006622
17	11	1.132343	1.087899	0.8964242	0.9847718
18	12	1.242084	1.197201	1.558062	1.267161
19	13	1.041393	0.9589889	0.6690134	0.7849755
20	14	1.156106	1.10392	1.008588	1.364268
399	393	1.45E+00	1.279048	1.353978	1.618607
400	394	1.136537	1.04767	1.078184	1.534208
401	395	1.039625	1.111613	0.7899141	1.26064
402	396	1.030138	0.9718295	0.6346787	1.352289
403	397	1.481446	1.293646	2.294173	1.354895
404	398	1.037834	1.041626	0.9621134	1.050103
405	399	1.052902	1.11E+00	1.15E+00	9.88E-01
406	400	1.162035	1.02406	0.8592102	1.139502

Chapter 48: Computing VAR for Forwards and Futures

Many corporations face the risk that their profit will greatly change when commodity prices or currency rates change. For example, a glass making company uses natural gas to heat their furnaces. They face the risk that the price of gas will increase, thereby increasing their costs. A drug company selling drugs in Germany faces the risk that a decline in the value of the mark will reduce the value of their German accounts receivable. **Futures and forwards** can be used to hedge commodity and exchange risk.

In this Chapter we give a brief introduction to futures and compute the VAR for an exchange rate future. In Chapter 49 we show how to use @RISK to determine optimal hedging policies.

Suppose you have just bought an ounce of gold for $30. The current price of a commodity such as gold is called the **spot price** of the commodity. If the price of gold increases, you make money because your gold is worth more. If the price of gold decreases, however, you will lose money. To reduce or **hedge** this risk you might sell or **short** an gold future. Suppose today is January 1, 2000 and you have sold or shorted a one-year gold future. This means that on January 1, 2001 you have a guarantee that you will be paid an amount (the current one-year futures price) and in return you must deliver on that date one ounce of gold. This obligation may be traded at any time on a futures exchange for the current futures price of a January 1, 2001 future. As time progresses, if the market deems gold more valuable the value of the gold you own goes up, but you lose money on your futures contract because you will have to deliver a more valuable commodity. If as time progresses the market deems gold less valuable you lose money on your gold, but the value of your futures contract increases because you will have to deliver a less valuable commodity. This discussion shows that by selling or shorting an gold future we can reduce the risk involved in holding gold.

Pricing of Futures Contracts

Simple formulas exist (see Chapter 3 of Hull (1997)) for the price of forward contracts. Forward contracts cannot be traded month to month. We will assume the formulas for forward prices apply to futures prices. Let S = current spot price of a commodity and r = risk free rate. Then ignoring storage costs and convenience yields the price of a futures contract expiring at time T is given by

$$F = Se^{rT} \quad (48.1).$$

For a forward contract written on an exchange rate let rforeign be the risk free rate in the foreign country. Then the price of a futures contract expiring at time T is given by

$$Se^{(r-rforeign)T} \quad (48.2).$$

We now show how to determine the VAR for a futures contract written on the German mark.

Example 48.1

It is September 5, 1997. We have just bought a 12-month futures contract on the German Mark. In one month how can the value of this futures contract change? Our work is in the file *forwardmark.xls*. See Figure 48.1.

Figure 48.1

	A	B	C	D	E	F
1	September 5 1997					
2	Current US Rate	0.0555				
3	Current German rate	0.03483				
4	$/marks current rate	0.5545				
5	Current Futures Price	0.566081				
6	Duration of contract(years)	1	**Corr Matrix**	Ger rates	US Rates	IR Parity error
7	Next month US rate	0.0555	Ger rates	1	0.05	0.14
8	Next month German Rate	0.03483	US Rates	0.05	1	0.13
9	Next Month $/mark rate	0.555452	IR Parity error	0.14	0.13	1
10	Next Month futures Price	0.566077				
11	Duration of contract	0.916667				

The current 12 month future price is $.566081. Currently the US short-term interest rate is 5.55% and the German short-term rate is 3.483%. There are three keys to modeling next month's future price.

1) From (48.2) observe that at any time the price of a forward (and approximately a futures contract) is given by

$$Se^{(r-rforeign)t} \quad (48.2).$$

Where S = current spot exchange rate, r = current US short-term rate , rforeign = current foreign short-term rate, and t = remaining duration of contract.

2) The second key to our problem is interest rate parity. IRP implies that our best guess at next month's $/mark spot rate is

$$Current\ Spot * \frac{1+(r/12)}{1+(rforeign/12)}$$

See the end of the chapter for a brief explanation of interest rate parity.

3) The third key to our problem is to look at historical data to see how German and US rates change over a month. We found:

- Assuming a flat yield curve the standard deviation of monthly changes in US short-term rates was 7% of the current rate.

- The standard deviation of the monthly change in German short-term rates was 6% of the current rate.

- We also need to see how accurate interest rate parity predictions are one month in advance. For the mark we found the standard deviation of our one month interest rate parity forecasts were 3% of the current spot rate.

- Finally we need to know the correlation between month to month interest rate changes and the errors in our interest rate parity forecasts. We found this to be:

	C	D	E	F
6	**Corr Matrix**	Ger rates	US Rates	IR Parity error
7	Ger rates	1	0.05	0.14
8	US Rates	0.05	1	0.13
9	IR Parity error	0.14	0.13	1

We are now ready to model next month's future price. After remembering that the contract now has 11 months left we can use (48.2) to simulate the future price in one month after generating next month's spot rate in each country as well as next month's spot rate. Here's how we do it.

Step by Step

Step 1: In B1:B6 we enter the problem's current parameters.

Step 2: In B7 we compute next month's US short-term rate with the formula

=RISKCorrmat(D7:F9,2)+RISKNormal(B2,B2*0.07).

This formula ensures that next month's US rate has same mean as this month, a standard deviation equal to 7% of the current rate and is correlated with next month's IRP forecast error and German rate change according to E7:E9.

Step 3: In B8 we compute next month's German short-term rate with the formula

$$=RISKCorrmat(D7:F9,1)+RISKNormal(B3,0.06*B3).$$

This formula ensures that next month's German rate has same mean as this month, a standard deviation equal to 6% of the current rate. Also the change in next month's German rate is correlated with next month's US rate change and IRP forecast error according to D7:D9.

Step 4: In B9 we compute next month's $/mark spot rate with the formula

$$=RISKCorrmat(D7:F9,3)+RISKNormal(B4*((1+(B2/12))/(1+(B3/12))),0.03*B4).$$

This formula ensures that next month's spot rate will have a mean given by interest rate parity, has a standard deviation about this mean equal to 3% of the current spot rate. Also the change in next month's spot rate is correlated with changes in next month's interest rates according to F7:F9.

Step 5: In B10 we invoke (48.2) and compute next month's forward price with the formula

$$=B9*EXP(B11*(B7-B8)).$$

Step 6: We now select B10 as our output cell and run a simulation. Our output is in Figure 48.2.

Figure 48.2

	H	I
12	Name	Next Month futures F
13	Description	Output
14	Cell	B10
15	Minimum =	0.5086644
16	Maximum =	0.6269337
17	Mean =	0.5660869
18	Std Deviation =	1.71E-02
19	Variance =	2.92E 04
20	Skewness =	1.67E-02
21	Kurtosis =	3.00867
22	Errors Calculated =	0
23	Mode =	0.5597149
24	5% Perc =	0.5383316
25	10% Perc =	0.5442101
26	15% Perc =	0.5481554
27	20% Perc =	0.5515768
28	25% Perc =	0.5546693
29	30% Perc =	0.5569817
30	35% Perc =	0.5596049
31	40% Perc =	0.5616261
32	45% Perc =	0.5639719
33	50% Perc =	0.5658243
34	55% Perc =	0.5682461
35	60% Perc =	0.5702059
36	65% Perc =	0.572939
37	70% Perc =	0.5752767
38	75% Perc =	0.5776649
39	80% Perc =	0.5807303
40	85% Perc =	0.5839704
41	90% Perc =	0.5881432
42	95% Perc =	0.5937085

On the average, the futures contract we own will have a price next month of .566. There is a 5% chance the future's value could go as low as .538, a loss of .028/.566 or around 5%. Thus our one month VAR is 5%.

Note On Interest Rate Parity

If we invest $1 today in a US bank then in one month we will have

(1 + (current US rate/12)) dollars. (48.3)

If today we convert $1 to marks and invest it for one month in a German bank and then convert the marks back to $s we will have

(Current mark/$ spot rate)*(1 + (current German interest rate/12))*(1/((Spot rate mark/$ in one month) dollars. (48.4)

Setting (48.3) equal to (48.4) yields interest rate parity. (48.3) must equal (48.4) because if equality did not hold a trader could realize infinite profits.

Reference

Hull, J., *Options, Futures and Other Derivatives*, Prentice-Hall, 1997.

Chapter 49: Hedging with Futures

In Chapter 48 we briefly discussed how companies could hedge commodity and exchange risk with futures. The natural question is, of course, how many futures do you need to buy to adequately hedge your risk? In this chapter we show how to use @RISK to determine optimal hedging policies. Our goal will be to choose a hedging policy that minimizes the standard deviation of our total costs.

An Overview of Hedging

Suppose I need to purchase heating oil in November 2000. Also suppose that on June 8 of 2000 I purchase (**or go long**) a December 2000 future for a price of $1 per barrel. This gives me the right to receive a barrel of heating oil for $1 on December 8, 2000. Suppose the price of heating oil increases, and I close out my futures contract on November 1, 2000 and buy heating oil. What happens? The cost of heating oil increases (this is bad for me) but the value of the future contract increases (this is good for me) because I have the right to receive a more valuable commodity. If the price of heating oil drops between June and December what happens? The drop in the cost of heating oil reduces my cost of purchasing oil (this is good) but the value of the future drops (this is bad) because I have the right to receive a less valuable commodity. In short, going long the future has created a hedge that makes the change in the price of heating oil between June and December largely irrelevant.

Suppose I own an ounce of gold on June 8, 2000. If I sell or short one December 8, 2000 gold future at $400 what can happen? Shorting the future means I must deliver an ounce of gold (and receive $400) on December 8, 2000. If the price of gold increases, the value of my gold increases (this is good) but the value of my future drops (this is bad) because I must deliver a more valuable commodity. If the price of gold drops then the value of my gold drops (this is bad), but the value of the future increases (this is good) because I must deliver a less valuable commodity. Thus we see that shorting the future has created a hedge that makes the change in the price of gold largely irrelevant.

We now turn to a specific example of how to determine how many futures to purchase when hedging. We will deal with the previously discussed oil situation. Recall from (48.1) that given the current risk free rate r and the current spot price S a futures contract of duration T should sell for Se^{rT}. In reality, however, future prices will vary about this "expected price". Let's suppose that for oil futures, actual future prices average out to the prediction of (48.1) with a standard deviation of 5%. The other source of uncertainty is, of course, the spot price path of oil in later months. We will assume that future oil prices will be governed by a Lognormal random variable, so future spot prices may be modeled with (41.1).

Example 49.1

It is June 8, 2000. Glassco needs to purchase 500,000 gallons of heating oil on November 8, 2000. The current spot price of oil is $0.42 per gallon. Oil prices are assumed to follow a Lognormal random variable with $\mu = .08$ and $\sigma = .30$. The risk free rate is 6%. We are hedging the price risk inherent in our future oil purchase by buying oil futures that expire on December 8, 2000. How many futures should we buy? We assume the mean future price at any time is governed by (48.1) and the actual future price will have a standard deviation equal to 5% of its mean. We assume that on June 8, 2000 the December 8, 2000 oil future is selling for $0.43769. We also ignore movements in the interest rate.

Solution

Our work is in the file *oil.xls*. See Figure 49.1.

Figure 49.1

	A	B
1	Hedging	
2	Petroleum	
3	Risk	
4		
5		
6	June 8 oil price per gallon	0.42
7	r	0.06
8	volatility	0.3
9	oil drift	0.08
10	sigma of percentage variation of future from mean	0.05
11	future duration	0.5
12	December futures price on June 8	0.43769
13	gallons bought	500000
14	# long	600000
15	November 8 spot oil price	0.426169879
16	Mean of November 8 price of December future	0.428306065
17	Actual November 8 futures price	0.428306065
18	Bottom line	
19	Cost of buying oil	$213,084.94
20	Revenue from futures	$256,983.64
21	Cost of buying futures on June 8	$262,614.00
22	Total cost	$218,715.30

An Overview of Hedging

Step by Step

Step 1: In B6:B11 we enter relevant parameters.

Step 2: In B12 we enter the price of the December future on June 8 ($0.43769).

Step 3: In B13 we enter number of gallons of heating oil that must be purchased.

Step 4: In B14 we use a RISKSimTable to consider different choices (0, 100,000, 200,000, ..., 600,000) for the number of futures to purchase.

=RISKSimTable({600000,500000,400000,300000,200000,100000,0}).

Step 5: In B15 we use (41.1) to generate the November 8 spot oil price.

=B6*EXP((B9-0.5*B8^2)*(5/12)+RISKNormal(0,1)*SQRT(5/12)*B8).

Step 6: In B16 we use (48.1) to compute the expected price of the December future on November 8.

=EXP((1/12)*B7)*B15.

Step 7: In B17 we build in the 5% standard deviation of the actual future price from the expected future price and compute the actual price of the December future on November 8.

=RISKNormal(B16,B16*B10).

Step 8: In B19 we compute the cost of buying oil at the November 8 spot price with the formula

=B15*B13.

Step 9: In B20 we compute the revenue earned from selling our futures on November 8 with the formula

=B17*B14.

Step 10: In B21 we compute the cost of buying our futures on June 8 with the formula

=B12*B14.

Step 11: In B22 we compute our total cost (oil purchase cost) + (futures purchase cost) - (futures sales revenue) with the formula

=B19+B21-B20.

Step 12: We now select B22 as an Output Cell and run 400 iterations of 7 simulations (remember the =RISKSimtable). After merging the simulations we find the results in Figure 49.2.

Figure 49.2

	E	F	G	H	I	J	K	L
45	Futures bought	600000	500000	400000	300000	200000	100000	0
46	Minimum =	153722.1	175478.6	188876.9	176125.4	159278.3	1.41E+05	119502.7
47	Maximum =	258467.4	249375.8	259734.1	275567.9	305822.8	340563.8	375304.7
48	Mean =	217838.9	217708	217577.1	217446.2	217315.3	217184.5	217053.6
49	Std Deviation =	16188.65	11070.79	11839.02	17744.64	25430.14	33698.98	42209.73
50	Variance =	2.62E+08	1.23E+08	1.40E+08	3.15E+08	6.47E+08	1.14E+09	1.78E+09
51	Skewness =	-0.6915989	-0.1955315	0.3666323	0.4345655	0.4824924	0.5192108	0.5448452
52	Kurtosis =	4.070718	3.488647	3.234234	3.221479	3.260778	3.316812	3.364228
53	Errors Calculated =	0	0	0	0	0	0	0
54	Mode =	207027.1	225078.7	231190.8	221927.5	199803.4	215689	203427.8
55	5% Perc =	185996.2	199438	1.99E+05	190401.7	179992.7	168532.8	154357.9
56	10% Perc =	197790	204127.5	202524.8	195212.3	185606.7	176231.4	166168.9
57	15% Perc =	202295	206844.1	205053.7	198278	191313	182934	174107.3
58	20% Perc =	206585.6	209077.8	206935.3	201781.8	195622.8	188625.7	180832.8
59	25% Perc =	209333.2	210981.3	208831.6	205386	199694.2	192972.6	186879.1
60	30% Perc =	211391.9	212427.2	210877.8	207557.9	202797.9	197477.8	192431.4
61	35% Perc =	213426.1	213414.7	212591.6	209518.1	206919.2	202448.1	197747.5
62	40% Perc =	215160.4	215048.7	213725.1	212097.6	209456	206494.9	202872.7
63	45% Perc =	216710.2	216491.5	215698.3	214647.8	212609.1	210791	207828.1
64	50% Perc =	218941.1	217753.6	217180.7	216065	215110.5	213928	212874.4
65	55% Perc =	221690.2	219071.5	218494.2	218217.9	217400.4	217628.6	218253.1
66	60% Perc =	223845.8	220540.8	220416.2	220728.4	220538.2	222029	223702.7
67	65% Perc =	225432.9	221781.5	222166.1	223016.6	224173.8	226950.5	229503.2
68	70% Perc =	226727.4	223443.4	223589.6	225833.9	228746.2	232332.9	235605.3
69	75% Perc =	228571.1	225095.9	225179.4	228238.7	233031.8	237225.3	242470.3
70	80% Perc =	230739.8	226861.4	226882.2	232227	238459.7	244224.2	250453.7
71	85% Perc =	232825.8	228479.8	229423.6	235021.5	243295	252836.1	259996.7
72	90% Perc =	235872.7	231528.1	2.32E+05	2.40E+05	2.50E+05	2.62E+05	2.73E+05
73	95% Perc =	241728	235736.6	238242.5	247782.8	263235.8	277668.4	292647.1

Note that purchasing 500,000 futures minimizes the standard deviation of total cost. Purchasing 500,000 futures also appears to minimize the 95%ile of total cost. Note that if no futures are purchased, the standard deviation of cost is nearly 4 times the standard deviation of cost when 500,000 futures are purchased.

Remarks

Movements in the interest rate can be modeled using techniques discussed in Chapters 51 and 53. Commodity prices are often modeled as a mean-reverting process. See Chapter 51 for a discussion of mean-reverting processes.

Chapter 50: Foreign Exchange Options and Hedging Foreign Exchange Risk

In the file *Germanyvar.xls* you have a template that uses the BS model to price European foreign exchange puts and calls. Note that an additional input is the interest rate in the foreign country. Letting r = US interest rate and q = Foreign interest rate we can also price an exchange option (even an exotic via simulation) **by assuming the exchange rate ($s per unit of foreign currency) grows at a rate r – q.**

Example 50.1

On July 31, 1997 exchange rate was $.5445/ mark. Price of a European put option expiring on September 21, 1997 with exercise price $.53/mark was 0.23 cents.

What is implied volatility?

We have 500,000 marks coming on September 21 1997. If we buy 8 puts (each put is on 62,500 marks) how well have we hedged our exchange risk?

Solution - Part a

To begin we need the German interest rate. We can extract this from forward prices. See Figure 50.1 and file *Germanyvar.xls*.

Figure 50.1

	G	H	I	J
9	Forwards			
10	t		annualgrowth	
11	0	0.5445		
12	0.083333	0.5457	1.026769	
13	0.25	0.5479	1.025212	
14	0.5	0.5511	1.024389	
15			1.025457	

It can be shown (see (48.2)) that forward contracts on currency grow at rate r – q. We see that German forwards are growing by 2.5% per year so German rate must be 2.5% lower than US rate (5.1%). Thus German rate is 2.6%. Putting all our known inputs into the option template we may find the implied volatility of the $/mark rate using goal seek.

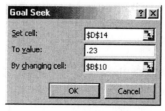

Thus we try to adjust the volatility (B10) so that cell D14 becomes .23. We find the implied volatility is 9.9%.

Figure 50.2

	A	B	C	D	E	F
1	Currency					
2	Option Template					
3				July 31, 1997 data		
4	Input data			Today's September put price		
5	Currency value in $s	$0.54		.23 cents		
6	Exercise price	$0.53				
7	Duration	$0.14				
8	Interest rate	0.051				
9	Foreign interest rate	0.026				
10	Implied volatility (stdev)	0.098567				
11				cents		
12				Predicted		
13		Call Price		1.86247		
14		Put Price		0.230096		
15	Other quantities for option price					
16	d1	0.839829		N(d1)	0.799498	
17	d2	0.802625		N(d2)	0.788904	
18				N(-d1)	0.200502	
19				N(-d2)	0.211096	

Solution - Part b

Step by Step

Step 1: We enter all input parameters in C3:C9. Note duration =52/365=.14.

Step 2: Assuming $/mark grows at rate (.051-.026) per year we can generate in cell C10 the September 21 $/mark price with the formula

   =C9*EXP((C5-C7-0.5*C6^2)*C8+C6*RISKNormal(0,1)*SQRT(C8)).

Step 3: In C14 we convert our 500,000 marks to dollars with the formula

   =C3*C10.

Step 4: In C15 we compute the payment (in dollars) received on September 21 from our put option with the formula

   =C12*62500*MAX(C11-C10,0).

Step 5: In C16 we compute the cost of the put option in September 21 dollars (remembering to compute its future value!) with the formula

   =EXP(C8*C5)*C4*C12*62500/100.

Note that price of put is in cents so we divide by 100 to go back to dollars!

Step 6: In C17 we compute our total $s received with the formula

$$= C14+C15-C16.$$

Step 7: To verify the option price we keep track of discounted cash flows for put in E8 with the formula

$$= EXP(-C5*C8)*MAX(C11-C10,0).$$

Figure 50.3

	B	C	D	E
1	**500,000 dm coming on september 21**			
2				
3	Payments	500000		
4	Put price today	0.23	cents!!	
5	r	0.051		
6	implied vol	0.0985		
7	r foreign	0.026		Discounted cash flow from put
8	duration	0.142466		0
9	$/dm today	0.5445		
10	$/dm on Sept 21	0.546065		
11	Put strike price	0.53		
12	**Puts bought**	8	62,500 dm/put	
13	$ value in September			
14	Payments	273032.6		
15	Put option received	0		
16	Cost	1158.386		
17	Total with hedge	271874.2		

By risk neutral valuation the expected value of this cell should equal the price of the put.

Step 8: We run 1000 iterations of @RISK with our output cells being C17 (Total value in dollars received with hedge), C14 (dollar value received with no hedging) and E8(discounted cash flows from put). Our results are in Figure 50.4.

Figure 50.4

	F	G	H	I
13	Name	Total with hedge	Payments	duration / [
14	Description	Output	Output	Output
15	Cell	C17	C14	E8
16	Minimum =	263841.6	236852.9	0
17	Maximum =	308271.3	309429.7	5.59E-02
18	Mean =	273220	273217	2.31E-03
19	Std Deviation =	8.50E+03	1.02E+04	6.12E-03
20	Variance =	7.22E+07	1.04E+08	3.75E-05
21	Skewness =	0.7969913	9.71E-02	3.491375
22	Kurtosis =	3.117573	3.057079	17.68259
23	Errors Calculated =	0	0	0
24	Mode =	263841.6	270082.7	0
25	5% Perc =	263841.6	256826.7	0
26	10% Perc =	263841.6	260311.5	0
27	15% Perc =	263841.6	262672.4	0
28	20% Perc =	263841.6	264606.8	0
29	25% Perc =	265112.4	266270.8	0
30	30% Perc =	266603.8	267742.8	0
31	35% Perc =	267999.8	269140.9	0
32	40% Perc =	269294.8	270453.2	0
33	45% Perc =	270589.1	271747.4	0
34	50% Perc =	271860.8	273019.3	0
35	55% Perc =	273140.7	274299	0
36	60% Perc =	274482.3	275593	0
37	65% Perc =	275809.7	276968.1	0
38	70% Perc =	277255.7	278386.1	0.00E+00
39	75% Perc =	278788.8	279947.3	0.00E+00
40	80% Perc =	280528.8	281687.2	6.90E-04
41	85% Perc =	282600.9	283733.4	4.62E-03
42	90% Perc =	285138.5	286296.9	9.24E-03
43	95% Perc =	289099.9	290178.9	1.62E-02

We see that without the hedge we could drop to $236,853. With the hedge we can only drop to $263,842. Mean payoffs with and without hedge are basically a wash. Note that simulation does verify the option price or .23 cents. Also note that if we hedge our 5%ile is almost $7000 higher than if we do not hedge.

Remarks

Of course, we could use the =RISKSimTable function to vary the number of puts purchased. This would help us determine the number of puts that gives the desired risk-return tradeoff.

Chapter 51: Modeling Mean Reverting Processes

Changes in foreign exchange rates or interest rates can greatly influence a company's bottom line. For example, increased interest rates greatly decrease car sales. Suppose the yen's value (in dollars) drops. Then US car manufacturers lose sales in the US because the price of a Japanese car in US dollars will decrease. In evaluating investment projects it is crucial to be able to model changes in interest rates and exchange rates. Many people believe that interest rates, inflation rates, exchange rates and many commodity prices follow a **mean-reverting process**. In this chapter we will fit a mean reverting process to US interest rates. Let I_t denote the interest rate at time t. Interest rates are said to be mean-reverting if there is a level L for interest rates with the following properties:

- If I_t is less than L we expect (on average) I_{t+1} to be larger than I_t. and less than L.

- If I_t is greater than L we expect (on average) I_{t+1} to be smaller than I_t and greater than L.

- If I_t equals L we expect (on average) I_{t+1} to equal I_t.

We can see that no matter what the current interest rate is, next period's interest rate will tend to be closer to L than the current rate. Hence the term **mean reverting process.** Why might interest rates be mean reverting? When interest rates are low inflationary pressures tend to build up which pushes rates up. When interest rates are high, the Federal Reserve Bank often lowers them to prevent a recession.

Simulating a Mean Reverting Process

Here is how to simulate a mean reverting process:

1. Run a regression with the dependent variable being the current period's interest rate and the independent variable being last period's interest rate (called the lagged one period rate). Suppose the resulting estimate is $I_t = a + bI_{t-1}$ + *(error term)*. Compute the residuals (actual rate - predicted rate) for each month. Check the number of times the residuals change sign. If the residuals are random, they should change sign around half the time. If the residuals change sign much less than half the time, our regression probably exhibits **positive autocorrelation** and should not be used. More formally, if we have n observations in our regression and the number of sign changes is smaller than

    $$\frac{n-1}{2} - \sqrt{n-1}$$ we probably have positive autocorrelation. Otherwise we are OK

    and can use the results of this regression to simulate future rates. If we do not find positive autocorrelation then we simulate I_t as a normal random variable with mean = our prediction = $a + bI_{t-1}$ and standard deviation = standard error

    of regression. It is easy to check that this process mean reverts to $L = \dfrac{a}{1-b}$.

    When I_{t-1} is less than L, we predict $L > I_t > I_{t-1}$; when I_{t-1} is greater than L, we predict $L < I_t < I_{t-1}$, and when $I_{t-1} = L$, we predict $I_t = I_{t-1}$.

2. If our first regression yields positive autocorrelation run another regression with the dependent variable being the current period's interest rate and the independent variables being last period's interest rate and the interest rate two periods ago (the lagged two period rate). Suppose the resulting estimate is $I_t = a' + b'I_{t-1} + c'I_{t-2}$ + *(error term)*. Compute the residuals (actual rate - predicted rate) for each month. Check the number of times the residuals change sign. If the residuals are random, they should change sign around half the time. If the residuals change sign much less than half the time, our regression probably exhibits **positive autocorrelation** and should not be used. More formally, if we have n observations in our regression and the number of sign changes is

    smaller than $\dfrac{n-1}{2} - \sqrt{n-1}$ we probably have positive autocorrelation.

    Otherwise we are OK and can use the results of this regression to simulate future rates. If we do not find positive autocorrelation then we simulate I_t as a normal random variable with mean = our prediction = $a' + b'I_{t-1} + c'I_{t-2}$ and standard deviation = standard error of regression. It is easy to check that this

    process mean reverts to $\dfrac{a'}{1-b'-c'}$.

3. Continue **lagging** back more periods until (hopefully) no positive autocorrelation is found.

We illustrate this methodology in the file *mean.xls*. Our goal is to simulate future one-year spot rates in US. We are given data from January 1988 to February 1998. See Figure 51.1.

Figure 51.1

	B	C	D	E	F	G	H
2						cutoff	49.0455488
3						total sc	41
4		US 1 year rate	Lag 1	Lag 2	Prediction Lag 1	Error	Sign Change
5	Jan-88	0.0699					
6	Feb-88	0.0664	0.0699		0.069632	-0.00323	
7	Mar-88	0.0671	0.0664	0.0699	0.066176	0.000924	1
8	Apr-88	0.0701	0.0671	0.0664	0.066867	0.003233	0
9	May-88	0.074	0.0701	0.0671	0.069829	0.004171	0
10	Jun-88	0.0749	0.074	0.0701	0.07368	0.00122	0
11	Jul-88	0.0775	0.0749	0.074	0.074569	0.002931	0
12	Aug-88	0.0817	0.0775	0.0749	0.077136	0.004564	0
13	Sep-88	0.0809	0.0817	0.0775	0.081284	-0.00038	1
14	Oct-88	0.0811	0.0809	0.0817	0.080494	0.000606	1
15	Nov-88	0.0848	0.0811	0.0809	0.080691	0.004109	0
16	Dec-88	0.0899	0.0848	0.0811	0.084345	0.005555	0
17	Jan-89	0.0905	0.0899	0.0848	0.089381	0.001119	0
18	Feb-89	0.0925	0.0905	0.0899	0.089973	0.002527	0
19	Mar-89	0.0957	0.0925	0.0905	0.091948	0.003752	0
20	Apr-89	0.0936	0.0957	0.0925	0.095108	-0.00151	1
21	May-89	0.0898	0.0936	0.0957	0.093034	-0.00323	0
22	Jun-89	0.0844	0.0898	0.0936	0.089282	-0.00488	0
23	Jul-89	0.0789	0.0844	0.0898	0.08395	-0.00505	0
122	Oct-97	0.0546	0.0552	0.0556	0.055116	-0.00052	0
123	Nov-97	0.0546	0.0546	0.0552	0.054524	7.62E-05	1
124	Dec-97	0.0553	0.0546	0.0546	0.054524	0.000776	0
125	Jan-98	0.0524	0.0553	0.0546	0.055215	-0.00282	1
126	Feb-98	0.0531	0.0524	0.0553	0.052351	0.000749	1

Step by Step

Step 1: In D6:D126 we compute the one month lagged interest rates by copying from D6 to D7:D126 the formula

=C5.

Step 2: We ran regression with Y RANGE C6:C126 and X RANGE D6:D126. This estimates a one period lagged model. The results are in Figure 51.2.

Figure 51.2

	L	M	N	O	P	Q
6	SUMMARY OUTPUT					
7						
8	*Regression Statistics*					
9	Multiple R	0.988431254				
10	R Square	0.976996344				
11	Adjusted R Square	0.976803036				
12	Standard Error	0.002534664				
13	Observations	121				
14						
15	ANOVA					
16		*df*	*SS*	*MS*	*F*	*Significance F*
17	Regression	1	0.032470123	0.032470123	5054.090682	2.4839E-99
18	Residual	119	0.000764518	6.42452E-06		
19	Total	120	0.033234641			
20						
21		*Coefficients*	*Standard Error*	*t Stat*	*P-value*	*Lower 95%*
22	Intercept	0.000609342	0.000859195	0.709201053	0.479586897	-0.001091947
23	X Variable 1	0.987444997	0.013889653	71.09212813	2.4839E-99	0.959942132
24	Rate =.000609+.987445*Lag Rate					
25	**mean revert to**					
26	0.048533785					
27	Month t risknormal(.0006093+.987445*Month t-1,.0025)					

Note in L26 we have computed that the one period lag indicates interest rates mean revert to a level of $\dfrac{.00609}{1-.98744} = 4.85\%$.

Step 3: We now check for positive autocorrelation. First we compute in F6:F126 our predictions by copying from F6 to F7:F126 the formula

$=\$M\$22+\$M\$23*D6.$

Step 4: In G6:G126 we compute the errors or residuals (actual rate - predicted) by copying the formula

$=(C6-F6)$

from G6 to G7:G126.

Step 5: Note that a sign change in the residuals occurs if and only if the product of two consecutive residuals is negative. With this observation we determine if the first two predictions yield a sign change by entering in H7 the formula

$=If(G7*G6<0,1,0).$

Copying this formula to H8:H126 determines if each pair of observations yields a sign change.

Step 6: In H3 we compute the total number of sign changes (41) with the formula

$$=SUM(H7:H126).$$

Step 7: We have 121 total observations in the regression. The cutoff for positive autocorrelation is computed in H2 with the formula

$$=60\text{-}SQRT(120).$$

Since we had 41 sign changes and the cutoff is 49, we do have positive autocorrelation. We now must run regression including a two period lag.

Step 8: In E7:E126 we create the two period lagged interest rates by copying from

$$=C5$$

from E7 to E8:E126.

Step 9: We now run a regression with Y RANGE of C7:C126 and X RANGE of D7:E126. We obtain the results in Figure 51.3.

Figure 51.3

	M	N	O	P	Q	R	S	T
29	SUMMARY OUTPUT							
30								
31	*Regression Statistics*							
32	Multiple R	0.991202265						
33	R Square	0.98248193						
34	Adjusted R Squ	0.982182476						
35	Standard Error	0.00222909						
36	Observations	120						
37								
38	ANOVA							
39		*df*	*SS*	*MS*	*F*	*Significance F*		
40	Regression	2	0.032604633	0.016302317	3280.908981	1.7537E-103		
41	Residual	117	0.000581354	4.96884E-06				
42	Total	119	0.033185988					
43								
44		*Coefficients*	*Standard Error*	*t Stat*	*P-value*	*Lower 95%*	*Upper 95%*	*Lower 95.0%*
45	Intercept	0.000949308	0.000758605	1.251387236	0.213289529	-0.000553068	0.002451685	-0.000553068
46	Lagged 1	1.458274678	0.080648153	18.0819352	1.12593E-35	1.298555249	1.617994108	1.298555249
47	Lagged 2	-0.47492628	0.080581465	-5.893740965	3.72129E-08	-0.634513637	-0.315338924	-0.634513637
48								
49		Month t = .000949 +1.450*Month t 1 -.475*Month t-2						
50	Mean revert to	0.057010015						
51		Month t is risknormal(.000949+1.458*Month(t-1) -.47493*Month(t-2),.002229)						
52								

Columns I-K contain the autocorrelation check for this regression. From Figure 51.4 we find that this regression has no significant positive autocorrelation and we may use the results of this regression to simulate future interest rates. In N50 we computed level to which interest rates mean revert (5.7%) with the formula

$$=N45/(1\text{-}N46\text{-}N47).$$

Figure 51.4

	I	J	K
2		cutoff	48.59129
3		total sc	54
4	Prediction Lag 2	Error	Sign Change
5			
6			
7	0.064581	0.002519	0
8	0.067264	0.002836	0
9	0.071307	0.002693	0
10	0.075569	-0.000669	1
11	0.07503	0.00247	1
12	0.078394	0.003306	0
13	0.083284	-0.002384	1
14	0.080122	0.000978	1
15	0.080794	0.004006	0
16	0.086094	0.003806	0
17	0.091774	-0.001274	1
18	0.090227	0.002273	1
19	0.092859	0.002841	0
20	0.096576	-0.002976	1
21	0.091993	-0.002193	0
22	0.087449	-0.003049	0
23	0.081379	-0.002479	0
24	0.075923	0.005877	1
25	0.002764	-0.000564	1
26	0.081971	-0.002071	0
27	0.078427	-0.000727	0
122	0.05504	-0.00044	0
123	0.054355	0.000245	1
124	0.05464	0.00066	0
125	0.055661	-0.003261	1
126	0.051099	0.002001	1

Step 10: We may now model Month t interest rate as a normal random variable with mean (.000949+1.458*Month (t-1) -.47493*Month(t-2) and standard deviation .002229. See Figure 51.5. In C127:C132 we generate a path of the next six months of one year spot rates. Simply enter in C127 the formula

$=RISKNormal(\$N\$45+\$N\$46*C126+\$N\$47*C125,\$N\$35)$

and copy this formula to C128:C132.

Figure 51.5

	B	C	D
127	Mar-98	0.053498	
128	Apr-98	0.053745	
129	May-98	0.053917	
130	Jun-98	0.05405	
131	Jul-98	0.054162	
132	Aug-98	0.054263	

In a similar fashion, one can simulate a mean-reverting process for exchange rates, oil prices, etc.

Chapter 52: Simulating Exchange Risk-Valuing a Foreign Currency Swap

Suppose Company I can borrow dollars cheaper than Company II and Company II can borrow yen cheaper than Company I. Also assume that Company I needs yen and Company II needs dollars. Then it is beneficial for Company I to borrow dollars and Company II to borrow yen. Then Company I can "swap" their borrowed dollars for Company II's borrowed yen. The annual volume of currencies swaps (as well as interest rate swaps that involve swapping fixed interest rate payments for floating rate payments) runs into hundreds of billions of dollars. A fair value of a swap is the expected discounted value of the cash flows from the swap. See Chapter 5 of Hull (1997) for an excellent discussion of swaps. We now illustrate how to value a currency swap. After reading Chapter 53, it should be clear how to value an interest rate swap. Here is an example of valuing a currency swap.

Example 52.1
It is August 1997 and we have entered into the following swap: The notional amounts are 1200 million-yen and $10 million US. During August of each of the next three years we will pay 8% interest in dollars and receive 5% interest in yen. Of course, the notional amounts will be "swapped" at the end of the three-year period. Current exchange and interest rates are given in Figure 52.1

Figure 52.1

	A	B	C	D
1	3 year swap			
2	Japanese principal 1200 million yen			
3	US principal 10 million dollars			
4	pay 8% per year in dollars			
5	get 5% per year in yen			
6				
7	Month	Jun-97	Jul-97	Aug-97
8	Actual US 3 mo Rate	0.054	0.0525	0.05280
9	Actual Japan 3 mo Rate	0.012	0.011	0.00957
10	Exchange Rate predicted(yen/$)			138.00
11	Actual Exchange rate			138.00

Two questions of obvious interest are:
1) What is a fair price for the swap?
2) How much risk is involved in the swap?

Where is the Uncertainty?

The uncertainty about the outcome of this swap is due to the fact that future interest rates in Japan and US are unknown as are the future exchange rates. Once we model these sources of uncertainty we can compute the value in dollars of our payments received each August (by using the exchange rate when the payment is received) and then discount them back to today's dollars. We now turn to modeling the three sources of uncertainty. Our work is in the file *exchangesim.xls*. Following our work in Chapter 51 we will model both future US and Japanese interest rates as mean reverting processes.

Uncertainty in US Rates

Following our work in Chapter 51, we will model future US rates as a mean-reverting process where the interest rate during month t + 1 will be normally distributed with

Mean = .000949 + 1.458275*(Month t Rate) - .47493*(Month t - 1 Rate)

Standard deviation = .002229.

Under this assumption US interest rates mean revert to 5.7%.

Uncertainty in Japanese Rates

Following our work in Chapter 51, we will model future Japanese rates as a mean-reverting process. Our work is in sheet Japan of file *exchangesim.xls*. See Figure 52.2 and Figure 52.3.

Figure 52.2

	A	B	C	D	E	F	G
1						cutoff	36.85634924
2	Japan MR						51
3		Date	Jap Rates	Lagged	Prediction	Error	Sign Change
4		3/1/87	0.037416				
5	1	4/1/87	0.03827	0.037416	0.03737	0.0009	
6	2	5/1/87	0.039509	0.03827	0.038216	0.001292	0
7	3	6/1/87	0.038612	0.039509	0.039444	-0.00083	1
8	4	7/1/87	0.036514	0.038612	0.038555	-0.00204	0
9	5	8/1/87	0.039816	0.036514	0.036476	0.00334	1
10	6	9/1/87	0.041293	0.039816	0.039748	0.001545	0
11	7	10/1/87	0.037215	0.041293	0.041212	-0.004	1
12	8	11/1/87	0.043517	0.037215	0.037171	0.006346	1
13	9	12/1/87	0.035726	0.043517	0.043416	-0.00769	1
14	10	1/1/88	0.039816	0.035726	0.035696	0.004121	1
15	11	2/1/88	0.041954	0.039816	0.039749	0.002205	0
16	12	3/1/88	0.040431	0.041954	0.041867	-0.00144	1
17	13	4/1/88	0.036583	0.040431	0.040358	-0.00378	0
18	14	5/1/88	0.037217	0.036583	0.036545	0.000672	1
19	15	6/1/88	0.042259	0.037217	0.037173	0.005087	0
20	16	7/1/88	0.045832	0.042259	0.04217	0.003662	0
21	17	8/1/88	0.050333	0.045832	0.045709	0.004624	0
22	18	9/1/88	0.04945	0.050333	0.050169	-0.00072	1
23	19	10/1/88	0.050134	0.04945	0.049294	0.00084	1
24	20	11/1/88	0.056245	0.050134	0.049971	0.006273	0
25	21	12/1/88	0.055897	0.056245	0.056027	-0.00013	1
26	22	1/1/89	0.06529	0.055897	0.055682	0.009608	1
27	23	2/1/89	0.067456	0.06529	0.064989	0.002468	0
28	24	3/1/89	0.063748	0.067456	0.067135	-0.00339	1
29	25	4/1/89	0.066403	0.063748	0.063461	0.002942	1
90	86	5/1/94	0.022813	0.023125	0.023211	-0.0004	1
91	87	6/1/94	0.021875	0.022813	0.022901	-0.00103	0
92	88	7/1/94	0.020625	0.021875	0.021972	-0.00135	0
93	89	8/1/94	0.020625	0.020625	0.020733	-0.00011	0
94	90	9/1/94	0.021875	0.020625	0.020733	0.001142	1
95	91	10/1/94	0.0225	0.021875	0.021972	0.000528	0
96	92	11/1/94	0.022813	0.0225	0.022591	0.000221	0
97	93	12/1/94	0.0225	0.022813	0.022901	-0.0004	1
98	94	1/1/95	0.0225	0.0225	0.022591	-9.1E-05	0

Figure 52.3

	I	J	K	L	M
15	SUMMARY OUTPUT				
16					
17	*Regression Statistics*				
18	Multiple R	0.98280915			
19	R Square	0.96591382			
20	Adjusted R Square	0.96554331			
21	Standard Error	0.00067647			
22	Observations	94			
23					
24	ANOVA				
25		*df*	*SS*	*MS*	*F*
26	Regression	1	0.035237846	0.035	2607.04
27	Residual	92	0.00124351	1E-05	
28	Total	93	0.036481356		
29					
30		*Coefficients*	*Standard Error*	*t Stat*	*P-value*
31	Intercept	0.00029759	0.001037343	0.287	0.77485
32	X Variable 1	0.99083007	0.019405519	51.06	2.7E-69
33					
34	Mean reverts to	0.03245248			
35	Month t is normal with				
36	mean of .000298 +.99083*(Month t-1)				
37	standard deviation of .003676				

Autocorrelation does not appear to be a problem (number of sign changes exceeds autocorrelation cutoff), so from Figure 52.3 we find the interest rate during month t + 1 will be normally distributed with

Mean = .000298 + .99083(Month t Rate)*

Standard deviation = .003676.

Under this assumption Japanese interest rates mean revert to 3.2%. We also note that historically, Japanese and US interest rate moves have had a .40 correlation.

Exchange Rate Uncertainty

We will work with one-month time intervals. **Interest rate parity** tells us that our best forecast for the yen/$ spot rate one month hence is given by

$$(Current\ spot\ rate\ yen/\$) * \frac{1 + (current\ Japanese\ rate/12)}{1 + (current\ US\ rate/12)} \quad (52.1)$$

In the past the standard deviation of the errors in predicting exchange rates three months hence with interest rate parity has been 5% of the predicted yen/$ spot rate.

Note on IR Parity

If we invest $1 now in a US bank then in one month we will have

(1 + (current US rate/12)). (52.2))

If we now convert $1 to yen and invest it for one month in a Japanese bank and then convert the yen back to $s we will have

(Current yen/$ spot rate)(1 + (current Japanese rate/12))*(1/((Spot rate yen/$ in one month) dollars. (52.3)*

Setting (52.2) = (52.3) yields interest rate parity. If this equality did not hold traders could make infinite profits.

Simulating the Swap

We are now ready to simulate the swap! (*See Figure 52.4 and sheet Simulation of Exchangesim.xls*).

Figure 52.4

	A	B	C	D	E	F	G	P	AB	AN
2	Japanese principal 1200 million yen									
3	US principal 10 million dollars									
4	pay 8% per year in dollars									
5	get 5% per year in yen									
6					1	2	3	12	24	36
7	Month	Jun-97	Jul-97	Aug-97	Sep-97	Oct-97	Nov-97	Aug-98	Aug-99	Aug-00
8	Actual US 3 mo Rate	0.054	0.0525	0.05280	0.05301	0.05318	0.05332	0.05428	0.05517	0.05577
9	Actual Japan 3 mo Rate	0.012	0.011	0.00957	0.01120	0.00978	0.01139	0.01080	0.01197	0.01307
10	Exchange Rate predicted(yen/$)			138.00	137.51	137.03	136.53	132.25	126.74	121.50
11	Actual Exchange rate			138.00	137.51	137.03	136.53	132.25	126.74	121.50
12	$s paid(millions)							0.80000	0.8	10.8
13	yen received(millions)							60	60	1260
14	$ discount rate				0.99562	0.99124	0.98687	0.94794	0.89758	0.84926
15	net $s received							-0.3463	-0.32658	-0.4297
16	total value							-0.32827	-0.29313	-0.36492
17										
18							NPV received	-0.98633		

We proceed as follows:

Step by Step

Step 1: Enter given exchange rate and interest rate data in B8:D11.

Step 2: In rows 8 and 9 we generate future US and Japanese 90 day rates. We will use the =RISKINDEPC and =RISKDEPC functions to ensure that during each time period changes in Japanese rates and US have a .40 correlation. To generate the September 97 rate we enter in E8 and E9 respectively, the following formulas:

=RiskIndepC("Spot1")+RISKNormal(0.000949+1.458275*D8 0.47493*C8,0.002229) (gives US rate for September 97)

=RiskDepC("Spot1",0.4)+RISKNormal(0.000298+0.99083*C9,0.003676)) (gives Japanese rate for September 97).

Using a different name Spoti for each period ensures that the changes in US and Japanese rates for each period have a   .4 correlation. Of course, this is tedious to enter into the spreadsheet. For October 1997 we want Spot2 replacing Spot 1 etc. Best way to do this is copy the September, 1997 formulas and put the Spot2, Spot3 etc. in manually.

Step 3: In row 10 we use interest rate parity (52.1) to determine a prediction for future exchange rates (based on the last known interest rates and exchange rate). Our September 1997 prediction is obtained in E10 with the formula

$$=D11*(1+(D9/12))/(1+(D8/12)).$$

Step 4: In row 11 we compute the actual exchange rate using the mean obtained with interest rate parity and the 5% standard deviation of actual rates about interest rate parity predictions. Our September 1997 exchange rate is obtained in E11 with the formula

$$=RISKNormal(E10,0.05*E10).$$

Step 5: In rows 12 and 13 we enter the actual payments associated with the swap. We receive 60 million yen in August 98 and 99 and receive 1260 million yen in August 00. We pay $.8 million in August 98 and 99 and pay $10.8 million in August 00.

Step 6: In row 14 we compute the US discount factors based on the US interest rates. For September 1997 the discount factor is computed in E14 with the formula

$$=1/(1+(D8/12)).$$

In F14 we compute October 1997 discount factor with the formula

$$=E14/(1+(E8/12)).$$

Copying this formula across to G14:AN14 determines all future US discount rates.

Step 7: In row 15 we compute the net amount of dollars received each August. To do this we use the current exchange rate to convert yen received to dollars. The amount of dollars received during August 1998 is computed in P15 with the formula

$$=P13*(1/P11)-P12.$$

Copying this across to column AN creates our other net $ payments.

Step 8: In Row 16 we convert the $s received to today's dollars. To convert the August 98 dollars received to today's dollars we simply multiply (in cell P16) our payments by the discount factor.

$$=P15*P14.$$

Step 9: In cell P18 we compute the total NPV (in $s) of our payments with the formula

=SUM(P16:AN16).

This is the output cell for the simulation. The average value of this cell is the value of the swap.

Step 10: After selecting P18 as our output cell we obtained the simulation results given in Figure 52.5.

Figure 52.5

	AP	AQ
24	Cell	P18
25	Minimum =	-6.56
26	Maximum =	16.48
27	Mean =	-0.11
28	Std Deviation =	3.18
29	Variance =	10.10
30	Skewness =	1.10
31	Kurtosis =	5.38
32	Errors Calculated =	0.00
33	Mode =	0.16
34	5% Perc =	-4.42
35	10% Perc =	-3.73
36	15% Perc =	-3.20
37	20% Perc =	-2.67
38	25% Perc =	-2.30
39	30% Perc =	-1.98
40	35% Perc =	-1.63
41	40% Perc =	-1.26
42	45% Perc =	-0.92
43	50% Perc =	-0.59
44	55% Perc =	-0.20
45	60% Perc =	0.18
46	65% Perc =	0.60
47	70% Perc =	1.00
48	75% Perc =	1.54
49	80% Perc =	2.26
50	85% Perc =	2.95
51	90% Perc =	4.16
52	95% Perc =	5.52

Thus it appears that we should be paid $110,000 enter into the swap. There is a 5% chance that we could be down at least $4.42 million from this swap, so the VAR of the swap is around $4.42 million.

Remarks

Of course, we should update our mean reverting interest rate models with the most recent data. We might even used **weighted least squares** to estimate our mean reversion models. To use weighted least squares we would give more recent errors more weight and use Solver to find the coefficients that minimize the sum of the weighted squared errors.

Reference

Hull, J. *Options Futures and Other Derivatives*, Prentice-Hall, 1997.

Chapter 53: Simulating Yield Curve Movements Based on Historical Data

We now discuss how historical data can be used to forecast (and simulate) future movements in the yield curve. We will use the current yield curve to make forecasts for the yield curve at a future date (say in 3 months). We will find these forecasts to be biased upward. Then we will eliminate the bias for each point on the yield curve. From these forecasts we will create scenarios which are used to model movements of the entire yield curve. Then we will be ready to use @RISK to simulate future movements in the yield curve. Our data contains spot rates for 3 months, 6 months, 1 year, 5 years, 10 years and 30 years. See Figure 53.1 and file *advancedyield.xls*. Our data is for the years 1985-1992.

Figure 53.1

	A	B	C	D	E	F	G	H	I
2									
3									
4			FYGM3	FYGM6	FYGMYR	FYGT5	FYGT7	FYGT10	FYGT30
5	8501	1	7.76	8	8.33	10.93	11.27	11.38	11.45
6	8502	2	8.27	8.39	8.56	11.13	11.44	11.51	11.47
7	8503	3	8.52	8.9	9.06	11.52	11.82	11.86	11.81
8	8504	4	7.95	8.23	8.44	11.01	11.34	11.43	11.47
9	8505	5	7.48	7.65	7.85	10.34	10.72	10.85	11.05
10	8506	6	6.95	7.09	7.27	9.6	10.08	10.16	10.45
11	8507	7	7.08	7.2	7.31	9.7	10.16	10.31	10.5
12	8508	8	7.14	7.32	7.48	9.81	10.2	10.33	10.56
13	8509	9	7.1	7.27	7.5	9.81	10.24	10.37	10.61
14	8510	10	7.16	7.33	7.45	9.69	10.11	10.24	10.5

Interpolating to Find Current Spot Rates

We want to forecast spot rates three months in the future. This will involve computing the following forward rates:

f.25,.5   f.25,.75   f.25,1.25   f.25,5.25   f.25,7.25   f.25,10.25   f.25,30.25

To compute these forward rates we will need estimates (which we obtained by linear interpolation) of the following spot rates:

sp.25   sp.5   sp.75   sp1.25   sp5.25   sp7.25   sp10.25   sp30.25

For instance to obtain sp(.75) we simply take .5*spot(.5) + .5*spot(1). We do this in L5 with the formula

=(0.5/100)*(D5+E5).

To obtain sp(1.25) we take (15/16)*(spot(1)) + (1/16)*spot(5). We do this in M5 with the formula

=(15/1600)*E5+(1/1600)*F5.

Continuing in this fashion we compute other needed spot rates in N5:P5. To compute spot(30.25) we assume that spot rate will grow at

$$\frac{11.45 - 11.38}{20}$$

per year. Then we can construct the estimated sp(30.25) in Q5 with the formula

=(1/100)*(I5+(1/80)*(I5-H5)).

Figure 53.2 gives the implied spot rates computed by linear interpolation.

Figure 53.2

	J	K	L	M	N	O	P	Q
3	0.25	0.5	0.75	1.25	5.25	7.25	10.25	30.25
4	sp.25	sp.5	sp.75	sp1.25	sp5.25	sp7.25	sp10.25	sp30.25
5	0.0776	0.08	0.08165	0.084925	0.109725	0.112792	0.113809	0.114509
6	0.0827	0.0839	0.08475	0.087206	0.111688	0.114458	0.115095	0.114695
7	0.0852	0.089	0.0898	0.092138	0.115575	0.118233	0.118594	0.118094
8	0.0795	0.0823	0.08335	0.086006	0.110513	0.113475	0.114305	0.114705
9	0.0748	0.0765	0.0775	0.080056	0.103875	0.107308	0.108525	0.110525
10	0.0695	0.0709	0.0718	0.074156	0.0966	0.100867	0.101636	0.104536
11	0.0708	0.072	0.07255	0.074594	0.097575	0.101725	0.103124	0.105024
12	0.0714	0.0732	0.074	0.076256	0.098588	0.102108	0.103329	0.105629

Computing Forward Rates

We now compute the forward rate f(i,j), where i and j are measured in years. Recall from Chapter 12 that

$$(1 + s(i))^i (1 + f(i, j))^{j-i} = (1 + s(j))^j$$

Or

$$f(i, j) = \frac{(1 + s(j))^{j/(j-i)}}{(1 + s(i))^{i/(j-i)}} - 1$$

In R5 we compute f(.25,.5) for January, 1985 with the formula

$$=(1+K5)\wedge(K\$3/(K\$3-\$J\$3))/(1+\$J5)\wedge(\$J\$3/(K\$3-\$J\$3))-1.$$

Copying this formula from R5 to S5:X5 constructs the forward rates needed to forecast the yield curve three months into the future. See Figure 53.3.

Figure 53.3

	R	S	T	U	V	W	X
4	f.25,.5	f.25,.75	f.25,1.25	f.25,5.25	f.25,7.25	f.25,10.25	f.25,30.25
5	0.082405	0.083681	0.086764	0.111356	0.11407	0.114729	0.114822
6	0.085101	0.085776	0.088336	0.113157	0.11561	0.115917	0.114966
7	0.092813	0.092107	0.093879	0.117116	0.119432	0.119442	0.118372
8	0.085107	0.08528	0.087639	0.112086	0.114708	0.115189	0.115003
9	0.078203	0.078853	0.081374	0.105349	0.108487	0.109382	0.110828
10	0.072302	0.072952	0.075323	0.097973	0.102004	0.102452	0.104833
11	0.073201	0.073426	0.075544	0.098931	0.102846	0.103944	0.105313

Are Forecasts Biased?

In Columns Y-AE we compute (see Figure 53.4) the ratio of the actual yield curve value to the forecast made 3 months prior. If our forecasts are unbiased the average of these ratios should be near 1; if the average of these ratios exceeds 1, then our forecasts tend to be too low; if the average of these ratios is less than 1, then our forecasts tend to be too high.

Figure 53.4

	X	Y	Z	AA	AB	AC	AD	AE
2								
3	fudge	0.942178	0.954737	0.948847	0.968855	0.974377	0.978865	0.985639
4	f.25,30.25	error.25	error.5	error1	error5	error7	error10	error30
5	0.114822							
6	0.114966							
7	0.118372							
8	0.115003	0.964743	0.9835	0.972753	0.988719	0.99413	0.996257	0.998941
9	0.110828	0.878952	0.891853	0.888655	0.913774	0.927258	0.936013	0.961157
10	0.104833	0.748815	0.769754	0.774403	0.819701	0.843998	0.850625	0.88281
11	0.105313	0.831891	0.844276	0.834104	0.865405	0.885727	0.895048	0.913018
12	0.105919	0.913012	0.928315	0.919209	0.931189	0.940202	0.944401	0.952831
13	0.106428	0.981994	0.996548	0.995706	1.001297	1.003885	1.012182	1.012086

In Y3:AE3 we construct the average over all forecasts of the actual yield to predicted yield. To do this enter in Y8 the formula

$$=((C8/100)/R5)$$

and copy it to the range Y8:AE101. This yields actual yield/predicted yield for each month and point on the yield curve. Then we average each column's actual/predicted yields (in Y3:AE3) to get a fix on whether we are forecasting, on average, too high or too low. See Figure 53.4.

We find, unsurprisingly, that on average we are overpredicting each point on the yield curve. For example, for the three-month rate the actual yield is around 94% of the forecast. To make our forecasts unbiased, we can multiply each of them by Row 3 number. This is our fudge factor.

Now we create unbiased forecasts in the sheet Fudged by multiplying the forward rate forecast by fudge factor. Thus to forecast the three month rate we take $(.942)*f(.25,.5)$. Now the average ratio of actual to forecast is 1 for each yield curve point. To obtain the actual/predicted for .the .25 month yield curve point in April 93 we enter in Y8 the formula

$$=(C8/100)/(R5*Y\$2).$$

Copying this formula to Y8:AE101 generates the actual/predicted for each fudged forecast. See Figure 53.5

Figure 53.5

	X	Y	Z	AA	AB	AC	AD	AE
1	sigma	0.089153	0.089199	0.093532	0.08545	0.077389	0.071982	0.064302
2	fudge	0.942178	0.954737	0.948847	0.968855	0.974377	0.978865	0.985639
3		1	1	1	1	1	1	1
4	f.25,30.25	error.25	error.5	error1	error5	error7	error10	error30
5	0.114822							
6	0.114966							
7	0.118372							mad
8	0.115003	1.02395	1.030127	1.025195	1.020503	1.020272	1.017768	1.013496
9	0.110828	0.932894	0.934135	0.936563	0.943148	0.951642	0.956223	0.975162
10	0.104833	0.79477	0.806248	0.816151	0.846051	0.866193	0.868991	0.895673
11	0.105313	0.882945	0.884303	0.879071	0.893224	0.909019	0.914373	0.926321
12	0.105919	0.969044	0.972326	0.968764	0.961123	0.964926	0.964791	0.966714
13	0.106428	1.04226	1.043793	1.049385	1.033485	1.030283	1.034036	1.026832
14	0.105315	1.038152	1.045611	1.039342	1.010955	1.008875	1.006414	1.01155

We have also found the standard deviation of the percentage errors for each of our forecasts in Y1:AE1. Note that short-term rates are harder to predict than long-term rates.

Estimating Error Scenarios

Recall we have computed the actual/predicted yield in our forecasts in columns Y:AE of sheet Fudged. For example, the error in forecasting the .25 month rate for April 1985 is computed in Y8 with the formula

$$= (C8/100)/(R5*Y\$2).$$

As we have seen copying this formula to the cell rangeY8:AE101 generates all actual/predicted yields. As we will soon see, we view Y8:AE8, Y9:AE9, ... Y101:AE101 as 94 different "scenarios" for the variation of the yield curve about our predictions. These scenarios will drive our simulation of the yield curve. Our "error scenarios" are in Figure 53.6.

Figure 53.6

	Y	Z	AA	AB	AC	AD	AE
4	error.25	error.5	error1	error5	error7	error10	error30
5							
6							
7							mad
8	1.02395	1.030127	1.025195	1.020503	1.020272	1.017768	1.013496
9	0.932894	0.934135	0.936563	0.943148	0.951642	0.956223	0.975162
10	0.79477	0.806248	0.816151	0.846051	0.866193	0.868991	0.895673
11	0.882945	0.884303	0.879071	0.893224	0.909019	0.914373	0.926321
12	0.969044	0.972326	0.968764	0.961123	0.964926	0.964791	0.966714
13	1.04226	1.043793	1.049385	1.033485	1.030283	1.034036	1.026832
14	1.038152	1.045611	1.039342	1.010955	1.008875	1.006414	1.01155
15	1.024535	1.015385	0.997133	0.958168	0.956487	0.959406	0.963625
16	1.01283	0.993453	0.969811	0.900722	0.902027	0.904729	0.909445
17	1.000482	0.999236	0.98713	0.907404	0.90608	0.909602	0.905561

Running an @RISK Simulation of Future Yield Curves

We now show how our analysis enables us to simulate future movements of the yield curve.

Example 53.1

Suppose it is January 1, 1993. Let's simulate the yield curve for the next year (in three-month increments. Currently the yield curve is as follows:

- Three month-3.00%

- Six-month-3.14%

- One Year-3.35%

- Five Year-5.83%

- Seven Year-6.26%

- Ten Year-6.60%

- Thirty Year-7.34%

We can now set up a simulation that gives the yield curve on April 1, July 1, October 1 of 1993 and January 1 of 1994. See Figures 53.7-53.10.

Figure 53.7

	A	B	C	D	E	F	G	H	I
1	Forecasting 3 months ahead yield curve								
2									
3									
4		fudge	0.942178	0.954737	0.948847	0.968855	0.974377	0.978865	0.985639
5			1	2	3	4	5	6	7
6		Scenario	FYGM3	FYGM6	FYGMYR	FYGT5	FYGT7	FYGT10	FYGT30
7	Jan-93		0.03	0.0314	0.0335	0.0583	0.0626	0.066	0.0734
8	Apr-93	47.5	0.03515	0.036367	0.038962	0.063127	0.066181	0.068345	0.073688
9	Jul-93	47.5	0.040277	0.042033	0.044853	0.067992	0.069709	0.070637	0.073908
10	Oct-93	47.5	0.046929	0.048627	0.051293	0.072886	0.073181	0.072872	0.074059
11	Jan-94	47.5	0.053932	0.055591	0.058016	0.07772	0.076537	0.075008	0.074127

Figure 53.8

	A	B	C	D	E	F	G	H
12	Scenario#	FYGM3	FYGM6	FYGMYR	FYGT5	FYGT7	FYGT10	FYGT30
13	1	1.02395	1.030127	1.025195	1.020503	1.020272	1.017768	1.013496
14	2	0.932894	0.934135	0.936563	0.943148	0.951642	0.956223	0.975162
15	3	0.79477	0.806248	0.816151	0.846051	0.866193	0.868991	0.895673
16	4	0.882945	0.884303	0.879071	0.893224	0.909019	0.914373	0.926321
17	5	0.969044	0.972326	0.968764	0.961123	0.964926	0.964791	0.966714
18	6	1.04226	1.043793	1.049385	1.033485	1.030283	1.034036	1.026832
19	7	1.038152	1.045611	1.039342	1.010955	1.008875	1.006414	1.01155
20	8	1.024535	1.015385	0.997133	0.958168	0.956487	0.959406	0.963625
21	9	1.01283	0.993453	0.969811	0.900722	0.902027	0.904729	0.909445
22	10	1.000482	0.999236	0.98713	0.907404	0.90608	0.909602	0.905561
23	11	1.018103	1.012861	0.998454	0.913066	0.905948	0.902516	0.898167
24	12	0.969718	0.95909	0.951708	0.868851	0.856044	0.852957	0.844406
25	13	0.88715	0.879283	0.867767	0.826223	0.806221	0.806558	0.795739
26	14	0.911649	0.908683	0.912494	0.920082	0.90817	0.900758	0.852597
27	15	1.001688	0.996549	0.999285	1.046838	1.030371	1.019893	0.963166
28	16	1.014391	1.010341	1.013153	1.024284	1.027494	1.017086	0.996438
29	17	0.942113	0.929353	0.925895	0.922766	0.933222	0.94552	0.987741
30	18	0.873572	0.8842	0.89042	0.924415	0.956683	0.971131	1.020125
31	19	0.933428	0.933	0.948986	0.986934	1.021094	1.034593	1.072852
32	20	1.019448	1.012323	1.011232	1.012454	1.026723	1.026778	1.03844

Figure 53.9

	J	K	L	M	N	O	P	Q
4	0.25	0.5	0.75	1.25	5.25	7.25	10.25	30.25
5								
6	sp.25	sp.5	sp.75	sp1.25	sp5.25	sp7.25	sp10.25	sp30.25
7	0.03	0.0314	0.03245	0.03505	0.058838	0.062883	0.066093	0.073493
8	0.03515	0.036367	0.037665	0.040472	0.063509	0.066361	0.068412	0.073755
9	0.040277	0.042033	0.043443	0.046299	0.068206	0.069786	0.070677	0.073949
10	0.046929	0.048627	0.04996	0.052643	0.072923	0.073155	0.072887	0.074073
11	0.053932	0.055591	0.056803	0.059247	0.077572	0.07641	0.074997	0.074116

Figure 53.10

	R	S	T	U	V	W	X
6	f.25,.5	f.25,.75	f.25,1.25	f.25,5.25	f.25,7.25	f.25,10.25	f.25,30.25
7	0.032802	0.033677	0.036316	0.0603	0.064077	0.067011	0.073863
8	0.037586	0.038924	0.041807	0.064947	0.067493	0.069257	0.074083
9	0.043793	0.04503	0.04781	0.069622	0.070855	0.071449	0.074234
10	0.050328	0.051479	0.054076	0.07424	0.074104	0.073544	0.074303
11	0.057254	0.058242	0.06058	0.078768	0.077221	0.075529	0.074286

The idea behind our simulation is to use the spot yield curve of three months ago (see Figure 53.9) to generate forward rates (see Figure 53.10). For example, we use f(.25,.5) to generate 3 month rates, f(.25, 1.25) for one year rates etc.. Then we use the fudge factor to get a base forecast for the desired yield curve point. Then we randomly choose one of the 94 "scenarios" for the yield curves movement from columns Y:AE of Figure 53.4 (see Figure 53.8). The chosen scenario is used to simultaneously adjust the forecast for all points on the yield curve.

Step by Step

Step 1: To generate the chosen scenario (See Figure 53.7) for the April, 1993 yield curve enter in B8 the formula

$=RISKDUNIfORM(\$A\$13:\$A\$106).$

This gives each of the 94 scenarios the same chance of being chosen. We copy this formula to B9:B11 to create scenarios through Jan 94.

Step 2: In cell C8 generate the forecast for the .25 year yield curve point in April 1993 with the formula

$=R7*VLOOKUP(\$B8,\$A\$13:\$H\$106,C\$5+1)*C\$4.$

This takes the current forward rate forecast f(.25,.5) (in R7) times the relevant fudge factor (in C\$4) times the "scenario factor". The scenario factor is computed from

$VLOOKUP(\$B8,\$A\$13:\$H\$106,C\$5+1).$

We lookup the scenario off the DUniform in B8. Then we head down to the range where the scenarios are pasted (A13:H106) and read the resulting scenario movement from the second (C\$5+1) column. Copying this formula to the range C8:I11 generates all yield curve points for April 93, June 93, September 93, January 94.

Remarks

1. The key to this approach is noting that the scenarios let us maintain the relationship between various points on the yield curve. The values in a scenario (.25, .5,... 30) are highly correlated. For example, if the .25 number is greater than 1, almost surely the .5 and 1 year numbers will exceed 1, implying that our raw forecast for .25, .5, and 1 year rates were too low and need to all be adjusted upward.

2. If we want to generate, say, 6 month movements in the yield curve, then we would forecast six months ahead with forward rates f(.5,.75), f(.5, 1), ... f(.5,.30.5) . Then compute new fudge factors and error scenarios and run things through again.

Fixed Rate or ARM?

Suppose we need to borrow money and several different methods of paying back the loan are under consideration. Our methodology can be used to determine which method of paying back the loan is most advantageous. Simply choose the loan payback method that has the lowest expected cost of the payments when we simulate off today's yield curve. Here is an example:

Example 53.2

On December 29, 1997 the US yield curve was as follows:

Duration	Yield
3 months	5.391%
6 months	5.475%
One year	5.533%
Five Years	5.72%
Seven Years	5.74%
Ten Years	5.75%
Thirty Years	5.918%

You are going to borrow $20,000 to buy a new car. You will make 5 equal payments: one year from now, two years from now, three years from now, four years from now, and five years from now. You have been offered two possible loans.

- Fixed interest rate of 7%.

- An adjustable rate loan where each payment is computed on basis of a rate 2.0% higher than the value of the 3-month rate a year ago.

Which loan is a better deal?

Note: Use the Excel =PMT functions to determine what each of your payments are. For adjustable rate loan you will need to keep track of unpaid balance after each payment.

Solution

Our work is in the file ARM. See Figure 53.11.

Figure 53.11

	Y	Z	AA	AB	AC	AD	AE	AF	AG
6	Time in Future	Three Month Rate	Discount Factor	Fixed Payment	ARM Payment	Unpaid ARM Balance	Interest	NPV Fixed	NPV ARM
7	0.00	0.054							
8	0.25	0.059	0.9867						
9	0.50	0.059	0.97246						
10	0.75	0.062	0.95838						
11	1.00	0.064	0.94382	-4877.81	-4928.99	20000.00	1478.20	-4603.79	-4652.09
12	1.25	0.067	0.92888					0.00	0.00
13	1.50	0.070	0.91349					0.00	0.00
14	1.75	0.074	0.89768					0.00	0.00
15	2.00	0.077	0.88146	-4877.81	-5045.17	16549.21	1396.16	-4603.79	-4761.74
16	2.25	0.080	0.86485					0.00	0.00
17	2.50	0.083	0.84788					0.00	0.00
18	2.75	0.087	0.83057					0.00	0.00
19	3.00	0.090	0.81294	-4877.81	-5158.30	12900.20	1248.93	-4603.79	-4868.51
20	3.25	0.093	0.79504					0.00	0.00
21	3.50	0.097	0.77689					0.00	0.00
22	3.75	0.100	0.75853					0.00	0.00
23	4.00	0.104	0.74	-4877.81	-5250.56	8990.83	989.65	-4603.79	-4955.59
24	4.25	0.107	0.72134					0.00	0.00
25	4.50	0.110	0.70257					0.00	0.00
26	4.75	0.113	0.68374					0.00	0.00
27	5.00	0.117	0.66489	-4877.81	-5314.12	4729.92		-4603.79	-5015.59
28								NPV Fixed	NPV ARM
29								-23018.94	-24253.52

Step by Step

Step 1: We copy the simulation sheet to a new workbook and enter the given yield curve in C7:I7. Then future yield curves will be automatically simulated in rows 8-27. See Figure 53.11. The future yield curves were obtained by copying the formulas in C11:I11 to C12:I27.

Step 2: We recopied the time (relative to the present) to Column Y and the simulated three-month rates (to Column Z).

Step 3: In AA8 we compute the discount factor for payments received three months from now with the formula

$$=(1/(1+(Z7/4))).$$

In cell AA9 we compute the discount factor for payments received six months from now with the formula

$$=AA8*(1/(1+(Z8/4))).$$

Copying this formula from AA9 to AA10:AA27 computes discount factors for payments received at any time during the next 5 years.

Step 4: In AB11 we compute our annual payment if the fixed loan is chosen with the formula

$$=PMT(0.07,5,20000).$$

Copying this formula to AB15, AB19, AB23, and AB27 computes the fixed loan payments at the time they are paid.

Step 5: Column AD contains the unpaid balance on the ARM. We note that during any year the payment on the ARM is computed at a rate of 2% + the three-month rate from a year ago and keys off the unpaid balance on ARM. The first payment is computed assuming 5 payments remain; the second payment is computed assuming four payments remain, etc. Therefore our Year 1 payment on the ARM is computed in AC11 with the formula

$= PMT(Z7+0.02,5-Y7,AD11).$

Copying this formula to AC15, AC19, AC23, and AC27 computes the payment on the ARM at times 2, 3, 4, and 5.

Step 6: In cell AD11 we enter the initial unpaid balance on the ARM ($20,000). In cell AD15 we compute the unpaid balance on the ARM after the first payment with the formula

(Initial Unpaid Balance) - (Year 1 Payment - Interest on ARM at Time 1) .

Column AE will compute interest on unpaid balance. Therefore in cell AD15 we compute the unpaid balance on the ARM after the first payment with the formula

$=AD11+AC11+AE11.$

Copying this formula to AD19, AD23, and AD27 computes the Unpaid Balance on the Loan at times 2, 3, 4, and 5.

Step 7: In Column AE we compute our interest on the unpaid balance. Our payment at any time keys off the unpaid balance before the current payment is made. The interest rate is 2% higher than the three-month rate a year ago. Thus one year from now our interest is computed in AE 11 with the formula

$=(Z7+0.02)*AD11.$

Copying that formula to AE15, AE19, and AE23 computes unpaid interest each time a payment is made.

Step 8: In AF11 we compute the present value of the Year 1 payment on the Fixed Mortgage with the formula

$=\$AA\$11*AB11.$

Copying that formula to AF15, AF19, AF23, and AF27 computes present value of each Fixed Mortgage payment. Copying from AF11:AF27 to AG11:AG27 computes the present value for each Adjustable Rate payment.

Step 9: In AF29 we compute the NPV of the Fixed Mortgage Payments with the formula

=SUM(AF11:AF27).

Copying this formula to AG29 we compute the NPV of the Adjustable Rate payments.

Step 10: We now select AF29 and AG29 as our Output Cells. After running 1600 iterations we obtain the output in Figure 53.12.

Figure 53.12

	AI	AJ	AK
32	Name	NPV Fixed	NPV ARM
33	**Description**		
34	Cell		
35	Minimum =	-22689	-21541
36	Maximum =	-20074	-20816
37	Mean =	-21594	-21235
38	Std Deviation =	413	113
39	Variance =	170818	12671
40	Skewness =	0	0
41	Kurtosis =	3	3
42	Errors Calculated =	0	0
43	Mode =	-21985	-21369
44	5% Perc =	-22227	-21411
45	10% Perc =	-22114	-21378
46	15% Perc =	-22021	-21356
47	20% Perc =	-21942	-21331
48	25% Perc =	-21872	-21314
49	30% Perc =	-21814	-21298
50	35% Perc =	-21768	-21280
51	40% Perc =	-21721	-21265
52	45% Perc =	-21671	-21252
53	50% Perc =	-21619	-21238
54	55% Perc =	-21572	-21224
55	60% Perc =	-21517	-21210
56	65% Perc =	-21464	-21196
57	70% Perc =	-21402	-21177
58	75% Perc =	-21343	-21162
59	80% Perc =	-21277	-21146
60	85% Perc =	-21183	-21122
61	90% Perc =	-21057	-21093
62	95% Perc =	-20848	-21047

We find the expected payments from the ARM are $359 less than the payments from the Fixed Mortgage.

Valuing Interest Rate Derivatives

There are many derivatives whose payments are based on values of the interest rate(s) at a future time(s). For example, a **cap** guarantees that the rate a borrower pays is "capped" at a given level. For example, a 10% cap would mean a borrower pays the smaller of 10% and the prevailing interest rate. A **floor** places a lower limit on the interest rate a borrower must pay. The guiding principle in valuing an interest rate derivative is as follows: **an interest rate derivative is valued at the expected discounted value of its cash flows.** Of course implementing this idea requires that we have a model that can be used to generate future interest rates. Chapter 17 of Hull (1997) and Tuckman (1996) contain good discussions of interest rate modeling. We may also look at the VAR of an interest rate derivative as loss associated with the fifth percentile of the derivative's value. We illustrate these ideas with the following example.

Example 53.3

As we all know Orange County lost a lot of money in 1993. Was their loss really a large loss or was it well within the range of normal variation? We will model the interest risk associated with a two year **inverse floater** (Orange County owned billions of dollars worth of inverse floaters). Then inverse floaters paid every six months (beginning in July 1993 and ending in January 1995) a coupon proportional to .155-2 (floating three-month rate for six months ago). Assume the principal was $100 million. On January 2, 1993 the yield curve was as follows:

Duration	Spot Rate
.25	3.15%
.5	3.36%
1	3.7%
2	4.46%
3	4.94%
5	5.9%
7	6.29%
10	6.59%
30	7.32%

Value this derivative and calculate the VAR.

Solution

Our work is in the file *Inversefloater.xls*. In C7:I7 we entered the January, 1993 yield curve. See Figure 53.13. As with the ARM-Fixed Rate example, we begin by copying our simulation worksheet to a new workbook.

Figure 53.13

	Y	Z	AA	AB	AC
6	Date	3 mo Rate	Discount Factor	Payment	PV
7	Jan-93	0.0315			
8	Apr-93	0.037623			
9	Jul-93	0.043263	0.9829413	9.2	9.0430595
10	Oct-93	0.048259			0
11	Jan-94	0.053307	0.9608318	6.8474752	6.57927162
12	Apr-94	0.058415			0
13	Jul-94	0.063637	0.9345477	4.8386937	4.52199006
14	Oct-94	0.068965			0
15	Jan-95	0.074388	0.9043209	2.772543	2.50726865
16				Total value	22.6515898

We begin by copying the dates and the simulated three-month rates to Y7:Z15. Then we proceed as follows:

Step by Step

Step 1: In cell AA9 we compute the discount factor for the first inverse floater payment (received in July 1993) with the formula

$$=1/((1+(Z7/4))*(1+(Z8/4))).$$

In cell Z11 we compute in cell AA11 the discount factor for the second inverse floater payment (received in January 1994) with the formula

$$=AA9*(1/(1+(Z9/4)))*(1/(1+(Z10/4))).$$

Copying this formula to AA13 and AA15 computes the discount rate for other payments.

Step 2: In AB9 we compute the value of the first payment on the inverse floater with the formula

$$=MAX(100*(0.155-2*Z7),0).$$

Note that the payment keys off the six-month rate evaluated **six months prior to the payment date**. Copying this formula to AB11, AB13, and AB15 computes the value of each payment.

Step 3: In AC9 we compute the present value of the July 1993 payment on the inverse floater by multiplying the payment times the discount rate

$$=AA9*AB9.$$

Copying this formula to AC10:AC15 computes the present value of all other payments from the inverse floater.

Step 4: In AC16 we compute the total NPV of the inverse floater payments with the formula

=SUM(AC9,AC11,AC13,AC15).

Step 5: After choosing cell AC16 as our output cell we obtain the output in Figure 53.14.

Figure 53.14

	AE	AF
12	Minimum =	20.2565
13	Maximum =	41.499
14	Mean =	32.72242
15	Std Deviation =	$3.42
16	Variance =	11.68786
17	Skewness =	-0.3617958
18	Kurtosis =	3.014143
19	Errors Calculated =	$0.00
20	Mode =	34.95209
21	5% Perc =	26.74464
22	10% Perc =	28.23535
23	15% Perc =	$29.23
24	20% Perc =	29.96015
25	25% Perc =	30.5126
26	30% Perc =	30.95482
27	35% Perc =	$31.51
28	40% Perc =	31.98355
29	45% Perc =	$32.43
30	50% Perc =	32.98327
31	55% Perc =	33.42319
32	60% Perc =	33.82157
33	**65% Perc =**	34.2994
34	70% Perc =	34.69872
35	75% Perc =	35.14877
36	80% Perc =	36
37	85% Perc =	$36.20
38	90% Perc =	$36.88
39	95% Perc =	$38.13

We find a fair price for $100 million of this inverse floater to be $32.72 million. There is a 5% chance that the NPV of the payments would drop by at least 19%. In reality, Orange County lost 8% (more than one billion dollars) on these inverse floaters. Was this an astoundingly large loss? 8% of $32.72 million is around $2.6million. A loss of $2.6 million would leave the inverse floater's value at around $30.1 million. $30.1 million is between the 20%ile and 25%ile, so it appears there was a more than 20% chance that Orange County would have lost 8% or more on these inverse floaters.

Remarks

1. Most of the interest rate models discussed in the references are known as **arbitrage-free models.** Essentially, these models are calibrated so that they accurately price a variety of interest rate derivatives that are of long and short duration. The idea is that such calibration greatly reduces the chances that a combination of derivatives will be priced in an inconsistent fashion which allows arbitrage profits. Our model could be calibrated to accurately price derivatives by changing the weights given to each error scenario. See Tuckman (1996) for a lucid introduction to arbitrage-free models.

2. Of course, we should update our scenarios with the most recent available data.

References

Hull, J. *Options Futures and Other Derivatives*, Prentice-Hall, 1997.

Tuckman, B., *Fixed Income Securities*, John Wiley, 1996.

Chapter 54: Delta Hedging

A financial institution that sells options is at great risk. For example, if a Wall Street firm sells a call option there is no theoretical upper limit on the discounted cash value that the purchaser of the option will receive at expiration. **Delta hedging** (described with great clarity in Hull (1997) enables a firm writing options to control the riskiness of their position. Our example is based on Chapter 14 of Hull (1997).

Example 54.1

Suppose we have just sold for $300,000 a 20-week European call option on 100,000 shares of a non-dividend paying stock. The current stock price is $49, exercise price is $50, risk-free rate is 5%, and stock volatility is 20%. We assume the expected return from stock follows a Lognormal random variable with μ = 13% per year. Black-Scholes price for this option is $240,000 so it looks like we made a smart move selling option for $300,000.

The Risk

We are subject to grave risk. If price of stock increases to say, $60 we owe 10*100,000 = $1,000,000 and we lose $700,000. How can we hedge this risk?

Delta of an Option

The **delta** of an option is (approximately) the change in the value of the option that ensues if stock price increases by $1. Clearly a call option has a positive delta and a put option a negative delta. If stock is strongly in the money a call option has a delta of 1, if a call option is way out of the money the delta is 0. If we define

$$d_1 = \frac{ln(S/X)+(r+\sigma^2/2)(t)}{\sigma\sqrt{t}}$$

then the delta of a call option is $N(d_1)$ and the delta of a put option is $N(d_1) - 1$.

Here

$S = current\ stock\ price$

$X = exercise\ price\ of\ option$

$t = remaining\ duration\ of\ option$

$\sigma = annual\ volatility$

$r = annual\ interest\ rate$

$N = Normal\ cumulative;\ N(0) = .5, N(1) = .84$

How can we hedge the risk associated with selling the call option? Suppose at any point in time we own 100,000N(d_1) shares of stock. If the price of the stock increases by $1 our stock increases in value by 100,000N(d_1) and our obligations associated with the call also increase by 100,000N(d_1). Thus we are **delta neutral** towards a change in stock price. Suppose that **weekly** we adjust our holdings so that we always own 100,000N(d_1) shares of stock. In file **Delta.xls** we simulate the risk associated with this strategy. See Figure 54.1.

Figure 54.1

	A	B	C	D	E	F	G	H
1	Delta Hedging							
2								
3	Shares	100000		In week 1 for instance if stock up				
4	Today's price	49		$1 we lose around $52,000 on				
5	Exercise Price	50		option and gain $52,000 on stock.				
6	r	0.05		A perfect hedge (except for the				
7	sigma	0.2		fact that the delta changes during				
8	growth rate	0.13		the week!)!				
9								
10	Week	Stock Price	Delta	Shares Purchased	Cost of Shares Bought	Cumulative Cost	Interest Cost	Stock Held
11	0	49	0.52160473	52160.473	2555863	2555863.18	2458.743	52160.47
12	1	49.10376	0.52469944	309.47089	15196.19	2573518.1	2475.727	52469.94
13	2	49.20775	0.52797749	327.80487	16130.54	2592124.37	2493.626	52797.75
14	3	49.31195	0.53146312	348.563275	17188.33	2611806.33	2512.56	53146.31
15	4	49.41637	0.53518556	372.243555	18394.93	2632713.82	2532.673	53518.56
16	5	49.52102	0.53918041	399.485059	19782.91	2655029.4	2554.141	53918.04
17	6	49.62589	0.54349163	431.12232	21394.83	2678978.37	2577.18	54349.16
18	7	49.73098	0.54817427	468.263837	23287.22	2704842.76	2602.061	54817.43
19	8	49.83629	0.55329838	512.411635	25536.69	2732981.52	2629.131	55329.84
20	9	49.94182	0.55895487	565.648106	28249.5	2763860.15	2658.836	55895.49
21	10	50.04758	0.56526425	630.938132	31576.93	2798095.91	2691.771	56526.42
22	11	50.15356	0.57239062	712.63747	35741.31	2836528.99	2728.743	57239.06
23	12	50.25977	0.58056452	817.38947	41081.81	2880339.53	2770.889	58056.45
24	13	50.3662	0.59012251	955.799211	48139.97	2931250.4	2819.865	59012.25
25	14	50.47286	0.60158036	1145.78526	57831.05	2991901.32	2878.212	60158.04
26	15	50.57974	0.61577946	1419.90977	71818.66	3066598.19	2950.07	61577.95
27	16	50.68685	0.63421322	1843.37612	93434.92	3162983.19	3042.793	63421.32
28	17	50.79418	0.65987185	2565.86273	130330.9	3296356.88	3171.098	65987.18
29	18	50.90175	0.6999809	4010.90518	204162.1	3503690.05	3370.553	69998.09
30	19	51.00954	0.77913401	7915.31126	403756.4	3910816.97	3762.209	77913.4
31	20	51.11756	1	22086.5989	1129013	5043592.12	4851.94	100000
32								
33				Cumulative Costs	5043592			
34				Option profits	188244.4			
35				Revenue from Stock Sale	5111756			
36				Total Profit	256407.9			

We proceed as follows:

Step by Step

Step 1: In B1:B8 we enter the relevant information.

Step 2: In C11 we compute the current delta of the put with the formula

=NORMSDIST((LN(B11/$B$5)+($B$6+$B$7^2/2)*(20-A11)/52)/($B$7*SQRT((20-A11)/52))).

Step 3: In D11 we now compute the number of shares purchased ($100,000N(d_1)$) with the formula

=$B$3*C11.

Step 4: In E11 we compute the cost of purchasing the shares with the formula

=D11*B11.

Step 5: In F11 we compute the cumulative cost to date with the formula

= E11.

Step 6: In G11 we compute the interest cost associated with the money tied up in stocks with the formula

=(EXP($B$6/52)-1)*F11.

Step 7: In H11 compute our current stock holdings with the formula

=D11.

Step 8: In D12 we generate the Week 1 stock price using the lognormal distribution of stock prices:

=B11*EXP(($B$8-0.5*$B$7^2)*(1/52)+$B$7*RISKNormal(0,1)*(1/52)^0.5).

Step 9: Copy the formula from C11 to C12 to generate this week's delta.

Step 10: In D12 compute the number of shares we need to purchase to bring our holdings to $10000*N(d_1)$.

=(C12-C11)*$B$3.

Step 11: In E12 compute cost of shares bought by copying the formula in E11.

Step 12: In F12 compute our cumulative cost to date with the formula

=F11+E12+G11.

Step 13: In G12 compute our current week's interest cost (due to money tied up in stocks and interest obligations) by copying the formula in G11.

Step 14: In H12 compute our current stock holdings with the formula

$=H11+D12.$

Step 15: Copying B12:H12 to B13:H31 to generate the remaining 19 weeks.

Step 16: In E33 recopy from F31 our cumulative costs for the 20 weeks of hedging.

Step 17: In E34 compute our profits from the option with the formula

$=If(B31>50,300000-(B31-50)*\$B\$3,300000).$

Step 18: In E35 we keep track of revenue we earn by selling our shares of stock at the week 20 price.

$=B31*H31.$

Step 19: In cell E36 we compute Total profit (from writing option and hedging process) with the formula

$=E35-E33+E34.$

Step 20: We now ran 1000 trials with output cells E34 (option profits in Column K) and E36 (total profits in Column L). Our results follow in Figure 54.2.

Figure 54.2

	J	K	L
42	Cell	[delta.xls]Sheet1!E34	[delta.xls]Sheet1!E36
43	Minimum =	-2371416	-133582.4
44	Maximum =	300000	218017.6
45	Mean =	-3.17E+04	5.46E+04
46	Std Deviation =	4.49E+05	4.74E+04
47	Variance =	2.01E+11	2.25E+09
48	Skewness =	-1.605825	-0.4096479
49	Kurtosis =	5.480183	4.143471
50	Errors Calculated =	0	0.00E+00
51	Mode =	300000	5.56E+04
52	5% Perc =	-974599.1	-3.07E+04
53	10% Perc =	-697484.4	-1253.476
54	15% Perc =	-493854	1.28E+04
55	20% Perc =	-349408	2.17E+04

Note that the hedge has a higher mean profit and a lower standard deviation than the naked call. The hedge has only 10% of the standard deviation of the naked call. Note VAR of naked call is -$975,000 and VAR of hedged position is -$30,000!

It is clear that the delta hedging has substantially reduced our risk.

Chapter 55: Using the Risk-Neutral Approach to Value Real Options

The risk-neutral approach discussed in Chapter 40 is very powerful. It enables us to value many quantities which **derive** their value from an underlying asset. In most books, you do this by finding a combination of puts and calls which replicates the payoffs of what you are trying to value. We do not need to do this. Just use the lognormal to simulate the future value of the underlying asset (growing at risk-free rate) and then make your Output Cell be the discounted value of the payoffs you receive. The mean of your Output Cell is the value you seek. Here are six examples:

Example 55.1

The current price of IBM is 145 and 1/8. In 64 days Gerstner will be paid as follows: For every $1 increase in stock price up to $10 he receives $1 million; For every $1 increase in stock price over $10 Gerstner receives $500,000. What is a fair market value for Lou's option?

Solution

We need the volatility of the price of IBM stock. By looking at traded options we can estimate the implied volatility (see file *IBMvols.xls* and Figure 55.1).

Figure 55.1

	A	B	C	D
1	IBM OPTIONS	April	April	April
2	Current Price	145.125	145.125	145.125
3	Duration	0.175342	0.175342	0.175342
4	Volatility	0.327147	0.327147	0.327147
5	Exercise Price	140	150	160
6	Risk-free Rate	0.0636	0.0636	0.0636
7	d1	0.412352	-0.09128	-0.5624
8	d2	0.275362	-0.22827	-0.69939
9	N(d1)	0.659959	0.463633	0.28692
10	N(d2)	0.608481	0.409717	0.242153
11	Option Price(theory)	11.53395	6.50882	3.324504
12				
13	Option Price(actual)	12	6.25	3.125
14	Squared Error	0.217206	0.066988	0.039802
15				
16	SSE	0.323996		

In row 13 we have listed the price of three call options which expire in 64 days (exercise prices $140, $150, and $160). We have created a Black-Scholes template that, upon entering volatility in row 4 computes a Black-Scholes price in Row 11. We want to find a single volatility which best predicts these prices. We choose B4 to be our changing cell for volatility and minimize sum of
squared errors / (actual-predicted price)² for the three options (cell B16).

Our Solver Window is as follows:

Figure 55.2

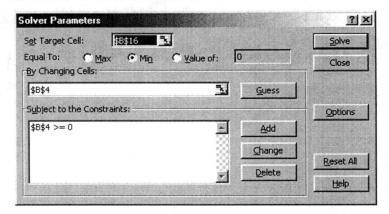

We find an implied volatility of 32.7%. We can now value our option. (See Figure 55.3 and file *Gerstner.xls*).

Figure 55.3

	A	B	C	D	E	F
1	Gerstner					
2						
3						
4	Current Price	145.125				
5	Volatility	0.327				
6	Riskfree rate	0.0636				
7	Duration	0.175342			Name	Discounted payoff
8	Normal	0			Description	Output
9	Later Stock Pric	145.3831			Cell	B11
10	Payoff(millions)	0.258143			Minimum =	0
11	Discounted payc	0.25528			Maximum =	47.52227
12					Mean =	6.374745
13					Std Deviation =	8.484468
14					Variance =	71.98619
15					Skewness =	1.281692
16					Kurtosis =	4.098358

Step by Step

Step 1: In B4-B7 we enter relevant parameters, including the implied volatility.

Step 2: In B8 we enter a Normal (0,1) variable with formula

$=RISKNormal(0,1).$

Step 3: In B9 we compute the stock price in 64 days using lognormal growth at the risk-free rate and known volatility

$=B4*EXP((B6-0.5*B5^2)*B7+B8*SQRT(B7)*B5).$

Step 4: In B10 we compute Gerstner's payoff with the statement

$$=If(AND((B9-B4)>=0,(B9-B4)<10),(B9-B4),If(B9-B4>=10,10+0.5*(B9-(B4+10)),0)).$$

This pays Lou $1 million per dollar increase up to $10 and $.5 million per dollar increase beyond that point.

Step 5: In B11 we discount this payoff back to the current time with the formula

$$=EXP(-B6*B7)*B10.$$

Step 6: After making B11 our Output Cell we find from Figure 55.4 that our best estimate is that the fair market value is $6.37 million.

Figure 55.4

	E	F
7	Name	Discounted payoff
8	Description	Output
9	Cell	B11
10	Minimum =	0
11	Maximum =	47.52227
12	Mean =	6.374745
13	Std Deviation =	8.484468
14	Variance =	71.98619
15	Skewness =	1.281692
16	Kurtosis =	4.098358

An Abandonment Option

Example 55.2

An asset is currently worth $553,000 and has an annual volatility of 28%. The risk-free rate is 5%. A year from now I may sell the asset for a salvage value of $500,000. How much is this abandonment option worth?

Solution

Let V = value of asset one year from now. Then a year from now option returns

$$Max(0, \$500,000 - V) \ (55.1).$$

If we let asset grow for one year at risk-free rate and with given volatility and take discounted value of (55.1) as our Output Cell, then the mean of our Output cell is the value of the abandonment option. Our work is in Figure 55.1 and file *Abadonment.xls*.

Figure 55.5

	A	B	C	D	E	F	G
1	**Abandonment**						
2	Abandonment value	$500,000.00					
3	r	Volatility	Current Price	Normal(0,1)	Price 1 year from now	Value of Option	Discounted value
4	0.05	0.28	$553,000.00	0	$531,741.78	0	0

We proceed as follows:

Step 1: In D4 enter a standard normal (mean 0, sigma of 1) random variable with the formula

=RISKNormal(0,1).

Step 2: In E4 generate the value of the asset a year from now using the lognormal random variable. The formula is

=C4*EXP((A4-0.5*B4^2)+B4*D4).

Step 3: In F4 we exploit (55.1) to generate the value of the option's cash flows one year from now with the formula

=If(E4<C2,C2-E4,0).

Step 4: In cell G4 compute the discounted value of the option's cash flows with the formula

=EXP(-A4)*F4.

Step 5: After choosing G4 as our Output Cell we find the option is worth $34,093.

Figure 55.6

	I	J
7	Name	Discounted value
8	Description	Output
9	Cell	G4
10	Minimum =	0
11	Maximum =	280536.9
12	Mean =	34,092.91
13	Std Deviation =	54,870.25
14	Variance =	3.01E+09

An Option to Postpone (Based on Trigeorgis (1995))

Example 55.3

The current risk-free rate is 8%. We can build a plant now costing $104 million and gain revenues worth (risk adjusted) $100 million. Revenues begin one year from now. Therefore current value of project is -$4 million and project does not appear worthwhile. Suppose, however, project's value has a 60% annual volatility and we can wait one year before investing in this project. What is the worth of this option? Assume that construction costs grow at the risk-free rate.

Solution

Our work is in Figure 55.7 and the file *Postpone.xls*. Let V = value of project one year from now. Then value of option to postpone is

$$=max(0, V - e^{08}(104)). \quad (55.2)$$

This is because we will invest one year from now only if the value of the project exceeds the cost (which one year from now will be $e^{08}(104)$).

Figure 55.7

	A	B	C	D	E	F	G	H	I
1	Postpone Investment								
2									
3									
4	r	Current value	Investment cost	Value with no option	Volatility	Normal (0,1)	Value One year from now	Cash flows in one year from waiting	Discounted value of cash flows
5	0.08	100	104	-4	0.6	0	90.4837	0	0

We now proceed as follows:

Step 1: Enter needed parameters in A5-E5.

Step 2: In F5 enter a Normal(0,1) with the formula

=RISKNormal(0,1).

Step 3: In G5 use the lognormal to compute the value of the asset one year from now with the formula

=B5*EXP((A5-0.5*E5^2)+F5*E5).

Step 4: In H5 we use (55.2) to determine the cash flows obtained in one year with the formula

=MAX(0,G5-C5*EXP(A5)).

Step 5: Discount the value of the cash flows back to time 0 in cell I5 with the formula

=EXP(-A5)*H5.

Step 6: Make I5 an Output Cell and obtain the following results.

Figure 55.8

	D	E
12	Minimum =	0
13	Maximum =	664.869
14	Mean =	22.1453
15	Std Deviation =	50.32
16	Variance =	2532.11
17	Skewness =	4.17166
18	Kurtosis =	31.0005

Thus the option to postpone improves our position by 22.14 - (-4) = \$26.14 million relative to our position if we did project without having option to postpone project.

Valuing the Option to Expand

We now modify Example 55.3 to show how we evaluate an option to expand a project.

Example 55.4

Assume you have the option to spend $40 million one year from now on a plant expansion that will increase the project's value by 50%. Value this expansion option.

Solution

Our work is in the file *Expand.xls*. See Figure 55.9

Figure 55.9

	A	B	C	D	E	F	G	H	I	J	K
1	Expand for 40 million by 50%?										
2											
3											
4	r	Current value	Investment cost	Value with no option		Volatility	Normal (0,1)	Value One year from now	Cash Flows in One Year	Discounted value of cash flows	Expansion cost	Expansion factor
5	0.08	100	104		-4	0.6	0	90.48374	95.72561	-15.634122	40	0.5

We proceed as follows:

Step by Step

Step 1: In A5:E5 and J5:K5 we enter relevant parameters for the problem.

Step 2: In cell F5 we enter

=RISKNormal(0,1).

This will help us generate the value of the project one-year from now.

Step 3: In cell G5 we generate the (random) value of the project one-year from now with the formula

=B5*EXP((A5-0.5*E5^2)+F5*E5).

Step 4: Note that if we choose to expand, our cash flows in one year will equal

1.5*(value in one year) - 40.

If we do not expand, our cash flows in one year will simply equal the value of the project. Therefore in H5 we compute our cash flows in one year with the formula

=MAX((1+K5)*G5-J5,G5).

Step 5: In cell I5 we compute the discounted value of our cash flows with the formula

=EXP(-A5)*H5-C5.

Step 6: We now select cell I5 as our output cell. After running 900 iterations Figure 55.10 indicates that with the option to expand our situation is worth an average of $14.08 million. Thus the option to expand improves our position over doing the project right away by $18.08 million.

Figure55.10

	D	E
9	Name	Discounted value of cash flows
10	Description	Output
11	Cell	I5
12	Minimum =	-91.8832
13	Maximum =	987.4983
14	Mean =	14.08345
15	Std Deviation =	95.02
16	Variance =	9029.213
17	Skewness =	2.609704
18	Kurtosis =	15.51571
19	Errors Calculated =	0
20	Mode =	-53.04
21	5% Perc =	-72.91
22	10% Perc =	-65.34437
23	15% Perc =	-59.19777
24	20% Perc =	-53.65549
25	25% Perc =	-48.32503
26	30% Perc =	-43.02106
27	35% Perc =	-37.73096
28	40% Perc =	-32.27309
29	45% Perc =	-24.77618
30	50% Perc =	-15.72217
31	55% Perc =	-5.884071
32	60% Perc =	4.850531
33	65% Perc =	16.87049
34	70% Perc =	30.53909
35	75% Perc =	46.76334
36	80% Perc =	66.62992
37	85% Perc =	92.33498
38	90% Perc =	128.8684
39	95% Perc =	194.7092

Valuing the Option to Expand

Valuing the Option to Contract

Now we modify Example 55.3 to value the option to contract a project.

Example 55.5

Instead of paying the entire $104 million plant cost now you must only pay $50 million now. A year from now you may pay the remaining $54 million cost (with interest) and obtain the full project value or you may contract the scale of the project by paying only $25 million. If you contract the scale of the project the project will be worth only 50% of what it would have actually been worth. Value this contraction option.

Solution

Our work is in the file *Contract.xls*. See Figure 55.11.

Figure 55.11

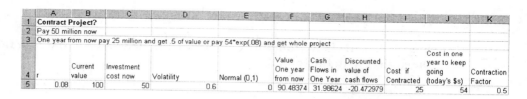

	A	B	C	D	E	F	G	H	I	J	K
1	Contract Project?										
2	Pay 50 million now										
3	One year from now pay 25 million and get .5 of value or pay 54*exp(.08) and get whole project										
4	r	Current value	Investment cost now	Volatility	Normal (0,1)	Value One year from now	Cash Flows in One Year	Discounted value of cash flows	Cost if Contracted	Cost in one year to keep going (today's $s)	Contraction Factor
5	0.08	100	50	0.6	0	90.48374	31.98624	-20.472979	25	54	0.5

We proceed as follows:

Step by Step

Step 1: Enter the relevant parameters in cells A5:D5 and I5:K5.

Step 2: In cell E5 enter

   =RISKNormal(0,1).

This random variable will be used in F5 to generate the value of the project in one year.

Step 3: In cell F5 we generate the value of the project in one year with the formula

   =B5*EXP((A5-0.5*D5^2)+E5*D5).

Step 4: In G5 we compute the cash flows from the project in one year. Note that if we contract the project our cash flows in one year are given by

.5*(Value of project) - $25 million.

If we do not contract the project our cash flows in one year are given by

(Value of Project) - $e^{.08}$*($54 million).

Since we can choose the better of these options in G5 we compute the cash flows from the project in one year with the formula

=MAX(F5-EXP(A5)*J5,K5*F5-I5).

Step 5: In cell H5 we compute the total discounted value of the cash flows from the project with the formula

=EXP(-A5)*G5-C5.

Choosing cell H5 as an output cell yields the @RISK output in Figure 55.12.

Figure
55.12

	D	E
		Discounted value of cash flows
10	Name	
11	Description	Output
12	Cell	H5
13	Minimum =	-68.05699
14	Maximum =	515.879
15	Mean =	-1.28
16	Std Deviation =	62.90
17	Variance =	3956.415
18	Skewness =	2.348511
19	Kurtosis =	11.81437

Our simulation indicates that our expected discounted cash flows with the option to contract are $-1.28 million. This improves our situation over immediately doing project by $2.72 million.

A "Pioneer" Option

Often companies enter into small projects that have a negative NPV. The reason for this is that participation in the smaller project gives the company the option to later participate in a larger project that may have a large positive NPV. Merck Pharmaceuticals, led by their CFO Judy Lewent (see Nichols (1994)) has "pioneered" the use of real option theory. Here is an example of this idea, again based on Trigeorgis (1996).

Example 55.6

Merck is debating whether to invest in a pioneer biotech project. They estimate the worth of this project to be -$56 million. Investing in the pioneer project gives Merck the option to own, if they desire, a much bigger technology that will be available in 4 years. If Merck does not participate in the Pioneer project **they cannot own the bigger project**. The big project will require 1.5 billion in cash 4 years from now. Currently Merck estimates the NPV of the cash flows from the bigger project to be $557 million. What should Merck do? Risk free rate is 10% and annual volatility of big project is 35%.

Solution

Our solution is in the file *Pioneer.xls*. See Figure 55.13.

Figure 55.13

	A	B
1	**Buying a Pioneer Project**	
2		
3	NPV of pioneer project	-56000000
4	Current NPV of new technology	597000000
5	Year 4 cost of New Technology	1.5E+09
6	r	0.1
7	Annual volatility	0.35
8	Normal (0,1)	0
9	Value of project in 4 years	697091803
10	NPV in year 4 of doing new Project	0
11	Discounted NPV of doing new project	0

We proceed as follows:

Step by Step

Step 1: Enter relevant parameter values in B3:B7.

Step 2: In B8 generate a standard normal that will be used to generate the value of the project in four years with the formula

$=RISKNormal(0,1)$.

Step 3: In cell B9 generate the value of the project in four years with the formula

$=B4*EXP((B6-0.5*B7^2)*4+B8*SQRT(4)*B7)$.

Step 4: In cell B10 we compute the NPV (in Year 4 $s) of doing the new Project

$=MAX(B9-B5,0)$.

This assumes, of course, that we only do the new project if it is worthwhile.

Step 5: In cell B11 we compute the value (in today's dollars) of doing the new project.

$=EXP(-4*B6)*B10$.

Step 6: We choose B11 as our Output cell. Our @RISK results (900 iterations) are in Figure 55.14.

Figure 55.14

	D	E
4	Name	Discounted NPV of do
5	Description	Output
6	Cell	**B11**
7	Minimum =	0
8	Maximum =	4.25E+09
9	Mean =	69,091,440.00
10	Std Deviation =	274,982,500
11	Variance =	7.56E+16
12	Skewness =	6.705864
13	Kurtosis =	65.36147

It appears that the value of the option to invest in the new project is $69 million. This more than outweighs the negative NPV of the Pioneer project, so we should go ahead with the Pioneer project.

Remarks

Chapter 21 of Brealey and Myers (1996) contains an excellent introduction to real options. The two books by Trigeorgis contain a comprehensive (though advanced) discussion of real options. We refer the reader to Luenberger (1997) for an excellent discussion of real options.

Of course, it is difficult to come up with volatility for a project. Looking at implied volatilities for companies in a similar industry may be helpful. Probably the best strategy is to use the =RISKSimTable to value the option for a wide range of volatilities.

The value of many projects (particularly in high technology industries) is probably best modeled as a **jump diffusion** process. See Chapter 41 for a discussion of the jump diffusion process. The author is working on applying jump diffusion processes to real option problems.

References

Brealey, R. and Myers, S., *Principles of Corporate Finance*, Prentice-Hall 1996.

Luenberger, D., *Investment Science,* Oxford Press, 1997.

Nichols, N., "Scientific Management at Merck: An Interview with CFO Judy Lewent," *Harvard Business Review*, Vol. 72 No. 1, pages 89-99, 1994.

Trigeorgis, L., *Real Options*, MIT Press, 1996.

Trigeorgis, L., *Real Options in Capital Investment*, Praeger, 1995.

Chapter 56: Pricing an American Option with Binomial Trees

We cannot use @RISK to price an American option because to determine the cash flows from the option we need to account for the possibility of early exercise. American options are usually priced with **binomial trees**. We divide the duration of the option into smaller time periods (usually weeks or months). During each time period the stock price either increases by a factor u or decreases by a factor d. We assume d = 1/u. Let delta t equal length of period in tree. The probability of an increase each period (p) is chosen in conjunction with u and d so the stock price grows on average at the risk-free rate r and has an annual volatility of sigma. We let q = 1- p be probability of a decrease during each period. To ensure that our tree matches the mean growth rate and volatility per unit time of an asset following a Lognormal random variable with parameters r and sigma we must choose (see Chapter 15 of Hull (1997)).

$$u = e^{sigma(sqrt(deltat))}$$

$$d = 1/u$$

$$a = e^{r*deltat}$$

$$p = \frac{a-d}{u-d}$$

$$q = 1 - p$$

We set up our tree in file *American.xls*. Let's price a 5-month American put with

- Current stock price = $50

- Exercise price = $50

- Risk-free rate = 10%

- Annual volatility = 40%

- Deltat = 1 month = .083 years

All this data plus the previous definitions of u, d, a, q, and p are input in the range A1:B13 of the spreadsheet. We have used range names to make the tree easier to explain. Our work is in the sheet pricing of file *American.xls*.

The Stock Price Tree

We begin by determining the possible stock prices during the next 5 months. Column B has today's (Month 0) price, Column C Month 1, etc.

Step by Step

Step 1: Enter today's stock price ($50) in B16 with the formula

$=B3$.

Step 2: By copying the formula

$=u*B16$.

from C16 to D16:G16 we obtain the price each month when there have been no down moves.

Step 3: To compute all other prices note that in each column as we move down a row the price is multiplied by a factor (d/u). Also note that for Month I there are I + 1 possible prices. This allows us to compute all prices by copying from C17 to C17:G21 the formula

$=If(\$A17<=C\$15,(d/u)*C16,"-")$.

As we move down each column, the prices are successively multiplied by d/u. Also, our formula places a "-" where a price does not exist.

The Optimal Decision Strategy

We now work backwards to find the value of the American Put. Remember, at each node the value of the put equals the **expected discounted value of future cash flows from the put.**

Step 4: At month 5 the option is just worth maximum (exercise price – current stock price). Thus we enter

$=MAX(0,\$B\$4-G16)$

in cell G24 and copy this formula down to G29.

Step 5: In Month 4 (and all previous months) the value of the option at any node is

Maximum(value from exercising now, (1/(1+(.1/12)))*(p*(value of option for up move),+ q(value of option for down move)).

For example, in F28 the value of option is

$$max(50 - 31.50, (1/1.0083)*(.507*(\$14.64) + .493*(\$21.93)) = \$18.50.$$

Since this maximum is attained by exercising now, if this node occurs we would exercise the option now. At the node in F26 the maximum is attained by not exercising. To implement this decision-making procedure we enter in cell F24 the formula

$$=If(\$A24<=F\$23,MAX(\$B\$4-F16,(1/(1+r\_*deltat))*(p*G24+(1-p)*G25)),"-").$$

Copying this formula to B24:F29 generates value of option for all possible prices during Months 1-4 and places a "-" in any cell where there is no actual stock price. In cell B24 we find the estimated value of the put $4.49. Of course, $4.49 is an approximation to the put value. As deltat grows small, however, our price will converge to the actual price of the put if the stock grew according to a Lognormal random variable.

Using Conditional Formatting to Describe the Optimal Exercise Policy

Assuming the stock grows at the risk free rate, how would we react to actual price changes? Suppose the first three months have down moves. We do not exercise during first two months but we exercise after third down move. Suppose first four months are down up down down. Then we exercise after the fourth month. To make this clearer, we use Excel's Conditional Format Option to format the spreadsheet so that cells for which option would be exercised are in bold face. We begin by noting that **it is optimal to exercise the option at a Month and price if and only if the value of the cell corresponding to the month and price equals (exercise price) - (stock price).**

To indicate the cells where exercising the option is optimal begin in cell G24 by selecting Format Conditional Format and enter the following:

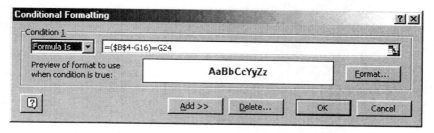

Then click on Format Bold. This dialog box ensures that if the option is exercised in the state with 5 up moves in period 5 then a bold font is used. The interpretation of

$$=(\$B\$4-G16)=G24$$

is that the format takes hold only if $(\$B\$4-G16)=G24$ which is equivalent to option being exercised. If we Edit>Copy cell G24 and Paste>Special Format to the range B24:G29, we ensure that any period and number of up moves for which exercise of the option is optimal will be indicated in bold font.

Figure 56.1

	A	B	C	D	E	F	G
1	**American Option**						
2	**Put**						
3	Current price	$ 50.00					
4	Exercise price	$ 50.00					
5	r	0.1					
6	sigma	0.4					
7	t	0.416667					
8	deltat	0.083333					
9	u	1.122401					
10	d	0.890947					
11	a	1.008368					
12	p	0.507319					
13	q	0.492681					
14		**Time**					
15	**Stock Prices**	0	1	2	3	4	5
16	0	$ 50.00	$ 56.12	$ 62.99	$ 70.70	$ 79.35	$ 89.07
17	1		$ 44.55	$ 50.00	$ 56.12	$ 62.99	$ 70.70
18	2		-	$ 39.69	$ 44.55	$ 50.00	$ 56.12
19	3		-	-	$ 35.36	$ 39.69	$ 44.55
20	4		-	-	-	$ 31.50	$ 35.36
21	5		-	-	-	-	$ 28.07
22	**Down Moves**						
23	**Put Value**	0	1	2	3	4	5
24	0	$ 4.49	$ 2.16	$ 0.64	$ -	$ -	$ -
25	1	-	$ 6.96	$ 3.77	$ 1.30	$ -	$ -
26	2	-	-	$ 10.36	$ 6.38	$ 2.66	$ -
27	3	-	-	-	$ 14.64	$ 10.31	$ **5.45**
28	4	-	-	-	-	$ 18.50	$ **14.64**
29	5	-	-	-	-	-	$ **21.93**

Sensitivity Analysis

Using one-way data tables it is easy to see how changes in various input parameters change the price of the put. We varied the annual volatility of the stock from 10%-70%. Figure 56.2 (a one-way data table with Input Cell sigma) shows how an increase in volatility greatly increases the value of the put. Increased volatility gives us a larger chance of a big price drop, which increases the value of the put.

Figure 56.2

	H	I
7	Volatility	4.489053
8	0.1	0.680146
9	0.2	1.91777
10	0.3	3.197364
11	0.4	4.489053
12	0.5	5.799995
13	0.6	7.104648
14	0.7	8.400682

Figure 56.3 shows how a change in the exercise price of the stock changes the value of the put. We used a one-way data table with input cell B4.

Figure 56.3

	K	L
7	Ex Price	4.489053
8	$ 45.00	2.139609
9	$ 46.00	2.609498
10	$ 47.00	3.079387
11	$ 48.00	3.549275
12	$ 49.00	4.019164
13	$ 50.00	4.489053
14	$ 51.00	4.980604
15	$ 52.00	5.484364
16	$ 53.00	5.988124
17	$ 54.00	6.52469
18	$ 55.00	7.092245
19	$ 56.00	7.733071

As the exercise price increases, the value of the put increases because an increased exercise price increases the number of values for which the put is "in the money".

Finally, Figure 56.4 shows that an increase in the risk-free rate decreases the value of the put.

Figure 56.4

	N	O
7	r	4.489053
8	0.01	5.300677
9	0.02	5.207424
10	0.03	5.114923
11	0.04	5.023183
12	0.05	4.932208
13	0.06	4.842007
14	0.07	4.752584
15	0.08	4.663947
16	0.09	4.576102
17	0.1	4.489053
18	0.11	4.405002
19	0.12	4.333566

This is because an increase in the risk-free rate makes the payoff from the put (which occurs in the future) less valuable.

Relationship to an Abandonment Option

Often an option to abandon a project may be thought of as a put. To see this in the current context, suppose the current value of a project is $50 million, the risk-free rate is 10%, and the project has a 40% annual volatility. Any time in the next five months we may abandon the project and receive $50 million. To determine the value of this abandonment option we would proceed exactly as we proceeded to value the put. We would have found the value of the abandonment option to be $4.49 million.

Computing the Early Exercise Boundary

Given the price of the stock today is $50 it would be nice to know, in advance what we would do (exercise or not exercise) for any given price during a future period. For example, would we exercise if Month 1 price were $42? If we have not exercised during first three months would we exercise during Month 4 if price were $40? Answering this question requires that we compute the **early exercise boundary** for each period. It turns out for each month there exists a "boundary price" p(t) such that we will exercise during Month t (assuming option has not been exercised) if and only if Month t price is less than or equal to p(t). Together p(1), p(2), p(3), p(4), and p(5) define the early exercise boundary for the put. To find the early exercise boundary it is convenient to make four copies of our original sheet. To copy a sheet put the cursor on the sheet name, hold down the left mouse button, and drag the sheet to another tab. We have renamed our four copies Ex Bound 1, Ex Bound 2, etc. In sheet Ex Bound 1 we determine p(1) as follows. The value p(1) for which we exercise during Month 1 if and only if p≤p(1) can be found by observing that **p(1) is the largest Month 1 price for which Exercise price - p(1) equals the Month 1 value of the option.** To find p(1) (see Figure 56.5) we proceed as follows:

Figure 56.5

	A	B	C	D	E	F	G
1	American Option						
2	Put						
3	Current price	$ 50.00					
4	Exercise price	$ 50.00					
5	r	0.1					
6	sigma	0.4					
7	t	0.416667					
8	deltat	0.083333					
9	u	1.122401					
10	d	0.890947					
11	a	1.008368					
12	p	0.507319					
13	q	0.492681					
14		Time					
15	down moves	0	1	2	3	4	5
16	0	$ 50.00	$ 39.19	$ 43.98	$ 49.37	$ 55.41	$ 62.19
17	1		$ 31.11	$ 34.91	$ 39.19	$ 43.98	$ 49.37
18	2		-	$ 27.71	$ 31.11	$ 34.91	$ 39.19
19	3		-	-	$ 24.69	$ 27.71	$ 31.11
20	4		-	-	-	$ 22.00	$ 24.69
21	5		-	-	-	-	$ 19.60
22		ex-price	$ 10.81				
23	Put Value	0	1	2	3	4	5
24	0	14.6728	10.81387	6.84145	3.096029	0.309755	0.00
25	1		18.89456	15.08723	10.81387	6.017455	0.63
26	2		-	22.28669	18.89456	15.08723	10.81
27	3		-	-	25.30891	22.28669	$ 18.89
28	4		-	-		28.00154	$ 25.31
29	5		-	-	-		$ 30.40

Step by Step

Step 1: In cell C16 insert a trial value for p(1). Note that the way we have set up the price tree ensures that the prices in B16 and C17 have no effect on the value of the put computed in C24.

Step 2: Assuming that the Month 1 price equals the value in C16, we compute in C22 the value if the put is exercised in Month 1 with the formula

=B4-C16.

Step 3: We can now use Solver to determine p(1). To find p(1) note that p(1) is the largest price (entered in C16) for which the value of exercising now (in cell C22) equals the Month 1 value of the option (computed in C24). Therefore the following Solver Window let's us compute p(1).

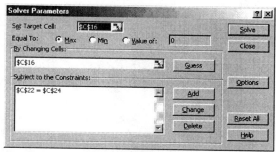

We find that p(1) = $39.19. Thus if the Month 1 price is below $39.19 we should exercise, otherwise go on. The reader should try a variety of Month 1 prices in B16 to convince herself that it is optimal to exercise for any price below $39.19 and continue for any price above $39.19. Of course, we are assuming that exercise can only occur at time =1, 2, ... 5, but it turns out that even if many more points of exercise were allowed, p(1) would be fairly close to $39.19. In a similar fashion we find the rest of the early exercise boundary to be the following:

Time	Exercise if price <=
1	$39.19
2	$39.41
3	$41.64
4	$45.28
5	$50.00

Simulating the Actual Cash Flows from an American Option

Now that we have computed the early exercise boundary, it is easy to simulate the actual cash flows generated by optimal exercise of the put. Our work is in file VAR.xls and Figure 56.6. We assume that the actual stock price follows a Lognormal random variable with μ = .20.

Figure 56.6

	A	B	C	D	E	F	G
1	American Option						
2	Put						
3	Current price	$ 50.00					
4	Exercise price	$ 50.00					
5	r	0.1					
6	sigma	0.4					
7	t	0.416667					
8	deltat	0.083333					
9	u	1.122401					
10	d	0.890947					
11	a	1.008368					
12	p	0.507319					
13	q	0.492681					
14	growth rate	0.2	1	2	3	4	$ 5.00
15	Ex Bound		39.19	39.41	41.64	45.28	50
16	Price	50	50.50251	51.01007	51.52273	52.04054	52.56355
17	Value if Exercised		0	0	0	0	0
18	Value to date		0	0	0	0	0

Step by Step

Step 1: In cells C16:G16 generate a 5-month stock price path by copying from C16 to D16:G16 the formula

$$=B16*EXP((\$B\$14-0.5*sigma^2)*(1/12)+RISKNormal(0,1)*sigma*SQRT(1/12)).$$

Step 2: Enter the exercise boundary in C15:G15.

Step 3: In C17:G17 we compute the cash flow from the put, assuming it has not yet been exercised by copying from C17 to D17:G17 the formula

$$=If(C16<C15,\$B\$4-C16,0).$$

These formulas ensure that if the current price is less than the exercise boundary we receive exercise price - current stock price. Otherwise, we receive nothing.

Step 4: In C18:G18 we compute the actual discounted payoff earned from the put. In C18 we compute the Month 1 payoff with the formula

$$=C17*EXP(-r\_*C14/12).$$

To compute the final discounted payoff received we copy from D18 to E18:G18 the formula

$$=If(C18>0,C18,EXP(-r\_*D14/12)*D17).$$

If the option has already been exercised, we retain the discounted value already received. Otherwise, we enter the discounted value (possibly 0) earned during the current Month. Then cell G18 gives the **actual discounted cash flow** from the put.

Step 5: We ran 1600 iterations with output cell G18 and obtained the output in Figure 56.7.

Figure 56.7

	H	I
13	Cell	G18
14	Minimum =	0
15	Maximum =	19.67661
16	Mean =	3.711043
17	Std Deviation =	4.89601
18	Variance =	23.97092
19	Skewness =	0.9425099
20	Kurtosis =	2.479961
21	Errors Calculated =	0
22	Mode =	0
23	5% Perc =	0
24	10% Perc =	0
25	15% Perc =	0
26	20% Perc =	0
27	25% Perc =	0
28	30% Perc =	0
29	35% Perc =	0
30	40% Perc =	0
31	45% Perc =	0
32	50% Perc =	0.00E+00
33	55% Perc =	0.4434712
34	60% Perc =	2.704098
35	65% Perc =	4.871075
36	70% Perc =	6.391032
37	75% Perc =	7.866961
38	80% Perc =	8.973576
39	85% Perc =	10.41997
40	90% Perc =	11.45398
41	95% Perc =	12.9345
42	Value	0
43	Percentage	53.75%

We find an expected discounted cash flow from the put of $3.71. By using the Target command (see I42 and I43) we find there is a 46% probability that the put will return a positive cash flow.

Chapter 57: Using Real Options to Value a Lease on a Gold Mine

Many investment opportunities involve decisions that are made at different points in time. If the value of the investment opportunities depend on the price of a commodity (such as gold price) then the risk neutral approach we used to value stock options can be used to value real investment opportunities. This approach to valuing investment opportunities is known as the **real option approach.** Chapter 21 of Brealey and Myers has a nice chapter (Chapter 21) on this approach. Luenberger (1997) has a nice discussion of real options in Chapters 12 and 16. We will base our discussion on Luenberger's gold mine example.

Example 57.1

GoldCo is trying to value a 10-year lease on a gold mine. Each year up to 10,000 ounces of gold can be extracted at a cost of $200 per ounce. The risk free rate is assumed to remain constant at 10%. The price received for all gold extracted during a year is assumed to equal the price of gold at the beginning of the year, but the all cash flows occur at the end of the year. The current price of gold is $400 and the future price of gold is uncertain. We model the future price of gold with a **binomial tree**. Each year we assume that gold will (with probability .75) increase by 20% and (with probability .25) decrease by 10%. The annual interest rate is 10%. What is the value of the lease?

Solution

Again we use the risk neutral approach. We need to find the probability (p) of an up move in gold prices, which makes gold yield the risk free rate. Then we use the gold price tree we create to find the expected discounted value of all the cash flows associated with the option. See Figure 57.1 and file *Gold.xls*.

Figure 57.1

	A	B	C	D	E	F	G	H	I	J	K	L
1	Simplico Gold mine			r	0.1	p	0.666667					
2				u	1.2	Cost	200					
3		Gold Prices		d	0.9							
4	Down moves	0	1	2	3	4	5	6	7	8	9	10
5	0	400	480	576	691.2	829.44	995.328	1194.394	1433.272	1719.927	2063.912	2476.695
6	1		360	432	518.4	622.08	746.496	895.7952	1074.954	1289.945	1547.934	1857.521
7	2	-		324	388.8	466.56	559.872	671.8464	806.2157	967.4588	1160.951	1393.141
8	3	-			291.6	349.92	419.904	503.8848	604.6618	725.5941	870.7129	1044.856
9	4	-		-		262.44	314.928	377.9136	453.4963	544.1956	653.0347	783.6416
10	5	-		-	-		236.196	283.4352	340.1222	408.1467	489.776	587.7312
11	6	-		-	-	-		212.5764	255.0917	306.11	367.332	440.7984
12	7	-		-	-	-	-		191.3188	229.5825	275.499	330.5988
13	8	-		-	-	-	-	-		172.1869	206.6243	247.9491
14	9	-		-	-	-	-	-	-		154.9682	185.9618
15	10	-		-	-	-	-	-	-	-		139.4714
16		Value										
17	Down Moves	0	1	2	3	4	5	6	7	8	9	10
18	0	2.41E+07	2.78E+07	3.12E+07	3.42E+07	3.65E+07	3.77E+07	3.71E+07	3.41E+07	2.78E+07	1.69E+07	0.00E+00
19	1		1.79E+07	2.07E+07	2.33E+07	2.52E+07	2.64E+07	2.62E+07	2.43E+07	2.00E+07	1.23E+07	0.00E+00
20	2	-		1.29E+07	1.50E+07	1.67E+07	1.79E+07	1.81E+07	1.70E+07	1.41E+07	8.74E+06	0.00E+00
21	3	-	-		8.82E+06	1.04E+07	1.15E+07	1.20E+07	1.15E+07	9.72E+06	6.10E+06	0.00E+00
22	4	-	-	-		5.61E+06	6.73E+06	7.40E+06	7.39E+06	6.42E+06	4.12E+06	0.00E+00
23	5	-	-	-	-		3.17E+06	3.97E+06	4.30E+06	3.95E+06	2.63E+06	0.00E+00
24	6	-	-	-	-	-		1.45E+06	1.98E+06	2.09E+06	1.52E+06	0.00E+00
25	7	-	-	-	-	-	-		4.37E+05	7.03E+05	6.86E+05	0.00E+00
26	8	-	-	-	-	-	-	-		3.65E+04	6.02E+04	0.00E+00
27	9	-	-	-	-	-	-	-	-		0.00E+00	0.00E+00
28	10	-										0.00E+00

To find p note that $p(1.2) + (1-p).9 = 1.1$. This ensures that gold yields, on average, the risk-free rate of return each period. Therefore we find

$$p = \frac{1.1 - .9}{1.2 - .9} = \frac{2}{3}$$

We now proceed as follows:

Generating Gold Prices

Step by Step

Step 1: We compute p in cell F1 with the formula

=(1+E1-E3)/(E2-E3).

Step 2: In rows 4 through 15 we generate the tree of gold prices for Years 1-10.
We assume that our revenue is received at times 0, 1, 9. Then in rows 18-28 we will generate the discounted expected value of cash flows from wherever we are to end of problem. For example, cell J18 gives the expected discounted value of cash flows (at beginning of year 8) received during the last two years of the lease (given price of gold is $1719..93). To begin we enter the current price of gold, $400, in cell B5.

Step 3: To compute the price for each year when there have been no down moves copy from C5 to D5:L5 the formula

$$=u*B5.$$

Note that as we move down one row in a given column, the price of gold is multiplied by d/u. Therefore in cell C6 we can compute the Year 1 price following a down move with the formula

$$=If(\$A6<=C\$4,(d/u)*C5,"-").$$

Copying this formula to C6:L15 generates all other gold prices and enters a "_" in cells where no price is defined.

Finding Value of Lease

We begin in Column K by finding value of lease at beginning of last year. Then we work backwards to find value of lease at earlier times. Remember at each node we will not mine any gold if the current price of gold is under $200.

Step by Step

Step 1: In K18 we compute the value of the lease at the beginning of year 9 if current gold price is $2063.91. Since we assume payments are received at end of year (based on beginning of year price) the value of the lease at Time 9 if gold price is at its highest level is

$$max(0,\frac{10000(2063.9-200)}{1.1})=16.94\,million$$

To implement this idea enter in K18 the formula

$$=MAX(0,(K5-\$G\$2)*10000/(1+\$E\$1)).$$

Copying from K18 to K19:K27 generates the value of the lease for all possible gold prices at the beginning of the last year.

Step 2: To work backwards to Time 8 we compute in J18 the expected discounted value of the lease if gold is at its highest price. Note that this value is given by

$$\frac{1}{1+r}\mathbf{max}(0,10000(current\,gold\,price-200))$$

$$+\frac{1}{1+r}(p(Time\,9\,value\,after\,up)+(1-p)(Time\,9\,value\,after\,down))$$

To operationalize this idea enter into J18 the formula

$=If(\$A18<=J\$17,(1/(1+\$E\$1)*MAX((J5-\$G\$2)*10000,0)+(\$G\$1*K18+(1-\$G\$1)*K19)*(1/(1+\$E\$1)))," - ").$

Copying this formula to B18:J26 computes the value of the lease for all other possible combinations of Year and gold prices. Note that a "-" is placed in any cell for which a value of the lease is undefined. We find the value of the lease to be $24.1 million.

Remarks

The key value of the real option approach is that it lets us value flexibility. If gold prices go down, we do not have to mine the gold.

For complicated "real option" problems, I would use a decision tree approach and model risk aversion by assessing a utility function. Precision Tree is well suited to this type of situation.

References

Brealey, R. and Myers, S., *Principles of Corporate Finance*, Prentice-Hall 1996.

Luenberger, D., *Investment Science*, Oxford Press, 1997.

Chapter 58: Valuing an Option to Purchase a Company

The binomial tree approach to valuing an option is very flexible. It can be used to value many "real investment options" such as an option to purchase, and option to contract operations and an option to expand. Here is an example of how to use the binomial tree approach to value the option to purchase a company.

Example 58.1

Corpco is currently worth $50 million. The value of Corpco has an annual volatility of 40% and the risk-free rate is 10%. During each of the next five years we will have the option to buy Corpco at the following prices (in millions):

Year	Purchase Price
Now	$40
1 year later	$41
2 years later	$42
3 years later	$43
4 years later	$50
5 years later	$70

Value the option to purchase Corpco. How sensitive is the value of this option to changes in volatility and interest rates? Determine a range of values for Corpco during each year for which you would purchase Corpco.

Solution

Our work is in file *Purchase.xls*. See Figure 58.1.

Figure 58.1

	A	B	C	D	E	F	G
1	**American Option**						
2	**to purchase**						
3	Current price	$ 50.00					
4							
5	r	0.1					
6	sigma	0.4					
7	t	0.416667					
8	deltat	1					
9	u	1.491825					
10	d	0.67032					
11	a	1.105171					
12	p	0.529335					
13	q	0.470665					
14		**Time**					
15	**Stock Prices**	0	1	2	3	4	5
16	0	$ 50.00	$ 74.59	$ 111.28	$ 166.01	$ 247.65	$ 369.45
17	1		$ 33.52	$ 50.00	$ 74.59	$ 111.28	$ 166.01
18	2		-	$ 22.47	$ 33.52	$ 50.00	$ 74.59
19	3		-	-	$ 15.06	$ 22.47	$ 33.52
20	4		-	-	-	$ 10.09	$ 15.06
21	5		-	-	-	-	$ 6.77
22	**Purchase Price**	$ 40.00	$ 41.00	$ 42.00	$ 43.00	$ 50.00	$ 70.00
23		**Purchase Value**					
24	**Down Moves**	0	1	2	3	4	5
25	0	$ 23.38	$ 41.69	$ 72.71	**$ 123.01**	**$ 197.65**	**$ 299.45**
26	1	-	$ 7.75	$ 15.66	**$ 31.59**	**$ 61.28**	**$ 96.01**
27	2	-	-	$ 0.51	$ 1.06	$ 2.21	**$ 4.59**
28	3	-	-	-	$ -	$ -	$ -
29	4	-	-	-	-	$ -	$ -
30	5	-	-	-	-	-	$ -

Step by Step

We use the same formulas to generate the possible values of Corpco that we used to generate stock prices in Chapter 56. **All we need to do is change delta t to 1, because we are looking at the value of Corpco at yearly time intervals.**

Step 1: We enter the yearly purchase prices in B22:G22.

Step 2: In Year 5 we will purchase if and only if Corpco value is at least as large as purchase price ($70 million). We therefore determine in cell G25 the value of the purchase option if each price move for 5 years has been up with the formula

=MAX(G16-$G$22,0).

Copying this formula to G26:G30 computes the value of the purchase option for all other possible Year 5 prices.

Step 3: Suppose it is Year t and there have been I down moves. Then the value at Year t of the option to purchase is given by

(58.1) Maximum (Current Value – Current Purchase Price, (1/(1+r)*(p*(Year t+1, I+1 up move value+q*(Year t+1, I up move value).

If Maximum is attained by Current value - Current Purchase Price, then we buy Corpco this year, otherwise we continue. To implement (58.1) we enter in cell F25 the formula

=If($A25<=F$24,MAX(F16-F$22,(1/(1+r_*deltat))*(p*G25+q*G26)),"-").

Copying this formula to B25:F30 computes the value of the purchase option for all possible Corpco values during Years 0-4.

From cell B25 we find the option has a value of $23.38 million. Assuming the value of Corpco actually grew at the risk-free rate we would wait until Year 3 and purchase if at most one down move occurred.

Step 4: To show in bold face the cells where purchasing Corpco is optimal use Conditional Formatting to enter the following format in cell G25

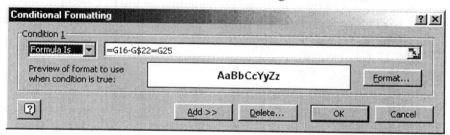

and select a bold-faced font. Using Edit>Copy>Paste Special Formats we copy this format to the cell range B25:G30. Now any cell in which it is optimal to exercise our purchase option will be noted in bold face. This is because it is optimal to exercise the purchase option if and only if (Corpco value - Purchase price) = (Current value of option).

Sensitivity Analysis

Running a one-way data table on the volatility and risk-free rate (using column input cells sigma and r_, respectively) yields the results in Figure 58.2.

Figure 58.2

	H	I	J	K
5	Sensitivity Analysis			
6				
7	Volatility	23.37825	r	23.37825
8	0.1	18.40191	0.01	18.08367
9	0.2	18.95871	0.02	18.59624
10	0.3	20.80347	0.03	19.16049
11	0.4	23.37825	0.04	19.75173
12	0.5	26.33766	0.05	20.34653
13	0.6	29.50719	0.06	20.94501
14	0.7	32.4609	0.07	21.54729
15			0.08	22.15349
16			0.09	22.76376
17			0.1	23.37825
18			0.11	23.99711
19			0.12	24.62052

Note that an increase in either the volatility or the risk-free rate increases the value of the purchase option. The risk-free rate, however, has little impact on the value of the option to purchase.

When Do We Buy?

For each year t we determine a "cutoff point" p(t) defined as follows. If Year t value of Corpco is at least as large as cutoff point, we will purchase (if we have not already done so) Corpco during Year t; if Year t value of Corpco is less than p(t) we will not purchase Corpco during year t. The value p(t) is simply **the smallest value during year t for which the value obtained by purchasing during year t is at least as large as the value of continuing onward.** We illustrate the determination of p(3). See Figure 58.3.

Figure 58.3

	A	B	C	D	E	F	G
1	American Option						
2	to purchase						
3	Current price	$ 50.00					
4							
5	r	0.1					
6	sigma	0.4					
7	t	0.416667					
8	deltat	1					
9	u	1.491825					
10	d	0.67032					
11	a	1.105171		Purchase if			
12	p	0.529335		value in year 3			
13	q	0.470665		>=$67.13			
14		Time					
15	Stock Prices	0	1	2	3	4	5
16	0	$ 50.00	$ 74.59	$ 111.28	$ 67.13	$ 100.15	$ 149.41
17	1		$ 33.52	$ 50.00	$ 30.17	$ 45.00	$ 67.13
18	2		-	$ 22.47	$ 13.55	$ 20.22	$ 30.17
19	3		-	-	$ 6.09	$ 9.09	$ 13.55
20	4		-	-	-	$ 4.08	$ 6.09
21	5		-	-	-	-	$ 2.74
22	Purchase Price	$ 40.00	$ 41.00	$ 42.00	$ 43.00	$ 50.00	$ 70.00
23	Value if buy				$ 24.13		
24	Down Moves	0	1	2	3	4	5
25	0	$ 19.34	$ 36.76	$ 69.28	$ 24.13	$ 50.15	$ 79.41
26	1	-	$ 3.85	$ 8.00	$ -	$ -	$ -
27	2	-	-	$ -	$ -	$ -	$ -
28	3	-	-	-	$ -	$ -	$ -
29	4	-	-	-	-	$ -	$ -
30	5	-	-	-	-	-	$ -

Step by Step

Step 1: Enter a trial Year 3 value for Corpco in cell E16.

Step 2: In cell E23 compute the value of purchasing in Year 3 with the formula

=E16-E22.

Step 3: The following Solver Window will determine p(3):

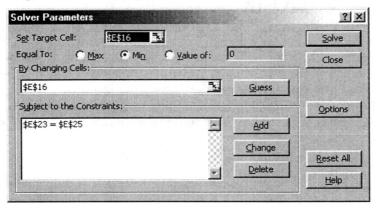

We seek the smallest Year 3 Corpco value (E16) for which it is optimal to purchase Corpco during Year 3 (it will be optimal to purchase Corpco if E23 = E25). We find p(3) = $67.13. Thus if we have not yet purchased Corpco, we should do so during Year 3 if its value is at least $67.13 million. In a similar fashion we find that there is **no value** for which we should purchase Corpco during Years 1 and 2. During Year 4 if we have not yet purchased Corpco we should purchase Corpco if its value is at least $57.83.

Chapter 59: M^2- A Risk-Adjusted Measure of Portfolio Return

For many years, the investment community has searched for a measure of return on investment that adjusts for the riskiness of the investment. Nobel Prize winner Francis Modigliani and his granddaughter Leah have developed a neat risk-adjusted measure of return on investment: M^2. Here is how M^2 works. We choose a benchmark investment such as the S&P index to which we will compare other investments. Suppose we want to compare a mutual fund which has been riskier than the S&P to the S&P. We reduce the risk (and return) of the mutual fund by adding an amount cash c to our investment. The amount c is chosen to reduce the variability of the combined portfolio (mutual fund + cash) so the variability on the combined portfolio matches the variability of the benchmark. Then the risk-adjusted return of the mutual fund is simply the expected return on the combined portfolio. Conversely, if we want to compare a mutual fund which has been less risky than the S&P to the S&P we increase the risk (and return) of the mutual fund by subtracting an amount of cash c from our investment. The amount c is chosen to increase the variability of the combined portfolio (mutual fund - cash) so the variability of the combined portfolio matches the variability of the benchmark. Then the risk-adjusted return of the mutual fund is again the expected return of the combined portfolio.

Spreadsheet Implementation of M^2

We will work with quarterly data so the end of a period is one quarter (3 months from now). Let

I = (random) value in one period of $1 invested now in investment.

B = (random) value in one period of $1 invested now in benchmark.

r = risk-free rate during next period.

c = cash added (or subtracted) to investment so combined portfolio yields same risk as benchmark.

If we invest $1 in investment and $c in cash the return on our portfolio is $\dfrac{I + (1 + r)c}{1 + c} - 1$ (59.1)

Thus we wish to choose c so that

$$\text{var}(\frac{I + (1 + r)c}{1 + c} - 1) = \text{var } B$$

Once c has been chosen to make the variance of the combined portfolio equal to the variance of the benchmark, the risk-adjusted return on our investment is just the expected value of

$$\frac{I + (1 + r)c}{1 + c} - 1$$

To illustrate the computation of M^2 we will compute M^2 for three mutual funds: Income Fund, T Row Price NH, and AIM Constellation for the period 1990-1996. The mean and standard deviation of quarterly returns on these investments as well as the S and P and risk free rate is given in file *Msq.xls*. See Figure 59.1.

Figure 59.1

	B	C	D	E	F	G
107	stdev	0.0566	0.0065	0.038848	0.10584982	0.103146904
108	mean	0.02773	0.0135	0.029689	0.045232143	0.051132143
109		S and P	T-Bill	Inc Fund	T Row Price NH	Aim Constellation

Note that the Income fund is less risky than the S&P so we will subtract cash from the Income Fund. On the other hand, T Rowe Price and AIM Constellation are riskier than the S&P so we will add cash to these investments to make them less risky. We proceed as follows:

Step 1: Enter trial values for cash added or subtracted to each investment in H77:J77.

Figure 59.2

	B	C	D	E	F	G	H	I	J	K
76										
77							Cash Inc	cash Rowe	cahs AIM	
							-0.30692	0.85745005	0.807038	
78		S and P	T-Bill	Inc Fund	T Row Price NH	Aim Constellation	Inc fund +	Rowe+cash	Aim+cash	
79	3/30/90	-0.0381	0.0202	-0.032	-0.0046	0.0298	-0.05512	0.00684891	0.025513	
80	6/29/90	0.00523	0.0202	0.0222	0.0876	0.1157	0.023089	0.05648296	0.073046	
81	9/28/90	0.07663	0.0191	-0.0816	-0.264	-0.2624	-0.12618	-0.13333103	-0.1367	
82	12/31/90	-0.1464	0.0177	0.0679	0.1353	0.1318	0.090118	0.08102582	0.080855	
83	3/28/91	0.13135	0.0155	0.0953	0.2797	0.2768	0.130633	0.15774394	0.160107	
84	6/28/91	0.09136	0.0143	0.0136	-0.0346	-0.0091	0.013304	-0.0120415	0.001336	
85	9/30/91	0.0332	0.0137	0.0585	0.1174	0.1605	0.078319	0.06955037	0.094958	
86	12/31/91	0.01199	0.0112	0.0533	0.1023	0.1606	0.071959	0.0602301	0.093862	
87	3/31/92	0.04161	0.0101	0.0159	-0.0204	0	0.018465	-0.00631627	0.004515	
88	6/30/92	0.01507	0.0094	0.044	-0.1009	-0.0933	0.059324	-0.04998436	-0.04744	
89	9/30/92	0.02232	0.0077	0.0404	0.0529	0.0612	0.054876	0.03203968	0.037312	
90	12/31/92	-0.013	0.008	0.0151	0.1925	0.1955	0.018264	0.10730863	0.111741	
91	3/31/93	0.04801	0.0075	0.0629	-0.0264	0.0087	0.087455	-0.01077309	0.008143	
92	6/30/93	0.00321	0.0077	0.0238	-0.0642	0.0532	0.030943	-0.03102305	0.032866	
93	9/30/93	0.01804	0.0076	0.0331	0.1181	0.0738	0.044377	0.06710679	0.044251	
94	12/31/93	0.04396	0.0078	0.0141	0.0533	0.0282	0.016874	0.03231305	0.019106	
95	3/31/94	0.02946	0.0083	-0.0448	-0.0371	-0.0154	-0.06833	-0.01612379	-0.0048	
96	6/30/94	-0.0637	0.0402	0.0066	-0.063	-0.0662	-0.00826	-0.01538148	-0.0187	
97	9/30/94	0.01628	0.0116	0.0261	0.1056	0.1013	0.032535	0.06219284	0.061226	
98	12/30/94	0.03077	0.0138	-0.0118	0.0055	0.0004	-0.02313	0.00932589	0.006379	
99	3/31/95	-0.0041	0.0149	0.0716	0.0982	0.0826	0.096706	0.05974956	0.052368	
100	6/30/95	0.09415	0.0144	0.0713	0.1296	0.1413	0.096486	0.07643304	0.084638	
101	9/29/95	0.09199	0.0137	0.0621	0.1786	0.145	0.083525	0.10248713	0.08637	
102	12/29/95	0.03459	0.0134	0.0587	0.0632	-0.0426	0.078757	0.04021532	-0.01759	
103	3/29/96	0.09376	0.0127	0.0303	0.0634	0.0569	0.038085	0.04000482	0.037169	
104	6/28/96	0.02854	0.013	0.0161	0.0615	0.0525	0.017478	0.03910607	0.034854	
105	9/30/96	-0.0217	0.0132	0.029	0.0411	0.0363	0.036005	0.02821251	0.025976	
106	12/31/96	0.10207	0.0121	0.0696	-0.0041	0.0086	0.095046	0.00339694	0.010181	
107	stdev	0.0566	0.0065	0.038848	0.10584982	0.103146904	0.056596	0.05659541	0.056596 stdev	
108	mean	0.02773	0.0135	0.029689	0.045232143	0.051132143	0.036843	0.03059999	0.034341 mean	
109		S and P	T-Bill	Inc Fund	T Row Price NH	Aim Constellation	1.68E-16	6.428E-15	1.68E-16	
110							Inc Fund	T Row Price	Aim Constellation	
111					Target					
112					6.7642E-15					

Step 2: In H79:J106 we compute the return during each period on the cash-adjusted portfolio. To do this copy the formula

$$=((1+E79)+(H\$77)*(1+D79))/(1+H\$77)-1$$

from H79:J106. During each quarter this uses (59.1) to compute return on combined portfolio for each investment.

Step 3: In H107:J108 compute the mean and standard deviation on the combined portfolio for each mutual fund by entering in H107 the formula

$$= STDEV(H79:H106)$$

and in H108 enter the formula

$$= AVERAGE(H79:H106).$$

Then we copy these formulas from H107:H108 to J107:J108.

Step 4: We now use Solver to determine the cash amount added (or subtracted) to each mutual fund which makes the combined portfolio have the same variance (or standard deviation) as the benchmark S&P. In H109:J109 we compute the squared value of the amount by which the standard deviation of each combined portfolio differs from the standard deviation of the benchmark. To do this copy the formula

$$=(H107-\$C\$107)^2$$

from H109 to H109:J109.

In cell F112 we create a target cell for Solver which keeps track of the sum of the square of the amount by which each combined portfolio's standard deviation differs from the standard deviation of the benchmark. To do this enter in F112 the formula

$$=SUM(H109:J109).$$

Choosing the cash added (or subtracted) for each fund to minimize this cell will ensure that each combined portfolio has the same standard deviation as the benchmark. Our Solver window is as follows.

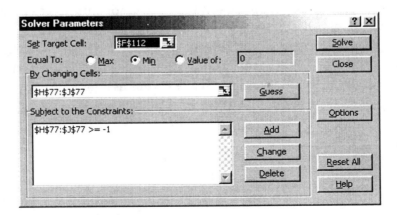

Note that we must ensure that cash "added" is at least -1.

From Figure 59.2 we find that we subtracted $0.31 from Income Fund. This "levers" a less risky fund to make it more risky. We added $0.86 to the T. Rowe Fund and added $0.81 to the AIM fund. These cash additions make these riskier funds less risky. As shown in Figure 59.3, all three combined portfolios have the same standard deviation as the S&P. All three combined portfolios have a higher mean return than the S&P. We find a quarterly risk-adjusted return of 3.7% for the Income fund, 3.1% for the T Rowe Price Fund, and 3.4% for the Aim Fund. Note that M^2 ranks the conservative Income Fund as the best of the three funds!

Figure 59.3

	C	D	E	F	G	H	I	J	K
107	0.0566	0.0065	0.038848	0.10584982	0.103146904	0.056596	0.05659541	0.056596	stdev
108	0.02773	0.0135	0.029689	0.045232143	0.051132143	0.036843	0.03059999	0.034341	mean
109	S and P	T-Bill	Inc Fund	T Row Price NH	Aim Constellation	1.68E-16	6.428E-15	1.68E-16	
110						Inc Fund	T Row Price	Aim Constellation	

Chapter 60: Maximizing Long-Term Growth-The Kelly Criteria

Suppose that at the beginning of each time period (say a month) you have n investments to which you may allocate money. Let X_0 = your initial capital and X_t = your capital at the end of period t. Then the t period growth rate is given by $\left(\dfrac{X_t}{X_0}\right)^{1/t}$. At the beginning of each month , what fraction of your money should you allocate to each investment in order to maximize the expected long-term growth of your money? Kelly (1956) solved this problem. Our discussion is based on Luenberger (1997). In order to maximize the expected long-term growth rate you should allocate your money among the n investments to maximize E(Ln (R)) where R = the one-period (random) return on your investment. If m = maximum E(Ln(R)), then the average per period rate at which your capital will grow is e^m. We now show how to use Solver to find the maximum growth rate (or **Kelly**) portfolio. Then we use @RISK to simulate the Kelly portfolio (and suboptimal portfolios) for 50 periods to show that the Kelly portfolio does indeed maximize expected long-term growth. Our example is drawn from Luenberger (1997).

Example 60.1

Each period you may invest your money in two places: Stock 1 and Stock 2 . Each Stock is equally likely to double or halve our money. Returns on the two stocks are independent. What asset allocation plan maximizes expected long-term growth?

Solution

The sheet Kelly of workbook *Kelly.xls* contains a Solver solution to the problem. See Figure 60.1.

Figure 60.1

	A	B	C	D	E	F	G
1	**Volatility Pumping**		Max E(Ln(R))				
2	weights	stock 1	stock 2	Total		e^m	1.118034
3		0.5	0.5	1	=		
4	Prob	Stock 1	Stock 2	Stock 1 Value	Stock 2 Value	Growth factor (R)	Ln(R)
5	0.25	up	up	1	1	2	0.693147
6	0.25	up	down	1	0.25	1.25	0.223144
7	0.25	down	down	0.25	0.25	0.5	-0.69315
8	0.25	down	up	0.25	1	1.25	0.223144
9						E(Ln(R))	0.111572

We proceed as follows:

Step 1: In B3:C3 we enter trial values for the fraction of our money allocated each period to each asset. In D3 we add up the total fraction of our money allocated with the formula

SUM(B3:C3).

Step 2: In A4:C8 we enter all scenarios that can occur during a period and their probabilities (each of the four scenarios has a .25 probability of occurring).

Step 3: Assuming we have $1 at the beginning of the period, in D5:E8 we compute the ending value (for each scenario) of the money placed in each investment. For each stock we compute the ending value of our capital by copying from D5 to D5:E8 the formula

=If(B5="up",2*B$3,0.5*B$3).

This formula ensures that if Stock 1 goes up, our money invested in Stock 1 doubles; otherwise our money invested in Stock 1 is halved.

Step 4: In F5:F8 we compute the factor by which our portfolio grew in each scenario by copying from F5 to F6:F8 the formula

=SUM(D5:E5).

Step 5: In G5:G8 we compute the logarithm of the growth factor for each scenario by copying the formula

=LN(F5)

from G5:G8.

Step 6: In cell G9 we compute the expected value of the logarithm of the one period return with the formula

=SUMPRODUCT(A5:A8,G5:G8).

Step 7: We now use Solver to find the asset allocation that maximizes the expected value of the logarithm of the one period return. Our Solver window is as follows:

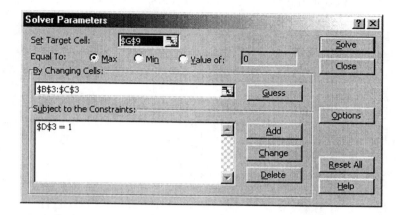

We maximize expected logarithm of one period return (G9) by changing cells B3:C3. Our changing cells must be non-negative (we assume we cannot short a stock) and add to one (D3 = 1).

From Figure 60.1 we find half our money should be allocated to each stock and m = maximum expected value of logarithm of one period return is .111572. We find e^m = 1.118. Thus the Kelly criteria suggests we can obtain a long-run growth rate of 11.8% per period by placing (at the beginning of each period) half our money in each investment. We now use simulation to verify this 11.8% growth rate.

Simulating Long-Term Growth

In the sheet simulation of file *Kelly.xls* we simulate the Kelly optimal portfolio (and several suboptimal portfolios) for 50 years. See Figure 60.2.

Figure 60.2

	A	B	C	D	E	F	G
1	%age stock 1	0.9					
2						Growth rate	1.25
3	Year	Beginning	Stock 1?	Stock 2?	Final Position		
4	1	$ 1.00	1.25	1.25	$ 1.25		
5	2	$ 1.25	1.25	1.25	$ 1.56		
6	3	$ 1.56	1.25	1.25	$ 1.95		
7	4	$ 1.95	1.25	1.25	$ 2.44		
8	5	$ 2.44	1.25	1.25	$ 3.05		
9	6	$ 3.05	1.25	1.25	$ 3.81		
10	7	$ 3.81	1.25	1.25	$ 4.77		
11	8	$ 4.77	1.25	1.25	$ 5.96		
12	9	$ 5.96	1.25	1.25	$ 7.45		
13	10	$ 7.45	1.25	1.25	$ 9.31		
14	11	$ 9.31	1.25	1.25	$ 11.64		
15	12	$ 11.64	1.25	1.25	$ 14.55		
16	13	$ 14.55	1.25	1.25	$ 18.19		
17	14	$ 18.19	1.25	1.25	$ 22.74		

Step by Step

We proceed as follows:

Step 1: In B1 we use a =RISKSimTable function to allow us to place 90%, 80%, 70%, 60%, 50%, 40%, 30%, 20%, 10%, and 0% of our money each period to Stock 1 (and the rest to Stock 2).

=RISKSimTable({0.9,0.8,0.7,0.6,0.5,0.4,0.3,0.2,0.1,0,0}).

Step 2: In B4 we enter our starting capital ($1).

Step 3: In C4:D53 we generate the (random) return on each Stock during each of the 50 periods by copying from C4 to C4:D53 the formula

=RISKDUniform({2,0.5}).

This formula makes the return on a stock during a period equally likely to be 200% or 50%. It also makes the returns during each period on the two stocks independent random variables.

Step 4: In E4 we compute our ending Year 1 position with the formula

=$B$1*B4*C4+(1-$B$1)*B4*D4.

This formula takes the amount invested in Stock 1 (B1*B4) and grows it by Stock 1's growth factor C4, and the amount invested in Stock 2 ((1-B1)*B4) and grows it by Stock 2's growth factor (D4).

Step 5: In cell B5 we compute period 2's beginning capital with the formula

$=E4.$

We now copy the beginning capital formula from B5 to B6:B53 and the ending capital formula from E4 to E5:E53.

Step 6: In G2 we compute the 50 year growth rate with the formula

$=(E53)^{\wedge}0.02.$

Step 7: We selected cell G2 as our output cell and ran 10,000 iterations of 10 simulations. The results are in Figure 60.3.

Figure 60.3

	I	J	K	L	M
16	Summary Statistics		e^m	1.118033989	
17					
18	Fraction in Stock 1	Name	Minimum	Mean	Maximum
19	0.9	Growth rate	0.7713071	1.051207	1.49334
20	0.8	Growth rate	0.8145967	1.083384	1.460428
21	0.7	Growth rate	0.8423573	1.10471	1.419048
22	0.6	Growth rate	0.8539677	1.11693	1.439228
23	0.5	Growth rate	0.8591393	1.120915	1.454944
24	0.4	Growth rate	0.8555224	1.116931	1.460204
25	0.3	Growth rate	0.8373724	1.104711	1.463715
26	0.2	Growth rate	0.7929758	1.083385	1.476475
27	0.1	Growth rate	0.7408566	1.051206	1.480781
28	0	Growth rate	0.6783022	1.004857	1.474269

As predicted by the Kelly criteria, allocating half our money each period to Stock 1 maximizes expected long-term growth. Note the surprising long-term growth rate (.4% in the simulation, 0% in theory) if all our money is allocated to a stock (Stock 2). This implies that putting all our money in either stock result in no long-term growth. So why does allocating half our money to each Stock result in nearly 12% growth? As Luenberger eloquently points out, the answer is **volatility pumping**. When a stock goes up we can invest some of the profits in the other stock. When a stock goes down, we tend to buy more "shares" of the stock. This is because we always have half our money in each stock. Essentially volatility gives use the opportunity to implement a buy low, sell high strategy.

References

Kelly, J. "A New Interpretation of Information Rate," *Bell System Technical Journal*, Volume 35, pages 917-926.

Luenberger, D. *Investment Science*, Oxford Press, 1997.